Praise for *The Cricket War*

'A fascinating account in masterly detail of an extraordinary episode in Australian cricket. Highly recommended' Peter Roebuck

'Haigh towers over the cricket writing landscape in Australia' *Guardian*

'Haigh shows a supreme gift for old-fashioned journalistic foot-slogging and the art of telling a great story with a brisk, unfussy narrative' Richard Whitehead, *The Times*

'The most detailed history of the 'war' so far' Michael Davie, the *Age*

'The reverberations of the war are still being felt in Australia and in world cricket. This book will be timely for all those who want to understand what took place in the still recent past – and what could well happen in the near future' Richard Cashman, the *Australian*

'Haigh writes with wit, perception and a pace that rivals Roberts ... *The Cricket War* is an example of what can be done with fine writing, thorough and imaginative research and a mature approach to sports book publishing' Mark Ray, *Sunday Age*

'Superbly researched and written' Ashley Browne, the *Age*

'There are various claimants to the title of 'world's best cricket writer', yet no dispute about who, today, is the best writer on cricket. This is the Australian, Gideon Haigh' Ramachandra Guha

ABOUT THE AUTHOR

Gideon Haigh is an award winning independent journalist, who has written for many publications over a career spanning thirty years; including the *Age*, the *Australian*, *The Times*, the *Telegraph*, *Wisden Cricket Monthly*, the *Cricketer, Observer Sports* and *World Cricket Watch* to name a few. He has published over thirty books, over twenty of them about cricket. Born in London, Haigh went to school in Geelong, and now lives in Melbourne.

THE CRICKET WAR

The Story of Kerry Packer's World Series Cricket

BY

GIDEON HAIGH

BLOOMSBURY

LONDON · OXFORD · NEW YORK · NEW DELHI · SYDNEY

John Wisden & Co Ltd
An imprint of Bloomsbury Publishing Plc

50 Bedford Square
London
WC1B 3DP
UK

1385 Broadway
New York
NY 10018
USA

www.bloomsbury.com

WISDEN and the wood-engraving device are trademarks of John Wisden & Company Ltd,
a subsidiary of Bloomsbury Publishing Plc

First published in Australia in 1993 by The Text Publishing Company
This edition published in 2017 by John Wisden & Co Ltd

Cover Image © Getty Images

Images from the author's personal collection unless otherwise stated

Gideon Haigh has asserted his right under the Copyright, Designs and
Patents Act, 1988, to be identified as Author of this work.

www.bloomsbury.com/wisden
Follow Wisden on Twitter @WisdenAlmanack
and on Facebook.com/officialwisden

British Library Cataloguing-in-Publication Data
A catalogue record for this book is available from the British Library.

Library of Congress Cataloguing-in-Publication data has been applied for.

ISBN: PB: 978-1-4729-5063-5
ePDF: 978-1-4729-5065-9
ePub: 978-1-4729-5064-2

10 9 8 7 6 5 4 3

Typeset in Stempel Garamond LT Std by Deanta Global Publishing Services, Chennai, India
Printed and bound in Great Britain by CPI Group (UK) Ltd, Croydon CR0 4YY

To find out more about our authors and books visit www.bloomsbury.com/wisden.
Here you will find extracts, author interviews, details of forthcoming events
and the option to sign up for our newsletters.

To remember my brother
Jasper Manton Oakley Haigh (1969–1987)

CONTENTS

INTRODUCTION

World Series Cricket has reached its fortieth anniversary – by convention an age of maturity and insight. Yet little by little, it grows harder to fully apprehend. Nobody under the age of fifty can have a coherent memory of the pre-existing cricket to which WSC afforded such a jolting contrast; to search for it in this visual age is to leave disappointed by the fragments of fuzzy footage on YouTube and the dearth of flavoursome archival photographs. Every couple of years, it seems, a documentary of sorts is produced, involving many of the same talking heads, mine included. But a bigger audience will have watched the dramatization of events, *Howzat!,* which brought flares and bushy moustaches back to television for two top-rating nights in 2012. Forty, let's remember, is also an age increasingly prone to the distorting lens of nostalgia.

Twenty-five years, meanwhile, have elapsed since *The Cricket War* was written, and it is in this version obtaining its first UK publication. It was the first book to revisit World Series Cricket since a handful published *in medias res,* and my interest was not, in fact, entirely welcome. Approaches to several key figures, on both sides of the divide, were firmly rebuffed; rather than nostalgia, there was at the time a general sense that sleeping dogs were best let lie. The Australian Cricket Board was still connected to WSC's remnants – by now rather resentfully – through its commercial ties with PBL Marketing, while the Channel Nine commentary box was full of WSC legatees. Kerry Packer himself had defied mortality, bouncing back from a severe heart attack with insouciant profanity: 'I've been to the other side, and let me tell you, son, there's fucking nothing there.'

For my own part, I was twenty-six, had been in print journalism eight years, and written one previous book. That's relevant insofar as I could recall cricket before Packer, remembered the passions the WSC insurgency had unleashed, and understood the cricket I was now watching to have been profoundly shaped by events fifteen years earlier: the passage of time had normalised day-night cricket with white balls, coloured clothes, and helmets; the strains of 'C'mon Aussie C'mon' were as familiar as an anthem. Yet somehow nobody talked about their origins. Of the 56,126 runs scored and 2364 wickets taken across WSC's two summers, there was precious little trace.

That, perhaps, is the part of the story it is now easiest to miss. Over the last decade, cricket fans have grown accustomed to a hectic rate of change, to the sway of commercial imperatives, and to the dictates of the mass market. Twenty20 is the game's killer app, India its candy mountain. While cricket did evolve between the end of World War II and the advent of Kerry Packer, reformers had always walked into stiff conservative headwinds. Seven years separated the innovation of one-day cricket at domestic level and its introduction internationally; a further five years elapsed before the inaugural World Cup; and between December 1975 and December 1978, there was not a single limited-overs international match in Australia.

In those times, cricket celebrated continuity. The Centenary Test in March 1977 marked the longest run of all, bringing together cricketers born as far back as the reign of Queen Victoria, while the teams of Tony Greig and Greg Chappell played for the delectation of Queen Elizabeth II – to whom Dennis Lillee irreverently proffered his autograph book. A few months later, some in cricket thought Greig, Chappell and Lillee fit only for Traitors' Gate. Cricket was going well, was it not? Crowds were large; stars were popular; sponsors were eager. But that was the point – it is why Packer coveted a share.

The Australian Cricket Board had for some years before been quietly on guard about 'private promotors', given short shrift to the few who had materialised, and sought to improve the lot of players within what they saw as prudent and responsible bounds. The pace of change outstripped such piecemeal measures. They never genuinely grasped their cricketers' grievances, which were as much about conditions as they were about pay. They never understood that amassing players represented less of a risk to Packer than losing players was to the established game: Packer could amortise the expenses of his cricket attraction across his Nine Network, while the establishment's solitary profit centre, international cricket – and within that only really Ashes cricket – sat atop a complex of costs. An attraction straining to sell itself was a jarring rival to a game that had never seriously tried; commentary that invited viewers into the action and thrived on conflict made a striking comparison to coverage that had by convention kept a deferential distance; yet after all that continuity, the public proved more than ready for a bit of change.

For players, the summers of WSC provided a glimpse of the shape of things to come. If day/night cricket was a powerful innovation, WSC mainly accelerated changes already afoot, such as the popularization of shorter formats, the intensification of scheduling, the predominance of fast bowling and the development of protective equipment. It also distributed its benefits unevenly, promoting an elite at the expense of the mass. For once Packer and the Australian Cricket Board made peace, neither had much interest in further significant enhancements of the terms of cricketers' employment. Without a collective bargaining agent until the mid-1990s, Australian first-class cricketers remained poorly paid – the recruiting agents of the South African rebel tours found them comparatively easy pickings. Without much incentive to change, Australian cricket itself rather marked time in WSC's aftermath: the casts changed, but the calendars and commercial formulae repeated *ad nauseum*.

At forty, however, the legacy of WSC, and Packer's personal reputation, look secure. A minute's silence before a Boxing Day Test marked Packer's final passing in December 2005; the following year the Australian Cricketers' Association inaugurated the Kerry Packer Award to 'recognise outstanding contributors to the ACA and its membership'; if the family and the network then parted ways, Nine remained 'the cricket channel'.

When Allen Stanford and Subash Chandra hove into view with their DIY cricket attractions soon after, they explicitly invoked the example of WSC – 'Chandra does a Packer' read the headline in India's *Business Standard*. When Lalit Modi launched the Indian Premier League in April 2008, he pioneered an intrapreneurship that owed more to the example of a Packer-style privateer than of any local peer in the Board of Control for Cricket in India. Outside capital has been made welcome in the T20 leagues of South Asia and the Caribbean; that Australia has advanced more cautiously might owe something to experiences forty years earlier.

This text of *The Cricket War* has not been revised from the first edition – it was only ever a second draft of history, and a prentice work. But I am glad to see it for all that – the events it chronicles were part of my initiation into cricket, as they have shaded all that I have watched since. When WSC reaches its fiftieth anniversary, the world will look different again. But I suspect that I shall still recognise the abiding influence of Kerry Packer and his colourful cohorts.

GIDEON HAIGH
Melbourne
April 2017

PROLOGUE

'Jesus, it's not going to work'

Ian Chappell rarely watched his openers' preparatory rites, but on the morning of 2 December 1977 he could not help studying Ian Davis. Moments before stepping into a crossfire of West Indian pace, Davis was a hyperactive blur.

'Wiz was getting ready and I watched him put on a thigh pad,' Chappell recalls. 'Then he got this other thigh pad and put it round his chest. But then he had a look at himself in the mirror and took it off. Then he put it back on. And took it off again.'

Davis turned to him seeking advice. 'Whatever you feel comfortable in, Wiz,' Chappell said lightly. But even he, after seventy-two Test match first mornings, could feel the weight of the occasion. Because this wasn't a Test.

It was fourteen months since Chappell had heard talk of an international cricket series independent of the game's existing rulers, and six since he'd signed a contract to play the Supertests of the upstart World Series Cricket.

He'd joined his rival captain Clive Lloyd in the centre of a cavernous football stadium on Melbourne's outskirts called VFL Park fifteen minutes earlier, and lost a toss superintended by Sir Garfield Sobers. A single in-house photographer had been on hand to record the occasion, and there seemed hardly a soul around. Fewer than 500 people were strewn round concrete tiers that could hold 80,000.

Accompanied by Rick McCosker as he ascended the ramp from the underground dressing room, Ian Davis was about to take in the same vacuum. Seven months earlier he'd joined McCosker on the first morning of the Centenary Test against England to the roars of more than 50,000 at the MCG. Now only the cap was different – gold rather than green – but he could hear his own breathing. 'Here I am, playing with all these great players,' Davis thought. 'And no one's here. Jesus, it's not going to work.'

As he watched McCosker take guard and West Indian Andy Roberts recede into the distance, the twenty-four-year-old collected himself. He felt in form. A stint of weight training had put muscle on his slender ten-and-a-half-stone frame. A few days earlier his captain had told Davis that he'd never seen him hit the ball so hard.

McCosker was more phlegmatic. In a week he'd be thirty-one, a late bloomer who'd taken five years to graft his way into the New South Wales side but then just a year to become a Test batsman. His mind was full of Roberts, who'd rolled him three times in four previous meetings. Roberts would be on him quickly, and he'd get nothing loose.

It was swift to be sure. Umpire Jack Collins had said 'Play', and that was exactly what he had to do, stabbing an exploratory short ball to gully. The second ball left him in the air, and kissed his committed bat on its way to Vivian Richards at third slip. West Indian cries filled the still air.

That was Roberts. Crestfallen as he was, McCosker admired the pace man's craft. 'Two to play at straight away,' he thought disgustedly, pulling off his gloves. 'It's not supposed to happen like that, but it does against Andy. One day he'll give me a half-volley.'

Vern Stone didn't know much about cricket, but WSC's general manager knew a bad start when he saw it. It was already a bad day. How could that stew at the gate with the photographers have happened? His offsider, Ern Steet, had been following orders to keep reporters from the square, but the priceless moment of WSC's first toss had been missed when it needed all the good publicity it could get.

Stone could imagine what his master Kerry Packer was now thinking. Taciturn among a group in the VIP area including Victorian

Governor, Sir Henry Winneke, the Sydney businessman was studying the empty stands with features tight. Stone's own face was red
as he passed the official response to requests for an audience. 'No
interviews today. Mr Packer wants to enjoy the cricket.'

The tall blonde figure by Packer's side, Tony Greig, could sense
Packer's distress as well. The South African-born cricketer had been
intimately involved with WSC for eight months and was closer to
Packer than any member of his star troupe. Now the curtain had
risen on the big occasion and there seemed more heads in the VIP
area than in the stands.

Ian Chappell tugged at his cap at the non-striker's end and turned
to studying Roberts' twenty-three-year-old scion Michael Holding.
His range was rusty, but the boy was quicker straightaway than in
Australia two years before, and getting faster by the ball.

What's more, he mused, Holding's front foot landed an unvarying
nine inches behind the front crease. 'Shit,' Chappell thought. 'Hope
he doesn't wake up to that. Better he bowls from nine inches further
away if he's going to bowl that fast.'

The captain re-examined the artificially grown and transplanted
pitch he'd first played on a week before against Greig's World XI. Its
salient feature – the junction of its two halves – was still easy to see.
The fuller length of the World's fast bowlers had saved him discovering what might happen if a ball pitched there. Today, likely as not,
he'd find out.

Chappell and Davis settled, Lloyd replacing Holding with Wayne
Daniel after three overs. Adopting his captain's businesslike cross-
step, Davis moved smartly into line, though he could still recall the
reason for his chest pad dilemma. Two years earlier he'd batted in a
Brisbane grade match for Toombul with a young wicketkeeper then
dossing in the Wooloowin flat Davis shared with the fast bowler Jeff
Thomson. Twenty-two-year-old Martin Bedkober had waved away
assistance after allowing the short ball to strike his chest. Then, to
Davis' horror, Bedkober crumpled.

'I'd been the one who'd organised for Martin to come to Brisbane
in the first place and he'd only been there a couple of months,' says
Davis. 'And I was the first bloke to find out he was dead. I can
remember going behind the curtain at the hospital and the doctor

telling me. And I can still remember what he had for breakfast that morning and sending his dirty washing home to his mother.' Davis looked up to see the slippery Holding reappear at the outer end.

Holding himself was apprehensive about second spells. A shoulder injury he'd carried for a year had still to heal, and he nursed it carefully. 'I could bowl fast for five or six overs but after that I could hardly lift my arm up,' he recalls. 'So those first couple of spells always counted. I knew I might not be able to come back for a second spell that day.'

He saw Davis moving swiftly back and across as he let go at 1–33, and was puzzled momentarily by the sound of crashing timber. The little opener pulled away, his eyes shut tight. He had hit his stumps. 'I can't understand it to this day,' Davis recalls. 'I felt I'd been going quite well but I guess I'd been creeping further and further back, just a few inches, to give myself extra time to play. I must have knocked nearly an inch of wood off the end of my bat.'

Now Holding had found his range, he zeroed in on the pitch's fault line. Greg Chappell's first delivery exploded from the crack and fizzed past his nose; his third did the same and bounced to gully from a flinching glove.

At first sight of the left-handed wunderkind, David Hookes, Holding swung to round the wicket. 'I was still learning, still experimenting,' Holding says. 'And I found it difficult to get the ball to straighten to the left-handers from over the wicket. It would pitch and go straight across the body. From round I could get the ball coming into them.'

Hookes scratched his guard, recalling that Bob Willis had recently used the same tactic against him in England. It took three balls to learn the differences. 'Bob was a fucking off-spinner compared to Michael,' he says. 'And that was as quick as Michael got that summer.' His off drive had barely commenced as his off stump toppled, Hookes stumbling forward like a man pushed down a flight of stairs.

The sight of Doug Walters joining him would normally have cheered Ian Chappell. But Dougie had looked out of sorts in practice, eagle-eye no longer quick enough to disguise his homespun technique. It was possible to enjoy one heel-clicking straight drive from Walters, but Chappell knew this was a different ball game. You had to pounce on anything loose and run like blazes, for Lloyd's fielding side contained no malingerers.

Sweating on 34 for two hours' graft as lunch approached, Chappell seized a Holding half-volley with relief. It skimmed in the air behind square leg, where Daniel had been sent to graze after his morning spell. The fast bowler's stoop was deceptively casual, the catch never in doubt.

As he headed for the players' race, Chappell noticed he had company. He recognised David Grant, an interviewer recruited to eavesdrop on players' self-diagnoses of dismissal, who was clearly intent on a word. Grant's morning preparations had been so rushed that he'd missed McCosker's early exit altogether. Chappell wasn't about to change his luck. Not today, or ever. The only sound Grant's microphone captured was that of the captain's bat echoing down the race as he passed.

Chappell was still in his pads when Walters joined him, outpaced by Roberts as he searched for runs in the gully. Chappell was surprised to hear Walters muttering. The man who of legend could resume a card hand interrupted by a duck was repeating: 'What a bloody shot.'

And a bloody score. At lunch, 6–66. 'We're in trouble,' Chappell could hear from players huddled round a television set in the corner. But it wasn't their own game they were discussing. Since midday, they had been tuned to the ABC, as Australia batted in their Test match against India at Brisbane's Woolloongabba ground. No daylight saving in the north and Dennis Lillee had been waiting for the telecast all morning.

It seemed like the easy way in to Peter Toohey. Although most of the names had been unfamiliar when he'd heard them, he'd flown from Sydney to Brisbane flanked by two very familiar presences.

Toohey's Western Suburbs club captain, Bob Simpson, had been feted all along his route back to the Australian captaincy; and his flatmate, the Waverley wicketkeeper Steve Rixon, had also been picked for his Test debut. Simpson had then told Toohey he'd be twelfth man: a chance to get used to the terrain without the risk of costly failure.

After a comfortable hotel breakfast that morning, though, the skipper had approached him. 'You're playing Pete,' he'd said simply. Kim Hughes, the West Australian, would carry the drinks.

Toohey had looked up to Simpson the moment he'd arrived at Wests as a gawky eighteen-year-old from Blayney in late 1972, and promptly been promoted to first grade. 'Then when I started making runs early the next season,' Toohey recalls, 'Simmo wrote about me in the *Daily Telegraph* as someone who should be playing for NSW, so it was very flattering. Simmo was a legend to a young player like me.'

Greatness was being thrust upon many that morning. Toohey saw six others about him playing their first Tests. Experience was at a premium. Three weeks after his twenty-sixth birthday, Craig Serjeant had learned that mixed form in three Test matches in England imbued him with the stuff of vice-captains. Though he'd not even played a Test on that miserable tour, Gary Cosier's eight previous caps gave him senior status and an unaccustomed opening berth. His partner, Victorian Paul Hibbert, had made his solitary first-class century a fortnight earlier.

Simpson won the toss from his Indian rival Bishan Bedi with a lucky American dollar and batted. The pitch was moist but might crumble, and India's opening bowlers Sharma Madan Lal and Mohinder Amarnath caused him few second thoughts. Only within sight of lunch after a rain-reduced morning session did things begin going amiss. Cosier's fretful cut had flown to second slip. Then Bedi's first gentle left-arm spinner had turned enough to catch a tentative debutant's edge from Queenslander David Ogilvie.

It could have been better than 2–33, thought Bob Parish, but it was the real thing. And that's what mattered. The Australian Cricket Board chairman didn't hurry when paged in the Cricketers' Club for an interstate call. He'd heard the news already from VFL Park. Ray Steele, ACB treasurer, had been watching GTV-9's broadcast of the 'First Supertest' at his Kew home and turned it off with mild satisfaction. 'I was pretty pleased to see he (Packer) didn't have too many in,' Steele recalls.

The Gabba, in contrast, was an establishment heartland. Mr Packer had waved his chequebook at ground trustees four months earlier, but they'd been unimpressed. Particularly at his threat of making members pay for the privilege of watching his stars. No-one was going to miss him. The ground's light rinsing hadn't deterred a crowd building towards 12,000.

Nothing evoked the split in cricket as thoroughly as the program being perused by patrons at the Gabba. The cover featured Jeff Thomson: the local boy who'd thought better of signing for the fraudulent game. Few thoughts were spared for Thomson's partner in speed, Dennis Lillee, whose image featured on the cover of the brochure on sale at VFL Park.

Lunch had been hard to palate for Serjeant. On resumption he would have seven balls from Bedi to take, and the misty rain's return was unsettling.

Serjeant was not even captain of his Nedlands club and, as a first-class cricket freshman, he'd declined a WSC contract offered in England. Now, though, there was only a forty-one-year-old separating him from Australian cricket's highest office. 'It had been a complete bolt from the blue,' he recalls. 'I'd no idea they'd been thinking about me for the job at all and, because there was still uncertainty about Simpson going to the West Indies after the Indian series, there was suddenly all this talk of me leading the team on tour.'

Bedi allowed him no long-range planning. Gliding in as soon as Serjeant had marked centre, he bubbled when the ball struck sharply from the rain-freshened turf. Australia's vice-captain watched as the solitary close catcher was joined by four others. For the next three balls, their arms and strangled cries surrounded him as Serjeant strained to stifle the turn. He elected to leave his fifth ball as it pitched outside leg stump, but its diagonal deviation caught his outside edge before arcing to Sunil Gavaskar at slip. 'I'm out,' Serjeant thought as he walked away. 'And I had no control over my dismissal at all.'

His captain walked into the same soggy trap and, despite reminiscent cheers, lasted five minutes before falling identically. The following over from Amarnath, Hibbert's first one and a half hours as a Test batsmen were through. 'We're in trouble,' could be heard round the Gabba as the newcomers Toohey and Tony Mann combined at 5–49, and there was no doubt which trouble was concerned.

Lunch at VFL Park had been uncomfortable. The blue-ribbon fare hardly befitted the sensation VIPs had of intruding on private grief.

Packer, moreover, wanted everything just so. He mixed marti-
nis personally when commentator Fred Trueman and wife Veronica
joined him, and disdained the Vickers Gin the barman offered. 'This
is no good,' he said. 'Is this all you've got? Son, I want the best gin.'
A bottle of Gordons was fetched.

Packer had publicly anticipated 15,000-a-day at his Supertests,
while Stone had heard predictions of a first-day crowd as high as
50,000. Cornell had bet on 30,000, a match aggregate of 105,000.
Another important WSC architect, retired Australian captain and chief
commentator Richie Benaud, had been more conservative: maybe
8000. But the throng did not get beyond 2847, whose tickets barely
covered the VIP catering bill. 'We ended up spending $17–18,000 on
food for the VIPs,' Stone recalls. 'Just for people to pick at, and most
of it was slung in the bin.'

Down in Benaud's commentary area, the sparseness of the crowd
was troubling even the GTV-9 cameramen. Confining crowd shots to
the few knots of spectators was considered, then rejected. The empty
seats could not be concealed. 'You couldn't hide them,' recalls director
Brian Morelli. 'And when the ball went up you saw them anyway.'

As Ray Bright and Rod Marsh padded up to resume, the
Australian dressing-room was still stuck on the ABC. Bright was
pleased to know that his Victorian mate Hibbert had lived up to his
ironic nickname Dasher, and knew he'd need similar stubbornness.

Concentrating on defence, the twenty-three-year-old hazarded
the odd fling when the ball was within range. 'Some pretty good players were already out,' he says. 'And I thought: "We're not going to
do much here if we just stick around". Everyone was treading warily
that day – like the first couple of days of the Centenary Test – so if
we had a go at a few we might be able to put a bit of pressure back on
the West Indies.'

The sight of the day's first bold strokes brought cheer to a lonely
crowd. Marsh hooked Daniel with vigour, while Bright took a dash
at Collis King. When Lillee hoicked an improbable six from Holding,
the scoreboard was for the first time occupied more deeply in its own
match than in relaying the scores from Brisbane.

Still, as the players adjourned for tea, the latest Brisbane bulletin
suggested that something had been reviving Australia there as well.
Who'd come good?

Toohey and Mann had taken the same approach as Marsh and Bright. If it was up, it had to go. The 41 they added in three-quarters of an hour took Australia within sight of the century and, although Bedi's attack struck three times again before tea, Toohey felt comfortable and keyed up despite the score of 8–122.

Such was the clatter of wickets, he'd barely had time to get nervous. like a schoolboy beneath his big green lid, Toohey had disarmed the Indians with his free-flowing shots. Bedi and his spin partner Bhagwat Chandrasekhar saw no harm in Toohey farming the strike as the innings went on. 'I guess the way I played they always felt they had a chance of knocking me over,' Toohey reflects. 'They didn't push the field back at the start of the over or bring it in at the end, so I was able to bat pretty normally and get most of the bowling.'

The novice stormed at the spinners after tea, in half an hour adding 43 of 44 Australian runs. Bedi was driven for six and Chandra cut adeptly, before the inevitable prearranged stumping snare. Toohey returned to a buzzing dressing-room, suddenly confident of Australia striking in the hour and a quarter remaining.

Jeff Thomson fancied his chances with the new ball. As a seventeen-year-old at Punchbowl High playing for Australian Schoolboys, he'd bagged a bundle of young Indians. For Wayne Clark, whom Simpson trusted to bowl into the wind, selection had been as much deliverance as delight. Like Serjeant, he'd turned WSC away a couple of months earlier for the chance to play Tests. 'When I was injured before the first Shield match and didn't get many wickets before the team was selected, I wondered if I'd made the right choice,' Clark recalls. 'I was relieved more than anything when I heard I'd been picked.'

In his second over Clark found the length to disturb the diminutive Gavaskar, ten Test centuries and all, into fending a short leg catch. A successful light appeal ended the day three-quarters of an hour early, but the faithful ovation told of relief at a day rescued and a cause honoured.

Rescue was well under way at VFL Park. A 49-run last-wicket stand between Max Walker and Len Pascoe had prolonged the Australian innings almost an hour beyond tea, to the extent that the last four wickets of the total had added 190 by its conclusion at 256. Leaving the television behind, Ian Chappell led his team into the field with a purposeful jog.

Pascoe was the second Punchbowl High boy entrusted with an Australian new ball that day, and he fancied his chances as strongly as schoolmate Thomson. Three years before, as a twenty-one-year-old scruff making his NSW Sheffield Shield debut in Perth, he'd asked Dennis Lillee to help him sort out a frenzied approach and non-existent follow-through. Now he was taking second over to the same man.

The West Indian openers Gordon Greenidge and Roy Fredericks went for him, ears pinned back. Nor could Pascoe get a foothold. Just as there was a tectonic split in the prefabricated pitch, the grass approaches had still to take root. Relieving Lillee, Walker found the same problem. 'You were like a dog in the passage with the rug gathering up under your feet,' Walker recalls. 'You'd be thinking: "I've finished my run and there's a couple of yards of raw dirt ahead of me".'

But Pascoe finally found his feet, piercing Fredericks' drive and pinning nightwatchman Holding on his stumps. Cheers from the terraces were isolated, but the Australian congratulations were genuine. With the West Indies 2–47 at stumps, the team had dragged itself back into the fight.

Friday 2 December 1977 saw Australian collapses – and recoveries – in two cities. Two rookies of twenty-three had proved themselves. Two apprentice opening bowlers had left teams in good heart by evening. Opponents and conditions alike had been wrestled and resisted.

But the manner of both matches had been entirely distinct. Australia had been foiled by speed in Melbourne, by spin in Brisbane. The atmosphere had been funereal at VFL Park, festive at the Gabba. Two commercial enterprises were in clear conflict, and dejected organisers to the south envied indulgent proprietors in the north.

It was too late to undo their rivalry, but too early to judge who would prevail. For Packer was unshakeable. As pressmen asked him what defeat felt like, he stiffened. 'I'm sorry gentlemen, but you've never been so wrong in your lives,' he replied.

'These are not professionals'

Three of the party landing in London on 29 May 1975 worked for banks back in Australia. Two were insurance salesmen and two accountants. An architect came with familiar companions, a teacher and a trainee engineer, although his friend the antique salesman could not make it. A real estate executive and a cigarette salesman kept spirits buoyant, especially in the company of a journalist.

The group was an Australian cricket team touring England, the second Ian Chappell had brought, and very much in the mould of its precursors: semi-amateur, part-time players, paid accordingly. It was an honourable tradition. Butchers, bakers and undertakers have blended beneath 'baggy green' and, more than any other nation's cricket lore, Australia's is written in team terms. With shorter hair and sharper razors, Ian Chappell's seventeen could have been stepping from a P&O steamer.

Chappell's grandfather Vic Richardson *had* led Australia forty years earlier, and the inherited characteristics showed. In his very first Test as captain at Sydney in 1971 against England, Chappell had been next in when a wicket fell five minutes before stumps. Although there is no time to get 'in' under such circumstances, and always ample to get out, the captain batted.

On twenty-seven of the forty-eight occasions he batted in the number-three slot for Australia, the score had not reached 20. Leaping to attention at the premature fall of a wicket, he seemed to seek walls to put his back to. His trademark became a hook of often premeditated defiance.

Illogical defiance, too. In the five minutes Chappell batted in Sydney, Australia might have lost a valuable top-order wicket. His powers against spin might occasionally have been better used at number five. And resolving to hook every bouncer 'as an example' *did* sometimes cheapen his wicket. The best of all possible captains would probably have attained Zen-like detachment, assessing the asset to be preserved, hour, state of wicket and match situation. Ian Chappell, rationally speaking, was too willing a self-abnegator to be a great captain. But the same attachment to cricket's anachronistic, highly irrational, damnably inspiring traditions made him a remarkable leader.

Chappell's on-field values circulated easily. Get in line. Don't walk, even on edging a catch, but accept the umpire's decision. Battle ends at stumps, and nothing on the field cannot be settled off it over 'a beer and a yarn'. Cricketers who made a modest ration of ability last were especially respected. Where the shades were grey, as in questions like sporting links with South Africa, he took the career cricketer's side: sport and politics were separate.

As Australia sought emblems in the Whitlamite nationalism driving and dividing Australia round Chappell, however, evidence of change seemed to be everywhere. 'In Bradman's day Sydney editors banned any reference to the play *Lysistrata*,' wrote Ray Robinson in his elegant appreciation of Chappell in *On Top Down Under*. 'By Chappell's time families could see Diane Cilento playing in Aristophanes' comedy on television . . . On the day Ian was reappointed skipper for the 1974–1975 Tests against England, an unwed mother Helen Morgan, twenty-two, was selected as Miss World.'

Chappell did indeed regard a spade as a fucking shovel. Cricketer's chins were not policed, and curfews were for college kids. Leg-spinner Kerry O'Keeffe recalls team meetings of elaborate simplicity: 'Ian would go through the other team by name. "Boycott?" "Bounce the cunt". "Edrich". "Bounce the cunt". "Willis". "Slog the cunt". "Underwood". "Bloody tight. Hard to get away. Slog the cunt".'

To drink all night and bat all day was the fullest expression of an insouciant circle, and Chappell was more supervisor than regulator. He told players when he assumed the captaincy that his hotel door would remain open until 3am. Those still socialising as that hour approached would remark that there was 'still time to go and see Bertie'.

Regulation, though, began at the gate. 'It pays a captain to be friendly with his men off the field,' Vic Richardson had written. 'But once they walk through the gate, there must be no doubt who is in charge.' And Chappell could be strict. Idiosyncratically. For sins the night before a 1975 tour match, for instance, all-rounder Gary Gilmour was sentenced to a session and a half of bowling, and a fielding beat from third man to third man. 'By tea, Gus was absolutely cactus, heaving his guts out,' a fellow tourist relates. 'And Ian grabbed a can, ripped off the top, and went over and stuck it in front of him. He just said: "Gus, I hope you've learned something today".'

And in the meshing of generations, the captain kept old gurus. With Bill O'Reilly, for instance, he would discuss their shared distrust of coaches. With Richie Benaud, who became something of a paterfamilias, he could talk over man-management and a mutual disdain for administrators.

It worked. At times, such as at the Oval in 1972, and at Port-of-Spain in 1973, magically. Like its predecessors, the 1975 team was a true ensemble. Only the captain and his brother, Doug Walters, Rod Marsh, Ashley Mallett, Dennis Lillee, and middle-order batsman Ross Edwards had made the 1972 trip; and the last three had in the interim known long absences from the team. Only five of the 1975 side had played more than twenty Tests. The still-fragile Lillee had survived only seventeen in four years as a Test opening bowler. Yet it played with a winner's flair. Its confidence was not yet arrogance, its unity not quite chauvinism, and it drew strength from praise and detraction alike. Injuries were ignored, apparently out-of-form batsmen played blinders, tailenders acquired defensive strokes for a day that had eluded them for a lifetime, medium pacers charged in believing they were expressmen. Faces changed, but the face of the Chappell era did not.

The 1974–1975 home summer left behind had been arduous and exhilarating. Never had Australian cricket seemed more robust.

Never had players felt their own semi-professional status more demeaning.

Entertaining, competitive cricketers, they were in demand abroad, while making Australia an attractive rendezvous for touring sides. Since Chappell's elevation, Australia had hosted a Rest of the World combination, Pakistan, New Zealand and England, while visiting England, the West Indies and New Zealand.

But cricketers remained voyeurs to their popularity. During the team's emphatic capture of the Ashes from Mike Denness's Englishmen in 1974–1975, less than 2 per cent of the bumper gate-takings came the cricketers' way, and the Australian Cricket Board held to the philosophy that true patriots would pay to play for their country. Home Test fees rose $20 to $200 between 1970 and 1975, while in the Whitlam wage surge Australian workers awarded themselves pay rises of a third.

Jack Fingleton had warned thirty years before that 'no ordinary mercantile concern could afford to carry a cricketer . . . incessantly absent from his employment', and it had only grown harder to hold an outside job. With unemployment reaching a post-Depression peak of 5.2 per cent after the 1974 credit squeeze, absentee athlete employees were a corporate luxury.

The formula lost appeal to the likes of Graham McKenzie, Keith Stackpole, Paul Sheahan and even Richie Benaud's talented twenty-eight-year-old brother John. Mallett and Ian Redpath – with businesses and careers at sensitive stages – continued only by assessing each tour and season as it arose. Through Ian Chappell Enterprises Pty Ltd, incorporated in September 1973, the captain was one of a kind in 'living from cricket', though most of his income came from advertising for Gillette, Chrysler and TAA, contracts for three books and a syndicated newspaper column. His actual earnings from cricket were 'fish and chip money'.

The ACB seemed, as it ever has, inept, niggardly, and heartless, though the tendency to cast the administrative class of the 1970s as villains is something of a convenience. They too were amateurs. Chairman Tim Caldwell could not attend an entire Test from 1932 until his retirement as an ANZ Bank executive in 1974. His successor Bob Parish had worked in the family timber business since 1932. Treasurer Ray Steele was a retired lawyer. And as the Sheffield Shield declined in the late 1960s, administrators understandably viewed big Test gates as something to salt away. Discontent about pay and conditions abided. A dispute during the Adelaide Test in February 1975 was averted only narrowly when the ACB rewarded players with a bonus and a credit to their two-year-old provident fund (which provided for a small 'tide-over' lump-sum payment to retirees according to their Test experience). Yet a more sustained increase in player payments met a blank response when Chappell sought it at the ACB executive committee. The meeting was nominally led by Caldwell, who had assumed the chair vacated by Sir Donald Bradman in September 1972, but Bradman's presence representing the South Australian Cricket Association was pervasive. 'When I came to the two matters on finance he sat forward, listening intently,' Chappell wrote. 'After I finished each point, he explained in his distinctive tone and in no uncertain terms that the board couldn't entertain such ideas.' The oft-quoted retort of board secretary Alan Barnes to press comment about player payments was: 'These are not professionals . . . they were all invited to play, and if they don't like the conditions there are 500,000 other cricketers in Australia who would love to take their places.'

Three senior West Australian members of the 1975 team – Marsh, Edwards and Lillee – provide a good peer sample at the end of three hectic years. Edwards recalls, for instance, their Perth flit at the end of the Sydney Test with Pakistan in January 1973 to deposit washing and collect luggage before returning two days later to embark on a Caribbean tour. With young families, all three were studying the bottom line of their endeavours.

Marsh, appointed third tour selector, was luckier than most: his employer, home-builder Realty Development Corporation, quite liked having an Australian cricketer on staff. Although he had clocked on barely eight days in eighty during the cricket season, RDC paid him his full salary. That said, he still earned $12,000 a year. In 1975, his professional golfer brother Graham – a regular guest in the Australian dressing-room in England – was the world's sixteenth ranked player and earned $US120,354.

Cricket for Edwards, a hard-working sweat whose father had played for WA, was a succession of crossroads. He had qualified as an accountant, but spent much of his cricket duty wondering if he would ever practise except as consultant to Ian Chappell and a few teammates. Tours were subsidised by letting his house, while wife Lyndall took their son to stay with her parents in New Zealand.

'I played from September 1971 to June 1973 without a break,' Edwards says. 'And by the end in the West Indies I was so physically exhausted I couldn't get past the teens when I batted. I remember one day when someone brought some food into my hotel room and I just couldn't stop eating it. My body was so starved of nutrition.'

Edwards returned to Perth financially depleted, too. 'I was wiped out,' he says. 'I was unemployed and had $10 in the bank. I had a wife and a son and I just couldn't go on ignoring our bank balance.' Omission from the national side in the summer of 1973–1974 allowed him some time to rebuild, but recall the following season and selection to tour was a sublime form of suffering.

Almost eighty weeks in the first five years of Dennis Lillee's first-class career had been spent overseas on representative duty and as a Lancashire League cricketer. A Commonwealth Bank teller until 1973, he'd been lucky after an unsuccessful investment in contract cleaning to find a job at a travel agency, Travel Time International.

Treatment for spinal stress fractures diagnosed in the West Indies that cost him the 1973–1974 cricket summer had pushed him into a bizarre dispute with the ACB when he was restored to the Australian team. The board had inscrutably ceased paying his bills the instant Lillee had rolled his arm over in Perth grade cricket just before Christmas 1973, and he had to visit Barnes to settle the matter. 'At one stage a doctor even offered me the chance to pay his account off at $1 a week,' he wrote. 'How embarrassing! It wasn't the amount of money it was the principle. I'd injured myself playing for Australia and I wasn't going to pay for the treatment that followed.'

The 1975 tour contract itself continued the steady decline in cricketers' earnings relative to average male weekly wages. As Braham Dabscheck of the University of New South Wales points out, the weekly income of the Australian team members on tour in India and South Africa in 1969–1970 had been 66 per cent above average male weekly earnings of the time; the margin had narrowed to 40 per cent by 1972, and in 1975 was a slender 13 per cent.

The contracts, though, were signed with the usual alacrity. Only Redpath decided he could not afford the further neglect of his

Geelong antique business. The 1975 schedule was as stimulating as any offered a devoted cricketer: a whistle-stop in Canada before a fortnight involved in cricket's first World Cup and a four-Test defence of the Ashes just seized.

Travel broadened the Australian mind. Their eyes were opened in the World Cup to one-day cricket's heady English surge. It was a discipline for which the tourists had little preparation: their primitive Gillette Cup state knock-out competition at home might limit them to one such sprint a season.

They were still headed only in the cup final by the West Indies. Despite the run-a-minute century by West Indian captain Clive Lloyd and the uncanny fielding sense of a twenty-three-year-old Vivian Richards, the result was in doubt until the day's 120th over in a Lord's twilight.

Cricket's full international flavour was savoured for the first time. Never had all Test nations (not to mention Sri Lanka and East Africa) been gathered in a single location, and the mingling Australians learned that times were tough all over. With British inflation running at 25 per cent that month, local Test fees were unchanged at £180. Tournament gossip was of an Indian businessman in London proposing a travelling sequence of all-star exhibitions.

Cricket-minded Indian businessmen were always 'well-connected' and 'had access to substantial capital', but private cricket enterprise seemed fanciful while boards of control had the run of venues. When the Chappells, Lloyd and Indian captain Bishan Bedi were among those canvassed at a London hotel while the Cup was under way, their advice was to obtain official sanction first. The cricketers heard no more.

The Ashes were satisfactorily retained on the strength of Australia's conclusive victory in the murk at Edgbaston, although the series again had a financial backdrop. Ian Chappell met Caldwell and tour manager Fred Bennett at the Waldorf on the rest day of the Oval Test and sought a review of the entire Test fee: not just the $200 match payment but the scrawny $50 in expenses and $35 for meals away from home. The first, he felt, should be at least $500, and he was annoyed at anomalies like the fact that hotel meals taken after restaurant hours because of practice sessions often left his men out of pocket.

The Waldorf had been privy to such meetings before. In 1968, his predecessor Bill Lawry had first suggested to manager Bob Parish that the ACB should contract players long-term, so that their finances would hinge less on fluctuating form and favour. Ian Chappell's 1972 tour had ended in a similar heart-to-heart with manager Ray Steele.

The gathering on 31 August 1975 was not a militant meeting. As Edwards observes: 'We were hardly in a bargaining position. We wanted to play for Australia. We'd based our lives round it. We said: "We want to keep playing. We think we're worth it. Can't you help us?"' Nor were the officials unsympathetic. Caldwell, about to yield his chair to Parish, had been a thoughtful and concerned listener. The likeable Bennett had heard many of the same complaints as treasurer for the 1972 trip.

But the captain was insistent. Poor pay might sap success. His team had already been denied Redpath's guiding hand at the top of the order. Now Edwards had chosen the Oval Test as his last and Mallett was toying with retirement. Chappell himself was considering at least standing down as captain. The winning Australian side was the ACB's prime asset. Some reinvestment in that asset was now politic.

He sensed his chance: the Ashes were in safekeeping, the hawkish Bradman was 12,000 miles away, and the forthcoming West Indies' tour of Australia guaranteed buoyant Test attendances and board profits for at least another year.

It was a persuasive case although the committee process would deny Chappell a decisive win. A week after Australia had the better of a protracted draw at The Oval, it had similar fortunes at the ACB's pre-season meeting at Cricket House in George Street, Sydney: match payments were doubled to $400, with a $25 increase in expenses and a $40 rise in meal allowances.

When Ian Chappell did relinquish his captaincy, he became 1975's second ex-captain. Mike Denness's exit amid the wreckage at Edgbaston, however, had not been as orderly. With England heading for its sixth defeat in eight Ashes contests, Denness himself suggested that a leadership change might be positive, and proposed the popular Tony Greig. The extroverted all-rounder seemed qualified as a leader: opportunistic, magnetic, and uncannily adept at getting up Australian noses.

Greig played cricket more in keeping with his South African nativity than his Scottish paternity. He was ambitious, too. Given two years by his father to make a cricket mark while wintering in England in 1965, he had joined Sussex, made a century on debut and sought British citizenship. As a clean-hitting, visibly competitive middle-order batsman and seamer, he made a virtue of his two metres in height.

While early skirmishes left some Australians chary of Greig, his brand of cricket was one to which Ian Chappell in particular could relate: mean on the field, generous off it. Profiling the South African for *Cricketer* magazine, Chappell wrote: 'As a person I like Tony. We've shared many beers after the day's play was over, which in turn hasn't stopped either of us from having a few choice things to say to each other in the middle in the heat of the battle.'

Despite his nationhood and combustibility, Greig also gained the confidence of authority. He grew close to the *Daily Telegraph's* influential Jim Swanton, who wrote of him in 1974: 'The degree to which Greig can subdue what amounts to an excessive and misguided enthusiasm is important for English cricket since, off the field, he is a strong and most likeable personality whom men will gladly follow. Given self-control he has all the ingredients of leadership, and one can see him as a natural captain of England.'

The English selectors were of a mind at Birmingham and named Greig captain for the balance of the series. And although he achieved more in style than substance over the ensuing three draws, he entered English imaginations as though he had recaptured the urn single-handed. *Wisden* saluted the 'many splendid qualities' of the 'tall, volatile captain of Sussex'.

Greig knew enough of Test cricket from his three years, however, to understand that his name would never be stencilled in. 'I'd got it from a guy who'd thought he was going to hang on to it for a long time,' he says. 'Who'd got it in turn from someone who thought he was going to hold on to it for a long time. And the same before him. Denness had got it when Ray Illingworth was sacked. Illy had taken it from Colin Cowdrey. I decided when I got the captaincy that I should never be in a position where I could be as let down as those guys seemed to be, when I knew a tenure could be ended by one bad report, one incident, one bit of foul language.'

With that in mind, he pursued endorsements and contracts restlessly, and in expansive mood spoke of becoming 'the world's first millionaire cricketer'. In England he even employed an agent of sorts in Reg Hayter – the man who thirty years before had introduced Denis Compton to Bagenal Harvey and Brylcreem – and had struck up a business friendship with Australian opener Bruce Francis while they were playing in South Africa in 1972.

When Francis organised in September 1975 for Greig to play for his venturesome Waverley Cricket Club, it was remarked that a deal of this kind was unusual for England's captain. It looked all the more peculiar when, with the help of advertising executive Ian Macfarlane, Greig made his name synonymous with Kelloggs and Waltons, spruiked pads and pantyhose, wrote a newspaper column and a book and almost incidentally took 70 wickets for Waverley. But Tony Greig was no ordinary holder of English cricket's top job.

It set the tone of the 1975–1976 cricket season in Australia that the top scorer in the annual charity match organised by Sydney's Spastic Centre at Drummoyne on 5 October was Bob Hawke, then in his pomp as president of the Australian Council of Trade Unions. The summer proved a high tide in Australian cricket's on-field success and recognition and a low point in its malfunctioning industrial relations. So profound became the problems that Hawke, despite the strife about to break loose in the Australian Labor Party with the Whitlam dismissal, was seldom far from a Test match that summer.

Australia, under Greg Chappell's leadership, firmly redressed its World Cup loss to the West Indies with a 5–1 Test series victory. Edwards' retirement and Walters' absence with a knee injury were more than compensated for by the valedictory feats of Redpath and Ian Chappell and the emergence of middle-order talent in Gary Cosier and Graham Yallop. Lillee and Thomson ruled the roost once more, aided and abetted by the maturing Gilmour, and there seemed few reasons that the younger Chappell, just twenty-seven, should not reign as long as his brother.

The summer bore better financial fruit for the Australian team. Their improved pay was funded comfortably from surging gates, and $150,000 staked by the tobacco company sponsor Benson & Hedges. New patrons like Queensland radio station 4IP also appeared. After seeking unsuccessfully to lure Dennis Lillee east, 4IP's cricket-crazy chief Ken Mulcahy eased local hero Jeff Thomson's homesickness for his native Sydney with a ten-year, $633,000 deal.

The money was strictly rationed, and the Dino Ferrari sports car beside which Thomson posed for promotional photos was leased, but the contract was talismanic for the fast bowler's peers. Players, it proved, had a commodity to trade beyond their skill. As Greig was discovering, a name could be a brandname. Before Thomson, 4IP had been just another radio station, barely audible beyond Tweed Heads. After his signing, it had a national profile.

The deal also meant much to its broker, David Lord. An energetically mediocre club captain at Mosman until 1973, Lord hoped to become a better businessman. A sometime ghost writer and editor of *David Lord's World of Cricket Monthly*, he became for press purposes after the 4IP deal Thomson's 'agent'.

Sparks from a short-circuiting cricket system, however, were detectable throughout 1975–1976. Mulcahy had caught Lillee at a tender time in October 1975: Lillee had been retrenched by Travel Time and was only kept in Perth by a friendly car-dealer, Rod Slater, who found him work selling Renaults and Peugeots.

Recalcitrance at Test level had also filtered down to first-class cricket, whose administrators made the ACB elite seem enlightened fabians. When *Cricketer* magazine editor Eric Beecher surveyed the top twelve players in each of the five Sheffield Shield states for his December 1975 issue, he was deluged. Only two of sixty respondents believed they were being offered 'sufficient financial rewards'. Only one more was against professional promoters being brought into the game.

Beecher commented soberly: 'The result of this poll should not be mass revolution. It does not signify need for drastic upheaval. But it does require patient understanding, genuine acknowledgement and a sincere attempt at remedying disenchantment clearly pervading dressing-rooms at present.' In fact, Beecher added for emphasis, for far longer: 'For decades, cricketers have been voicing their disapproval of administrators. The communication gap between the two factions seems to have broadened with the years. Administrators with short memories could think back to one of their most illustrious – Sir Donald Bradman – at loggerheads with officialdom at times during his remarkable career.'

The ACB had created one loggerhead at the beginning of the season by requiring written reports from umpires on player conduct after every first-class game. Ian Chappell had promptly raised another by a famous decision – more memorable in correspondence than the event – to lower his trousers to adjust his protector during an early season fixture. Then, more seriously, he made the 'communication gap' palpable by leading his South Australian team to the brink of a strike over Sheffield Shield selection.

The disputes were symptomatic. *Cricketer* had discovered that two-thirds of its sample believed poor pay and conditions would force them from cricket prematurely. More than half were finding cricket actively detrimental to their careers.

As discussion became freer and franker, it became audible to those outside cricket's core. Those of greatest importance, and closest in attitude and age to the players themselves, were a peculiar trio: the television comics Paul Hogan and John Cornell, plus Cornell's former confrere on Perth's *Daily News*, Austin Robertson.

Hogan had met Cornell in 1971, where they were in front of and behind the camera on the Nine Network's fledgling *A Current Affair*. Hogan was a lowly paid comic on the show still living in a Sydney Housing Commission home, Cornell its Melbourne producer hired by another *News* old boy Mike Willessee.

When Cornell extracted Hogan from his niggardly contract and fell out with Willessee in 1973, the pair combined as JP Productions on ATV-7's *The Paul Hogan Show*. Their TV sketch comedy echoed the era as faithfully as Ian Chappell's cricketers. With their stock characters, Hoges and Strop, the pair lionised lairs and wags whose street-smart charm redeemed them. JP also branched out into managing their entertainment discoveries, notably the singer Bob Hudson and a Playboy bunny turned model, Delvene Delaney, who became Cornell's girlfriend.

When Cornell left him at the *News*, Robertson was at his peak as a Westralian sport divinity. As full-forward at Subiaco, he had steadily outgrown being the son of the super-sprinter Austin senior. Schooled in the drop-punt by Neil Hawke, his 1210-goal pile still stands in the WAFL.

Robertson was the *News'* athletic everyman. In the WA Sheffield Shield side, for instance, he knew everyone from captain and vice-captain John Inverarity and Ian Brayshaw, youth cricket teammates, to the kid swing bowler, Mick Malone, half-forward flanker in Subiaco's 1973 premiership season.

When Robertson played his last game for Subiaco the following year and joined the *News* full-time, he'd been an obvious figure on whom Lillee could lean for small 'management' duties as the fast bowler became media property again on resuming Test cricket. Such business had long attracted Robertson, but Perth was a parochial promontory for the ambitious. In late 1975 he finally contacted Cornell and Delaney and told them he was coming to Sydney to 'get serious'.

Dossing in their Neutral Bay home and considering sports-management's horizons, Robertson startled Cornell by telling him Lillee scraped as little as $8000 from cricket every year. With his conviction that class acts should be paid class sums, Cornell recalled the exploitative $50 a week Hogan had been paid on *A Current Affair* five years earlier.

The genesis of World Series Cricket, as Cornell has related it, was an exchange as he and Hogan lounged in their Neutral Bay writing-room in their usual creative attitude: on their backs, feet up against the wall. Hogan repeated that someone should do something to reward the cricketers, and added as an afterthought: 'Why don't we do it ourselves? Contract the players and set up our own series?'

Some serious scuff marks were left on the wall as ideas were kicked round, but reality soon dawned. The closest they had come to cricket administration was organising a Variety Club celebrity challenge in January 1975 (Bob Hawke and Tony Greig among the star cast). They were basically sports fans, whom success had not spoiled to the degree that they could afford to buy a cricket team. Perhaps JP could manage a few of the guys: Robertson's cachet with players, and the contacts Cornell and Hogan had in business and the media seemed a useful package. Robertson contacted Lillee in Perth urging he meet Cornell, another savvy local boy made good.

The fast bowler was unsure he needed a full-time agent. Though he agreed to meet him at Perth's Parmelia Hilton, Lillee knew Cornell simply as Strop the golden-hearted imbecile. 'As I walked into that room,' Lillee wrote, 'I did expect Strop to jump out of his chair, the jaw to drop and sneaky laugh to follow.' Lillee was wooed, however, especially when Cornell extemporised of a cricket tournament of the world's best players. Lillee had thrived on the World Cup, and reckoned some similar one-day jamboree would sell in Australia. With board approval.

It was a refrain Robertson would find familiar in other preliminary contacts with players. When the JP alliance broached its concept with the Chappells, Lillee and Marsh at the team's Koala Oxford Hotel billet during the Fourth Australia–West Indies Test in Sydney in January 1976, they encountered a weary response. Says Ian Chappell: 'I'd heard these things a few times before, and I just thought it'd go the same way as the rest of them. And if they disappeared I wasn't going to be jumping up and down.'

The Chappells still preferred to think of reform by sanctioned routes. Jack Nicholson topped the celebrity register at Melbourne's Hilton Hotel during the Sixth Test, but the most significant guest for the Chappells was Bob Hawke. The ACTU president joined a dinner round-table about the state of the cricketing nation with Marsh, Rick McCosker and former Australian batsman Bob Cowper.

McCosker was an officer with the Rural Bank of NSW in Newcastle, and had succeeded Edwards as the team's unofficial treasurer. Cowper, who ten years before had compiled an indelible 307 across the road at the MCG against Mike Smith's Englishmen, had put a stockbroking career at Guest and Bell ahead of cricket in 1970 and was now a henchman of takeover merchant John Elliott.

Test players were keen to depute an 'official liaison officer' to represent them at the ACB. In time, he might speak for all first-class players if they could evolve some sort of 'trade union'. Privy to his sharp mind as an adjacent slip-fielder during the 1960s, Ian Chappell imagined Cowper in the role. Cowper himself had felt strongly enough in 1974 about the calibre of Australian cricket's management to seek election as the VCA delegate of his Hawthorn-East Melbourne club. He'd felt even more strongly when he'd missed out. But Cowper's business acumen might even cut ice with another stockbroker in Sir Donald Bradman.

'You've been raped for years,' Hawke agreed, but he counselled caution. Hint of a 'trade union' to the ACB would provoke thoughts of the Eureka Stockade. English cricketers had made their ten-year-old Cricketer's Association acceptable to the Test and County Cricket Board by choosing a 'liaison officer' above suspicion in president John Arlott. Cowper would have to radiate the same rectitude.

Beecher gave the idea oblique approval in *Cricketer*. 'Cricket in Australia needs a mediating force between the two groups and . . . negotiations have been taking place for such a post to be filled by an eminently suitable person. His appointment could mark a new era in relations between the two volatile groups and a new deal for Australian cricketers.'

A different appointment at that same Test, however, proved more significant. Lillee had become the first client of the embryonic JP Sport. Press calls were fielded, interviews arranged, a Renault commercial filmed at the South Melbourne Cricket Club on the rest day, to fit round Lillee's cricket. Lillee and Thomson in that Test were creating a first. Australia's first 'managed' opening pair featured Lillee in Cornell's corner, Thomson in David Lord's.

One 'new deal' was in motion, but so was a newer one. And the first sign that the latter would gather up the former came when Cornell rang Lillee in Perth to ask his client whether he'd ever heard of a businessman called Kerry Packer.

2

'You think this is a fucking democracy, do you?'

Having last left Australia on a very traditional tour, the Chappells flouted convention on their next. And the Australian-accented International Wanderers XI they marshalled for a 'fact-finding' visit to South Africa with Richie Benaud bespoke frustrations the trio felt beyond the parsimony of a local board. Abandoned to politicians, they felt, South Africa's cricketers might as well start erecting rugby uprights.

Ian Chappell's calls for South Africa's reacceptance in Test cricket had already seen him branded a Pretorian envoy, but his sensibilities could not accept the likes of Barry Richards, Graeme Pollock, Mike Procter and Eddie Barlow languishing 'where the rest of the world cannot marvel at their talent'.

The thirty-year-old Richards, following summers from Natal province to Hampshire county, could feel his game slipping. 'I was at the stage in my career of saying, what I am doing here?' he says. 'You think about that marvellous word "marketing". Standing round at parties saying hello to people seems very appealing.' He kept it quiet when he began experimenting with lenses to correct myopia in his left eye: 'You let that get around and people start to write you off.'

Exercising professional rights had become a preoccupation. Pollock, Richards and wicketkeeper Lee Irvine appalled Benaud by boycotting early games for more money. But it was a measure of the Springboks' frustration: if cricket was to be their labour, they'd not go short.

It was sufficient for Australians to be beneath a Chappell banner. As well as enticing Lillee, Walker, Gilmour and Mallett, Ian had picked out the twenty-five-year-old Victorian fast bowler, Alan Hurst, and Greg his twenty-two-year-old Queensland colleague, Martin Kent, to buttress the squad.

Teacher Hurst risked the sack to spend the three weeks abroad. When approval for his unpaid leave was not processed in time, he counted on a cricket buff education minister Lindsay Thompson ignoring that a Victorian teacher was doing good cricket works abroad.

Hurst did very good works, earning favourable comparisons with Lillee in the Wanderers' song, to the tune of the timeless 'My Ding-A-Ling': 'Dennis and Alan bowl real fast/You don't see the ball, you just feel the draft/And even with your box on it don't half sting/If they catch you on your ding-a-ling.' He left his mark on Richards, too, knocking him cold at Kingsmead with a ball the batsman ducked into as one of his experimental lenses came adrift. The batsman deliberately made light of the blow by coming back a few hours later to bat with his usual felicity. 'He played as though nothing had happened,' Hurst says. 'Players you see hit, usually the last place they want to go near is the ground.'

Kent's impending marriage was accommodated by making the trip his honeymoon, and he drubbed 155 in Johannesburg. Pollock's 124 in the same match left Kent determined to remain in his high company. 'I was amazed by his driving,' Kent recalls. 'Fielding in the covers I was just running over to the gutter and picking them out'

Ian Chappell noted also a composed eighteen-year-old among his opponents. Kepler Wessels' pad-lined technique exasperated the visitors. When Gilmour acidly told the youth to discard his bat and oil his buckskins, Chappell also approved the teenager's silent response.

The rest of his 'fact-finding' depressed him. Multi-racial cricket was a mirage, and South African cricket might become one. 'Right now South Africa's cricket future is in the balance,' he wrote. 'Once the cream of their cricket bow out, there will be some big gaps left . . . and that sadly could signal the end of cricket of any real class in South Africa.'

Feted throughout South Africa, Dennis Lillee returned to Perth with a fuller self-estimate. Sums of $30,000 had been dangled to entice him into spending a season there, and his mind returned to Cornell's telephone conversation.

Kerry Packer? Dennis Lillee had let the name pass, even when Cornell mentioned that the businessman might bankroll a global one-day bash. But, while it is hard to conceive of an eighteen-stone six-footer being so, the public Kerry Francis Bullmore Packer was still smaller than life.

The house of Australian Consolidated Press Holdings that his leonine father Sir Frank had built was considerable: with the twin television stations TCN-9 Sydney and GTV-9 Melbourne and their affiliates, plus a dozen magazines from *Australian Women's Weekly* to the *Bulletin*. After Sir Frank's death in May 1974, Consolidated Press's deputy chairman Harry Chester (executor and trustee of Sir Frank's estate), had rung round executives to advise them: 'Your new boss is a young man of whom I have high expectations. You should treat him the same way as you treated his father.'

That was, with deference. 'Kerro', as Chester alone called him, emerged as sharing many of his father's attributes and prejudices: tyrannous, generous, impulsive, instinctual, and knowing no fury as intense as perceived disloyalty.

While Packer trusted Chester implicitly – he once withdrew from the purchase of a magazine on the basis of a nightmare Chester had – he left the rest of his executives in a state of exhilarated fear. The mandatory nature of their lunches at Consolidated Press when Packer returned from abroad was even enforced by memo: 'On the day I return from overseas I expect all my executives to be here, so they can inform me of what has been happening during my absence. If not, I expect to know why they will not be available before I go away. World tours or other trips will be cancelled.' He consumed ideas simultaneously, like the cigarettes he would sometimes chain-smoke four at a time in different ashtrays round a room.

Such was the pace of change Packer set. Disposal of the *Daily Telegraph*, the launch of *Cleo* and relaunch of the *Weekly* had transformed Consolidated Press by August 1975. But GTV-9 and TCN-9 had their problems. And that was where Dennis Lillee came in.

Cornell was a natural intermediary. One of Packer's first actions on his father's death had been to try and lure *The Paul Hogan Show* back from the Seven network and – though the 'handshake deal' he'd struck with Hogan and Cornell was successfully challenged in court – their regard was mutual.

But the careers of Lillee and Packer had been interlacing anyway. Lillee returned to big cricket for Western Australia against South Australia in the Gillette Cup at Perth's WACA Ground on 19 October 1974 in Australia's first colour television cricket telecast (just twelve days after colour test patterns began). Lillee's exertions in the ensuing Ashes series had been captured in colour by the ABC and – as was the fashion – by commercial stations content to carry it non-exclusively: all three in Perth, for instance, had covered sessions of that city's Test.

Packer's problems were twofold. A decade-long decline in 'sets-in-use' as television's novelty wore thin had been exacerbated in 1973 by the Whitlam government's local content points system. Television's audiences were dwindling at the same time as costs were rising, because of the expense of producing local drama, current affairs and comedy.

Packer needed colour as answer to the first, and sport to remedy the second. The chase for sport telecast rights as cheap, attractive, local television was an industry trend. In the three years from 1973 sport rose from barely 5 per cent of commercial network time to nudge 8 per cent.

Packer, however, was interested in more than mere accumulation. He liked golf, and when he endowed and televised the Australian Open for the first time in October 1975, he expressed much of his vision of televised sport. There had to be stars, so Packer staked prize money of $35,000 through the *Bulletin* (and he would multiply this fivefold in collaboration with W. D. & H. O. Wills a year later to ensure winner

Jack Nicklaus's return). Star-gazing also required quality telescopes. Imported American producer Mac Hemion, director Brian Morelli and technical manager Warren Berkery were told not to miss a hole. With forty cameras and radio mikes, they did not.

Golf was good commercial TV: popular, prolonged and (unlike football or soccer) containing comfortable advertising breaks. But cricket was irresistible: longer, with even less motion, and naturally embroidered ad slots.

Packer was not alone in his fondness for cricket. Reginald Ansett's 0–10 network signalled its interest by sharing the 1974–1975 Gillette Cup with the ABC. But the ratings prize was exclusivity: the ABC's World Cup final telecast claimed an outrageous twenty-one ratings points at the far-from-prime time of midnight. A full five-day Test, moreover, contained at least 350 advertising spots and had local content weighting the same as thirty hours of other catchpenny entertainments like quiz shows.

Although the ABC's latest three-year deal with the Australian Cricket Board was up for renewal at the end of the 1975–1976 season, cricket's sudden appeal for commercial television was not an ACB preoccupation. Since the Victorian Cricket Association had sold the ABC television rights in 1956 for £25, the national broadcaster had ritually agreed a non-exclusive deal before commercial bids were solicited. As ACB treasurer Ray Steele says: 'The commercials were interested occasionally, but we got sick of them. When I used to meet FACTS (Federation of Australian Commercial Television Stations) and the ABC together, all they did was keep the price down and then back off anyway.'

The ACB's capitalist thoughts were mainly of the sponsorship money welling up with tobacco companies (whose television advertising was to be silenced from September 1976). Packer's expression of interest in Test rights in February 1976 accordingly nonplussed its television sub-committee of Steele, Parish and Victorian Len Maddocks. He could be dealt with later.

By the time Packer and Consolidated Press executive Alec Baz were granted an audience in Melbourne on 22 June 1976, in fact, the ACB had given the ABC its imprimatur for another three years. Nothing was yet signed, but Parish had shaken on the $210,000 contract with ABC deputy general manager Clem Semmler.

Packer's memoir is well known: 'I had just walked in the door when Parish said they'd sold the non-commercial rights to the ABC. He knew why I was there, why I'd come to Melbourne. He knew too that I didn't want to share with the ABC . . . it's obvious even to Blind Freddy that if you have a choice of watching ABC without commercials and a commercial station, you watch the ABC.'

Steele recalls Packer's rejoinder when offered the sop of exclusive commercial rights: 'That's no good to me. Come on now, we're all harlots. I know you haven't signed the contracts, what's your price?'

Words to an unpaid administrator have been more honeyed. 'We might not have done that, but we've shaken hands on it,' the ACB treasurer said. 'We've had meeting after meeting and offer and counter-offer, and we wouldn't let them down.'

Packer, however, sought some hidden harlotry. 'I told them I'd pay $1.5 million for a three-year exclusive contract when the ABC's contract expired in three years – I told them I'd sign then and there – half a million a year for three years. It was a lot more money than anyone had ever offered them . . . I could tell by their looks.' Slack-jawed Parish and Steele knew that such an income stream virtually matched the ACB's annual surplus. Parish said he would see about it. In three years.

Packer had expected rather a lot of the ACB. But the meeting confirmed his prejudgement of the ACB and ABC as clubmates. His father had once advised him to join any club he wanted to join before he was thirty-five: after that too many people wouldn't like him. Now he was thirty-eight, he might have to think about founding his own.

Cricket tailored for television had English precedent in Bagenal Harvey's wandering all-star Cavaliers XI. Thanks to Rothmans' sponsorship and BBC coverage from 1965, their festive Sunday afternoons had become nice little (charitable) earners. Profits were split between administrators, ground authorities and cricketing saints like Warwickshire stalwart Tom Cartwright, who reaped £3295 from a single Edgbaston game in June 1968.

But, in 1969, an envious Test and County Cricket Board had beguiled Rothmans' tobacco rival John Player and the BBC in

1969 to support a 40-over-a-side county league. 'It was inevitable I suppose that someone else would want to get in on the act,' the former English captain Ted Dexter wrote in memoriam. 'However it was a harsh and clumsy decision by the counties to prepare so actively for their own version of the Sunday bonanza . . . without so much as a thank-you.' Having proved Sunday cricket's saleability, the Cavaliers perished on outlying non-first-class grounds under the waning gaze of independent broadcasters.

Packer's exploration of the Cavaliers concept was stimulated by former Australian Test captain Bob Simpson, just appointed New South Wales Cricket Association promotions adviser and fantasising of a Cavalier culture in Australia. Simpson's proposal to TCN-9 in July 1976, for a scattering of games blending stars with old-stagers, struck a chord with Packer's yearning to 'do cricket properly', as he had 'done' golf.

Simpson was a cricketer in business, rather than vice versa. Since retirement in 1968, he had actually suffered the commercial indignity of becoming the only former Australian skipper convicted for breaching the Companies Act. Falling in with the Slater Walker asset-stripper Ian Murray, he had agreed in January 1973 to front one of Murray's illegal trust shuffles. In saving his client from any more than a fine and costs, Simpson's silk Alex Chernov had subsequently conceded his client's naivety with a 'king of kings of the financial world'.

Returning to the company of cricketers, Simpson had enjoyed brokering promotions of Brut 33 toiletries for the Australians and West Indians in 1975, and his letter to the NSWCA in August 1976 outlining the Cavaliers brimmed with enthusiasm:

> First-class and Test cricket has been televised in a pretty stagnant way . . . Nothing out of the ordinary is attempted and, as a result, viewers are seldom given an insight into the personalities of the players taking part. TCN-9 believe . . . that viewers want more from their coverage than this. Coverage of the Cavaliers will be heavily personalised, with a great deal of pre-recorded material interposed with the live coverage: eg personal tactics of bowlers and batsmen will be pre-recorded and played as that bowler runs up or the batsman takes strike . . . This type of coverage will we believe have a great impact.

Packer did as well. Whatever form it took, he had a cricket venture in mind. On 16 August 1976, he registered a business name for it: World Series Cricket Pty Ltd.

The lessons of Harvey's Cavaliers, however, were clear. The idea had thrived as long as it had traditional cricket's indulgence. Ted Dexter attributed their demise to being 'fouled up by pettifogging authority at every turn', and denial of key players by 'the heavy establishment finger'. Simpson's proposal similarly hinged on official approval, and dealing with authority condemned one to its glacial pace and occasional caprice.

Although Simpson continued to work on the authorities, he soon had a rival for Packer's attention: JP Sport. John Cornell and Austin Robertson had arranged a rough and ready *World Masters Snooker Championship* for the Nine network in July, and Cornell was in touch with Packer again as October 1976 began when Paul Hogan's Seven contract finally expired. As they agreed to a $500,000 contract for eight Hogan specials, Cornell mentioned an interest in cricket.

Hearing names with which he could conjure, the businessman was immediately of a mind. 'Why not do the thing properly?' Packer prodded. 'Let's get the world's best cricketers to play Australia's best?'

Just as top golf required Jack Nicklaus, cricket to his specifications required Chappells and Lillees. And Packer's feeling for cricket was also somewhat secondary to his sense of nationhood. He often reflected on the nobly futile way his father had warred for the America's Cup a decade before. 'My father got sick and tired of everyone thinking of Australia as kangaroos and tennis players,' he would say. 'That's why he challenged for the America's Cup. And the promotion Australia got out of the America's Cup was enormous, absolutely enormous.'

Although it was Cornell and Robertson who received Packer's commission to develop the World Series Cricket idea, the businessman did Simpson the courtesy of laying a sketch of an international breakaway tournament before the former Australian captain.

Their two-hour meeting at GTV-9 in Melbourne a few weeks later excited Simpson. 'Promotionally,' he wrote, 'this was close to what I had been dreaming about for many years.' But, as Packer fished for his thoughts of what a star cricketer's contract might cost, Simpson felt the tear between 'my love for the game as I had known it, and the chance to participate in what was shaping as a gigantic promotion. I left the meeting promising to keep in touch, but I think we both knew deep down that we weren't made for each other.' And Simpson's suggestion that Packer call Ian Chappell was thoughtful but unnecessary.

Ian Chappell had passed a busy winter polishing memoirs, preparing to commentate for o–10 on Pakistan's forthcoming tour and to play club cricket with North Melbourne for a couple of seasons. But JP Sport's first response to interest from Packer had been to contact Bob Cowper, who wrote in October 1976 to the ex-captain.

Cowper advised Chappell that Packer was 'looking for support' for private cricket sponsorship, reporting: 'You might just reflect on the thought of twelve-week contracts between $20–30,000 and let me know your reaction.' Having earned $5000 from cricket in his final summer, Chappell's reply was: 'Thanks.'

Chappell knew also that his response would be echoed by his familied former colleagues. Greg and wife Judy and the Lillees were both expecting second children during the season. The Marshes and McCoskers had two small boys each, the Walters a six-month-old son, the Walkers and Gilmours each young daughters. Even the footloose Thomson had just announced December marriage plans.

Walker was alone in having a professional qualification: a much-deferred architecture degree. McCosker, Gilmour, deputy wicketkeeper Richie Robinson and the young batsmen Martin Kent and Ian Davis worked in banks. Gary Cosier, the eleventh Australian to make a Test century on debut in December 1975, was unemployed until he found a vague promotional role at Adelaide radio station 5AA.

Packer was in good humour when Robertson summoned Chappell to Consolidated Press for a first meeting late on a Friday evening. Stockinged feet on the desk of his plush office in Sydney's Park Street, Packer studied Chappell's Western-style boots with cheery dubiousness. 'Cowboy, are you?' he said, before offering the former Australian skipper a seat. 'Now, who do you want in this fucking team of yours?' When Chappell pointed out that his brother now led

Australia, Packer retorted: 'You think this is a fucking democracy, do you?'

Chappell reeled off the core of the current team, before hazarding a few extra names he'd promoted for *Cricketer*. Bruce Laird, a methodical opener he'd taken to England in 1975, came to mind. So did Rob Langer, Laird's even less fashionable Perth colleague, and he gave warm wraps to his two young International Wanderers, Kent and Hurst.

In *Cricketer* Chappell had revealed misgivings about Gary Cosier. 'I must confess I've still to be convinced that Cose is ready for Test cricket,' Chappell wrote. 'He appears to be overweight and I wonder how hard he is prepared to work at his batting at this stage.' Given the choice by Packer, he thought Cosier dispensable.

As Chappell proposed his ideal squad, Packer nodded and chimed in. He demurred only when his guest enthused about resurrecting Ross Edwards, Ian Redpath and Ashley Mallett. Mallett left Packer cold. Compromise was reached. The off spinner would 'try out' for the troupe by bowling an over to the businessman at Barry Knight's Sydney cricket school. If he could knock Packer over, Mallett was in.

With Packer's underwriting and Chappell's endorsement, Cornell and Robertson spent December 1976 sketching a 1977–1978 series between Australian and World combinations interwoven with the planned Australia–India Test matches. For World leaders, two big names stood out: Tony Greig and Geoff Boycott.

Greig was a popular figure in Australia. As he had proved with Waverley in 1975–1976, he sold. And Boycott, though hibernating mysteriously from Test cricket, was ironically now following Greig's footsteps as the club's hired hand for 1976–1977, as Greig led England in India.

When Robertson persuaded Boycott to meet Packer, however, the Yorkshireman was evasive. Boycott left his audience holding a draft contract. Packer left holding the popular – if shallow – view that Boycott was a self-centred gold-digger. It was not a good start but Boycott had the reputation, for better or worse, of being one of a kind.

The 1976–1977 cricket summer should have been one of concord. While the ACB had paled at the prospect of a 'liaison officer', it had instituted a 'player sub-committee' made up of Sheffield Shield captains whose inaugural meeting in Adelaide preceded the First Test against Pakistan in December 1976.

Greg Chappell saw the meeting as important. During his first season as Australian captain he'd presided over a dressing-room whose thoughts increasingly seemed elsewhere. 'Players were becoming so heavily committed to their personal promotional pursuits,' he wrote, 'that it wasn't uncommon to see half the team race off on the eve of a Test to engage in this type of activity: even to the extent of licking ice creams or pumping petrol.' Their success, in the wake of Thomson's 4IP deal, worried him: 'Almost overnight players were being transformed from once a week hobby entertainers to the status of needing full-time managers to look after their affairs.' He wanted the ACB to take charge.

Rod Marsh, WA's captain, was more querulous. Why was Benson & Hedges paying pocket money to be patron of the Australian cricket team? The ACB was now speaking in millions, but B & H's owner Amatil was 'laughing all the way to the bank'.

Visiting Amatil director Barry Smith in the wake of the meeting, Parish sought an answer to both points that also satisfied the ACB's criterion of not depriving the game itself. Parish and Smith agreed to a separate $350,000 layer of B & H sponsorship entitling it to the role of 'exclusive sponsor' of the Australian team.

Amatil could now be sure that the team did not turn up puffing Marlboros (for Philip Morris) or Winfields (for Rothmans) while the effect on the peppercorn Test payments of seasons past would be dramatic. Though the base $400 Test fee did not change, it did not have to: it would be dwarfed by bonuses that made $2000 a Test match a possibility.

To some extent, however, the ACB was playing to an empty gallery. While the scheme would be supported by an overwhelming player vote, it could not redeem past sins of administrative omission. While Chappell was pleased, and would write that Australia 'led the world' in player rewards, Marsh was just reasonably satisfied: Amatil was 'obviously frightened that the board would go to another firm'.

Their differing perspectives were evident in the First Test: Chappell looked on in slight bafflement as Marsh, with Cosier, ducked a victory target of 56 runs from 88 balls. Marsh had seen his duty as ensuring that the marathon bowling of Lillee and Kerry O'Keeffe was not wasted.

Looking back on six years of Ian Chappellism, the Australians had reached something of an autumnal stage. Greg was an altogether different captain. Unsure of his ability to lead by inspiration, he concentrated on example. Where Ian believed in individual intuition, Greg leant on spoken truths. Where Ian had handled player problems privately in what the team called 'ego trips' to the bar, Greg was more inclined to lectures. 'Ian never ranted and raved at anyone on the field,' says Gary Gilmour. 'At the end of the day he'd just look at you and you knew you hadn't done the job. Greg got stuck into guys more, which I found harder to get used to.' The team was responding by becoming more like itself; harder, surer, closer-knit and, as Adelaide showed, as intent on preserving its record as enhancing it. Optimising one's own effort was now balanced by emphasis on not letting down another's.

That clannishness was still immensely motivating, piercing even the pain barrier. The First Test's greatest drama was a tragic injury to Jeff Thomson in a collision with teammate Alan Turner as they chased Zaheer Abbas's vertical pull shot. The fast bowler's shoulder was dislocated. But, though his pain was blinding without a regular morphine supply, Thomson insisted on joining his teammates for Christmas at the hotel. Gloomy prognoses were dismissed by the vision of returning. 'I'm glad they said all that,' he would tell a biographer. 'It got me all worked up.' Cricket had many laws. The Australians were superimposing some of their own.

The Nine network was reaching a similarly vital juncture. *The Sullivans* and *The Young Doctors* – which Packer launched in a fortnight in September 1976 – were ruling the ratings by Christmas. But such luxuries had to be subsidised. The former – a quality period soap – cost him $70,000 an hour.

The solution was more sport. He was especially drawn as the year ended to the TCCB's auction of rights for BBC coverage of Australia's forthcoming cricket tour of England, a process that of custom involved one bidder in the ABC. Confident that the perpetually straitened national broadcaster could not match him, Packer finally tendered a firm £75,000 on 6 February 1977.

His fury knew no bounds, however, when he learned that Parish had endorsed the ABC's £53,000 bid and seemed likely to sway the TCCB. It was what he would call the ACB's 'second knifing'. Executive Lynton Taylor was sent to London with instructions to sew the deal up within a week, and won the TCCB contract by effortlessly doubling Consolidated Press's bid. The ABC cowered further as Packer promptly repeated the tactic with the three foreign grand slam tennis tournaments.

Packer's cricket spending, though, had just begun. With the businessman's chequebook and Ian Chappell's list, Robertson had dropped into the strange landscape of unity and division that was Australian cricket in 1977.

His route began in his home town with his client Lillee on 10 January. Fresh from routing South Australia for 125 with 5–44, the fast bowler signed another JP Sport contract, this one promising him $105,000 for three seasons' work. The next day Lillee could meditate on his move when he finished the match early with 5–37.

Robertson next tried Ross Edwards, captain of Fremantle in the local grades. As another Westralian ignorant of Robertson's patron, Edwards went to rustle more detail on Packer at his oil company employer Woodside-Burmah. JP Sport, he learned, was a $2 company, though Packer was worth a bit more: a request for a list of his media interests met with the response that there 'wouldn't be enough paper.'

After calling on Redpath in Geelong, Robertson returned to Sydney to weigh up World selections. Pakistanis were perused as they concluded their tour with a Test win at the SCG. Imran Khan's 12 wickets left a forceful impression, and Ian Chappell agreed to accompany Robertson to Pakistan's next stop in the West Indies to court the players on both teams.

After his sad sights on the Wanderers tour a year earlier, Ian Chappell urged early contact with South Africans. Graeme Pollock was soon tantalising countrymen with talk of Australian summers. 'Don't sign a new contract for next season over here,' he told Procter. 'Something's going to happen in Australia that'll interest you.'

With Greg Chappell and Doug Walters in mind, Robertson and Cornell headed on 25 February for Auckland, where Australia was playing its Second Test against New Zealand. With the ACB's Tim

Caldwell in town, their cover story was that they were dealing with Lillee over a contract for *A Current Affair*.

Lillee, enjoying his role, advised that Max Walker be sounded out. The Victorian was being wooed by Tasmania for its maiden Sheffield Shield season in 1977–1978, and must know to hang fire until the Packer possibilities developed. Lillee muttered a few enigmatic words out of earshot in the back of the team bus. The Victorian got the message.

Caution remained a watchword. On the Test's first evening, Marsh walked into his captain's room for a chat but found him renewing acquaintance with JP Sport. An embarrassed Chappell explained that he couldn't actually say what they were discussing, but Marsh did not linger. If Austin Robertson was planning something he'd know soon enough.

The captain perused the offer carefully. 'As for detail,' he says, 'there really wasn't any. There was going to be a breakaway group. The players would be talked to and, if there was sufficient response, the cricket authorities would be approached and an attempt made to have it done under the auspices of the traditional controlling bodies. But a lot had to be done on trust. On both sides.'

It looked good: his five-year contract was sweetened by a scheme to buy and lease-back Chappell's house. He agreed to respond at Australia's celebratory Centenary Test against England at the MCG in a fortnight. The captain's mind raced as he went to bed. Because he was batting the next day, he rang for a sleeping pill.

Robertson and Cornell cornered Walters in a quiet janitorial alcove at the Eden Park ground. With Hoganesque timing, Cornell broke the ice: 'Doug, d'ya reckon you can lend me a couple of bucks.' Hand in his trouser pocket, Walters was officially 'approached'. The pair left with *A Current Affair's* new star reporter sprinting from the fence as he gathered eleven New Zealand wickets.

Cornell was at GTV-9 three days later to chaperone a different television recruit. He and Hogan were about to launch their new series on the station, and the pair's availability for advertising campaigns was probed. No, not interested. Too busy.

Even with Robertson in room 206 at Perth's Parmelia Hilton on 4 March, Ross Edwards was a fussy accountant. Given JP Sport's financial structure, could he have Packer's written guarantee its debts would be honoured? And what about rules? And pitches? But he promised an answer at the Centenary Test.

So did Robertson's next Parmelia guest, Barry Richards. He had been breaking batting records for the Midland-Guildford club while coaching, endorsing a local car yard and commentating with television station TVW-7 and radio station 6KY. The South African actually had a WACA television assignment the next day, though it was the silence that was eloquent. Tony Greig's Englishmen, a day after arriving from Colombo, were warming up against WA for the Centenary Test. Richards' co-commentators were Ian Chappell and Richie Benaud, on the field Marsh and Lillee. Despite the imminent confluence of their careers, they passed not a word.

The only words exchanged followed Robertson's other contact: twenty-six-year-old Perth swing-bowler Mick Malone. Though they'd been football colleagues, Malone's Parmelia invitation baffled him. 'Austin was kind of a legend, because I'd just been starting at Subiaco,' Malone recalls. 'So it wasn't as though I knew him well. I got the impression Dennis had had a lot to do with my being picked and I really didn't need much more. I'd always thought of myself as a Sheffield Shield player, maybe on the fringe of the Test team, but I never saw myself in front of 100,000 people at the MCG.'

Although Robertson offered him the cheapest contract he would extend – $57,000 for three years – Malone was not about to refuse. 'I went to the WACA straight after and the first person I saw was Dennis. I knew I wasn't allowed to say anything but I mentioned: "I've just spoken to Austin". And he gave me a thumbs-up sign, just a sign that I should go for it.' Malone did.

One hundred years in the making, the Centenary Test crowned the ACB's summer. Beginning on Tuesday 8 March when Parish met the morning Qantas flight from London disgorging the first of 111 cricket guests, the match was a twelve-day exultation: spell-binding cricket at the MCG by day, rousing fellowship at the Hilton by night.

Cornell was in town, specifically to shepherd Hogan through his GTV-9 launch press conference. 'G'day,' Hogan began. 'I'm real glad to be workin' for GTV-9 this year, and I'm also quite grateful for the chaff bag full of money they're givin' me.' Then it was down to Robertson's penthouse suite at the Windsor Hotel to ensure that a few cricketers paraphrased the line.

McCosker was JP Sport's first guest. Now a Test regular and sure of his English plane ticket, McCosker was notionally at his peak, but he considered Robertson's $67,500 three-year package carefully. 'Obviously they weren't going down the batting order,' he recalls. 'I was told that other players had been approached and I knew that Chappells and Lillees would be signed well before me.'

McCosker discussed it with his wife Meryl on match morning. Granted paid leave while touring England two years before, he would shortly be revisiting on unpaid leave. As a part-time Rural Bank official he could never prepare for their future. As a professional athlete, he would be spared worrying what might be round the corner. As it happened, he rounded one of those corners before noon: his jaw was broken by England's Bob Willis in the Test's first hour.

Opening partner and Commonwealth Bank employee Ian Davis cabbed to the Windsor quickly two days later. Just married at twenty-three, just back in the Australian team, he was looking forward to corners. 'I was told that all the main blokes had signed,' Davis recalls. 'And that Ian Chappell was coming back I thought was great. Basically I just wanted to be with the blokes.'

Like Davis, New South Wales teammate Kerry O'Keeffe had been a youthful prodigy on his Test debut in 1971. But just six months before the Centenary Test he'd been on the point of retiring: carting beer for half a year did not seem a long-term career and O'Keeffe had given himself a season. On 9 November 1976, the last morning of a Shield game with Victoria, he had taken a telephone call from a friend. 'Good luck today,' he told O'Keeffe. 'You're probably playing for your first-class life.'

A gimmee long-hop that day producing the first of 6–50 had deferred destiny. With an increasing incidence of skill he'd taken 5–30 against WA the next week, and resumed an interrupted Test career. But, reflecting on the offer in his hotel room, he could see no alternative to signing: 'I'd gone from a casual brewery truck worker who was going to give it one more year to a Test player against Pakistan. But in the end I was still a casual labourer and, although I was enjoying my Test cricket, I was twenty-eight and I didn't know where I was heading.' A day later he did.

The day after flattening England for 95, Lillee and Walker strolled across the parkland round the MCG in the twilight. Walker learned at last that he'd passed up a Tasmanian future for an offer of $75,000 over three years, and welcomed Robertson to his hotel room. Greg Chappell, Walters, Redpath and Barry Richards had completed their contracts, and Robertson finally chased down Ross Edwards.

It had been a harder choice for the retired Edwards than he'd imagined. The money was nice, but was he up to it? 'There's a lot of good players signing,' he thought. 'And there've been half a dozen Australian sides since I played. Do I need this hassle? Maybe I did pretty well to fit my career in when there weren't too many real quick blokes around.' Robertson looked at him in mild exasperation: 'Look, are you going to sign or not?'

It had to be done. 'Of course I am,' Edwards smiled. 'Give me the pen.'

Finally, there was Rod Marsh. Because Marsh had always been counted in, he had not been approached before Robertson found him at tea on the final day. And as it happened, Marsh felt especially willing. A proposal he had made for strengthening the team's provident fund had been cordially received by Parish, but then rejected by the ACB on the eve of the Test: it had legal advice that income tax laws made the scheme unworkable. Believing Parish had all but guaranteed it, Marsh felt deceived. 'I went off my brain completely,' he recalled. 'There was only one bloke responsible and that was Bradman . . . How else could it have happened?' Was he in? You bet he was.

Taking his position alongside Chappell, Marsh burned to say something but stuck to his secrecy clause. The Test twined them until, in lengthening shadow at 5.12 p.m., Lillee took his eleventh match-winning wicket: Alan Knott lbw for 42. As captain and vice-captain savoured the atmosphere, Marsh observed: 'I guess this'll be the last time we play here for a while.' When Chappell responded blankly, Marsh laughed: 'You know what I bloody well mean.'

Not that it meant anything to the uninitiated Gary Gilmour trotting behind them. 'I heard Marshy say it, but I had no idea what was going on,' he says. 'I'd seen Austin Robertson and Cornell in New Zealand. But I'd assumed they were there because Austin was mates with Dennis.'

Robertson's presence in the dizzy dressing-room afterwards intrigued Ray Steele. 'He was a mysterious bloke,' Steele says. 'I was never really introduced to him, but I noticed he was spending a lot of time round the players.' Robertson distributed envelopes containing $75,000 in signing-on cheques cagily: 'Here are your theatre tickets fellers.'

Pressmen were demanding audiences with the game's heroes: Marsh, the century-making wicketkeeper; Derek Randall, the plucky Brit whose 174 had brought England to within 46 runs of victory; the twenty-one-year-old David Hookes who, on his Australian debut, had slugged Greig for five successive boundaries. And most of all, Lillee. Was it now true that the need to rest his broad back would prevent him touring England? As his agent, Robertson organised a 7.30 p.m. press conference at the GTV-9 studios in Bendigo Street, Richmond.

Before leaving, though, Robertson asked Ross Edwards to introduce him to Tony Greig. With Boycott ducking any commitment to a contract, the English captain was the obvious World leader. Edwards tapped Greig's shoulder: 'I've got someone who wants to meet you. Let's find somewhere quiet' Greig heard that the Sydney businessman, Kerry Packer, would like to meet him, and agreed to pay a visit when in Sydney in a couple of days.

A taxi awaited Robertson and Lillee, and cameras festooned GTV-9's executive bar when they arrived. Yes, Lillee confirmed, his name would not be in the Australian touring team to be announced that evening. His back was buckling after his 93-wicket season. Lillee would instead be Nine's expert on the Tests that winter and *A Current Affair's* celebrity reporter. 'I feel sad about it, but I've learned in cricket you've got to take the breaks,' he said. 'Both ways.'

A couple of days later, Greig would be muttering much the same to himself.

Tony Greig left the Centenary Test in garlands, a model guest who had even deposited a 'Thank You Melbourne' letter with the *Age* newspaper. Seated in first-class on his Sydney flight – courtesy of Mr Packer – England's captain accepted a succession of compliments and congratulations. Fellow-passenger New Zealand Cricket Council Chairman Walter Hadlee looked forward to seeing him lead England's tour of New Zealand the following February. Greig said likewise, although one could never be sure of these things.

He was keen to meet Packer, whatever was in mind. Packer was in Sydney and in the media: two places Greig could see his career leading. And, as an aspiring 'millionaire cricketer', meeting one of the former after so many of the latter was clearly a step forward.

Welcoming him at his Bellevue mansion on the Saturday, 19 March, Packer was a sensitive host. Ian Chappell was a retired rebel, but Greig could easily feel a cat's paw. 'You've done a bit of work for us, haven't you?' the Australian said as they adjourned to Packer's study.

Had he? Greig wondered. So he had. Kelloggs had inserted a four-part guide to 'Cricket: The Tony Greig Way' in the *Women's Weekly* a month before, and Greig confessed he'd not known the magazine's ownership.

The particulars came at a rush: Packer wanted him for his circuit, and was offering $90,000 over three years. Greig's involvement would be as deep as he chose. He could be a paid consultant and, at the end of it all, further a career at Consolidated Press. In a whirl Greig asked for 'a stay of execution', and sought the counsel of Waverley friends Ian Macfarlane and Bruce Francis.

Execution, Greig knew, it would be. He had relished his captaincy in India, but remembered how close he had come to resigning against the West Indies nine months earlier. He pondered his thirty years, and uncertain future beyond a further five. Waltons and Kelloggs had opened possible post-cricket career paths, but Packer's Consolidated Press was a go-ahead outfit.

Reuniting with teammates Mike Brearley, Bob Willis and Graham Barlow at a Sunday barbeque thrown by sports hypnotherapist, Arthur Jackson, Greig was animated. Brearley would in hindsight recognise Greig's words to Willis – that if the fast bowler stayed fit 'there was no limit to the amount of money he might make' – as his first inkling of World Series Cricket.

The South African was indeed bewitched. When Ian Chappell was unable to free himself of post-season work with Qantas to accompany Robertson on the planned Caribbean recruiting, Greig volunteered. His Sussex committee had urged him to rest before the English season, and this seemed gainful employment. A week after the Centenary Test, Greig was planning to live out his Kelloggs slogan for Kerry Packer: 'Bring the whole team round to breakfast.'

3

'Where do I sign?'

In the disorienting blur of familiar faces round Tony Greig as he alighted at Victoria Station on 30 March 1977, the voice of Thames Television's Eamonn Andrews arrested him: 'Tony Greig. *This Is Your Life.*'

It sure was, and over the next three hours it flashed before his eyes. His agent Reg Hayter had slipped a sham appointment 'discussing an ITV sporting program' into Greig's diary, and the ruse had worked. Painfully well. Greig faced everything he stood to lose. His English teammates mingled with family members flown from Queenstown, his coaches, counsellors and kindergarten teacher. There was even Teki Manzei, the elderly African retainer who had bowled to a barefoot Greig during his South African childhood. Greig learned that the kind conspiracy had been engineered at the Centenary Test. He could not, of course, tell a soul about the planning in which he was now immersed.

Greig had dreaded such encounters. How could he face Alec Bedser and Ken Barrington, managers of his successful Indian campaign? And Jim Swanton, his stentorian *Daily Telegraph* advocate? With a steady gaze, Greig decided, and recalls:

That was where the deceptive side of it came. That was pretty difficult to handle. People who I was close to like Barrington and Bedser. If I'd have said anything to those guys, they would have been obliged to go to Lord's. Those chaps would depend on Lord's in some ways for the rest of their lives, as managers, selectors or coaches. There was Swanton, too, who'd been very good to me. How do you sit these guys down, as a South African with a Scottish father, and say: 'This is the real world. This is something you've got to adapt to. There is competition and it won't go away'? But I was on a new path in my life. And the strategy was to make sure that Greg Chappell's team made it to England intact. If I let the cat out of the bag, that wouldn't be certain.

Greig kept his poise. In an interruption in filming he even buttonholed Derek Underwood: he would call the spinner next morning about 'something big' that would interest him. Underwood, Kent colleague Alan Knott and Greig's Sussex teammate John Snow learned that they were to meet at London's Churchill Hotel on the evening of Easter Monday, but still the secret remained in its select circle. Even Teki Manzei, who stayed with the Greigs in Brighton a fortnight after his unexpected arrival, sensed only perpetual whirl. It was with Greig's brother Ian that 'Tackies' did most sightseeing.

Greig, of course, was just passing through. Two days later he booked into Port-of-Spain's Trinidad Hilton, where he met Robertson and Consolidated Press's veteran secretary John Kitto.

As the Fourth Test of Pakistan's West Indian tour commenced at Queen's Park, the Australians were equipped for safari. Their contracts were baited by a forty-five-minute cassette tape on which Ian Chappell attested JP Sport's bona fides. Greig camouflaged his involvement as native guide by carrying a Sussex contract for the emergent all-rounder Imran Khan.

Imran was also presented with a JP Sport contract, as were his cousin Majid, captain Mushtaq Mohammad and deputy Asif Iqbal. Rotating Tests and domestic cricket with English county careers, their cricket on the run prepared them for anything. Asif, Robertson's first guest after the third day's play, had dashed home from Kent to begin three Tests against New Zealand on 9 October 1976 with 166

in Lahore, then sparked November's Pentangular Trophy with 196
for National Bank against Pakistan Airways. Three Tests and two
Test centuries had followed his touchdown in Perth on 15 December,
and he would finish ten weeks in the Caribbean with 135 at Sabina
Park in a fortnight. Three days later he would captain Kent against
Surrey at Folkestone. Retirement beckoned, perhaps as a National
Bank executive . . . until he saw Robertson.

Mushtaq, fast making the Test a personal landmark with 171
runs and eight wickets, had been hoping to play Sheffield Shield
in 1977–1978 as a relief from leading Northamptonshire. Majid
and Imran, reassured by Greig that their Test careers would not
be jeopardised, signed their $75,000 three-year contracts with
equal flourish.

Warned by Mushtaq to beware 'an Australian businessman
called Robertson', Clive Lloyd was soon accepting a dinner invitation from the enigmatic visitor. The West Indian captain was into
his fruit salad by the time the $90,000 three-year offer came up,
but nearly choked. Chappell's recorded voice came as an important
endorsement, but Lloyd sought time to discuss the offer with his
wife Waveney.

Sir Frank Worrell might have been featured on the Barbadian
dollar, but no West Indian had grown rich through cricket. Lloyd's
Testmen remained virtually the only West Indians who could count
themselves professionals, and their abiding dependence on county
cricket careers bothered their captain. Staleness had characterised
his team during its 1–5 series defeat in Australia in 1975–1976. The
fulcrum of his attack, Andy Roberts, had been fatigued from carrying Hampshire's attack during the 1975 English season, and arrived
for the Pakistan series sore from a spell with NSW. The West Indies'
3–0 defeat of England in between had owed much to the players'
confinement to national duties.

Lloyd himself was thirty-three and wedded to life as a West
Indian Lancastrian for as long as tottery knees allowed. 'I had seen
the plight of many a great West Indian cricketer of the past following
their exit from the game and it was not particularly comforting,' he
recalled. 'Several had been forced to continue playing in the leagues
in England, while Caribbean governments had created coaching
posts for others. I did not see myself following either course, and

here now was an opportunity to earn and invest the kind of money which would allow me to be confident of my future after my playing days were over.'

By the time he returned to Robertson and Greig to sign his contract, the Antiguan alliance of Roberts and Viv Richards had been signed. Novelty had worn off the county contracts they had signed in 1973 with Hampshire and Somerset respectively, and they would rarely be better placed to sell themselves as professional sportsmen. Recognition of their 1976 record feats – Roberts' sprint to 100 Test wickets inside thirty months and Richards' 1710 Test runs – had so far been confined to their appearance on Antiguan stamps.

Last stop was Kingston, Jamaica, on 6 June where Roberts' twenty-three-year-old fast bowling partner Michael Holding was convalescing from a groin injury. Eight months before, Holding had disappointed Greig by rejecting a £10,000 Sussex contract. Again he was coy:

> I was at University and that came first. I remember telling a journalist in Jamaica that, whenever my studies clashed with a Test series, they would have to look for another fast bowler. I was not interested in county cricket, that grind. I played because I loved it. Andy had been used at Hampshire, bowled into the ground, because he was such a great wicket-taker. Touring with so many guys who played county cricket I knew what it was like.

Greig assured him that this would be different. While Holding might have to carry a county, he would never have to shoulder the World. The Jamaican's one insistence, when he heard that he might be sharing a dressing-room with South African cricketers, was a clause voiding the contract if it did not receive a prior blessing from his Prime Minister Michael Manley.

Manley was as fervent an opponent of sporting links with South Africa as he was a lover of cricket. He went as far as accepting county contacts between West Indians and South Africans as an occupational mishap, but no further. 'I agreed with Manley's stance,' Holding says. 'And I told Tony I could not be involved with any South Africans who had not at least played county cricket. Nor would I like to be involved.' Kitto hastily drafted the clause, and Greig undertook to contact Manley. But this strange political posture – that some South Africans were more equal than others – would come to plague the Packer organisation.

As Robertson and Kitto headed back to Sydney, Greig left Kingston for London where he planned to meet two 'unequal' South Africans in Pollock and leg spinner Denys Hobson. They were assembling at Greig's behest at the Churchill on the Easter weekend with countrymen Barry Richards, Eddie Barlow and Mike Procter. Greig proceeded. The wheels of politics would always grind exceeding small. Packer's were now at speed.

The momentum in Australia had gathered one recruit Ian Chappell felt indispensable. Packer called the venerable Richie Benaud on 6 April 1977 at the Coogee apartment that housed D. E. Benaud and Associates, retaining the consultancy that former Australian captain ran with his wife Daphne. The Benauds warned Packer about how the establishment would receive a rival:

> Their reaction in the first instance will be to contact one or two players and sound them out to find out what is going on; and their second reaction will be one of disbelief . . . They may come back to you then and suggest a meeting but, before that, we would strongly advise against any statement calculated to provide ammunition for them in criticism of the players. It will be the players who will come under fire on the basis of 'letting down Australia'.

Chances of a welcome were slim:

> Although the matter has remained confidential to date, it is doubtful there will be no leak between now and the announcement. It is equally doubtful that the ACB will be thoroughly delighted at the thought of Australia's players taking part in matches other than under their control. We believe it is important from the public relations point of view that you contact the ACB before making an official announcement, so they cannot say they and the game have been snubbed.

The Benauds reminded Packer that he had a lot of enemies.

> As this is a Channel Nine exclusive production there will be resistance from other media, despite the quality of the players. That can partly be overcome by performances on the field, but you shouldn't think there won't be some sniping from all areas of the media. It's not a national happening as in the Australian Open Golf where everyone wants to boost the event. Newspapers will almost certainly send their No. 1 writer to the Australia–India Test if there is a clash. No. 2 man will cover the commercial event. The way around that might be to avoid a clash of Test match dates, so that the top writers cover the whole summer, rather than a whole tour as is now the case.

Above all, the Benauds concluded, antagonists needed to be disarmed before they began. Packer had spoken of organising a coaching scheme for New South Wales country boys with the local association to be run by Barry Knight, and had budgeted it as much as $200,000. Tie the announcement of the two together, and the venture might be sweetened.

Richie Benaud would shortly be leaving for England, where he'd been a BBC television commentator since the end of his playing days in 1963, but left Packer a draft letter to the ACB along conciliatory lines:

> In keeping with our policy of boosting sport in Australia, I am writing to advise that my organisation will be staging a number of cricket matches during the 1977–1978 cricket season. It is proposed that these matches, to be played in each capital city, will be between teams of Australian players and players from other cricketing countries, the latter making up what could be called a World XI.
>
> To enable as many sports followers as possible to view these games, it is proposed to televise them throughout Australia on our network. As you know we have established an outstanding television technique for golf in the Australian Open, and it is hoped that now in cricket we shall be able to provide an equally outstanding coverage for the hundreds of thousands who will be watching

throughout the country. This is all part of our forward planning for sport and follows our recent announcement of a $200,000 coaching scheme for country boys in NSW. We are looking forward to an exciting summer. If your board has any further thoughts on how we could cooperate in assisting cricket and providing entertainment for the spectator and stay-at-home television fan, we should be pleased to hear from you.

Success of an 'independent' circuit would stand or fall on the quality of pitches and grounds, and no curator in Australia strictly fitted the bill of agriculturalist cum alchemist necessary to conjure wickets from the 'non-cricket' grounds it would be played on.

As he prepared for his English trip, Greg Chappell recommended instead someone he thought might rise to the occasion: groundsman at his Woollongabba home ground, John Maley. A thirty-year-old apostle of WACA curator Roy Abbott, Maley had first come to notice in Brisbane by resurrecting Toombul club's notorious mud-pile at Oxenham Park. Maley's two seasons taming the Gabba's mangrove had further impressed Chappell.

Robertson had actually called Maley in January, obliquely seeking his thoughts on prefabricating pitches. The challenge of doing it that Robertson put to Maley at the Gabba engaged him immediately: he signed a $50,000 three-year contract, handwritten on JP Sport notepaper. He would in all likelihood be surrendering a Test ground, but he would be taking on a test tube.

The magic ingredient, of course, was television. Planning a family holiday in the UK for June, TCN-9 sports director Brian Morelli was bemused by an exchange with a station executive. 'You're going to England aren't you?' he said. 'While you're there, take a look at how the BBC do the cricket.'

'Hmmm?' said Morelli. 'Are we going to be doing some cricket next summer?'

'Just go and have a look.'

Packer's project remained top secret at least until Chappell's team were in England. Benaud's letter could then be sent, a simultaneous Anglo–Australian news release made, and a puff piece published by *Bulletin* editor Trevor Kennedy. With the Ashes tour under way, punitive administrative actions – like the sacking of captains or recall of teams – would seem clumsy.

Greig returned to a country at a peculiar crossroads. As the Queen celebrated twenty-five years on the throne, loyalists were planning thanksgiving services and bonfires to illuminate the land end-to-end. Sporting events willingly took the royal seal, none more so than cricket with its so-called Jubilee Test Series.

But it was a strikebound isle, in which a million working days were being lost a month and the Labour Government of Prime Minister Jim Callaghan had seen prices rise 70 per cent in three years. Cricket's antiquity had rarely seemed more reassuring. Colin Cowdrey summed up the Centenary Test in *The Times*: 'It has been heady stuff and it will be much the same in 100 years from now.' Correspondence from an MCC member in the *Sunday Times* three weeks later looked forward to 'long summer days of grace and tranquillity . . . sitting, watching, eating sandwiches, drinking and sleeping'.

Barlow, Procter, Pollock, Hobson and Barry Richards were contrastingly agitated at the Churchill in Portman's Square, just near Marble Arch, when Greig met them on Easter Monday, 11 April 1977. Richards had already enlisted, and the rest itched to. Barlow would not wait for the carefully prepared introductory address. 'Where do I sign?' the all-rounder asked.

The Englishmen arriving were also willingly led. Snow was at the end of a career frequently estranged from England's selectors. A victim of selection fashion despite his 250 Test wickets, Underwood welcomed contracted security. The intensely religious Knott felt it all 'a wonderful answer to prayer' after a succession of winters away from his family. Only Greig's entreaties to the Test and County Cricket Board on his behalf had enabled him to take his wife Jan on the Indian tour, and the Knotts had sought divine guidance since returning home. The respect all four had for England's skipper deepened, for he had most to lose. As Underwood reminded him: 'On your own head be it.'

Over the next three days, Greig oversaw their signatures with Consolidated Press's London chief, King Watson. The following week began with his English team being toasted by the Anglo-American Sporting Club in London, two pre-season friendly matches against

Kent at Hove and a dash to Quaglino's on Wednesday, 20 April, to introduce Knott to the dinner presenting the keeper with the Walter Lawrence Trophy for the fastest century of the 1976 season.

Only there did Greig's facade slip. After enthusing to Swanton at length of the Indian tour, Greig invited the sage to stay with him in Brighton. 'Something big for the players' was in the wind, and Greig would like to explain aspects of it.

But Greig was swallowed by the English season proper two days later and the invitation was never formalised. 'It would be nice to go and do all these things in a more palatable fashion,' Greig says today. 'But things don't happen that way. Opportunities arise and you take them.'

Opportunities taken by thirteen of its seventeen members, the Australian team was finally in the air. Cricketers had kept coming right to the last moment.

Having skipped cricket to swot for Adelaide College physical education exams just five months before, David Hookes had left the Centenary Test as a student prince. His five centuries in three Sheffield Shield games and boyish good looks were fit for front pages and centrefolds.

Among callers in the next fortnight were the television variety hosts Ernie Sigley and Don Lane offering their management skills, and Hookes turned to his South Australian mentor Ian Chappell for advice. Chappell had a ready answer: have a yarn with John Cornell first.

With Hookes planning a trip to Newcastle for a demonstration game, he arranged to meet Cornell at his Neutral Bay home on the Thursday before Easter, 7 April. As they paced bayside walking tracks, Hookes was filled in. 'The best players were already involved,' Hookes recalls. 'And as far as losing my place in the Test team was concerned, John intimated there was a chance I could do both if the board acted accordingly.'

There was added inducement: he would be advanced two-thirds, rather than one-half, of his first-year fee when he signed so he could bring forward plans to marry his fiancee Roxanne Hewitt, a psychology graduate. Hookes joined on Easter Tuesday and, granting an interview to *Women's Weekly* in which he remarked cryptically: 'There's a lot of luck in this game, and you take it when you can.'

Robertson returned from Kingston with a fortnight to lasso the Australian team. The selectors had scattered a few surprises in the Ashes party named as an epilogue to the Centenary Test, of whom ten had not previously toured England.

Some were pleasant. With unflagging self-belief, Jeff Thomson had surged through a fitness test. The constitution and spirit of his boyhood Bankstown friend Len Pascoe had also brought him to notice. Robertson wanted both.

The exclusions were noteworthy, too. The left-handed opener Alan Turner, in the country's best XI for fifteen Tests before the Centenary Test, found he was now excluded from its best seventeen. And Gary Gilmour, having left Melbourne apparently assured of his tour berth, was also stuck wintering in Australia.

He'd limped through the season with a bone injury incorrectly diagnosed as an achilles strain, but been relaxed by the poker faces of selectors in the dressing-room after the Centenary Test. Until, that is, he was driving across Sydney Harbour Bridge on the way back to Newcastle that evening. 'I turned on the radio and they were reading out the Australian team,' he recalls. 'And I wasn't in it. I'd been in the team for the whole summer, played all the Tests, had been speaking to the selectors two hours before but they hadn't said a word.'

Robertson had both of them short-listed, and ultimately passed over only four of the seventeen tourists: the doubted Gary Cosier, the junior West Australian batsmen Kim Hughes and Craig Serjeant, and the veteran Queensland medium pacer Geoff Dymock preferred to Gilmour.

Cornell flew to Melbourne on Easter Monday, reuniting with Rod Marsh at the MCG where the keeper joined the colours while watching a Hawthorn–Richmond football match. Robertson then visited the Greensborough home of Marsh's shadow for the English tour, Victorian captain Richie Robinson, leaving him twenty-four hours in which to decide if he would perform the same function for JP Sport.

'When he told me the players who had been signed, I realised that, if there was a ban and I stayed where I was, I'd probably be one of the first offered the Australian captaincy,' Robinson says. 'But I weighed it up. So many of my contemporaries were involved, obviously believed it was the right thing to do and important for cricket, that I decided I'd pass that opportunity up.'

Robinson signed the same day as Robertson visited the Spotswood residence of his twenty-two-year-old state teammate Ray Bright. The left-arm spinner, yet to play a Test, had been on the periphery of the Australian side since 1974. 'I rang Ian Chappell,' Bright recalls. 'And basically what he said was good enough for me.'

On Tuesday 19 April 1977 the pair met Max Walker at Melbourne's Tullamarine Airport for the hop to Sydney, where they were to assemble with the rest of the Australian players and where Robertson was obtaining the signatures of Thomson and Pascoe.

Robertson then sought Gilmour. The aggrieved all-rounder signed with alacrity when chased down at the Newcastle Leagues Club. His only strike was Turner, awkwardly placed as a senior accountant at Benson and Hedges, the ACB's sponsors, and having thoughts of leaving cricket altogether anyway.

Australian manager Len Maddocks was cheerfully ignorant as he addressed a last supper in Sydney: thirteen of his retinue would be revealed once in England to have signed contracts with another boss. 'I'm going to England to have a good time,' he told them. 'And I hope you blokes are, too.'

Craig Serjeant was momentarily perplexed. 'Have you signed?' Richie Robinson had muttered as the pair changed for practice at Lord's. Signed what?

'I beg your pardon?' Serjeant replied. It didn't matter, the Victorian said. Only vaguely aware who was in their camp when they arrived in London, the Australians seethed with secrets. 'We were a vulnerable group of part-time cricketers to whom someone had offered money,' Kerry O'Keeffe reflects. 'For many of us that was a new experience.'

David Hookes knew at least that Cosier had not been approached, and joined a little half-heartedly in birthday celebrations for his Adelaide friend on 25 April. Two days later the pair were playing their first innings on English soil at the traditional one-day frolic against the Duchess of Norfolk's XI by Arundel castle.

A relaxed Greg Chappell had shaken hands with Tony Greig before another toss, and watched his young batsman hint at the talent of which he'd spoken glowingly on arrival. Serjeant made a firm fist of opening with 65, Hughes compiled a crisp 28, and 6000 spectators left the sylvan scene with a few new names to ponder.

But there was ample time in damp pavilions thereafter as a semi-permanent squall trailed the visitors around. One chilly day's play was possible in the team's opening first-class fixture against Surrey at The Oval, five fragmented hours against Kent at Canterbury.

Had there been less chance of introspection, and less opportunity for journalists to mingle among players, the Packer story might have taken a different turn. Its organisation might then have been seen as a commercial convenience, rather than as an act of espionage. As it was, Len Maddocks enjoyed a dinner party at Jim Swanton's Canterbury home with Chappell, Marsh and Walker little knowing the storm that would break about him two days later.

Chappell and Greig tossed at Hove for Australia's game against Sussex on Saturday, 7 May 1977, more as a ritual than a preparation. Hovering rain would banish players within an hour.

At least the tourists knew they would be spared the shabby confines of the Dudley Hotel that evening: Greig planned to repay Australian hospitality by throwing an elaborate party for the whole touring entourage, players and press, in a marquee at his new Brighton home. He'd even imported Foster's Lager for the occasion.

For the journalists Peter McFarline and Alan Shiell, who were pooling their intelligence after detecting whispers of some autonomous cricket carnival during the Australian summer, rain was convenient. They knew that English journalists had scented the same story and were satisfied with their information. Pro forma denial from Greg Chappell was sought and furnished. 'You can say this,' he told them. 'It sounds like an interesting proposition. I'd like to know more about it before committing myself.'

The pair headed for the Dudley to file the details that they had for the *Age* and the *Australian* respectively. When McFarline told Snow he was about to publish, Greig's party became a party line. He called Packer. He called Hayter. He called his World team members, who were scattered round the counties for John Player League games on the Sunday. Greig himself was leading Sussex against Yorkshire, although he tracked down Hayter beforehand to dictate a statement. 'There is a massive cricket project involving most of the world's top players due to commence in Australia this winter,' it read. 'I am part of it along with a number of English players. Full details and implications of the scheme will be officially announced in Australia later this week.'

A piquant duel was played out at Hove as journalists pieced together what they could from Greig's statement and their own prior intelligences. The Sunday fare of Sussex versus Yorkshire became Greig *contro* Geoff Boycott. After Boycott had played an *andantino* 36 in 24 overs with 29 singles, Greig's *allegro* 50 from 36 balls won the match with an over spare. And as they passed in the carpark later, Greig advised the Yorkshireman to beware an interesting story he expected in the next day's papers.

The Australian stories were just hitting the streets, sketchy but startling. McFarline's 'greatest cricket show on earth', naming two-thirds of signatories, carried the forecast of an unnamed English player that Packer's plan would be 'the biggest explosion in cricket since W. G. Grace'. McFarline's only mistake was his choice of season: in Melbourne, Collingwood Football Club's Saturday victory was the big story on Monday 9 May, and the *Age* secreted his twenty-three terse paragraphs on an inside back page of the sports section while it panted: 'Once again Collingwood is a great side, and coach Tom Hafey has told his players there are bigger and better things to come.'

Reading Shiell's front-page story in the *Australian* in Adelaide, Ian Chappell called a friend, car-dealer Graham Ferrett. 'Let's get out of town,' he said. 'Something big's about to blow. I'll explain later.' In a country pub over a counter lunch, Ferrett was admitted to the circle whose story was about to girdle the cricket globe.

Marsh, Walker and Malone alone avoided the helter-skelter. Greg Chappell had cleared them to honour invitations to the Amsterdam Cricket Club. But when Marsh rang his Perth home for Mother's Day, his wife's warning that news was oozing from the Australian media sent the wicketkeeper out early the following morning to gather the English papers.

In a thorough and well-informed story of the 'dogs of cricket' by the *Daily Mail's* Ian Wooldridge, the trio finally saw the full relief. 'Rod and I had played shield with each other and practised together all this time and we'd never mentioned it,' says Malone. 'And Max hadn't said a word. It was a case of each looking at the other one and saying "So, you are in".'

4

'How come you're worth all that money?'

Gary Cosier headed instinctively for the bar. If any of the team were about on the Sunday, 8 May, the odds were they'd be propping up the Dudley's run-down tavern.

But only Len Maddocks, tour treasurer Norm McMahon and the familiar face of ABC broadcaster Alan McGilvray were in evidence. Len was clearly fretful, Norm unusually self-absorbed, and McGilvray looked like he'd lost his best friend. As Cosier watched, the agitated manager ran to answer a phone call. 'Where are the boys?' Cosier asked, wondering if he'd missed something.

That he'd missed much he discovered when he found the team clustered round two tables in the Dudley's restaurant. Eyes followed him as he crossed the room to join his mate Hookes. 'What's going on here?' he asked.

'Don't you know?'

'No idea.'

Hookes explained: over the past couple of months, thirteen of them had signed secretly with someone called Kerry Packer for a series in Australia against a World team. Hookes saw Cosier's hurt. Three weeks earlier they'd flown side-by-side from Adelaide to

Sydney and Hookes had not said a word. 'I didn't know whether you were in or not,' Hookes told him. 'We weren't allowed to tell anybody. None of us knew who'd been invited and who hadn't.'

So what was happening now? 'We don't know,' Hookes replied. 'We don't know whether we're going to be allowed to continue the tour or whether we can play when we get home or what.'

As word spread, in fact, people seemed to know less. Details of the 'televised Tests' were scarce. Newspapers trawled files for information on Packer, Kerry, as opposed to Packer, Sir Frank.

A Monday press conference Packer and Cornell called at Consolidated Press proved more declaration of intent than detailed statement. At least Packer seemed quotable. 'We'll do all we can to co-operate with the cricket board,' he told the press. 'And, if they cooperate with us, there is no reason why Test cricket as it is now will be affected. But, if they don't co-operate, they'll walk straight into a meat mangler.'

Packer apologised for not informing Parish in advance. A courier carrying the Benaud letter had been marooned by striking Sydney air-traffic controllers, and would not arrive in Melbourne until evening. The *Age* delivered to his home in Lorene Court, Toorak, was Parish's sole intelligence as he and Australian Cricket Board secretary Barnes briefed Maddocks at the Dudley in Brighton. Defectors must know they were out of bounds: the ACB was Australian cricket's promoter and would act against enemy aliens. Otherwise, silence was to be observed. Maddocks obediently called an Australian huddle in the Hove dressing-room to press the point.

Trapped between players, administrators, press and a bare-knuckled businessman, the manager was particularly pained by Ian Chappell's involvement. Maddocks had helped entice the former Australian captain to his North Melbourne club for the 1976–1977 summer. Though Chappell *had* hinted at a 'big cricket' comeback in 1977–1978, he'd never mentioned captaincy of an outlaw XI.

No writer caught the moment better than John Arlott in the *Guardian*. His shorthand for Packer's proposal – the 'circus' – quickly became common coinage. 'Circus cannot match Test,' he wrote on Monday, 9 May. 'It is virtually certain that if a circus scheme were launched in competition with Test cricket, it would fail.

The English cricketing establishment could almost certainly destroy any such threat to the international game.'

Arlott had empirical support for his view that Australians would rally to boycott Packer's games: The rest of the World series in lieu of South African Tests in England and Australia had been poor crowd pullers.

> They have been raised on the age-old hostility of Australia versus England, the more recent spectacular series with the West Indies, and some exhilarating matches with Pakistan. If the members of the international teams were banned from both domestic and representative cricket in their own countries, they would rapidly become meaningless as performers.

Arlott, moreover, could not be dismissed as a blimp. As president of England's Cricketers' Association, he was 'the player's choice'.

The Australian Eric Beecher echoed Arlott in *Cricketer Annual*: 'Do they honestly believe such a trumped-up exhibition will interest cricket watchers . . . fattened on a diet of real Test matches?' He deplored that 'a band of money-hungry mercenaries' and 'shrewd commercial manipulators' were 'holding the game to ransom'.

Greig's 'mercenaries' met varying receptions. Kent chairman Walter Brice told Knott, Asif and Underwood at Canterbury that he could not interfere in their winter engagements. When Test and County Cricket Board chairman Doug Insole and secretary Donald Carr sought out Knott and Underwood as Kent played Middlesex at Lord's on Wednesday 11 May, they seemed conciliatory. They wanted to know more about Packer. 'Does he need a manager?' Insole asked.

Procter, however, found Gloucestershire's Tony Brown terse: he could play for Mr Packer if he wanted, but probably wouldn't for the county if he did so. And press hovered round Greig at Hove, even after the Australians left for Southhampton, like the clouds that doused Sussex's next match against Lancashire.

His Wednesday press conference upstairs in the adjacent Sussex Cricketer Hotel was strained. Greig tried to remain buoyant amid questions of growing hostility. 'This summer is in the hands of Lord's,' he said. 'In the winter it is in the hands of a possible compromise between Lord's and Packer. I will myself do anything possible to get them talking.' Reporters were still waiting when England's captain returned from answering Carr's statutory Lord's summons next day. 'A friendly chat,' he reported lightly. 'The topic of the England captaincy was touched upon but not in any great depth.'

'For the first time in my life,' Greig would write, 'I experienced the odd sensation of knowing that many of my listeners did not believe a word I was saying . . . When I insisted that cricket would benefit in the long-term, they stared and muttered as if I was a creature from another planet.'

As Carr and Insole reported to English cricket's superincumbent UK Cricket Council on the Black Friday afternoon, Henry Blofeld of the *Guardian* and Ted Dexter of the *Sunday Mirror* found Greig sheltering from the rain and chain-smoking in the Hove captain's room.

'What do you think they'll do?' Greig asked.

'I think you'll lose the captaincy,' replied Dexter. 'But I expect they'll let you go on playing.'

'Well,' said Greig, 'I knew that might happen when I went into this.'

UKCC chairman Freddie Brown donned the black cap when its meeting dissolved at 5.30 p.m., saying that Greig had 'inevitably impaired the trust' vested in him by acting as Packer's agent. Carr called Greig with a heavy heart: he had promoted the Testless youngster for the 1971–1972 World tour of Australia, and managed Greig's first English tour to India and Pakistan the following year.

A cosy Ashes summer had taken a week to shatter, and Greig's nominal successor, vice-captain Mike Brearley, was shaken by a journalist alerting him to the sacking. 'I don't want the job,' he thought. 'I just want to play. Should they have sacked Tony?'

Although the thirty-five-year-old Cambridge scholar had led Middlesex to a shared County Championship crown and played two Tests in 1976, he owed his sudden suitability predominantly to his predecessor . . . with a little help from Geoff Boycott.

When the prodigal Yorkshireman scorned an offer of the vice-captaincy for England's Indian tour, Greig had proposed Brearley.

'I liked Brearley and I liked the way he operated with me,' says Greig. 'I'd give him a problem and he'd go away and think about it, and always come back with something practical. I wouldn't have taken him to the West Indies, because he wasn't really a great player of fast bowling. But he had good footwork and played the spinners well in county cricket, so you could count on him for a few runs as well.'

Premature grey hairs and a degree in moral philosophy cloaked Brearley in a cerebral air, and he collected himself over the next fortnight as the scarcity of alternatives underscored the logic of his succession. Carr finally made the appointment formal on 25 May 1977, though Brearley did not feel inclined to speak of his 'reign'.

Packer's *Bulletin* had unprecedented circulation as it hit Australian newsstands that week. No administrator was fully informed without Trevor Kennedy's 'The Great Cricket Story: The Inside Facts'.

It was Lord's first measure of the men rapidly spoiling their season, and of their vision. Kerry Packer and the 'shrewd little hardhead' John Cornell emerged as unblinking revolutionaries. 'Probably the most imaginative piece of sports promotion ever devised,' Kennedy began. 'A staggering coup . . . expected to provide the greatest boost Australian cricket has ever received . . .'

The revelation that temptations had been dangled and accepted at the Centenary Test was like discovery of a marital infidelity, and Kennedy's implication that authorities were bereft of imagination and did nothing to 'boost' the game they ran was galling.

Again, though, it was a small measure. Aside from the players and the will, Packer's proposal had little substance: there were thirty-five cricketers but no itinerary, a groundsman but no grounds, a vague management structure but no managers, and six months to pull it together. JP Sport remained a $2 shelf company, share capital now divided between Consolidated Press's Television Corporation subsidiary and the Cornell-Robertson-Hogan alliance, designed to 'act as promoter for a series of cricket matches to be held in Australia and elsewhere'. World Series Cricket Pty Ltd remained a business name registered with the New South Wales Corporate Affairs Commission.

Groundlessness was addressed, fleetingly, when Packer followed up an idea from Michael Winneke, the barrister son of Victorian governor Sir Henry, who had helped Robertson draft contracts during the Centenary Test. Winneke had suggested Packer use the capacious VFL Park football ground in Waverley, twenty-five kilometres out of Melbourne. He knew that the league was struggling to justify the seven-year-old, $42 million arena in its isolated corner of the city. The idea of cocking a snook at the Melbourne Cricket Club would also appeal to it.

VFL boss Allen Aylett was indeed enthusiastic as he welcomed the helicopter disgorging Packer and Cornell at 5.45 p.m. on Tuesday 24 May. It would shortly be light-up time for the ground's four floodlight towers which, after a stadium tour, illuminated a night football match between Footscray and South Melbourne as the party dined.

It rained, though the VIPs were able from their executive balcony to admire the power of 1000 lux. 'The lights are so good,' Aylett quipped, 'you could even play cricket here at night.'

Packer himself switched on. If the light tower shadows could be eliminated by extra floodlighting, it might work. 'How much do you want for the ground?' he asked on the spot.

Aylett had no idea. '$250,000?'

'Sounds fair to me,' Packer replied.

'We'd also want a share of the catering and parking,' Aylett added hastily.

'No, $250,000 it is,' Packer replied. 'That's what you said.'

The spontaneity left Aylett breathless, and he hastened to stitch the deal up by phone next morning. Packer spent five minutes pondering a three-year ballpark offer of $825,000, but the result was the same. 'We didn't really know what VFL Park was worth,' Aylett wrote, 'but our take was close to the million mark and . . . from zero to a million in 12 hours seemed a good deal to me!' Aylett even picked up a job: official cricketers' dentist.

Other territorial claims, though, required a full-time manager, preferably someone skilled in promotion, nimble with finance and steeped in cricket. The best candidate Ian Chappell could suggest was thirty-one-year-old Victorian Cricket Association secretary, David Richards. A Monash University economics graduate, Richards had pioneered the VCA's promotional push with the daring appointment of consultants International Public Relations and more recently made the Centenary Test run like clockwork with ideas he'd picked up on a winter trip to the United States.

Chappell also floated Bill Lawry, now a senior manager at Malleys Whirlpool in Melbourne. In contrast with his hangdog air as a skipper, Lawry had an active promotional mind. He'd been instrumental while in England in 1968 in persuading insurer V&G to become Australia's first one-day cricket sponsor.

When Richards turned Packer away, though, GTV-9's David Evans recommended Consolidated Press's radio network boss Vern Stone. The smart, career-conscious Stone had propelled Melbourne's 3AK to the top of the ratings after coming from Perth's 6PM in 1973, and was known to have ideas above his stations. At Packer's Sydney summons, Stone dashed from Perth with a click of the heels.

The job offer of general manager of World Series Cricket, however, tore Stone: he found cricket mystifying. Packer reassured him: he would have the services of a cricket-literate administrative controller in Brian Treasure, a former Perth grade cricketer who had become Michael Edgley's partner in the city's Entertainment Centre.

'Look son,' Packer said, 'you're a young bloke, you're ambitious, you've done a good job. And it suits me that you don't like cricket. Basically I want someone to look after my money and to get this show on the road, because it's one hell of a job.' After an arm-twisting dinner at the Sydney Hilton with Evans and TCN-9's Sam Chisholm – who stressed the folly of rejecting their boss – Stone agreed.

But the new WSC organisation was still waging phoney war. Packer's preliminaries were enlarging the threat, not embedding it. Withdrawal remained optional if those television rights came loose. So what about a third team? And a fourth? Could Cornell and Robertson rustle enough Englishmen or West Indians to impersonate England and West Indies XIs? The latter, so used to changing allegiances, were very feasible. And the West Indies Cricket Board of Control had been the authority least vehement in response to WSC.

Robertson contacted Lloyd – then in a Manchester hospital awaiting knee surgery – to ask him for a list of his own preferred sixteen.

A bigger WSC meant more Australian and World players, so Ian Chappell and Tony Greig were asked for more names.

It was still, nonetheless, the no-obligation route. Buying more talent committed Consolidated Press to no more than paying out a few cheap contracts if the ACB capitulated. In the meantime, the Test nations faced matches without their best players and – however united the front the International Cricket Conference projected – had grounds to fill. Packer was a television man first, a cricket impresario second, if indeed at all.

Five days after watching night football in a ground designed for 80,000, Packer, Cornell and Robertson arrived to watch a Sunday of county cricket in a Hove ground that could not hold 10,000. Greig was captaining Sussex against Mike Procter's Gloucestershire and it was a chance to peruse the merchandise. 'I'm very excited about cricket and I've never seen Procter play before,' Packer told Blofeld. 'I hope to see him bat today.'

Although David Frost's ITV interview program was his one London appointment, Packer hoped to meet the Lord's elite. 'Whether you like it or not,' Blofeld was told, 'I have influence given to me by the top players in the game who thought they were getting a raw deal.'

Packer got his first wish – Procter took 4–26, then stroked his team to victory with an unbeaten 29 – but not his latter. With detail so scarce, the ICC was merely confused. 'It was difficult,' as secretary Jack Bailey wrote, 'to avoid the temptation of thinking Packer would go away. How could he sustain . . . worthwhile cricket matches in Australia? It was as if he didn't understand that 'authorised cricket' held the world copyright on the game and its organisation.'

Intelligence on Packer was almost as scant. When it came to Australian benchmarks, there were Rupert Murdoch and Rolf Harris (whose show was screening on BBC1) . The *Sunday Times's* reviewer for the Australian edition of the *Oxford Dictionary* was Sir Les Patterson.

Packer's inquisitors on *The Frost Programme* – BBC TV commentator Jim Laker, and the *Sunday Times* columnist and former Sussex captain Robin Marlar – reflected the mixed and muddied feelings. The former was a passionate moderate, friendly with Benaud if distrustful of Greig. The latter was more irascible, and known, in writer Don Mosey's words, as a man of 'strong and often peculiar views on a number of subjects'. Packer was, in Marlar's eyes, a self-publicising 'rich provincial' with a traitorous South African lackey.

It made great television. Marlar could not contain himself. 'Our life, of which cricket is a part, is entirely about *behaviour*,' he spluttered. Packer's contrastingly logical responses were leavened with humour that won the applause of a partisan studio audience. Asked whether he would be upset if his 'managing director' defected to a rival (as Tony Greig had done as chief of English cricket), Packer saved himself from an answer with a quip: 'I am my own managing director.' Marlar, as *Sunday Times* television columnist Dennis Potter wrote, was left 'trying to play a straight bat to a raspberry'.

As Lord's remained inscrutable, Packer flew Lloyd from Manchester to London to scan his West Indian sixteen, sending a liveried limousine to ferry him to the Dorchester Hotel. He also phoned Barry Richards during a match at Guildford for his opinion of Gordon Greenidge, his opening partner at Hampshire. As Richards was watching the West Indian make a double-century, it was not hard to be positive.

Greenidge bolted to Park Lane, and his countrymen also signed with zeal. While WSC money provided a decent upper-middle income in Australia, in the West Indies it conferred tycoonhood. At Caribbean rates of exchange, a $A20,000 a year contract was up to forty times the average per capita income. As the West Indian writer Tony Cozier puts it: 'When you put the fee in front of them, their first reaction would have been: "That's impossible." They were being offered the chance to earn in a few seasons what it would have taken them their whole career to earn playing Tests.'

Robertson and Cornell travelled invisibly in England as they hunted the county careerists: batsman Alvin Kallicharran, all-rounders Bernard Julien and Collis King, and the young fast bowlers Wayne Daniel and Joel Garner. Cornell, at Derby to poach Julien, sat unrecognised even as Strop amid a crowd heckling Knott and Underwood. 'He was quite an important man in the Packer set-up but no one at the ground had any idea who he was,' Knott recalls.

'Seen from the player's box he looked on that day as an unobtrusive spectator.'

To comb the Caribbean, Packer contacted the sporting impresario incarnate, Mark McCormack, who recommended him one of his trustiest IMG aides: Alistair Johnson, the Scottish accountant who ran Arnold Palmer Enterprises. In a week, Johnson rounded up batsmen Lawrence Rowe and Roy Fredericks, spinners David Holford and Albert Padmore, and the team's indispensable wicketkeeper and senior pro Deryck Murray. The only elusive name was one over which Packer had stumbled: the uncapped Leeward Islander Jim Allen. Islands were upturned – he was meant to be a bulldozer driver – until he was traced to a Welsh league.

Greig recommended Pakistani Zaheer Abbas as a World squaddy, and he signed at the Dorchester without hesitation. The contract made him 'whistle'. But, though Greig, Knott and Underwood had been picked 'on merit' to play for Brearley in three Prudential oneday games against Australia, potential English recruits were hemmed in daily by talk that Packer men would be frozen from county cricket. Knott was manhandled as he went into bat at Chesterfield by a spectator swearing: 'How come you're worth all that money?'

For Dennis Amiss, it was a matter of pride. He had been upset at omission from the original list, thinking: 'Why haven't they asked me. Aren't I good enough?' With eleven Test hundreds in fifty Tests, he assuredly was. But as Warwickshire's dressing-room became the country's fiercest anti-Packer bunker, he would wonder what the miff of the moment had got him into.

The bar of Manchester's Grand Hotel, Australia's billet for the first Prudential match on 2 June, emptied at word that Packer's skirmish with Robin Marlar was on television. Jammed in dressing-rooms by rain, it had been hard to avoid thinking about an employer none had met.

On the field, even the team's seniors were struggling. Left behind initially to nurse his mending jaw, Rick McCosker's arrival had been delayed until 15 May by the same strike that had grounded the Benaud letter. The bat seemed foreign as he opened the innings at Bath three days later, as did the sight of two metres of Bajan brawn tossing the new ball from hand to hand.

McCosker's introduction to Joel Garner lasted five balls, but he would become accustomed to his face. Playing that day as Somerset's guest on release from a league contract with Littleborough two months after his Test debut, Garner was about to sign a Packer contract.

A fortnight of skinny scores later, McCosker's early fall at Old Trafford in the Prudential match left Australia 2–2. England passed its puny 169 with ten overs to spare. At Edgbaston, the side folded for just 70. Greg Chappell called an anxious team dinner at the Waldorf before the final game at the Oval on the Bank Holiday Monday, 6 June, although only his century and heavy rain helped Australia to a consolation win.

As Australia headed for Dublin for a game against Ireland hosted by Guinness, however, Chappell vanished. He was still with friends on the Isle of Man when his players – poured onto their Aer Lingus flight back to London and then bussed all night to a Brentwood hotel – slumped sleeplessly against Essex.

With the First Test days away, Chappell's absence was ill-timed. But it would not be the last time Chappell sought refuge, and his Test selections betrayed his anxiety. The search for experience turned Richie Robinson into opener. The captain himself could not avoid being a bashful number three, for Walters had yet to pass 40 on tour. Thomson similarly had just seven first-class wickets.

In London for the ICC's emergency meeting at Lord's on 14 June, Parish and Steele at the budget Westmoreland Hotel in St John's Wood Road kept a distance from their team at the Waldorf in Aldwych. It was hard for them not to feel let down. Parish remembered Greg Chappell's pleasure at the Benson and Hedges sponsorship deal. And Lillee had just published his *The Art of Fast Bowling,* including a cricket philosophy to gratify any official: 'I know I grumble now and then, but I appreciate that cricket owes me nothing . . . I realise that I have enjoyed a red-carpet-ride to cloud-nine.'

'It had left a taste in my mouth,' Parish recalls. 'And it was a rather bitter taste. I felt there'd been a certain amount of under-handedness by the players involved.' Adds Steele: 'It was a fait accompli as far as I was concerned. I didn't want to hear explanations. The players hadn't thought it through.'

After the ICC resolved to issue Packer an invitation on 23 June, administrators then joined crowds magnetised by the Lord's Test. A satisfactory rubber seemed in the offing. Though McCosker remained luckless and Robinson's overenthusiastic swinging emphasised the batting's brittleness, Thomson found fire and Pascoe and Serjeant showed debut promise.

Greg Chappell could finally compare notes with brother Ian, who had arrived as a journalist. Gary Gilmour was covering the game for the *Newcastle Sun;* while Ross Edwards was leading a package tour. Brian Morelli had made it, breaking his family holiday to check on BBC sport-coverage conventions. And a face in the crowd on the fourth day shared his interest: director John Crilly.

Crilly's had been a longer, stranger journey than most. He had impressed Cornell as a director on Hogan projects and moved on to produce documentaries on Lillee and Marsh at Perth's STW-9, but ignored the Packer palaver until Cornell called him a few weeks earlier. 'You know I said I might be working with you again?' Cornell had said. 'I've got a job for you I don't think you'll be able to resist.'

Cornell had judged him well. After nineteen years directing boxing, football and cricket, Crilly was fascinated by Cornell's futuristic vision of televised cricket and flew straight to Sydney. The pair kept nightwatch on TCN-9's BBC telecasts of the first three days of the First Test at Cornell's Neutral Bay home, deriding the reverent camera work and deadpan commentary.

Cornell foresaw 'personality' coverage, from advertisements evoking players as individuals in their natural habitats to audio recordings giving their responses to certain cricket situations (being dropped, scoring a hundred, avoiding a duck, etc). Would Crilly go to England and do it? Ian Chappell and Tony Greig would give him an entree. The rest was up to him.

England was coming back firmly in the match when the jet-jaded Crilly stumbled into the Lord's press box just before 4 p.m. on Monday, 20 June to ask Ian Chappell for an introduction to Greig. He knew it might be a little difficult. The South African was next in.

Before Crilly knew it, however, Chappell was matter-of-factly leading him through Lord's catacombs to England's dressing-room door. Bob Willis politely fetched Greig, who appeared in his pads wearing one batting glove. 'This is unreal,' Crilly thought. 'The dressing-room is the holy of holies, you never speak to a batsman about to go in. Here I am talking to the great Tony Greig and he's about to go in to bat.'

They discussed Crilly's mission and arranged breakfast the next day, but an appeal cut them short. Brearley was out, after adding 132 with Bob Woolmer. 'Sorry John,' said Greig. 'Gotta go now. I'll see you tomorrow morning.' The now-obligatory hooting followed Greig as he marched out, though Crilly's arrival may have been a good omen: Greig's 91 assured England's fair share of the draw.

Address list in hand, Crilly and an English film crew began their star search. Asif, Mushtaq, Greenidge, Zaheer and Amiss responded for the tape recorder; Andy Roberts was filmed dashing deer-like through a Hampshire forest, Eddie Barlow captured among his pigs in Chesterfield.

The director reunited with Greig nine days later at Hove, where the South African's Sussex attack was being mauled by Somerset's Viv Richards. The Australian's intention had been to film Imran Khan – cooling his heels because of a clearance dispute with his former county, Worcestershire – strolling along Brighton beach. But, when Imran was delayed, Crilly's crew settled for watching a Richards double-century spangled with six sixes and twenty-one fours.

Their reverie was disturbed finally when Greig strolled coolly to the sightscreen by which they were filming to point out the arriving Imran. Jeers followed as the crowd twigged, and a Sussex official who'd offered free entry charged Crilly £30 as he left.

Packer himself was unmistakeable as he, Consolidated Press lieutenants Lynton Taylor and David McNicholl and an uncomfortable-looking Benaud, pulled up at the Grace Gates at Lord's two days after the First Test for his ICC audience. He'd not been taken by his invitation's reference to the ICC as the 'sole promoter of international cricket', but was determined not to enter as ogre.

Packer was attentive as ICC chairman Tagge Webster methodically listed conditions for sanctioning the series: WSC must be truncated to run as a six-week spectacle under ACB direction so as not to disrupt traditional cricket. Benaud added soothing words. But, with the parties at touching distance after an hour and a half, Packer renewed his ambit claim: exclusive television rights.

Benaud took Packer for a stroll round Lord's for the next forty minutes as the ICC deliberated. The WICBC was keen, and Steele half-inclined to leave the door ajar. 'He'd come across reasonably well,' Steele recalls. 'And I think Parish and I probably erred in agreeing to go along with some of the things the ICC said. We felt there'd be some people at home who wouldn't be very happy if we accepted Packer's offer.'

Webster emphasised, though, that the ICC could not be dictated to. And united they stood. Secretary Jack Bailey fetched Packer from the Long Room, and the Australian was told he could bid for the rights like everybody else when the ABC contract expired. 'Is that satisfactory to you?' asked Webster.

'No sir,' the Australian said.

'Then there is nothing further to discuss,' the ICC man said with finality.

Packer communed with himself as he left, then spat his response at waiting scribes. 'Had I got those TV rights I was prepared to withdraw from the scene and leave the running of the cricket to the board. I will take no steps now to help anyone. It's every man for himself and the devil take the hindmost.'

Packer's parting shot echoed. Critics seized it as proof of special villainy. 'So much for the protestations that he had come into cricket to improve the lot of the downtrodden first-class cricketer!' sniped Jim Swanton 'His players one and all, not least his truculent spokesman Tony Greig, were seen to be mere pawns in a local commercial dogfight.' He called on the cricket world to reply as one: 'And the devil take K. Packer!'

Benaud winced, dashing Taylor off a memo:

Please when you get to Australia start making love not war. The press has been desperately bad from the public relations point of view over that statement and the devil bit. As it is our job to pick up the pieces I'd like to think a more gentle approach could be evolved. With that statement already made, cricket authorities have gained a great deal of sympathy.

But the public relations setback was greatest among Packer's WSC Australians. Had he really been prepared to walk away? If every man was for himself, were they destined to be the hindmost? 'There'd been the comfort of thinking that the control boards were going to be approached and that was now gone,' says Greg Chappell. 'And I knew there was a fair amount of disquiet among especially the younger players about what they'd actually signed up to do.' A strong general had always been necessary for a team with ten first-timers in England, but the captain was feeling less and less like one.

5

'War situation'

When John Crilly finally caught the Australians up on 10 July 1977, they were three days into an Old Trafford Test gone wrong. By the rest day, when he arranged to collect Australian thoughts for the 'Cornell tapes', England were 139 ahead with a wicket in hand.

Partaking of a bath of beer and spirits that the director filled in a hotel room, players played cards as they took turns taping. 'By the time we got through it we were absolutely shit-faced,' Crilly recalls. A couple of days later, in a bar in Kingston, Jamaica, on the next leg of his journey, he noticed a blackboard carrying the Test score from England. The Australians, Chappell aside, had been brushed aside by Underwood on the fourth day and beaten by nine wickets. Crilly blanched: 'Was I responsible for that?'

Crilly's employer certainly wasn't helping. Packer's recruiting had recommended on Test eve when Robertson called Craig Serjeant – quickest of the young Australians coming to terms with English conditions – to ask if he was interested in a contract. When his coach Ken Meuleman in Perth and his parents urged him not to accept, Serjeant asked Robertson to come back if he was still making runs in a year's time.

It was at Old Trafford, too, that Gary Cosier first remembers
silences that his presence provoked from WSC signatories discussing
their latest news, and his exclusion from whispered instructions in
mixed company like the tour coach. Then on the Test's first morning, Greg Chappell met an ashen Tony Greig who'd just received
a call seeking comment on Packer's death in a car crash in Sydney.
Though he checked with his brother to be sure, Chappell told him
it was probably a hoax. 'Dead?' grunted Packer, when Greig finally
contacted Consolidated Press in Sydney. 'Well I'm not, am I?'

But, while the 1977 Australians are regarded as the team Packer
poisoned, they would have struggled in a sun-kissed summer with a
favouring wind. Generational problems in the team had been some
time coming.

The team photo is allusive. The nine players in the back row had
eighteen Tests between them. Among the team's nominal seniors in
the front row, only the captain and vice-captain Chappell and Marsh
were genuinely risk-averse selections: Walters had never succeeded
in England, McCosker's jaw might not have healed, Thomson was
a medical miracle, and none of Walker, O'Keeffe or Davis had been
first-choice players a year earlier. Premature Australian retirements
in the preceding two years had divided the team before Packer's inter-
cession. As Ian Davis remembers: 'There was literally no middle age
in that side. You had me and Hookesy, and Serj and Kim Hughes in
our early twenties, and then all these other guys round thirty. Unless
you were a very strong personality, you were just in awe of them.'

Kerry O'Keeffe felt the nexus give way:

The band of experienced players played in accordance with their
own unique overview of the game and couldn't really relate to
young struggling players. Kim Hughes in particular was yearning
for an experienced player to take him aside and talk him through
every shot, and that wasn't the nature of Chappell, Walters and
Marsh. They couldn't see the gripe. If you're getting caught
at long-on for 94 regularly then you should be able to suss out
yourself that there are easier ways to reach 100. So there was a
shortcoming among the senior players, but also a naivety among
the youngsters.

Greg Chappell was an apprentice captain, still fumbling with his tools, and unused to failure. Arriving for the *National Times*, Adrian McGregor wrote of Chappell's 'altered state':

> As courteous as ever, but with an air of having jammed his finger in the dyke . . . Yet sitting with younger players it was clear they were undergoing a crisis of confidence, confused at being led by Greg into an apparent dead-end.
>
> Greg had begun a sheepdog role, nipping at their heels. He maintained this role even at parties, shepherding players round arguments, calling for music if the action became too boisterous. I could see how the schoolmasterly metaphor came about.

The captain pined for the do-it-yourself ethos of his brother's time: cricketers who didn't need to be told. Richie Robinson's unsuccessful selection as opener at Lord's, for instance, hinged less on his suitability than on his captaincy of Victoria, previous English tour and the fact that 'if he was asked to open the bowling he would jump at the chance'.

As his virtuoso skill proved insufficient to inspire, Chappell withdrew. The senior players closed ranks round him, instinctively protective but inadvertently widening their distance from the ranks. Everyone felt aggrieved, nobody felt responsible, individual isolation was universal. Cosier recalls:

> It got to the stage where you only saw the senior players on the field. I only wanted to talk to someone about the way things were going on tour – not even about my own situation, that was between me and the selectors – but there was no bastard around to talk about it to. Greg just disappeared. Rod, who's a magnificent communicator, wasn't really round much. So it ended up that poor old Doug Walters tended to cop the lot.

Because everyone seemed to represent a faction, no criticism was trusted as objective. Maddocks, as the obvious establishmentarian, could do no right and his flagging organisation sapped morale. 'Len Maddocks just lost interest in us,' Davis recalls. 'His organisation got worse and worse. His attitude was: "You let me down, you've been disloyal, you've walked out on the board".'

Amid the mayhem, Craig Serjeant arrived at the 20 July tour match at Edgbaston unaware that he was opening. In his five minutes notice, he learned that his kit had been left at the hotel. Spectators watched as McCosker proceeded to the centre alone as Serjeant frantically borrowed equipment before running out still tying his pads. The breathless duck that followed was almost predestined. Australia next day took the field with ten men, Maddocks having freed reserves Dymock and Malone to attend a Rohan Kanhai benefit breakfast. Bob Willis' brother David, a club wicketkeeper, had to make a cameo appearance as substitute.

Rumours spread, after the unexpected arrival of Jeff Thomson's manager David Lord and lawyer Frank Gardiner, of at least one of the young signatories jumping ship. Robertson called Chappell in Birmingham to obtain what was an unauthorised statement of solidarity. Lillee began telephoning regularly with words of encouragement and unity.

The estrangement of the team's leaders showed when Pascoe led discussion at a 22 July meeting at Leicester, urging elders to a more motivated approach in tour games. Marsh replied that a few of the young players should try to motivate themselves a bit more. As the hapless Maddocks ventured the uncontroversial view that everyone was a little to blame for the team's dilemma, even Greg Chappell, Marsh immediately threatened to flatten the captain's first critic.

Charges that the Australian team was picked along Packer lines were levelled at tour selectors when Serjeant's omission for Robinson for the Third Test at Trent Bridge four days later eliminated its last 'non-rebel'. Chappell burst into Marsh's room at Nottingham's Albany Hotel with a hail of expletives. 'You know what those bastards have written about us now?' the captain spat. 'They reckon we've gone and picked a team of Packer players. It just never even occurred to me.'

This time Marsh was a pacifier: 'Well I was going to say something when we picked Richie. Someone was always going to say that.'

Chappell's rage, ironically, reassured Cosier. He was an accidental eavesdropper, lying on Marsh's bed but unseen round the corner, as he collaborated writing team ditties. No, he felt, Packer wasn't the root of the problem. If only it had been that simple.

The name Packer could not, however, be erased from newspaper front pages. On Wednesday, 27 July, the day before the Trent Bridge Test, the Australians passed papers round the Albany plastered with their mug shots. 'Banned!' and 'They Face Axe!' screamed the banners.

Reports were of an International Cricket Conference ultimatum issued the previous evening at Lord's: WSC players would be barred from all first-class and Test cricket if they did not shred their contracts before 1 October 1977. Though the Test and County Cricket Board's Doug Insole and Donald Carr had received Queen's Counsel's advice that enforcement would be legally difficult, the counties were passionate. Glamorgan's Ossie Wheatley went into the TCCB minute book expressing the view: 'Our duty is to drive this wedge of uncertainty into the players' mind.' Insole echoed: 'War situation. We must make sure this thing does not get off the ground.'

The ICC was not as united as it appeared. Jeff Stollmeyer and Allan Rae of the West Indies Cricket Board of Control had received a Churchillian admonition from chairman Webster for their dissent: 'Wars are not won by appeasement.' When the view was reiterated over lunch by the Australian Cricket Board's Tim Caldwell and the New Zealand Cricket Council's Walter Hadlee, the pair had accepted need for at least the appearance of unanimity. Establishment lobbyists at Nottingham targeted Thomson, Hookes and Davis.

Lord and Gardiner had arrived with gloomy news for their client: liquidators had been appointed to the two Allsports sporting goods stores in Brisbane in which, seven months earlier, Thomson had invested his 4IP cash with brother Greg and friend Ashley Colbert. Creditors were chasing $30,000. But, by signing with Packer, Thomson had jeopardised his ten-year radio contract. He couldn't do both, and Gardiner harped on WSC's uncertainties.

Thomson accepted the bald choice, and visited Chappell after the team dinner to say he was probably going to pull out. Half an hour later the captain's phone was ringing with requests for comment, and he asked the Albany switchboard to stop calls to his room at midnight. With the Third Test starting next day, he didn't care if Packer called.

Lord acclaimed the withdrawal. 'This will be the beginning of an exodus from the Packer circus,' he said. 'The players themselves have just followed each other like sheep without thinking about it. But suddenly they have had an attack of brains.'

Thomson was encircled by reporters on 28 July as he confirmed: 'I'm tearing up my contract. I was with a bunch of lads at the time and it seemed OK' His appearance at the crease just before tea was greeted by an ovation, but the capacity crowd of 22,000 could afford to be charitable: Australia, having batted encouragingly on a blameless pitch, had lost 7–54 in the afternoon session.

Adelaide businessmen were sought to contribute to a war-chest for Hookes' retrieval, while Davis took careful stock of a telephone call from Tim Caldwell, whom he knew from the Northern Districts grade club he'd joined as a Nowra teenager. 'We're only interested in you young blokes, you and Hookes,' Caldwell said. 'If things work out for you, you could be Australian captain in a few years' time.'

'Shit,' the young opener thought. 'Maybe he's right.' He'd never discussed the decision over with anyone, not even his parents, and now his first-class career might be ending at twenty-four. Davis, Walters, O'Keeffe and Pascoe contacted their former Sheffield Shield teammate Mick Hill, now a Newcastle lawyer, who was then in England on an Old Collegians' tour. Could he come to the Albany and have a look at their contracts?

Hill arrived, and took Doug Walters' contract to an Australian silk on sabbatical at Cambridge for an opinion on the players' legal bondage. There might just be a way out. But tactics were becoming more important than torts. When as a friendly gesture Hill confidentially passed Gardiner a copy of the contract it appeared the following day on the front page of the *Daily Mail*. Hill squirmed as a mole was suspected. 'I think at that stage the establishment had only seen extracts of the contract, not a whole one,' Hill recalls. 'I was shitting myself.'

As its reception for Thomson showed, the Trent Bridge crowd was making instant heroes. None outshone Geoff Boycott. His three years of Test self-exile were forgiven the moment he reappeared in his dark blue cap, and forgotten completely when he marked his return with a century.

McCosker is haunted by the reprieve he granted Boycott at slip when the Yorkshireman was 20, going on 107. 'I still have nightmares about it,' he says. So fallible was Australia's catching that Chappell thought it almost unfair: 'I said to Rod Marsh during Saturday's play that it seemed we were being paid back for the previous five years when everything that had gone in the air had been plucked safely out of it.'

Australia's decline was charted alongside the establishment ascent. Business rallied round a London-based cleaning business entrepreneur and former umpire, David Evans, who spoke of a corporate pool to pay Test bonuses to loyal English players.

Lord failed to woo Len Pascoe. Though Test cricket was a dream realised for the fast bowler, the suggestion that he would naturally want to follow his Bankstown pal Thomson felt vaguely insulting. But Lord was widening his net. At lunch on the third day, he reappeared in the press box to announce he'd rescued West Indian Alvin Kallicharran from the Packer clutch with a 4IP offer to come to Queensland. Kallicharran explained his decision to preserve a county career at Warwickshire as 'playing safe'.

Which was something the Australians seemed incapable of doing in their second innings, the long-suffering McCosker excepted as he mirrored Boycott's 107. And journalists could hardly wait for England's second win three overs after tea on 2 August. Kerry Packer was back in town.

Tony Greig beat most of them to the Dorchester, where Packer was headquartered with John Cornell and Lynton Taylor in a suite already crawling with lawyers studying the ICC ban.

Packer had anticipated the challenge. At a crucial meeting in Sydney with Cornell, Robertson, Vern Stone and Brian Treasure on 21 July he had resolved – against Benaud's advice – to short-circuit any ban by scheduling their 'Super Tests' on the same days as the Tests in different cities. The players would not be free for Test selection whatever the ICC's course.

It was a defiant strategy, and a perilous one. Packer had already stuck his neck out with crowd forecasts of 15,000 a day. Coinciding with a true blue Test, WSC could look pretty drab on the grounds that Stone was now negotiating to rent.

But the ICC's self-appointment as cricket's 'sole promoter' could not go unchallenged, and barring signatories from first-class cricket appeared an unenforceable restraint of trade. Lord had also to be stopped. Consolidated Press, it was decided, would back Greig, Snow and Procter in a High Court challenge to the ICC.

Procter took Greig's call in a Bristol restaurant, and pulled into Park Lane just after midnight. Snow arrived from Brighton in time for breakfast with Packer the following morning. With a phalanx of lawyers, they extracted an interim injunction against the ban and against Lord's infiltrations.

Packer was still simmering. He hit the phone to Kallicharran, threatening him with a breach of contract suit. Defectors? He'd leave them 'barefoot and bankrupt'. Even Cornell fell out momentarily with the Consolidated Press boss, feeling 'shitty as hell' at being ordered by an 'absolutely raving' Packer to be in the lobby of the Dorchester in fifteen minutes. Cornell decided to take forty. As he told Chris Forsyth, however, the protest was mute because Packer took longer. 'He didn't arrive for some two hours,' Cornell lamented. 'He'd got caught up in something else.'

Women's Weekly's editor, Ita Buttrose, recalled perhaps the only person to placate Packer was the Savoy Grill maitre'd. Fielding Packer's complaint one evening that his Krug was too warm, the waiter remarked: 'You look familiar, sir. Would your name be Packer? Ah, I remember your father always liked the champagne chilled.'

Australian fuses were also short on a tortuous bus journey to Sunderland after the team's Trent Bridge loss. Walters was to lead them against Minor Counties – with Chappell, Marsh and Thomson mourning in private – but young players bailed him up in the bar that evening. Who was in charge? Greg and Rod? Doug? The board? Packer? And how come Ian Chappell was apparently welcome to hitch a lift on the coach when he chose?

Walters took it on the chin, where he bore stitches two days later from a rising delivery that hospitalised him. O'Keeffe became Australia's fourth captain on the trip with the side reduced to a dejected dozen that included Walker as a hobbling substitute despite a cortisone injection in the knee. Minor Counties showed no more mercy than England and won the game after two declarations.

Arriving in Leeds on 10 August for the Fourth Test, Brearley had some sympathy for the Australians. As victories had brought his confidence into line with his competence, he had been an anxious conciliator. He would not hear of tit-for-tat reprisals. Before his team's pre-match dinner at the Dragonara Hotel, for instance, he insisted to David Evans that any Test bonus the cleaning millionaire organised must include Greig, Knott and Underwood.

England's captain feared a last Australian hurrah: 'I am sure Chappell and his side set out, like any self-respecting team, saying, in effect, "if this is our last fling, let's show them".' And Brearley's team were determined to prosecute. 'None of us felt sorry for Greg Chappell's side,' wrote Bob Willis. 'They were outclassed in every department, and it was good to be able to grind them down in the same way that they had played in previous years.'

Boycott liked no mission more in front of his home crowd than eternal vigilance. He was set on becoming the first man to achieve his 100th first-class century in a Test, and the on-driven boundary with which he reached it an hour after tea on the first day virtually retrieved the Ashes at a stroke. As patriots forded the boundary to surround their northern hero, Australians visibly sagged.

Having spent two and a half hours conspiring with Greig, Boycott spent another two and a half with Knott, and he lingered until tea on the second day compiling 191. Low cloud arrived between innings and, as the ball misbehaved, the first five Australians lasted no longer than it had taken Boycott to settle in.

The same familiar poses were struck: Davis inert, Walters chest-on and bat adrift, Hookes anchored in his crooked defensive push. Brearley caught Chappell's deflated drive at slip. Just 36 runs were added the following morning before Australia followed on, and Chappell's stiffer second-innings resistance was undermined by a rogue replacement ball. 'I remember Greg standing with his hands on his hips,' Brearley wrote, 'incredulous that even this should go against him.' Australia lost Hookes in worsening light, and Walters moments before an offer to go off, and had only Robinson left of its specialist batsmen when rain curtailed the day.

Packer was a disappointed patriot at the Dragonara, comparing notes with Ian Chappell and Greig as the Australians sank without trace, but keeping a discreet distance from his players. He accompanied Ian Chappell on the 14 August rest day to a press 'Test' on Harrogate's pretty ground and revealed rudiments of technique for seven balls in an unconquered two.

Party lines were relaxed as, standing beside the *Australian*'s Alan Shiell, Packer caught the TCCB's Peter Lush from David Lord's bowling. Greg Chappell and Hookes were faces in the crowd. Their first sight of Packer suggested only that he had a good pair of hands.

Ian Chappell exerted bustling authority despite the match's informality. When voluble locals began heckling Packer from the boundary, the player turned pressman silenced them with a few choice words. He continued in the same vein in the evening when he joined Packer for dinner at the Dragonara with Greig, *Guardian* gadfly Henry Blofeld and his two female companions. Blofeld recalled Ian Chappell taking his boss to task for tardiness approaching Ashley Mallett: Packer had yet to honour his offer of facing a trial over from the off spinner.

Packer took the chiding in good part, even when Knott and Underwood (also dining in the restaurant) were called on to corroborate. 'We'll see,' Packer said mildly. 'We'll see.'

In their separate worlds next day, Ashes victors and vanquished had only Packer as a common influence.

As the Englishmen ducked their own champagne corks on the Headingley balcony, Greig came to Brearley upset. Chief selector Alec Bedser had just asked him whether he would be available to tour Pakistan and New Zealand that winter. Of course, he would not, and it sounded to Greig like a threat to exclude him from the final Test team at the Oval. Brearley reassured him: he'd press the selectors to stick with the victorious outfit.

The pair then kept an appointment with Ian Chappell in Packer's Dragonara suite, to which Brearley had invited David Evans. Steak sandwiches, beer (for the players) and soft drinks (for Packer) were consumed as Evans was awaited. 'Post-Test languor had set in,' Brearley wrote. 'Ties were loosened, and jackets discarded.' Evans was a pinstriped incongruity as he arrived at around 9 p.m.

The TCCB was known to be beating the bushes for a Test cricket sponsor in 1978, and Evans and Brearley sounded Packer out: if he agreed to join Evans' partnership, they would try to persuade Lord's to drop the ban. Packer seemed willing, floating the figure of £50,000 and offering to withdraw his court action to allow breathing space to settle his differences with the authorities. Evans agreed to take the package to Lord's. Brearley recalled:

> None of us was sanguine. I felt that the TCCB would not be persuaded by an offer of money; the fundamental argument between the two worlds could be summed up in the Australian Board's horror at Packer's saying, 'Come on gentlemen, there's a little bit of the whore in all of us when it comes to money'. Moreover, the English authorities would feel that a year's time would be a year within which he (Packer) could strengthen his position.

Brearley was right. Evans was ignored.

The colours in the bar of Australia's billet at the Post House Hotel showed no sign of blending either. On one side of a table sat Marsh, on the other Gary Cosier and Kim Hughes, with Kerry O'Keeffe uneasily torn between factions. Hughes, who'd been desperate to play in the Test, suspected that Robinson had been preferred because he was close to the team hierarchy. Marsh denied it.

Though O'Keeffe had little time for Hughes, he had shared his bafflement. He'd also sympathised when the twenty-three-year-old moaned at receptions that nobody would offer him advice, although O'Keeffe had been careful to suggest no more than that the youngster beat the system by getting hundreds. Hughes had been out four times between 80 and 100 on the trip.

Hughes pressed his luck. Marsh must at least admit the error of Robinson's selection at Lord's, and added: 'Skull thinks so too.'

'Hang on, Kim,' O'Keeffe interjected, 'I didn't say that.'

But Marsh glared as he asked angrily: 'Do you think we were wrong to pick Richie as an opener at Lord's?'

That was another question, O'Keeffe thought, and he might as well come clean. 'Well,' he said slowly, 'as a matter of fact, I do.'

That tore it. Marsh rose angrily, tears in his eyes. Hughes was one thing – the kid was obviously drunk – but O'Keeffe was another. Marsh stormed from the bar. Kerry O'Keeffe did not play again on tour.

At the Waldorf two days later, a dozen Australians also faced their futures. Were they really rebels? If so, whose was their cause? Few had met the man most English papers called simply a 'TV magnate'. Now on 17 August 1977, it seemed, there was a chance to meet Mr Kerry Packer. Taxis shuttled from the Waldorf to the Dorchester, where their boss waited to receive them.

Hookes was especially anxious. His phone had run hot with calls from Adelaide as locals rallied to 'Keep Hookesy At Home'. Blandishments, big dollars and the South Australian captaincy were there if he quit WSC. Cornell busied himself pouring beers before Packer marched in, all bonhomie and business.

His lecture was pointed, and personal. 'The only thing that's going to make this thing work is our bond,' he said. 'And our loyalty and our commitment to one another. The only way I'll make money is if I give it everything. The only way you'll make money is if you do the same.'

After three months in which addresses had been mostly swipes at slackness, it sounded like the Sermon on the Mount. 'Is there any reason why we shouldn't play cricket for World Series?' a prowling Packer asked. 'Look, if Thomson and Kallicharran want to go that's fine, we're not going to chase them. We don't want guys who don't wanna play, we'll let 'em go.'

He began circling the room, eyeing each individual. 'Is anyone here having second thoughts? Is there anyone who thinks what they're saying is right, that you're a "disapproved person"?' Each player was fronted. 'Are you in?' Each assented.

'He'd lined us up and made it clear,' Davis remembers. 'He'd coughed the dough up and he intended us to be loyal. I think it put me back on the path to World Series. After that I just thought: "I'm committed. I'll stick with it".'

Malone was excited: 'Packer's physical presence was awesome. And because he was so direct and forthright, he came across as a powerful individual whose side you wanted to be on. What he said was really relevant to us: that we were all in it, that we had to make it work to make money out of it. At the end I felt really confident.'

Packer paused before turning to Hookes, who seemed doubtful. 'Kerry asked him again with a firmer voice,' Walker recalls. 'And Hookesy kinda coughed and said he was.' But Hookes was not swayed: 'At the end of it, he was still just a businessman to me. Not a billionaire or anything like that. And I was probably going through a stage every twenty-one-year-old goes through of being a bit of a smart arse.'

He returned to the Waldorf to find his friend Cosier disconsolately in the bar. Nobody, of course, had told Cosier, Serjeant, Hughes and Dymock of the meeting. Coming downstairs they'd met Maddocks wondering: 'Where are the boys?'

'It wasn't that the meeting was happening,' Cosier recalls. 'What disappointed me was that nobody said to us: "We've got this meeting down the road to go to. Sorry you can't come, but we'll meet you in the bar afterwards". It wasn't the fact that we were in the bar. The real hard part was that they weren't in the bar with us.' But this was a team that had never truly been united.

The Oval, England's usual final Test venue, is accustomed to farewells. Sir Donald Bradman denied in 1948 that its salute had anything to do with Test cricket's most mythologised duck. Applause as Greg Chappell embarked on his uncertain future was equally genuine, but no one could quite decide if Tony Greig, Alan Knott and Derek Underwood were taking genuine curtain calls. The crowd hissed Greig regardless.

As teammates at the Clarendon Court Hotel were aware, Greig was still very much in Mr Packer's pay. Just before the pre-Test dinner on 24 August he invited Bob Woolmer and Bob Willis to his room for a nightcap afterwards. The subject was obvious.

Greig had asked Knott to join him as an advocate but, joining them at 11.30 p.m., Woolmer was already sympathetic. From membership of a fervent anti-Packer faction on Kent's team bus in midseason, Woolmer had come around. He recalled past injustices at the Test selection table, like omission at Headingley two years earlier, apparently to accommodate a token Yorkshireman.

'You know what we're doing,' Greig stated simply.

'Yes,' said Woolmer. 'I'm right behind you.'

In principle anyway. Despite centuries in three consecutive Ashes Tests, Woolmer was unsure he fitted the 'top bracket'. TCCB Test payments also seemed about to surge from their £210: Evans was broking a £1000-a-Test deal for players with Cornhill Insurance not unlike Australia's Benson and Hedges underwriting.

Greig urged Woolmer to think of other cricketers. Woolmer's defection would help the fair pay fight. 'I thought you were all for it,' Greig said disappointedly. Woolmer said he was. It was whether it was all for him.

Woolmer had barely left to consider his position when Willis arrived. The ritual was repeated for the Warwickshire fast bowler, still relishing his best Test summer, and ended the same way. Derek Randall had already been privately courted. All reported to Brearley the following morning, Woolmer surest he would follow.

Although the Australians fared better at The Oval, their tour came full circle in a damp draw. Some of the Australians made the best of what might be their last Test. Hookes sparkled during his 85. Debutant Mick Malone was a medium-pace metronome for 47 overs at the Vauxhall end while claiming 5–63. But they were dispassionate pleasures. 'Greg just kept throwing it to me,' says Malone.

Others were merely glad to see the end. Serjeant, again reluctant opener, approached the wicket uncertain whether to take strike to Willis. 'Might as well get it over with,' he thought. He did not last the over.

English players adjusted themselves to divergent winters: the TCCB crowd were destined to tour Pakistan and New Zealand under Mike Brearley, Underwood, Knott, Amiss for Australia under Greig. As they parted at The Oval, Underwood told John Lever to give his regards to Hyderabad's insanitary Sainjees Hotel, then shared a cab with Ian Chappell. 'Guess I'll be seeing you in Australia,' he said, before thinking of Chappell's willingness and success in sweeping him. 'You and that bloody broom.' With Knott, Woolmer and Greig, the spinner had headed for a county match: the first hat-trick of his career at Hove on 31 August included Imran and Snow and was complemented by Woolmer's century.

A meeting of the English Cricketers' Association at Edgbaston on Monday, 5 September, showed the members' equivocal – according to Greig, contradictory – outlook. Almost four-to-one in favour of banning Packer players from the county game, a clear majority called on the ICC and TCCB to negotiate a truce.

But the TCCB had set its stall so utterly it had even wrong-footed David Evans. Evans called Woolmer after the Fifth Test, imploring him not to sign until he met Cornhill's chairman at Luton Football Club on Gillette Cup Final day.

But that Saturday, 3 September, was also selection day for the Pakistan tour party, and the TCCB's Donald Carr interrupted a party at Woolmer's home enquiring of the Kent batsman's availability. Hoping that Evans would call before the team was finalised, a perplexed Woolmer said that, on balance, he probably wasn't. He turned on the BBC's Gillette Cup *Grandstand* in the afternoon to find that the TCCB had proscribed him. 'That's typical of the way they handle things,' said an exasperated Evans when he called a little later. 'It serves them right. You go and play.' Party guest Greig signed Woolmer virtually on the spot.

When Hampshire denied Gloucestershire the County Championship the following Friday at Bristol, cheering locals consoled their inspiring captain Procter. Visiting players gathered to sing 'Auld Lang Syne' round Greenidge, Roberts and Barry Richards. Three days later, the players met again at the Dorchester with WSC's other county players to receive winter work schedules from Lynton Taylor.

6

'Just like old Aussie, eh?'

'Hi fellas,' read the handwriting on the corner of the newsletter. 'Being closely involved with the preparations for the Super Tests over the last couple of months, there is no doubt that the series will be a resounding success . . .'

On Austin Robertson's JP Sport bulletin, forwarded on 22 July 1977 to all WSC's recruits, the scrawl was recognisable as Dennis Lillee's. Whatever was happening in England, they were assured, the organisation awaiting them effervesced with ideas.

Lillee had been captivated by Packer at their first meeting at TCN-9, while he remote-commentated the Tests. The business-man percolated with plans, and called Lillee constantly from home while watching the telecasts to exchange notes. 'Some of the chats lasted from the minute I'd gone off-air after doing the lunch-time comments through to a few minutes before I had to prepare for the afternoon tea comments,' Lillee wrote. 'And sometimes he'd have been on the line for an hour before lunch, and then again after tea.'

Packer had been stunned by the ease of recruitments, but the mix of good sport, good television and good patriotism was mesmeric. He expected, even fed off, refractory opposition. Money was immaterial. As Packer had told Australian Golf Club members six months earlier, when offering to bankroll Jack Nicklaus's

Kensington course redesign for the Australian Open: 'I don't give a stuff what it costs.'

Though Packer's word was law, Consolidated Press's commitment remained spasmodic. Harry Chester, his deputy chairman and 'details man', policed the bottom line vigilantly. When Vern Stone called him to ask for a budget, Chester replied: 'There isn't one, son. We've already spent several million dollars, we've got to start to rope it all in. We've got to get some direction.'

WSC took on corporate substance on 17 August, when the name registered a year before was conferred on JP Sport. Stone and Brian Treasure also needed help. Chris Forsyth, a freelance journalist with a maverick streak and a classmate of Packer's at Geelong Grammar, came aboard as press officer. Viv Jenkins became official photographer. Graeme McDonagh, the Mullins Clarke and Ralph adman cutting a dash for GTV-9, supervised advertising. Mike Treloar, an Albert Park clothes designer for GTV-9 and HSV-7 personalities, became costumer. Treasure circularised players for their measurements.

Team managers were located for the Australian sides: Treasure found an experienced Perth grade cricketer, Geoff Forsaith; Benaud recommended the genial Adelaide car-dealer Graham Ferrett; Forsyth introduced Stone to a friend in flooring chemicals, John Curtain.

Mike Denness was delighted at Greig's offer of an Australian summer with his family managing the World side. Denness's English dismissal in 1975 had been followed by retrenchment at Kent, and he hardly genuflected to Lord's. The West Indians' steward would be Dr Rudi Webster, a Barbadian radiologist at Melbourne's Alfred Hospital dabbling in sports hypnotherapy, and a long-time familiar of touring Caribbean cricketers.

World Series Cricket soon became, though, a cricket team of eleven captains. Packer was overlord. CPH executive Lynton Taylor carried almost as much weight. Chester's memos were dreaded. Nine network chief Len Mauger and his station bosses Sam Chisholm and David Evans ran independent briefs, while consultants kept a constant chatter. The BBC's David Kenning advised on television coverage. Jack Nicklaus's golf course agronomist Fred Bolton – in Sydney supervising Kensington course's redesign – was consulted on pitches. Trail-blazing American tennis promoter Jack Kramer was asked for reflections on chaperoning touring athletes.

Bob Cowper and the shrewd ex-Test spinner John Gleeson sat with Benaud, Robertson and Forsaith on a 'governing committee' framing series rules, and John Cornell retained a mysterious mission as floating creative catalyst.

There was even Sir Garfield Sobers, whom Greig persuaded Packer to hire as a senior WSC statesman. At home playing for Barbados, Nottinghamshire and South Australia alike, Sobers epitomised the mobile professional player. He was also Greig's hero. Everyone was in charge, and the hard graft remained to be done. Where was WSC playing, for a start?

Although trustees at the Brisbane and Sydney Cricket Grounds withheld their headquarters, Stone had complemented Melbourne's VFL Park with the Sydney Showground by the end of June, and isolated similarly off-piste grounds in Perth and Adelaide: Gloucester Park (owned by the Western Australian Trotting Association) and Football Park (home of the South Australian National Football League).

There was also sufficient suggestion of bush hospitality in the next four weeks for Stone to surround his capital city itinerary of six Super Tests and dozen one-day International Cup matches with a preliminary rural rota of Country Cup matches.

The Super pitches needed, however, were still taking seed in John Maley's mind. He turned to former Gabba curator Jack McAndrew, then mowing wickets at Brisbane Church of England Grammar School, to discuss nurturing instant pitches in concrete cradles over heating wires and suction pumps. Soil was sifted with an Adelaide botanist, Roy Bond. In New South Wales, dry wamberal soil could be crushed near the Showground; in Victoria it was dug from the famous Merri Creek; in South Australia it was ploughed from a housing development; in the West it was retrieved from a Waroona farm (100 kilometres south of Perth) where an access road had to be hacked to withdraw it.

There was an added complication. While pitches could be grown in situ at the Showground and Gloucester Park, football footfall kept Maley from work in Adelaide and Melbourne until September. Wickets would have to be cultivated externally and transplanted. Engineer Aldis

Birzulis was retained to build glasshouses from Victorian Department of Agriculture blueprints. Their twenty-five-tonne concrete trays were sunk on the last day of July, but question of their transfer recurred like a jarring refrain.

Though Cornell's science-fiction notion of levitating them to the centre on an air cushion to avoid damaging the surrounds had gained respect from repetition, Stone's hovercraft survey with Birzulis ended gloomily with a small private firm in the Adelaide suburb of Parafield. 'It was a tin shed, thirty metres by forty,' Stone recalls. 'A couple of nice blokes, one an ex-submarine captain. There were these little hovercraft they made for surveyors, about three metres by five, running round in the fields outside.'

'Man, I'm depressed,' he told Birzulis on the plane back to Melbourne. 'We can't do this in three months. They haven't even been tested. These are twenty-five-tonne trays.'

Birzulis calmed him. 'Don't visualise a hovercraft carrying a pitch,' he said. 'The wickets become the hovercraft. The rubber gets strapped to the block, and then we have four minicraft powered by turbines that pump air into that curtain. And we'll use a steel cable system to guide it along.' Well, it sounded feasible, and it was what the brass wanted, so Stone commissioned the Parafield firm to go ahead.

Packer grasped the nettle personally when WSC kept promises to Michael Holding to seek a blessing for West Indians playing among politically sensitive 'non-county' South Africans, Graeme Pollock and Denys Hobson. But although he took Clive Lloyd to lobby at Kingston's Jamaica House in July, Packer got no joy from Prime Minister Michael Manley and special adviser Owen Karl Melhado. Even after what Manley called a 'lengthy, plain and humorous' discussion with an 'amiable pirate' of 'ready wit, iron will and an automatic good sense', the socialist leader stuck to the word of June's Commonwealth Heads of Government Meeting discouraging sporting contact with South Africa.

Local politics was simpler to influence. Sharing Packer's view that the thirteen-member SCG Trust was just a 'group of crusty old men sitting behind closed doors' when it turned Super Tests away, Premier Neville Wran went into bat advocating full utilisation of public facilities. On 25 July 1977 he sacked the trustees, reconstituting the body as the Sydney Cricket and Sports Ground Trust. WSC's offer of $20,000 a day for thirteen days' usage was confidently resubmitted.

Stone despaired at his ever-evolving attraction. Pollock and Hobson had to be deleted from the cricket cast list in a sixteen-page glossy for potential advertisers at a $25,000 Sydney Hilton promotional dinner a fortnight later. Then, so did Thomson, though it was too late to remove Kallicharran when he withdrew. The Showground remained WSC's Sydney estate, subject to amendment.

Paul Hogan mastered ceremonies, amplified by Treasure and Lillee, with a videoed address from Packer. With surrender of the Ashes days away, another film narrated by Ian Chappell featuring Lillee, Ross Edwards and Ian Redpath promised: 'You haven't seen the real Australian team in action.'

Network salesmen, however, found few corporate allies as they peddled $3.5 million in sponsorship 'opportunities'. No one wanted to fork out $400,000 for Super Test naming rights, and a revised $220,000 offer of advertising spots and perimeter hoardings had to be packaged.

Packer again took charge, with a personal luncheon circuit. 'Those who take advantage of our initial cheap offers will be taken care of over the next few years,' he promised one group. 'Those who haven't have been photostatted.' Old contacts were asked to rally. Berger Paints – sponsor of JP Sport's *World Masters Snooker* the year before – coughed up first. Then household goods firm Reckitt and Colman approved involvement of its Samuel Taylor subsidiary. A final few cut contra deals: McDonald's Family Restaurants would hand out player posters, SPC-Ardmona would festoon cans with cutout mug shots for pasting on a scrapbook-style *Women's Weekly* poster, while Qantas and Hertz Rent-A-Car knew circuses did not travel on magic carpets. Chris Forsyth's tart observation was that 'the novelty of it all was giving Australian businessmen their usual chance to distance themselves as far as possible from anything original or innovative'. Seducing the spectator fell to Graeme McDonough, who blanketed newspapers, while Cornell took responsibility for television advertising and awaited fruits of John Crilly's northern odyssey.

Crilly left England for the West Indies on 12 July with a series in mind of Caribbean candid camera shots of Super Test stars at play.

Vexed by his English film crew's £500-a-day bill, he appealed to the patriotism of a freelance Australian cameraman, Bob McDonald, in offering him the fortnight's work. 'There'll be first-class flights, first-class hotels, first-class food, the whole lot, and I'll pay you £200 a week in cash,' Crilly had told him. 'But it'll only be the two of us. Just like old Aussie, eh?'

'Done,' came the reply.

They'd had a rare glimpse of the recumbent West Indian: from the rambling Holding household with its mix of generations and earthen floors, to the seething Slim's Disco recommended by Collis King where only mention of the cricketer's name saved them from going the way of all honky trash. Were the locals the celebrity stock of legend? Those dusky maidens in Port-of-Spain had been happy to pose round a daiquiri-swilling Deryck Murray, but only a frozen ice salesman had recognised Lawrence Rowe near a Kingston bar at which he'd assured them mobs of groupies might make it 'a bit dangerous'.

By Crilly's return to Sydney, though, Cornell had become worried about an approach too unfamiliar to average cricket watchers and preferred the director's more conventional playing sequences. Crilly spliced a sequence of WSC's finest – the Brilliant (Clive Lloyd), the Double Century-Maker (Viv Richards), the Veteran (Doug Walters), etc – and recommended his friend Dean Reynolds to read the suitably hyperbolic Cornell commentary.

Reynolds' baritone sounded ideal as it echoed round a subterranean Sydney studio, where Cornell and Crilly oversaw the sixty-second sessions after dark. But Cornell never wanted less than perfection, never more than the minimum amount of sleep. Reynolds' vocal cords turned raw as take upon take was dustbinned by Cornell behind the glass in the sound booth.

As the clock ticked past 4 a.m., he became the first man WSC had literally rendered almost speechless. 'Crikey, what's the problem?' Crilly asked the sound engineer with whom he was sitting in the studio. 'We've been going eight hours and they've all sounded fine to me.'

'Well, we're listening to it back on this tiny speaker here,' the engineer replied. 'Because John's in the sound booth and he can hear everything: every rustle of paper, every breath and every sibilance.'

Crilly's eyes rolled as he turned toward the booth. 'Awww Christ, John! Don't you realise? We don't need you listening to it on that system. People don't hear it like that on TV.' Cornell twigged. Tapes rewound. Yes, that one at 8 p.m. would do nicely. Cornell never judged an advertisement in the sound booth again.

But then both McDonagh's newspaper ads and Crilly's television trailers faced an audience even stricter: the Trade Practices Commission. Citing an insert in the *Weekly's* last September issue pumping the Super Tests and their personnel from 'Australia', 'the World' and 'the West Indies', the Australian Cricket Board saw the cheeky pictures of Rod Marsh, Ian Chappell, Alan Knott and Clive Lloyd in their national colours, the use of the word Tests' and the offer of the 'highest possible standard of cricket played under accepted and traditional cricket laws' as flouting section 52 of the Trade Practices Act. The ACB's Federal Court action, Forsyth would recall, had 'such a profound effect on the WSC administration that the whole venture might easily have been stillborn'.

The ACB marketed Tests, WSC something else. The *Weekly* insert, the ACB alleged, amounted to 'misleading or deceptive conduct'. 'It was an ambush,' said Forsyth. 'And, like all well-mounted ambushes, it caught the entire WSC operation on the wrong foot.'

McDonagh was silenced, and Crilly and Cornell's nocturnes were now followed by daybreak journeys to Sydney's Federal Court building with their latest commercials as lawyers squabbled over the antiquity of the phrase 'Test match'. After Justice St John's interim injunction on 30 September 1977, two of their six commercials were killed, a third restrained.

When Wran's new SCSG Trust endorsed WSC's ground offer the same day, it seemed almost fated to the Equity Court challenge from the NSW Cricket Association. WSC was immobilised. With six weeks to hold public attention while lawyers argued, appealed and amended, it bobbed like a clipper in the doldrums.

When his impetus was most needed, Packer was in London for his skirmish in the High Court with the International Cricket Conference. WSC, Greig, Procter and Snow were plaintiffs against, the Test and County Cricket Board and chairman Doug Insole – the ICC had no legal 'personality'. A bodyline barrage of lawyers and twenty-one star witnesses was gathered to impress Justice Sir Christopher Slade.

Sole absentee was Sir Donald Bradman. Ray Steele arrived in his stead. 'He was such a shrewd little bugger of course,' Steele chuckles. Nobody relished the fiery court wicket with hostile Queen's Counsels from both ends: WSC's Robert Alexander downwind, the ICC's Michael Kempster coming uphill but making Greig flinch as testimony began. Ross Edwards was struck at how detested Greig had become. 'Jeez, he was like Lord Haw-Haw,' says Edwards. 'He was very bad meat.'

'For some reason, I felt like a criminal,' Greig recalled. 'Especially when I was first attacked by the opposition counsel. My initial impulse was to tell all our opposition to go and jump in the lake ... It became a battle, with the opposition trying to pull me apart and Alexander protecting me.'

Snow and Procter took their turns, before Packer's 3 October appearance. Confirmation of a two-year budget for WSC of $12 million turned heads, as did insistence that he was a cricket aficionado: 'Contrary to popular opinion, I have always liked cricket, and was always rather resentful of the fact that I wasn't coached properly.'

Ross Edwards followed his new employer into the stand, then Knott was watched by Kent confederates Asif and Underwood as they rostered a round-the-case watch. 'I remember regretting that I declined the opportunity to sit while giving my evidence,' the wicketkeeper wrote, 'not realising that I would be in the witness box for two hours.'

As Henry Blofeld put it, the ICC was chasing a big first innings. 'He (Packer) had created the impression of a businessman trying to do the best for his company, only to find that he had been frustrated by a lot of crusty old establishment figures who obviously did not know one side of a balance sheet from the other.'

While the WSC contingent banqueted in Park Lane and tripped to Royal Ascot, Ray Steele spent a frugal fortnight in the Westmoreland. 'At midday Packer would take his party off to some private place for a slap-up lunch, while we went across the road to a pub for a counter lunch.' Having expected three days in London in toto, Steele actually had three days in the stand. Dry humour sustained him. 'I've heard the only way to get out of a Packer contract is by becoming pregnant,' he advised the judge. West Indian, Pakistani and New Zealand officials preceded the ICC's Jack Bailey and the TCCB's Donald Carr before an incredulous Greig heard that Geoff Boycott was padding up.

Boycott's sudden thickness with Lord's after three years' estrangement caused Greig as much chagrined amusement as their mutual endorsement of St Peter cricket equipment. When Greig rang Boycott to ask if he would collect some bats for him from a Birmingham trade fair, the South African could not resist jibing: 'By the way Geoff, we're looking forward to throwing a bit of mud at you when you give evidence.' Greig cringed at Justice Slade's rebuke when Boycott's testimony began with an account of the conversation. This was, he was told, 'not a cricket match'.

As the Yorkshireman settled smoothly, however, it became not unlike one. His counsel Kempster he classed as a 'sort of medium-pacer', Alexander as 'a spinner if ever I saw one, alert and wily'. Boycott's observations that 'a man cannot serve two masters' mingled with the effective northern wisdom that players opposing the ban were 'wanting the penny and the bun'. 'He was reluctant to leave the witness box when his evidence was finished,' Blofeld observed, 'feeling he could do more to help the establishment.'

Boycott's fellow Yorkshireman Ray Illingworth, Cricketers' Association secretary Jack Bannister, and Worcestershire secretary Mike Vockins completed 137 hours of evidence. Long closing remarks by Alexander and Kempster left Justice Slade on 7 November with 'a certain amount of work to do'.

The sole court where Packer had jurisdiction was one where he felt himself a discerning judge: television. Impressing the magistrate fell to producer David Hill, directors Morelli and Crilly and technical manager Warren Berkery.

Journalist Hill had been poached from the ABC on the strength of his innovative *Sportsnight* program. Photography buff Morelli, in contrast, had turned up at TCN-9 in August 1956 before it had even begun broadcasting with a yen to be a cameraman. The first of few brushes with cricket had left one lingering impression: filming a 1956 testimonial game at North Sydney Oval, Morelli had been infuriated at the wearisome wide shots he had to shoot. 'I could have stood at the bus stop with the two teams and I would never have recognised them,' he says. 'They were just white blobs.'

Crilly nursed similar frustrations. Why did everything have to be straight on, when phenomena like run-outs, no-balls and stumpings were intelligible only from side-on? He remembered playfully filming a match between the World and Australia in 1971–1972 from this angle and in the space of an afternoon capturing three stumpings.

Three years later he'd also become a replay devotee on a sponsored journalist's tour of Canada. Baseball coverage there swivelled 'isos' – isolation discs enabling directors to pick salient replays from specific individual cameras – with electronic elan. Wiring the Australian Open Golf had made Berkery a similar technophile. With eight cameras, the co-operative planned to give their cricket quite indecent exposure.

As at the Open, Packer took overseas counsel. The BBC's David Kenning cost $10,000 and was not received with complete cordiality as he toddled round Hill's outside broadcast vans with a gin and tonic in hand, but his eight-page 'Some Thoughts on the Television Coverage of the Super Test Series' became an important reference. Packer had his own ideas: long-irked that half a day's overs were filled by 'batsmen's arses', he wanted every ball filmed from behind the bowler's arm.

Hill, Crilly, Morelli and Berkery filled their own suggestion box. The producer was a ringmaster with an eye and ear for spectacle. As he had at State of Origin Rugby League, Hill proposed rock music overtures to a day's play. A boundary-riding interviewer, David Grant, was hired from Perth's TVW-7 to buttonhole batsmen as they left the field. 'I want to know about why the bloke got out,' Hill said. 'We're a long way away in the grandstand, we're not allowed out there, and we need to know. Not twenty bloody minutes later in an interview, but when it actually happened.'

Morelli and Crilly sussed angles from which the game should be shot and evaluated suitable cameramen on the basis of previous work in other sports and entertainments. Warwick Bull was a steady sort: he could start on the 'straights'. Ian Monahan had the reflexes for mid wicket. Greg Cameron's excellence on the high-altitude 'cherry-picker' camera at the golf, suggested him as a 'follow' cameraman chasing the lofted hook and panting fieldsman. Berkery rejoiced in his Chyron, an electronic device which could project a Digital computer scoreboard on-screen at the end of each over. Morelli suggested illuminating the names of not-out batsmen.

Already armed with Crilly's taped interview segments, Cornell pressed for the full aural experience. Players carrying their own microphones proved unworkable, but sound man Colin Stevenson believed microphones stuck in the pitch might eavesdrop as effectively.

Richie Benaud sought commentators to lend him suitably authoritative support. Though Jim Laker declined Packer's terms after their *Frost Programme* meeting, his BBC colleague Fred Trueman was cooing within a week: 'He's a great feller this Kerry Packer, you know, sunshine. He's gonna be puttin' on some great stuff this winter.' Austin Robertson asked the melodious West Indian Tony Cozier to come for the first half of the summer, then interrupted Bill Lawry in his pigeon coop and his former Victorian colleague Keith Stackpole at work at Philip Morris with offers of summer employment. A good scorer was a must and the BBC TV statistician Irving Rosenwater seized the winter work, explaining to appalled acquaintances that: 'If I hadn't taken the job, Bill Frindall would have been in there like a shot.'

Creative tension crackled between the irreverent Hill, the artistic Morelli and the more traditional Crilly as they travelled cross-country surveying WSC's estates. VFL Park, Gloucester Park, Football Park and the Sydney Showground had never hosted cricket before, so none had a guide book for apprentices.

Differences came to a head at Football Park one morning when Hill and Crilly disagreed over the right height for a camera tower. In front of thirty crew, their tensions exploded. 'You're a cunt,' Hill shouted. 'You're always right, aren't you? Know it all!'

'And you're a bloody Johnny-come-lately who doesn't know anything about cricket,' Crilly shouted back. 'It's gotta be high enough for the camera to see over the top of the umpire's hat.'

The crew held its breath as Hill ascended the tower to judge for himself. 'Okay,' the producer called out finally. 'You're a cunt. You are right!' Hill's concession did much to clear the air. They had, after all, a long way to travel together.

The public would be the arbiters, Bob Parish told the ACB's private annual meeting at Sydney's Cricket House on 6 September 1977, adding only: 'Let's hope our friends stay with us.' That was as emotional as the chairman became. Parish's name was not his only hint of the ecclesiastical: his tongue rolled out references to 'the year nineteen-hundred-and-seventy-seven'.

It was his second chairmanship. Parish had been fifty when appointed for a three-year term in 1966, turned sixty-one two days before the Packer news broke, and was a benign, if remote, figure-head for a gentle gerontocracy.

Ian Chappell had warned Packer in a 6 May memo of the ACB 'attack' he anticipated: 'They will say they've been doing it for the glory of the game etc. One of the things they will try and put over is that we will be a flash in the pan, plundering players, money, and leaving cricket an empty shell in three years.' In fact Parish's 9 May letter to Consolidated Press advising that 'no good purpose would be served by a meeting' remained the ACB's sole correspondence. Legal jabs emitted by an 'emergency committee' of Parish and his two previous chairmen, the New South Welshman Tim Caldwell and Sir Donald Bradman of the South Australian Cricket Association were no more than a continuance of ACB policy toward private promoters. 'Lots of people in boom times wanted to put on a match here and there,' says Steele. 'But they had no obligation to the game or interest in it. They just wanted to make money. If they got hold of the proceeds of a match on a big ground they could obviously pay the players a lot of money, which would make them discontented.'

In his analysis for Packer, Benaud had advised against underestimating the ACB:

> The board of fourteen have in their number Bob Parish as chairman, a tireless worker; Sir Donald Bradman, a brilliant administrator and businessman, director of several boards; Ray Steele, solicitor and one of the best administrators in the world. There are weaknesses because the structure demands a certain number of representatives from each state but they will close ranks on a matter of this kind.

They were, though, thin ranks. An umbrella group of volunteers elected to promote and profit from Test matches on the states' behalf, the ACB's Trade Practices Act self-definition was 'an unincorporated association constituted by state associations' involving a 'small administrative body with little property or funds of its own'. Not only had it no executive officer, it did not even have an office: its half-dozen clerical staff perched at the Victorian Cricket Association in Jolimont Street near the MCG, and the NSWCA's Cricket House in George Street, Sydney.

Although Packer seemed the rebel assailing the establishment, it was the ACB that had the scale of a guerrilla army. Secretary Alan Barnes inhabited a Cricket House office virtually bomb-proofed with paper. Legal advice came from Graeme Johnson of the Melbourne law firm Hedderwicks. Promoting Australia's Tests with India was delegated in November to the VCA's Dave Richards, who was granted $25,000 to retain consultants at Sportsplan Marketing. Their slogan, 'The Indians Are Coming', might have pleased Packer. As an aficionado of Westerns, he knew that cowboys generally win.

7

'If you fuck it up we could lose the whole $12 million'

Max Walker's wife Tina answered the door at their Doncaster home in mid-September 1977 to find Victorian leg spinner Jim Higgs cloaked in darkness. The medium pacer cum architect had been expecting Higgs, who wanted to examine some technical drawings for his civil engineering class, and turned on the porch light. 'Oh, right, go for it,' he said. 'Look at whatever you want.'

Higgs was clearly uncomfortable. 'Look mate,' he said. 'Can you turn out the light? I've been told I'm not supposed to be here. The VCA reckons we shouldn't talk to you blokes.'

None of World Series Cricket's Australians had feared strangulation by ticker-tape at home. Some had delayed return from England: Greg Chappell and Rod Marsh had accompanied Ian Davis to Amsterdam to represent the 'Elephants' on the mats against the Netherlands, before turning tourists with their wives in Sardinia for a week.

Hostility toward them as 'disapproved persons' still smarted. Having sacked Chappell as a state selector while he was in England, the Queensland Cricket Association offered $15,000 to void the contract on which he'd been lured to the state from Adelaide in

1973. Though Chappell asked to be considered for state selection, he came no closer than a Gabba afternoon tea with QCA chairman Norm McMahon as Queensland played Victoria on 4 November. McMahon, who was Greg's tour treasurer in England as well, steered uneasily around the topic. Chappell refrained from mentioning it.

The role of iconoclast fitted Greg Chappell badly. 'All of the guys that had signed would have put themselves in the traditional camp,' he says. 'We had a great respect for the game. Always have done, always will. We weren't challenging the game, we were challenging the way it was run.'

Old friendships were strained. Even employers became abrasive. At the Rural Bank, McCosker found the atmosphere chill. 'It seemed that everyone involved in WSC should be treated with a fair amount of disdain,' he says. 'It was certainly the view of some of the management that I was now a rebel and should be treated like one.'

Official Australian Cricket Board response had been subtler. In fact, its 6 September meeting briefly raised hopes: it would seem that if players were free for Test cricket and able to honour commitments to Benson & Hedges as sole team sponsor, they would be picked.

They weren't and they couldn't, though, so they wouldn't be. Even if not involved in overlapping Super Tests, the players' B & H deal in January 1977 meant that the moment two or more team members observed clause 3 (10) of their WSC contract – stipulating they 'participate by personal appearance in team group photographs and TV programmes and/or advertisements' – they were exiling themselves from Test cricket.

'When it came to the crunch,' Parish recalls, 'the players had banned themselves. They couldn't be part of WSC and perform their duty to Benson and Hedges. An individual could do basically as he wished but as soon as there were two or more they implied they were part of a team.' As Austin Robertson and Brian Treasure completed WSC's last round of signings, the alternatives were clear. One could be an establishment pillar or a circus animal.

That did not deter West Australians Rob Langer and Bruce Laird, of whom Ian Chappell had written highly, or Greg Chappell's Queensland protege Martin Kent. Nor was their brother Trevor discouraged, just as he was about to play for Perth club Scarborough. Ian was also gratified to learn that Packer had offered terms to

Ashley Mallett – although time had never permitted that trial over after all – and even Australian masseur Dave McErlane.

McErlane was dear to the Chappells for his doughty temperament and impish humour. His physical strength in dressing-room wrestling was a byword. McErlane's twenty years at the New South Wales Cricket Association bothered him when Ian Chappell asked but Packer was difficult to deny. 'You're not coming with us Doc?' the businessman said. 'Would some money change your mind?'

It did. 'I wasn't stupid,' McErlane recalls. 'I'm not too good with words, but I can count.'

Quick bowlers, with fewer recent Test opportunities, were less eager. Even after meeting Treasure at his Bassendean home ground Hillcrest Oval and considering his school teacher's stipend, the young West Australian medium pacer Wayne Clark decided that Test cricket was too near and dear. He'd dreamed of it since being taught as an eight-year-old by Australian fast bowler Laurie Mayne.

'The money was good, and we weren't well off,' Clark recalls. 'But I called the ACB, and they said I had a 95 per cent chance of playing Tests that summer. Whereas I'd be banned and I might end up playing in Ballarat if I signed. There was also a credibility thing with friends. WSC was sort of a rebel thing to do and I knew I'd probably have to quit teaching to do it.'

The Victorian Alan Hurst, with two Testless tours behind him, also turned Robertson away. 'The offer would have to have been unbelievable really,' says Hurst. 'I was just desperate to play for Australia. I said to myself: "I've got my whole life to make a mark in whatever field I want, but this is my one chance to play for Australia. I have to make the most of it".'

The net had to be cast further. The chance to play for Ian Chappell, his old state captain and mentor, convinced the rangy paceman Wayne Prior in Adelaide. And a friendly call from Robertson to his Perth mate Graham McKenzie, then coaching Claremont-Cottlesloe, coaxed him from retirement. 'I was thirty-six and it was a bit of a bonus,' McKenzie recalls. 'I would probably be earning more from a season of WSC than I did in all the years I'd played for Australia.' The wages of sin were that, two days after joining WSC, Prior lost the job that the South Australian Cricket Association had arranged for him at Adelaide car dealer United Motors. And McKenzie had to leave his post at Claremont because of the widening WSC embargo in club competitions.

Umpires also proved hard to entice. When distinguished Australians Lou Rowan and Max O'Connell, and the Englishmen Dickie Bird and David Constant all turned WSC down, the ranks of retired referees had to be perused. Westralian Gary Duperouzel, Queenslander Peter Enright and Victorian Jack Collins eventually joined the West Indian Douglas Sang Hue.

The stain of WSC was the quickest route to a free Saturday in Melbourne. Ian Chappell's unhappily brief North Melbourne stay ended. Ian Redpath's two decades at South Melbourne were terminated. Max Walker ended a decade at Melbourne when an open vote to omit him from the side was opposed only by his state colleague Jeff Moss. Walker's three-page thank-you note and request for clearance to a lesser competition received a one-line reply: 'Your transfer application has been granted.'

Walker then achieved publicity by having to guest with five clubs in six different competitions in order to stay ahead of the contagion of prohibition. At Old Scotch Collegians, having changed from the boot of his car, the dizziness of his decline hit home. 'I was still tying up my boots as we were going out and shaking hands with Tom and Dick and Harry,' he recalls. 'In six months I'd gone from crowds 65–70,000 in the Centenary Test to two blokes, one lady and a dog.' Even Jack Collins was compelled to quit Footscray's committee.

In the West, Dennis Lillee's insistence on practising and coaching at Melville earned it a $5 fine. Melville was then alone opposing a ban proposed by Midland-Guildford, ironically the club that had welcomed Barry Richards a year before. Ross Edwards, assured by Fremantle that it would resist Midland's motion, felt betrayed. 'What happened?' he says. 'I mean, Fremantle had obviously been got at before the meeting and they'd wilted. I can tell you I was very pissed off.'

The pressure on David Hookes in Adelaide, although his sympathetic West Torrens club had named him captain, was unremitting. Entreaties from Australian selector Phil Ridings and a financial package more than twice the size of his WSC contract seemed to offer all the security he could want. He began to buckle, and in early October flew to see Packer with a financial adviser and resignation speech memorised. 'He just laughed at me,' says Hookes. 'Well, perhaps not laughed, but he made it clear that there was absolutely no way I could pull out. And if I did I'd end up paying him 90 per cent of my salary for the rest of my life. My name had been used in the advance promo material, so I'd be sued for damages.' Three weeks later when Gary Cosier was best man at Hookes' low-key wedding, the pair finally knew they were headed separate ways that summer.

WSC players fared better in Brisbane and Sydney. Unable to enforce a ban under its constitution, the QCA had to 'request' that clubs do the decent thing, but Martin Kent and Greg Chappell reeled off some gallingly routine centuries for their defiant Sandgate-Redcliffe and South Brisbane teams. Rick McCosker, Doug Walters, Len Pascoe and Ian Davis survived four Sydney grade rounds before the boom fell. Round one of competition proved especially watchable, with 108 by Western Suburbs' R. B. Simpson against Penrith.

Bob Simpson found his return to grade circles particularly gladdening. On 9 September he'd lunched at the Angus Steak Cave with the ACB's three-man 'emergency committee', having offered them his aid and comfort while Australia had been abroad.

Over lunch, the retired forty-one-year-old had been officially offered the captaincy of Australia a decade after relinquishing it. Sir Donald Bradman's was the voice Simpson heard clearest. The knight recalled his own position in 1945. He'd been content to pull stumps, but agreed to lead Australia as it recovered 'from the ravages of war'. With Australian cricket at war, an old general seemed expedient.

It was a remarkable reacceptance at the ACB's bosom. He had not been close to the board since his retirement, and some officials were chary of Simpson's commercial bent. A year before, of course, he'd tarried with Packer himself. Now Simpson was back in the inner sanctum, and his appointments to lead New South Wales and Australia were announced simultaneously. Polarities could not have been defined more sharply: sacred sportsman versus profane promoter. At Simpson's 11 October Cricket House press conference, journalists broke into applause.

A surprise well-wisher calling from Brisbane amid the fifty interviews of Simpson's first two days in the job was Greg Chappell.

And Ian Chappell forecast success in *Cricketer*. 'I've got tremendous admiration for the man,' he wrote, 'and I can't see why he can't do well this summer against an Indian attack which doesn't possess anyone above medium-pace . . . as a batsman Simpson rates as one of the best I've seen.'

All the same, the elder Chappell remembered Simpson advising him against the hook at an early stage of his career, a move against his instincts that he brazenly reversed after a season. And their mutual admiration was limited even at this stage. Simpson wrote:

In assessing the impact Ian Chappell made on Australian cricket, I find the easiest way to describe the transition which occurred under his command as being one where he took the team from the yachting-jacket set and brought it into the jean generation . . . Chappell in the early days of his captaincy was a bright, new and somewhat bumptious personality who was able to relate to the youth of Australia. He epitomised their attitudes and was prepared to thumb his nose at the establishment, which he did time and again by his casual attire and irreverence to tradition.

Ray Steele's seasonal address at the VCA on 24 October 1977 at last opened the great divide publicly. Referring to his nemesis only as either 'Packer' or 'the private promoter', Steele told his audience: 'There's a place for that kind of cricket . . . some place like Siberia.'

Packer was in an ashtray-filling mood at Consolidated Press four days later when he met with WSC's inner circle: the Benauds, Robertson, Treasure, press officer Chris Forsyth and the television men Hill and Berkery. The boss was emphatic about detail. The cap peaks for the player's uniforms were too short. Not enough videodiscs? Get more, and make sure you have what you want.

Richie Benaud reported from his governing committee on trailblazing playing conditions. From South Africa, where the experiment had been tried four years before in the country's local one-day trophy, it was borrowing the idea of circles restraining the ritual scattering of deep fielders in limited-overs matches. It was also demanding 75 rather than 65 eight-ball overs between new balls and promoting lenience toward fast bowlers on the front-foot no-ball law (a rule that Benaud despised).

Benaud worried aloud that the Laws of Cricket themselves might have a legal character. The MCC did hold their copyright. It would be important to play a form of stand-alone rules 'based on' the Laws to avoid still further legal troubles. These were already acute. The High Court action in London still had two weeks to run, the NSWCA was pulling the SCG beyond Packer's reach in the NSW Equity Court, and the ACB still had him pinned down in the Federal Court over whether he could touch the sacred 'Test'. WSC television advertisements that had been running for three weeks displayed the scars: the players shown were in limbo, no final schedule or venues could be promoted, and all had been viewed and amended by the Federal Court. If there was legal avenue open against WSC, Packer knew it would be probed. 'Get the legal side straight,' he told Forsyth. 'If you fuck it up we could lose the lot – the whole $12 million.'

The newly arrived Greig saw the $12 million at risk as his helicopter overflew VFL Park that day. He told pressmen it could be one of cricket's greatest stadia. Privately, sight of its gaping hole where a pitch should be had demoralised him. 'How the hell are we going to play on this?' he thought.

Wicket installation in Melbourne and Adelaide was, indeed, badly behind schedule. The pitches were flourishing in the greenhouses, but the hovercraft caused laughter wherever general manager Vern Stone went. 'Sounds fantastic,' said a friend in the Perth building industry when he heard the notion. 'Fantastic bullshit. It'll never work.' Army and Navy experts advised likewise, if more militarily.

Stone fumed when he flew to Adelaide to find the hovercraft team years from completion. 'I don't care about overtime,' he demanded. 'Get your men working twenty-four hours a day on it. We'll pay the bill. These things have got to be ready on time.'

Precautionary investigation of installation options dismayed him further. Cranes, perhaps? Too heavy. Helicopters? Too small. Then Stone received a report from soil scientist Roy Bond: drought conditions in Perth were killing the Gloucester Park pitch.

Lawyers could help them find a way round the restrictions on the phrase Super Test and Australia. The Federal Court seemed to find 'Supertest' satisfactory, and the guise WSC Australians and such apparently passed muster. Stone had then found WSC a home, block-booking ninety-five rooms at George Frew's sprawling, mock-Tudor Old Melbourne Inn for the first cricketing arrivals in three weeks.

A Country Cup itinerary was also finalised: team managers Graham Ferrett and John Curtain had taken Austin Robertson on a 12,000-kilometre car journey round a dozen cities registering interest in WSC. Concentrating on districts where sympathetic regional press could be expected, they organised co-promotional deals with local sponsors for a fourteen-match tour.

But the only relief Stone heard to the eccentricities of Birzulis' hovercraft had come from an enigmatic Waverley resident, introducing himself as a retired French army engineer who had seen service in Burma. 'Low-loaders,' he muttered. With tyres deflated and run overnight on a steel track over hessian sacks, damage to the ground should be minimal.

Stone was sufficiently intrigued to check with Brambles General Transport, and, when engineer Terry O'Brien confirmed the advice as informed, set Birzulis a strict agenda. Packer was coming to Melbourne on 2 November for the 3AK Christmas lunch at the Melbourne Club, and would like a pitch as a present.

It should have been a private process, but Chris Forsyth had invited the press for what became a very public debacle. Arriving by helicopter with Packer and Harry Chester that day, Stone's heart plummeted. 'I could see clouds of dust coming out from the greenhouse and people running round all over the place,' he recalls. 'I was shell-shocked. There wasn't meant to be anyone there.'

Packer growled: 'I thought this was meant to be private.'

'So did I,' the executive squeaked. Birzulis, standing by his overheated hovercraft, surrendered to Brambles.

Packer, in fact, never saw his pitches laid. He flew to Perth to lecture on the future of cricket with Lillee and Edwards at a Melville fund-raiser at Park Towers. Then he admired the terrain of his other estate – Kensington golf course – which he circled on a buggy with Jack Nicklaus.

As Brambles jemmied Maley's trays into Football Park on 8 November, Packer was in transit for a fishing trip on Lake Taupo in New Zealand with Nicklaus, golfer Jerry Pate and Tony Greig. And next morning, WSC finally filled the hole in his life at VFL Park.

Shaky laughter filled a Hertz minibus bound for Waverley just after 7.30 a.m. on Tuesday, 15 November 1977. The WSC Australians had left the Old Melbourne fifteen minutes earlier and headed towards VFL Park for their first practice session on the Packer payroll. Except it was at St Kilda Football Club's Moorabbin ground.

The bus reversed, but there was no turning back for the players. Practice, for once, looked good. Being 'disapproved persons' had taxed their ingenuity and patience. The skipper had set the example of turning out for village green teams as obscure as Pulteney Grammar Old Boys in Adelaide. Ian Davis had prepared for impending physical challenges by weight-training and a month facing Len Pascoe on a Bankstown concrete pitch with boxes of composite cricket balls, hard as rocks. Lillee and the West Australians had played a convivial charity match at Kalgoorlie and even managed a clandestine net with Tasmania's greenhorn Sheffield Shield team in Perth.

But it had been hard, especially in Adelaide where Bishan Bedi's Indians had begun their official tour. Even attending nets on Bedi's invitation, Prior was treated like a quisling. Only Phil Ridings troubled to cross the floor when Hookes attended the Indians' mayoral reception.

The word 'professionalism' was pervasive. Many players had ditched their outside careers. McCosker and Gilmour had left their banks, Malone had quit his school and Walker his architecture partnership. 'I had a planter box to do when I got back from England,' Walker remembers. 'It was up to scheme twenty-seven for Parliament Place, and I figured I didn't want to design a planter box I'd designed before. Suddenly pro cricket looked really good.'

Martin Kent and Gilmour had turned up with fingers already broken – the former missing a slip catch in a Brisbane club match with Sandgate, the latter playing in a Newcastle rugby league semi-final with Carlton-Merriweather – but were told they could see doctors in Melbourne. Ian Chappell wanted his team together.

In his room 413 at the Old Melbourne, with Cornell, Benaud, Geoff Forsaith and Graham Ferrett looking on, Chappell gave his orders for the day... and the decade. 'This thing is good,' he'd said. 'We're here to stay. Not just for one year, or three years, but ten years and more. And you've got to get that in your minds from here on in.' Solidarity was stressed. 'We have to sell our product and the way to do that is to make sure it's the best. We can do that by helping one another to improve his game.'

On Chappell's request, they stepped from the bus in creams. Each was issued four WSC shirts from Michael Treloar Uniforms, one pullover and sleeveless, and one tour cap each. Pascoe was first to the ball box, McCosker first into pads, in front of a few hardy pressmen and Moorabbin early-risers.

Greig arrived to pose for action shots with Lillee snapped by Adelaide promotional photographer Milton Wordley, and in room 413 that evening John Newcombe appropriately underscored their new commercial discipline. Tracing his experience of the tennis star as salesman, he described how ten years before he'd become part of the 'Handsome Eight' of Lamar Hunt's World Championship Tennis tour as 'Newc' the player-personality. 'When I started to have a court personality like the one I had in private, more people turned up to watch me play,' he explained. Ian Chappell might do something similar. 'The way he scratches his crutch before a ball's bowled must be a turn-on for women. Image is important, no matter what the traditionalists say and how much they hate it.'

The Australians heard more evangelism on 16 November from Ron Barassi, coach of 1977's Victorian Football League Premiers North Melbourne. The fundamentals of professionalism? Attitude, commitment and responsibility to the man paying the bills. 'That's the man you're playing for, that's the man who is going to control your future. You've got to give him everything . . . Anything else is wrong and unfair.'

It had a resonance to Richie Robinson who had been drafted for the 75-over-a-side practice match commencing that day to lead the Australians' second-stringers. It was a long-term assignment. 'Things were moving so quickly I can't even remember who told me I had the job, but it was a bit of a let-down,' he says. 'In all the years I was

Rod's deputy, I never ever resigned myself to not getting in there if his form faltered, or as a batsman.'

Robinson consoled himself by throwing Lillee a new ball at 10.38 a.m. The fast bowler accelerated as free admission turned a few hundred heads into 5000. Bright bagged five wickets in the afternoon, Marsh and McKenzie half-centuries of differing finesse. Seven thousand the next day saw Ian Chappell's XI squeeze home by five runs in spite of Davis's fluent 124. Ordinary cricket balls came soft to his bat after a month of Pascoe's pummelling.

Barassi had caused mild indigestion with his insistence that 'perfect practice' required 'perfect practices'. Even in diet. No more pies, milkshakes and hamburgers. Ian Chappell was studied carefully: he loathed running, and eschewed push-ups on the basis of the Nicklaus dictum that they interfered with a golf swing. 'Well I'm going for something to eat,' he said in his familiar deadpan. 'Anyone want to join me for a pie, a hamburger and a milkshake?' Revolution would clearly come at his pace.

The seafood fare was typically sumptuous in the Old Melbourne's Haymarket room on Monday, 21 November for WSC's welcoming banquet for the newly-arrived internationals, their families and press. Packer, having left the Australian Open in David Graham's custody the previous day, was now a cricketophile on High Table with Cornell, the team captains, Benaud, and Sir Garfield Sobers.

Packer pointed a few barbs at the NSWCA, which on the Friday had finally denied him the SCG, but was otherwise softly spoken. 'No I don't wish any ill to the touring Indians,' he stressed. 'Unlike the ACB I would like to see both series prosper.' He posed for photographers with Sobers, whose unimpeachable name was to bless a trophy at stake in Supertests between West Indies and Australia – as their official Tests were played for the Sir Frank Worrell Trophy – in an effort to communicate WSC's message: past and future blending to create cricket present. That was the idea anyway.

Aiming to please, Packer lavished a buffet on his practising players the next day, too. 'The Pakistanis couldn't believe it,' Walker recalls. 'I can just see Mushie tucking in; he must've just come from the curried goat and the fried rice. And it got like that everyday, the sort of stuff you might get in a superbox. After a week the little feller was like a tadpole.'

Packer mixed cheerfully at the session. 'Carrying a bit of extra weight Procky?' the businessman bantered.

'You get the pads on,' Procter replied. 'And I'll show you how fit I am.'

Procter, indeed, felt hollow on the cold Melbourne Thursday as he took the new ball on his WSC debut at VFL Park for Tony Greig's World XI against the Australians. Twelve thousand had watched the Aussies play their two-day scratch match, but no more than 200 seemed interested in paying for similar privilege.

'Just a practice match' was the official response, and the concept *was* only in miniature. Hill's cameramen rehearsed for closed-circuit monitors. Pitch microphones were in use for the first time, as technicians experimented with ways to fade out the saltier of the players' expressions. But the 2449 who joined Packer at various times looked all the fewer for their vast surrounds. 'Truth was a little loose on that day, actually,' Forsyth wrote. 'What had been billed as the start of the WSC competition had suddenly, surreptitiously and inexplicably, changed into what were termed by Packer and others as trial games.' The new press box resounded with phrases of indifference. *The Times'* John Woodcock summed it up: 'If history was, indeed, being made, it passed almost unnoticed.'

The first semi-official century from Ian Chappell, made mostly during a rearguard with Bright, came in virtual silence. The news was bleaker from Football Park in Adelaide, where Graham Ferrett had taken the West Indians and a World team led by Asif Iqbal. Fewer than a thousand were watching Dennis Amiss make a dogged 81.

Packer did not enhance attraction there the next day as he applauded the second semi-official century. More than half of Clive Lloyd's 140 came in boundaries, but barely 650 acclaimed it.

Packer did not sleep that night, although not for reasons some might have suspected. Justice Slade was due to pass High Court judgement on the International Cricket Conference ban and, with his lawyers overwhelmingly confident of victory, Packer consented willingly to a BBC telephone interview when the decision was known.

His honour handed out a greater hammering even than Clive Lloyd. The ICC's only gratification came in Justice Slade's observation that cricket administrators were a thoroughly decent breed who 'believed that they acted in the best interests of cricket'. The judge could also understand sense of betrayal at Greig's recruiting role, but retaliation had 'strained the bounds of loyalty'. In fact, they should have foreseen events: 'The very size of profits made from cricket matches involving star players must for some years have carried the risk that a private promoter would appear on the scene and seek to make money by promoting cricket matches involving world-class cricketers.'

It was an outright victory whose full implications took time to emerge. In fact at the outset it seemed a little empty for players uninvolved in county cricket. Even if they weren't 'disapproved persons', there was still a gulf to cross before their 'approval'.

But the setback for the ICC was palpable. New chairman David Clark would have to touch members for $320,000 costs. 'We were well and truly stuffed,' ruminated the Test and County Cricket Board's Doug Insole. Packer hung up on the BBC to wake Greig at the Old Melbourne. 'I just thought you'd like to know,' he said. 'We've stuffed them.'

'I'll get back to you,' said a drowsy Greig. So would many others.

Packer gave a convincing impression of tired triumph the next day at VFL Park, although he was not foolish enough to suggest the ICC would reopen negotiations: 'It would be easier to get an audience with the Pope and I'm not Catholic.' He even sat placidly through two takes of an interview for GTV-9 after the film unspooled at the first attempt.

He was stirred only by the sight of John Woodcock. 'One of the enemy,' he grunted.

'It's true,' said *The Times* writer. 'I've been against what you have been trying to do. But I would nonetheless like to congratulate you on a considerable victory.'

Packer was unmoved. 'I can see from your face how sincere you are. I've read some of your stuff. You've never been prepared to give me a chance.'

'I don't know,' Woodcock replied. 'I thought I said some good might come of it.'

'Good might come of evil?' sniffed the Australian. 'I don't think that's much of a compliment.'

Ian Chappell had been buoyed by his century. In his 1976–1977 grade season for North Melbourne, he'd not passed 94. 'I'd never been so long without a hundred,' he remembers. 'I'd been starting to think: "Jeez, maybe I'm getting a bit old for hundreds".' Then a better Saturday crowd of 3472 brought colour to Ian Redpath's cheeks during a celebratory 152. He chirpily performed shoulder rolls after twice lifting Albert Padmore into the stands.

Chappell felt that the outside pressures were bringing his team together. The Australian contingent that Richie Robinson and John Curtain led fifty miles down the highway to Geelong on 28 November dressed sprucely for a mayoral reception and performed coaching duties obediently on the outfield of Kardinia Park. They also convened a meeting at their Travelodge Hotel digs to discuss travel arrangements. It didn't seem proper to be sharing a bus with the West Indians they were playing the next day.

There were still going to be setbacks, and the game sadly ended Redpath's promising season. Falling in a delighted, dishevelled heap after claiming Lloyd's wicket, the local Geelong boy broke his achilles tendon.

But good vibes predominated. Packer helicoptered in to declare that Redpath would be paid in full for the season, and spectator Ian Chappell had a substitute in mind straight away. Graeme Watson, the versatile all-rounder who had quit cricket in 1975 to pursue architecture, had been playing with Greg at Souths. He deserved to be a WSC benefactor. Martin Kent's comeback 40 in a glove tailored to protect the three breaks in his finger had been promising. And Australia had won by 49 runs. It might turn out a real cricket contest.

Justice Slade's judgement had, of course, flashed round the world. Emergency meetings of the West Indies Cricket Board of Control were particularly careworn. Jeff Stollmeyer, who had voted against his instincts, recalled: 'Although . . . we tried to explain our position and that of the ICC and of the dangers which lay ahead for the future of international cricket, Kerry Packer became something of a hero and his "more bread for players" syndrome carried the day.'

News also reached Brearley's England side practising in Rawalpindi. 'All the talk is about Packer,' confided manager Ken Barrington in a letter home. 'It was a shock judgement. It's going to be a real problem unless they all get together.'

Within the ACB, the very fact that WSC was at the crease had raised the ante. When state captains attended the year's first meeting of the players sub-committee, the mission with which Ray Steele charged them was recorded in the minutes: 'The current year (is) of vital importance, and the established players should be aware that they are fighting for the survival of cricket.'

8

'Half a house brick at a hundred miles an hour'

For two days, Australia's clashing cricket attractions in December 1977 at VFL Park and the Gabba proceeded in symmetry. Both Test and Supertest Australians seized unlikely first innings leads. The former were 125 runs to the good with seven wickets standing as Sunday 4 December dawned, the latter 180 with six.

The public relations battle had, however, been a no-contest: aggregate attendance in Brisbane would hit almost 32,000, while a meagre 13,000 Melburnians came the twenty-five kilometres from city to Waverley to watch World Series Cricket. Kibitzers, come to bury WSC not to praise it, became offerers of condolence. Wrote Tony Lewis of London's *Daily Telegraph*: 'I can see how much the players love it and feel sorry for them that no-one wants to watch. Only time can help it, but time, too, might end it.' Eventually the phoney wars would seem to affect the real ones. Bob Simpson succeeded on still-agile feet against spin to the north. Ian Chappell was harpooned by a shooter on treacherous turf to the south.

The irony was that WSC could hardly have concocted better fare or finale, with the West Indians winning a tense, low-scoring match thanks mostly to their Antiguan axis of Richards and Roberts.

During a first-innings 79, Richards appeared almost to will Lillee and Pascoe to his strengths. Ever-faster, ever-shorter, the bowlers seemed dupes. It required a lightning strike to cut Richards down, a bottom-edge from Hookes' chinaman that Marsh caught between clenched thighs. And when Hookes interceded again to stem Richards at 56 on the last day, the South Australian's catch at deep square leg seventy metres from the bat briefly restored his team's hopes.

But Roberts, by this time, had done too much to lose. Evicting Walters and Hookes to begin Australia's Sunday slump, he took charge five hours later when his team trembled 46 runs from victory with three wickets standing by wordlessly promoting himself above an edgy Holding. An hour of scampered singles with Deryck Murray, and Roberts hoisted Bright beyond long-on to win the game. 'One of the facts of life was that over the years I was dobbed for a few sixes,' Bright recalls. 'And that was as big as any of them. Andy had this short sharp jolt of a backlift, though they always went a long way back.'

Writing of his team's spirited 16-run victory at the Gabba a couple of days later, Bob Simpson invoked the Tied Test he'd played seventeen years before. His youths had taken three hours to budge from their dressing-room. But VFL Park's absence of ceremony, and stake beyond the $16,667 prize money, left the *Daily Mail's* Ian Wooldridge ruefully indifferent. 'The Supertest players needed no excuses to be made on their behalf,' he recognised. 'Their match featured some colossal cricket. It would be uncharitable to suggest that the big top caved in on Mr Packer's circus. All that happened was that barely a single dinkum Australian paid it more than abstract attention.'

There were many explanations. VFL Park was too far away, there were a host of rival attractions (Australia had been beating Italy in the Davis Cup, too), the $5 admission was too steep, and big-ticket pre-Christmas cricket in Melbourne had never been attempted. But the possibility that grandstand finishes needed the right grandstand haunted WSC.

Tremors occurred. Manager John Curtain resigned, bemoaning lack of cricket know-how in WSC's administration. Then Packer actually sacked Chris Forsyth for unpacking his heart to a journalist, before being persuaded to reconsider.

Packer had also to farewell two of VFL Park's guests. The blacklisted Springboks Graeme Pollock and Denys Hobson had been brought within yards of international competition, but knew they were to be 'excused' WSC duty. Pollock, who had compiled twin hundreds for Eastern Province against Rhodesia a week before, left publicly lamenting 'scheduling problems'. Hobson spoke of a sore shoulder that would last the whole summer, though no one noticed him greet the New Year with bags of 5–65 and 6–49 for Western Province.

Gary Gilmour, Mick Malone and Kerry O'Keeffe, with Richie Robinson's Australians playing the World in the Country Cup at Rockhampton's Cricket Association Ground during the First Supertest, talked over their individual realities as reservists. 'We realised that if we'd stayed with the board we would have been golden-haired boys,' Gilmour says. 'Instead we were playing at Rockhampton, so it was hard to know if we'd made the right choice.'

O'Keeffe recollected his exchange with Marsh after the loss of the Ashes:

> I thought that fateful night was coming back to haunt me . . . I was never fully forgiven. In trying to put a case I hadn't agreed with I'd been seen to side with it. I didn't want the limelight. I'd always loved Sheffield Shield. I loved its values, and I really missed it. To face bowling up-country, knowing *Wisden* was never going to record it, frustrated me enormously.

They rejoined colleagues at Adelaide's Hotel Australia, where Chappell was trying to train his gaze on weekend International Cup matches. Net sessions were driven. VFL Park videos were replayed. A team rota was organised to involve peripheral personnel on the Saturday and Sunday, 10 and 11 December.

Previously, of course, there had been a rousing green-and-gold cap and patriotic following. Now bonding was essentially contractual and spectators scarce. Vern Stone was asked to install teams on separate hotel levels. Managers Geoff Forsaith and Graham Ferrett agreed that players sharing buses should at least travel in separate seat blocks. While WSC was theoretically an expression of the player as individual agent, there was very recent example in England in 1977 of disunity's dangers.

Packer remained a visible figurehead. 'There was hardly a morning when you didn't hear the chopper in the car park,' Walker recalls. 'It'd give us the tomtits frankly, because it threw dust over all the cars, but Kerry was always there.' To allow reciprocation in Adelaide, Cornell grouped the Australians after practice to singalong for a birthday video he was making for 'The Boss's' fortieth in a week's time.

The Australians were still tentative, though, and rusty in one-day drills like pacing an innings and bowling for dots which World and West Indian players knew by heart. Derek Underwood coiled round the Australian top order on the Saturday, undisturbed by Marsh's promotion to number three as a left-handed pinch-hitter, then Roberts and Daniel allowed them only ten scoring shots from their last 40 balls on the Sunday.

Beaten twice in two days before barely 4000 people, Robinson, Gilmour, Edwards, Davis and Hookes barely had time to shower before joining Lillee, Laird, Kent, Pascoe, Mallett and Trevor Chappell on an Ansett Fokker Friendship to Albury for a Country Cup match the following day. 'This is going to be horrendous,' thought Ferrett. 'The guys have been playing all day and they haven't eaten, and we've only got this propeller thing to get them to Albury.'

'Why don't we make it into a bit of a party?' he asked Cornell, and was authorised to invest in a chicken and champagne spread. By the time they hit Albury, the Australians had dubbed their outback duty 'The Champagne Tour'. Thin times lay ahead, but the name stuck.

Tony Greig and Ian Chappell shook on it. No bouncers. It seemed a fair precaution on Wednesday 14 December 1977 as they tossed at VFL Park for a new ball game within the new ball game. They were beginning in light but the World and Australians would finish their 40-overs-a-side in floodlight. It was a hurriedly arranged affair, untelevised because it was not part of any WSC competition, and the captains agreed to go a little easy. Greig was pleased to bat on calling correctly. Fielding floodlit had to be simpler than batting.

Night cricket had an antiquity in Australia. But the members at Western Suburbs in Sydney who in 1932 had practised on specially prepared pitches at Concord Oval had been confounded by evening damp and thrown away their white ducoed balls.

They'd been on at least one right track. White balls, WSC discovered, stayed basically white against the black sightboards regardless of scuffing and rotation. Orange balls went brown, red-and-white balls tended to vanish.

Alchemy in the air had even attracted a crowd rather than a clique to VFL Park: 6449 was the final count. Buoyed when he and John Cornell arrived by helicopter at the 'dinner break', Packer allowed spectators to gambol on the ground. Cornell had liked this 'village green' practice in New Zealand nine months before, and it seemed a worthwhile break with custom as players for the first time had a full evening meal in an underground restaurant.

As 14,000 watts illuminated VFL Park in the twilight, Packer and Cornell grew even jollier. They could 'see it'. The white ball zipped from the hand and scooted across the outfield with startling clarity. As Ian Chappell added 104 for Australia's first-wicket with Rick McCosker, Packer and Cornell examined the WSC calendar to reschedule some other VFL Park fixtures as evening fare and prime-time viewing.

Ian Chappell even smiled for the first time that summer. When his frustrated rival captain personally broke the bouncer bar and was pulled for four by McCosker, Chappell told him: 'If you want to bowl bouncers Greigy, we'll turn the lights off for you.' Underwood was the only worry and took four wickets as evening moisture fell, but Greg Chappell lent victory a festive air in the last hour with an unbeaten 59. His off-driven six from Mushtaq brought victory on the tick of the appointed 10.30 p.m. finishing time.

Packer and Cornell were already circulating. Marsh was cautious: the ball was hard to see against the batsmen's white clothing. The umpires had not granted an lbw: white balls striking white pads were difficult to judge. But 'The Boss' was able to give his first poised press conference of the new season. 'For the first time in a lifetime of watching cricket, I could see the ball from the moment it left the bat,' he said. 'It must be a great innovation for cricket and I can't see why it can't be used all the time.'

Even the *Age,* militantly traditional, ran a front-page picture story ('The Atmosphere was Electric') with a back-page match report ('Night cricket switches on the crowd'). 'Even though WSC did not get out of the blocks as its starter would have liked,' it wrote, 'under the power of 1000 lux the revolution took on some meaning.' It noted importantly that traditional cricket fans were less in evidence than 'the family element surrounding VFL Park'.

Eric Beecher, whose *Cricketer* was about to pack a punchy January 1978 issue headed 'The Great Packer Yawn', also ruminated. His report of the game secreted the words 'bright' and 'breezy', and in his book *The Cricket Revolution* he would see the evening as a turning point: 'Just as the sun seemed to be setting on WSC's first disaster-filled season, someone turned on the lights.'

Richie Benaud was off-duty as commentator that night, but on-duty as a historian. He fielded Greg Chappell's final six, pocketing the first white ball for presentation to the SCG Museum.

There was something about Andy Roberts. Word got round that he carried a preserved bull's penis. Word got round that the walkman tape that engrossed him on air routes was a chant of 'Kill the Whites'.

Even if one decided Roberts was merely shy, an opponent needed to know the Antiguan's peculiar cricketing habits. The second-most important thing about his bouncer was its speed. The most important was to expect it immediately after a very slow 'sucker' bouncer. And he didn't seem to mind the victims of that sinister 'left-right combination'.

English memories of Roberts and partner Holding from the West Indies' 1976 visit had been the main reason for Dennis Amiss and Tony Greig lugging what from a distance seemed like large chamber pots: visored white helmets.

Amiss carried a lump left in the back of his head in May 1976 by Holding in fading light at Lord's. In July 1976, Greig had been introduced to cricket fear while parrying Roberts, Holding and Daniel on a diabolical Old Trafford pitch. 'It was the first time in my career that I had felt really frightened,' he wrote. 'It was also the first time I almost gave up.'

Greig had had Bill Swanwick, a Nottingham maker of protective equipment for epileptics, take a wax mould of his head for a skullcap to fit beneath his cap. Mike Brearley had pursued the idea as far as wearing a Swanwick design from April 1977.

Watching Brearley, Amiss finally took the step of designing a full-blown, motorcycle-style helmet with businessman Peter Beniman and a Birmingham company called Vellvic. To Amiss and Greig, Australia seemed a very good place to test-drive.

You tried to be polite while Roberts was round anyway. Even county teammate Barry Richards would respond to Roberts' morning greeting with: 'And good morning to you, *Mister* Roberts.' And when Roxanne Hookes, having a casual balcony breakfast on the morning of Friday 16 December at Sydney's Chateau Commodore, saw Roberts pass on his way to the Showground for the first day of the Second Supertest, she made a point of complimenting him on his fashionable blue pants. Her husband might be facing him that day.

Although McCosker fell to Roberts' fifth ball, caught by Lloyd from Gordon Greenidge's fumble, the Antiguan did not command the stage at once. Ian Chappell's firm shots had restored Australian heart against Holding and Daniel, when spectators saw first evidence of the new West Indian depth. Chappell stood tall to stay over a square cut from Holding, but a figure standing taller in the gully picked it up almost playfully. Joel Garner.

Presented with Supertest selection on his twenty-fifth birthday, Garner could obviously field, and when he joined the attack himself proved he could bowl as well. Greg Chappell's drive was skewered to third slip and the day's two Australian newcomers, Martin Kent and Bruce Laird, swept away; the former's edge lodging unluckily in Murray's glove from Greenidge's tentative hand and Lloyd's knee.

From 5–89, however, the Australians rallied. Roxanne Hookes began watching her husband and, with 7200 spectators, to swing along with his strokes. The marauding Garner dropped short and was poached for 17 runs in an over. Holding, slower on his second breath, went for five intoxicating fours in his first over when recalled. Even Roberts seemed negotiable when Lloyd roused him and, so sweetly was Hookes harmonising with Marsh just after tea, that the Antiguan seemed reluctant to continue. 'I've had enough,' he told Lloyd.

'Just three overs Andy, fast,' the captain asked. His bowler shrugged.

'Did you hear that?' said Hookes to this partner. 'If we can see Andy off, we'll be right. Just concentrate on seeing Andy off.'

As the South Australian recalls with the clarity of a road accident victim, the slow bouncer arrived. 'Andy bowled me a 'lolly gobble bliss bomb' first up and I got that away all right,' he says. 'But the next one made a mess of me.'

A couple of feet shorter, several yards faster, it caught the hooking Hookes flush on the jaw despite his two hours at the crease, 81 runs and 14 fours. His head resounded, his body completing a full circle that ended in a semi-balletic swoon. 'And,' intoned Benaud gravely, 'he's in trouble.'

Murray was first to reach him, Hookes recoiling from his touch as he spat blood. Fielders were magnetised and Marsh charged from the non-striker's end. Only Roberts, chasing the ball from his follow-through, remained locked in his private thoughts.

As manager Rudi Webster bustled from the West Indian rooms, Packer himself was hastening to the Australian dugout. He was waiting among them when the bloodied, bare-headed Hookes was lowered gently on Doc McErlane's treatment table. Roxanne Hookes held her breath.

The newcomer Laird, a Supertestman just three years out of Perth club cricket, was transfixed. 'I'd never seen a broken jaw before,' he says. 'And I can still remember the splinters of bone through the blood on the floor of the dressing-room when Hookesy was brought in. They were like little bits of glass.'

Packer was the twenty-two-year-old's ambulance driver, his Jaguar ignoring traffic lights, for the one-mile journey to St Vincent's private hospital. A double fracture of the jaw and cheekbone was diagnosed, a five-week fracture in Hookes' season prescribed.

The Showground crowd spoke in bereaved whispers as Ray Bright came out to bat. 'Mmmm,' he muttered as he arrived at the crease, 'bit of blood in the old blockhole today.' Roberts adduced his edge and bowled a retreating Lillee before his second wind was spent, and only Marsh and Walker in a half-century stand pushed the total past 250. Lillee and Pascoe had 24 deliveries at Greenidge and Roy Fredericks that evening, and went for 31 dizzying runs.

As Hookes underwent surgery on the Saturday, so did the Australians. The scalpel was Viv Richards' 88, after the home side had almost revived with three early wickets. Pascoe pitched just short to the Antiguan and watched the ball disappear for a six, driven straight off the back foot. Fourteen other fours laced his two-hour innings. Lloyd and Murray endured, and bowler-fielder Garner proved he could bat as well.

Greenidge's first-day fumbles reflected a vital fact of Showground life. It was fast. Balls from groundsman John Maley's bounce gauge rebounded as though from marble. 'John had a piece of wood with a jam tin, that dropped the ball from a height of ten feet or so,' Kent recalls. 'He'd pull a string and bounce at different lengths up to see the bounce was uniform. At the Showground it was: three feet high all the way.'

Laird and a tin-hatted McCosker had twenty minutes merry hell that evening, but reduced the West Indian lead to 46 before they were parted. The Australians were 19 in credit with only two casualties when Garner began his first spell on the third day.

Still to acclimatise to his altitude, the Australians ran out of breath. Greg Chappell at once edged to Lloyd, who this time palmed the ball to Greenidge. In Garner's next over – the last before lunch – Lloyd caught Kent solo at ankle level. In his first over after the break, McCosker's deflection was too late to elude leg slip and Bright's footwork too slow to escape a yorker. Marsh was neatly held by Greenidge to become the fifth loss in nine runs. This time there was no retaliatory Hookes.

Lillee, Walker and Pascoe wasted the 69 they grafted with an hour and a quarter of thoughtlessness attacking Greenidge and Fredericks. Although Pascoe managed to strike Fredericks on the shoulder, the left-hander was as tender as tungsten and added 86 with his partner. Brainless bowling, brawny batting, and the West Indians had won the Sir Garfield Sobers Trophy with half an hour of the third day remaining.

For WSC it was another humiliation. Attendances had actually kept pace with those in the concurrent Perth Test, but the premature finish meant that four Super days had now collected gates of zero. The West Indians had collected more than $33,000 in less than six days work, the Australians nothing.

The rub for Ian Chappell was that this seemed to reflect the sides' merit. Fuse burned to a stub, he spent his spare days at the Chateau Commodore lugubriously. Odd phenomena occurred at such times. John Crilly remembers his poolside group looking up at an opening sixth floor window: Chappell had found his room-service meal cold and, with a stroke of his arm, swept a steak, plate, tray, phone, coffee pot and utensils out the window. Piqued management left them floating in the pool for three days.

The weekend David Hookes was struck proved a notable one in the history of the cricketing head. Packer promptly sought the name of Amiss's helmet-maker and had a batch ordered that evening from Birmingham. In Sunday's Country Cup match at Canberra's Manuka Oval, where Robinson's Australians were playing against the World, Bob Woolmer established Kerry O'Keeffe as the first batsman caught by a helmeted fielder camped in Vellvic canopy at short leg.

The most significant event, however, was occurring on a road between Sydney and Surfers Paradise. Tony Henson, who had recently acquired a company called Coonan & Denlay specialising in equestrian caps, heard news of Hookes' mishap on the radio as he drove north for a family holiday. As a club cricketer (and fast bowler) he'd thought deeply about Rick McCosker's broken jaw nine months before. Word that Packer was placing big orders overseas stopped him at a call box to put colleague Arthur Wallace at C & D's factory, in Parramatta Street, Ashfield, in touch with WSC.

Wallace was pessimistic in reporting a meeting with Marsh and Austin Robertson when Henson returned to work. 'It can't be done, Tony,' Wallace said. 'They want us to make something that can withstand half a house brick at a hundred miles an hour.' And Wallace was strictly right: that would need an astronaut's helmet.

But Henson persisted. Because most head blows were glancing, a helmet need only deflect impact rather than absorb it. And protection without compromising cricket aesthetics had to be feasible. Something, perhaps, like the polo helmet with cardboard 'visor' that early in the new year he put half-jokingly on his wife's head.

School holiday crowds in Perth for the next instalment in Simpson's comeback saga – another tense Australian victory – offered WSC one sop: Rob Langer's long-awaited ticket out. The West Australian Education Department had declined to offer him even unpaid leave after he signed (which it had done for Sheffield Shield games), and Langer had been excused WSC duties during term times in the belief he would not be at front rank of selections.

But with Hookes and Redpath rubbed out, and Walters in apparent eclipse, Langer was promotion material when he touched down in Canberra on 16 December. 'I literally got off the plane, went to the ground and ten minutes later was out there playing,' he remembers.

After anti-apartheid protesters spilling onto Manuka Oval to deplore South Africans playing enlivened Langer's deep-fielding, his 26 and 50 in two meek Australian batting performances were above the mean. He was then well placed when Ian Chappell came to Mildura personally to scout for talent as the Australians met the World again on 21 December.

The captain was in no mood to see the first three chances of the World innings at City Oval fluffed. As Robinson recalled: 'Practically every player in the team bore the brunt of his abuse over that two-day game and his criticism was not at all unjustified. Chappell . . . above all is aggravated by players making fundamental or basic errors.'

Players strove to impress, though Wayne Prior bowled almost too furiously in the 35°C heat. Dismissing Majid Khan, Asif Iqbal and Greig, he had helped reduce the World to 7–182 when his leg cramped. The Australians wilted with him, and Alan Knott and Imran Khan added 129 in two and a half hours to inflate their total to 352. A few of the Australians even managed to annoy their management that night by yarning into the small hours at the Mildura Inlander Motor Inn while toasting Walters' thirty-second birthday. It was not a cheery bunch rejoining battle the following day.

Temperatures touching 40°C that compelled drinks breaks every half hour sharpened the Test-like intensity. When Imran loosed a violent and voluble opening spell, Chappell thrashed back. He advanced on John Snow, twice flipping him beyond mid wicket for six, and batted past lunch with Davis adding an opening 165. Three quick wickets then left Rob Langer in the frame.

Four years' frustration at the Test periphery eddied up as he applied himself. At last, he felt, he would not merely be an object of distant binoculars: 'One thing I'd been attracted to in WSC was that the people picking the teams weren't up there sitting miles away. They were actually on the ground with you.'

Only after an abstemious two-and-a-half-hour 50 did he gamble. In consecutive overs, Greig and Underwood disappeared over square leg for sixes. The West Australian cursed himself when bowled by Snow for 90. 'I played a bit across it,' Langer remembers. 'And even John Snow chastised me for playing a shot like that and missing the hundred.' But the West Australian's 10-run shortfall meant less to Chappell than further failures for Walters and Kent.

The World lost lividly. Imran struck Ashley Mallett a sickening blow to the back of the head with just two runs separating the teams. Manager Ferrett blessed his invitation of a cricket-loving local doctor and ambulance personnel. At Mildura Base Hospital, Mallett learned he'd been within an inch of a paralysing spinal injury. It had not been a sunny couple of days.

The Old Melbourne Inn was an eye in the cyclone, already a refuge from care and controversy. Its downstairs 'noise room' offered cheap drinks and jukeboxes, 'Mum's' milk bar down Flemington Road a renowned chocolate milkshake.

Visitors were struck by its hermetic atmosphere. 'I only went there twice,' Henry Blofeld wrote, 'and each time it seemed like they were all corralled in this rambling old coaching inn, as if they feared they might be contaminated if they so much as stepped beyond its boundaries.'

But, unlike touring hotels of yore, the Inn was more than a staging-post. By Christmas 1977, it was home from home for eleven families, and facilities like WSC's creche were appreciated by cricketers accustomed to long absences from family and friends when on duty. Families could also accompany touring players on discounted fares, and received concessions on room rates. 'Accommodation was up a cog from what we were used to,' says Walker. 'Kerry did everything well. The impact of his financial status was everywhere and players really enjoyed it.'

'We were being spoiled rotten really,' Mick Malone recalls. 'Outside of WSC, there's always been the idea of establishment versus players: the traditional image of the captain marching into the committee room and saying "You're all a bunch of dickheads".

Now we were like celebrities.' Managers Forsaith, Webster and Mike Denness pooled resources on a rainy 25 December for the first WSC Christmas. Eddie Barlow squeezed into a Father Christmas outfit to distribute gifts, while Greig and Collis King were unlikely limbo-dancing contestants.

Greig was in mixed spirits. His South African countrymen were features of a comfortable International Cup win on Christmas Eve. Barry Richards sacrificed a century by holing out on the cover boundary for 95. Beginning with an outswinger that removed Greenidge's off stump, Mike Procter had then been irrepressible with the ball.

But Greig's intimacy with WSC made him uniquely sensitive to its stresses. A mere 3147 had dotted VFL Park on a day when 3549 loyalists watched Bob Simpson and the Test cubs Peter Toohey, John Dyson and Paul Hibbert play an MCG Sheffield Shield game. WSC's pre-Christmas schedule of twenty-seven days' in town and country had drawn just 84,000 people and looked worse when rain ruined VFL Park International Cup games the next two days. The GTV-9 crew almost overturned their outside broadcast van in the headlong flight for the next fixture at Football Park.

The South African actually spent the day before that 28 December International Cup game in Adelaide representing WSC at a fourteen-hour meeting proposed by David Lord. But the time for talk had passed. The Australian Cricket Board's resolve was stiffened as soon as WSC left Melbourne, when the city's climate turned traitorously balmy for the Australia–India Test match. In spite of the visitors' victory, some 82,217 people would attend.

ICC secretary Jack Bailey, an ACB guest, felt in the 'front line'. 'The atmosphere almost held a whiff of cordite,' he wrote. 'All the talk was of beating Packer. There was no question over the determination of Bob Parish and his colleagues ... At that time, there was a Churchillian mood about them.'

9

'We cannot afford to let this man down'

Despite his usual pre-match routine of half a dozen beers and an early night, Ian Chappell woke with a start in Adelaide after only a couple of hours. The Third Supertest at Football Park was eight hours off, but sleep felt impossible. All he could see in his mind was being hit in the head by a cricket ball. 'What the hell are you thinking about that for?' he seethed at himself. 'You've gotta go out tomorrow and face Roberts and the rest of them.'

In the previous fortnight he'd seen South Australian compadres Hookes and Mallett laid low, but it wasn't like him to lose sleep over such acts of God. He'd even made a point of lunching next to Imran in Mildura. 'As a professional sportsman you've got have the ability to cancel that sort of thing out,' he philosophises. 'You've got to be able to argue with your wife in the morning, when she might have said "I won't be here when you get home", but still get in your car, go to the ground and face Roberts and Holding and Garner and concentrate on what's going on.'

Studying his hotel-room ceiling, he recalled Paul Sheahan's advice: Don't resist negative thoughts; follow them with something positive. He'd gone a while without a century. Today would be his day.

Chappell's first duty on 31 December 1977 was pleasant. He told Rob Langer he'd been picked for what he could consider his Test debut. His second duty was successful. He won the toss from Clive Lloyd for the first time and batted on what he knew to be a slow pitch and a slick outfield.

Still the captain's mind wandered when he joined Bruce Laird in the fourth over, but it was his day. Michael Holding's frail shoulder finally gave way, and Lloyd's decision to omit Wayne Daniel for off spinner Albert Padmore reduced the West Indians to a pace pairing of just Roberts and Garner. Laird's solidity freed Chappell to focus on his inner game, and the captain reproved error as his opponents found a rewarding length elusive.

The opener was 19 at lunch, but Chappell was past his half-century and later saw Langer reward his faith. Padmore and Collis King were feasted on. As Garner's thrust petered, Chappell cut three boundaries in an over, and a trademark pull for four from that bowler raised the first Supertest century in four hours. Greg Chappell, demoted to break the bunching of right-handers, rediscovered touch to ratify Australian ascendancy at 3–261. Back at the Hotel Australia, the New Year's Eve entertainment organised by John Crilly was a casino night around an improvised roulette wheel and a print of *Deep Throat* for the West Indians.

Although a day in the sun, opponents drooping, had been routine at the Chappell era's peak, these were not the old days. Of custom there had also been a vast crowd to soak it in. But Richie Benaud's commentators had spent a listless day searching for spectators to kindle atmosphere. Brian Morelli recalls finding most of the 3000 congregated in the grandstand, because the general aluminium seating was too hot to sit on.

Packer, in a baseball cap to protect his sensitive skin, was among fewer than 3500 who came to watch the home-town brothers extend their partnership to 120 on New Year's Day. 'Once he looked back over his shoulder,' wrote John Benaud, Richie's brother on Sydney's *Sun*. 'Did he catch a glimpse of the devil that he once urged to take the hindmost?'

The Australians disappointed him. The elder Chappell was athletically caught by substitute fielder Jim Allen mishooking Garner after six and a half hours, and only Kent settled after Roberts ended Greg

Sale of the century: Greg Chappell's Australian cricket team assemble ahead of the Centenary Test at the Melbourne Cricket Ground in March 1977. Only Gary Cosier, in the middle of the back row, would not have signed with Kerry Packer by the time the Ashes tour commenced the following month.

Not one of us: Tony Greig at Hove to represent Sussex against the Australians, where Packer's recruitment went public. His defection would cost him the captaincy of England.

Young men in a hurry: Austin Robertson and John Cornell of JP Sport, who brainstormed what became World Series Cricket, then became its chief recruiting agents.

JP Productions Pty. Ltd.

~~82B/8 Kippax St., Surry Hills, Sydney, N.S.W. 8010 Australia. Phone: 818 2081, 818 2068~~

12 Artarmon Rd., Willoughby, NSW 2068.   Phone 958 1555

M E M O

TO: Mr. Kerry Packer

6th May, 1977

Ian Chappell said the main areas of the Board's attack would be on the following points:

1. <u>Private enterprise taking over cricket</u> - (They will say they've been doing it for the glory of the game, etc. One of the things they will try and put over is that we will be a flash in the pan, plundering players, money, and leaving cricket an empty shell in 3 years.

2. <u>The traditions of cricket</u> - (What about the Centenary Test, etc.)

3. <u>The grounds</u> - (Can you create a Test watch atmosphere at a Showground?)

4. <u>The wickets</u> - (The possibility of somebody being seriously injured.)

<u>PEOPLE TO WORRY ABOUT ON THE BOARD</u>

1. Parish
2. Steele
3. Maddocks
4. Bradman (Not on the Board, but they are certain to seek his advice.)

<u>POINTS TO MAKE</u>

1. Brought I. Chappell, Lillee, Redpath, and Edwards back.

2. Stress our coaching plan in N.S.W., to extend to other states in time.

3. Perhaps some financial grant should find its way back into cricket at a junior level, or assist with cricket equipment.

Points to make: Via JP Sport, Ian Chappell warns Kerry Packer of pitfalls ahead – a prescient memo.

Packer versus England: Kerry Packer challenges his antagonists on television (with David Frost, above) and at law (with Tony Greig, in the High Court, right). He proved a formidable opponent.

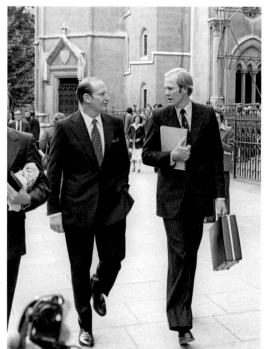

Packer versus Australia: As World Series Cricket commenced, the Australian public proved hard to woo, despite the credibility of Ian Chappell and Clive Lloyd (top left, tossing before the First Supertest) and the charisma of Dennis Lillee (top right). The bare terraces of VFL Park proved a stark background to a photoshoot for the McDonald's fast food chain (above).

The Brotherhood: Ian (above) and Greg Chappell (below), formally retired from Test cricket, found the Supertests hot to handle. The West Indians, whom they had seen off 1–5 in 1975–1976, had made giant strides.

Exiles: Pariahhood took different shades for different signatories. World Series Cricket hastened the fade of Max Walker (above left), slowing down in a faster world, and continued that of Graeme Pollock (above right), unable even to take the field because of West Indian objections – although, publicly, paid out in full.

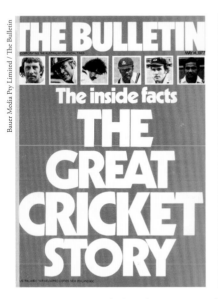
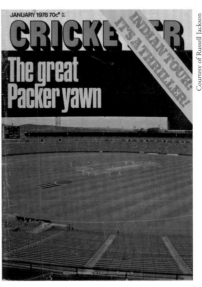

Cover point: Kerry Packer's media properties such as the *Bulletin* (left) covered his cricket ambitions generously; the mainstream cricket press, such as *Cricketer* (right), was more sceptical.

The boys light up: The first WSC day/night match, Australians v World, on 6 December 1978, drew more than 6000 spectators to VFL Park – the earliest glimpse of a crowd.

Glamour quotient: Most telegenic of Packer's assets, David Hookes, bounced back from a broken jaw to model a new batting helmet (left); most photogenic, Cornell's wife Delvene Delaney, partook of the merchandise.

The fun of the fair: Christmas 1977 at the Old Melbourne Inn pits Tony Greig against Collis King in a limbo dancing contest (above); dinner chez Packer in Vaucluse pits the boss's son James against Asif Iqbal and Derek Underwood (below) on a sheet pitch.

Victory in Sydney: After a summer in the ersatz surrounds of the Sydney Showground (above), WSC began its second season at the Sydney Cricket Ground itself, bathing in the new floodlights: with a crowd of nearly 50,000, it made itself instantly at home (below).

C'MON AUSSIE C'MON b/w ESTABLISHMENT BLUES

Classical and Pop: Richie Benaud (above left, with Tony Cozier) provided WSC with a credible voice, Alan Morris and Alan Johnston of advertising firm Mojo with a stirring new anthem (above right). By Christmas 1978, the tide of public opinion had turned (below).

THANKS McPACKER

MEMO TO:	ALL PLAYERS
	TEAM MANAGERS
FROM:	BILL MACARTNEY
DATE:	DECEMBER 28, 1978

It seems we are gaining a substantial number of new fans who traditionally may not have come within the bounds of Cricket followers.

Women are a significant and important example.

So, to continue the flow of "different" information and give the feature writers something to talk about, I would like to tell them about the injuries gathered by professionals in the "gentle" game of cricket.

For that purpose, could you list the injuries you've suffered during the course of your career, and what sort of incidents, in brief, caused them.

I'm talking about injuries more serious than pulled muscles or strains.

If you can jot them down and hand them to the team managers, it will be appreciated.

Bill Macartney

Bill Macartney
PUBLICITY DIRECTOR

A (wo)man's game: Injuries impaired human assets, but they provided grist for World Series Cricket's machismo mill: publicity director Bill Macartney took advantage.

A kid's game: World Series Cricket identified children as an influential part of cricket's audience and tried hard to make them feel wanted.

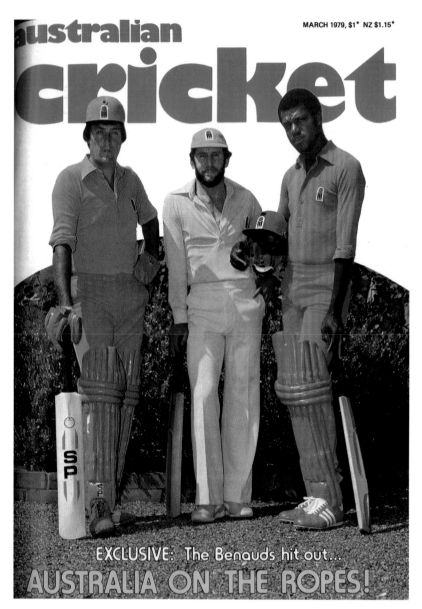

MARCH 1979, $1* NZ $1.15*

australian cricket

EXCLUSIVE: The Benauds hit out...

AUSTRALIA ON THE ROPES!

On with the motley: Colour television cried out for coloured clothing and, on 17 January 1979, World Series Cricket premiered it at the SCG. The World's Bob Woolmer in electric blue, Australia's Ian Chappell in wattle yellow and the West Indies' Colin Croft in coral pink leap from the cover of *Australian Cricket*.

A. ACB is the national Australian association responsible for the organisation and supervision of the game of cricket in Australia including the arranging of Test Matches between Australia and other countries and the arranging of interstate cricket matches.

B. ACB is constituted by the various cricket associations of the States and the Tasmanian Cricket Council which are responsible for the organisation of cricket within their States for players from junior cricket through to selection for State teams.

C. Publishing and Broadcasting Limited is a member of the group of companies which includes WSC and PBL.

D. WSC has since 1977 promoted cricket matches using contracted players.

The pipes of peace: As Australia and the World XI played off in 1979's Supertest final (Bruce Laird batting, below left), World Series Cricket and the Australian Cricket Board began the long journey towards a 'peace agreement' (above). It left Kim Hughes (below right) at the head of an Australian team in India on borrowed time.

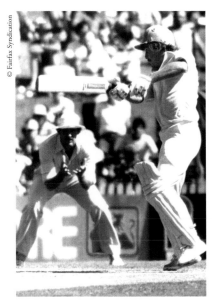

BENSON and HEDGES
1989/90 CRICKET
PROGRAMME

O my Chappell and my Lillee long ago: As official marketing partner of the Australian Cricket Board, Packer's PBL Marketing kept WSC's logo and nomenclature alive another twenty years (above left), even vestiges of its most popular slogan (above right); Packer has also inspired epigones like Subash Chandra (right), who founded his made-to-TV cricket spectacular in 2007.

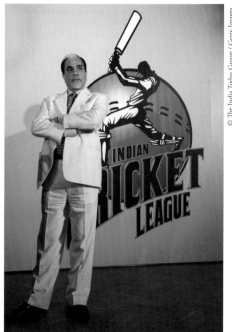

Chappell's three-hour 90. An hour before tea the West Indies were threatening to pass the Australians' 388 by stumps.

Lillee's season of struggle was becoming an unspoken byword. His five wickets thus far had cost 60 runs each. Because Lillee gathered so much locomotion from his approach, he was tormented by rough run-ups that felt like 'ploughing through sand'. Opponents sensed his discomfort, and Roy Fredericks and Gordon Greenidge used their nine overs before the break to exploit it: 73 runs included thirteen boundaries.

When Ian Chappell gambled on his brother's medium pace, however, his fortune would have bankrupted Crilly's roulette wheel. Aided by doubtful caught-behind decisions against Fredericks and Rowe, the flutter proved worth 5–20. Lillee, at last, celebrated a Richards edge. At a hurried corridor conference when his rivals were rounded up for 145 on Monday, Ian Chappell acknowledged the improbability of it all by declining to enforce the follow-on. Now it was time to graft.

The stubbornness that Bruce Laird's captain had seen in England in 1975 was suited to West Indian challenge. The opener glowed when bruised. 'Bruce I'd seen a bit of,' says Chappell. 'And if there was ever a guy you wanted to send out to blunt fast bowling, it was Stumpy.' Laird spent a neat four and half hours at his century and, while the West Indians worked steadily through his partners, no declaration came until their target exceeded 500.

The visitors, Chappell knew, retained the ability to astonish. Langer was dumbstruck when Bernard Julien tumbled into his full-blooded hook just behind square leg. Even watching the replay, he could not comprehend it: 'I tried to do everything right. I can remember rolling my wrists to keep the ball down and I really middled it. We had a drink later and I think he was still wondering how he'd caught it.'

Richards and Fredericks drove headlong for an hour and a half, and Australian fielding frayed as their stand reached 129. Laird at mid wicket was feeling a misfielding culprit when he dived Julien-style for Fredericks' pull and rose, baffled, with the ball. Richards stood alone as Lillee and Bright winkled out his partners over the next three hours. The soft hum of resurgence was maintained by the visit of David Hookes, who lived within sight of the park in West

Lakes. Jaw wired, he patted back underarms in the nets among a knot of well-wishers.

Winners at last, the Chappells, Lillee and Marsh could overlook the fact that a 190-run Test defeat of the West Indies two years before, virtually across the road at Adelaide Oval, had attracted a crowd nine times the meagre 15,210 of this 220-run triumph. Their team had earned $16,667 this time, of course, against $3000.

World Series Cricket itself, though, could not neglect comparison. Football Park, in which John Maley had invested thousands of hours, was deleted as a venue. It was a desperate advance guard WSC sent to Perth to promote three International Cup matches.

Vern Stone's confidence that the pattern would break in the West was that of a native. WSC could almost call Perth a company town. Cornell and Robertson, Stone and Treasure, Maley, Forsaith and Crilly called it home, as did Lillee and Marsh, Langer and Laird, Malone, McKenzie and Ross Edwards.

Perth had gone without a Test the previous summer despite its recent abundance of cricket talent. And crucially, WSC had twice its usual television grip: STW-9 shared a program-buying cartel with TVW-7 and both would be telecasting the games.

If, that was, they were ready to be telecast. WSC's itinerary had stretched taut resources. Complete resurfacing of the salt-riddled Gloucester Park square had been necessary, as had outside purchase of water because of Perth's summer drought. Fred Bolton had been flown from Kensington golf course to design a new reticulation system for the ground, and Packer himself had joined in mowing the outfield to make the pacing park a camp fit for cricket. Even the sceptical Blofeld saluted the effort: 'The transformation was astonishing, for when I first saw the park the day after I arrived in Perth it had been converted into an attractive cricket ground with the boats on Perth Water at one side giving it a pleasant atmosphere.'

Gloucester Park's other life left producer David Hill little margin for error: it was hosting the $100,000 Benson and Hedges Cup trot the night before the game, and WSC did not gain official custody of the venue until midnight on Saturday 7 December.

'It was only a day match the next day so we didn't have much time,' remembers Brian Morelli. 'The scaffolders went in the minute they finished.' Richie Benaud was to preview from his eyrie at 10.20 a.m. local time and, as dawn broke, gantries were still strewn in pieces across the track. It was not until 10.10 a.m. that Hill was sure WSC would make it to air.

The pre-match politics were familiar. 'It was the same stuff as usually happened,' Stone recalls. 'Mysteriously, people emerged to put parking tickets on cars. Police banned liquor going in to our ground while they were letting it into the WACA. But we had a queue. We'd been opening the gates and waiting an hour for people to turn up. This time they were lined up.' More than 13,000 Perth patriots arrived; easily a WSC record.

The Australians played, unfortunately, like a team happier with privacy. Against a West Indian pace attack supplemented by Wayne Daniel and Bernard Julien, the home side stumbled to 121 from 28 overs. Lillee then crooked an ankle in his fifth over on the uneven surface. His hobbling retirement on the shoulder of his father Keith completed a poor day's salesmanship.

Early rain discouraged spectators the next day as well, trimming 20 overs from the Australians' match against the World, but a faithful 9000 approved 87 from stopgap opener Greg Chappell and a three-wicket victory. The West Indians' defeat of the World on Monday brought Perth's three-day turnout to almost 29,000: a healthy 6000 more, in fact, than the ACB's five Test days there.

Perth had two unavoidable bum notes. With characteristic lack of fuss, Robinson had decided he did not want to be first among seconds: he resigned the captaincy of the Australians' Country Cup side. 'I think if I had a real beef with WSC it was that I was made captain of that second XI,' he says. 'It was logical, I suppose, because I had the experience with Victoria, but I thought it was a bit wrong that they hadn't told me when I'd signed. I would always have joined but, with all the extra duties a captain handles, I would have held out for a bit more money if I'd known I was it.'

The team elected Ross Edwards in his stead, again a man who never said no, and his first match at Maitland gave Robinson a chance to prove he could still be counted on. Their decisive unbeaten partnership of 65 came beneath a vault of inky cloud after a freak electrical storm that upended a sightscreen.

The other bum note – to Forsaith, Ferrett, Denness and Webster – had Packer's signature: a few locals seemed to have mislaid their contract clause requiring promotional devotion.

One of the first commitments WSC players had honoured was posing for a grand team photo mingling with 'Ronald McDonald', the clown mascot of the fast-food chain distributing the poster. Wayne Daniel and Len Pascoe had giggled through a television commercial, but there had since been several truants when marketing was mentioned. Chris Forsyth found Lillee, Marsh and Malone particularly difficult when press duty called: 'Each was willing . . . if the financial incentives were great, but for the occasions when no money was available they were decidedly disinterested.'

Humbler souls, especially 'Champagne Tourists', were more willing. Edwards remembers visiting four McDonald's outlets in a morning: 'When we realised it wasn't as though we were going to pull any big crowds, we went round saying g'day to the staff.' In country centres, co-promoters were recompensed for air fares and accommodation by the availability of players for personal appearances. 'We'd go to Fred's Shoe Store and there'd be a sign outside saying "Come and meet the WSC cricketers!",' recalls Edwards. 'We'd sign autographs and press the flesh, and it was great really because the cockies'd all be saying it was the first time they'd ever seen dinkum, competitive cricket.'

It was quaint for Graham McKenzie, no longer a household name seven years after his last Test: 'The kids had never seen me play, maybe never heard of me. Occasionally I'd hear a dad say: "You'd better get his autograph. I was a fan of his when I was a boy".'

Foreigners were happier celebrities, especially South Africans otherwise confined by county cricket. 'We were all bright-eyed and bushy-tailed at being "on-tour",' Barry Richards says. 'While money was important, it was exposure to international cricket that we valued.' Mike Procter wrote: 'Cricketers must be the hardest sportsmen to please – they moan about having to get places on time, about the food and having to do a few promotions for their employer. As far as I was concerned, I was lucky to be there.'

The roles Greig modelled, meanwhile, caused tension. At Sydney's Chateau Commodore prior to the Fourth Supertest between Australia and the World, he intercepted Barry Richards en route to a photo session with the Murdoch-owned *Daily Telegraph*, offering $160 for a store-opening appearance instead.

Forsyth was furious: Greig should have known better. WSC needed all the publicity it could get, and not one Fairfax reporter had been sent to Adelaide or Perth. Richards, too, settled for the unpaid front-page. 'In those days, it was the sort of money you'd think about,' he says. 'But it wasn't going to make or break anyone.' Greig stalked off with a sneer: 'If you want your picture in the paper so much instead of earning $160 I can't help you.'

The West Indians, meantime, savoured their success. At last they felt true professionals, secure in their station. 'We were kept as a unit for a long time,' says Michael Holding. 'Because the senior players had the men they wanted, you knew your place was not under threat and that you could do the job that you had to do.' Chests also swelled with outside recognition:

> Kerry Packer gave us pride. At that time we were just starting to climb the ladder and had a great team in the making, and the fact that Packer and whoever advised him would gamble on us was important. And Kerry Packer himself, I remember him coming into our room and kicking up a storm when we did not play our best. He knew what we could do and let us know what he thought, and that appealed to us. We thought: 'We cannot afford to let this man down.'

Holding's was a superbly balanced pace generation: its sprinters and endurance runners could be rotated perpetually. Nor was theirs a random violence. Laird remembers his pet cut falling into disuse. 'They were so disciplined,' he says. 'You got no width at all: I can't remember cutting them more than half a dozen times in two and a half years.'

Rick McCosker was teased forward. 'I'd always been a back-foot player, so they kept it up to me,' he recalls. 'These guys weren't mugs you know, they had a plan and they stuck to it.' Ian Davis, bombarded when recognised as a front-foot driver, realised he was receiving what Australians had given: 'It was "Cricket 2000" in 1977. We were a pretty aggressive side and, because the directive was that there was no limit on short-pitched bowling, everyone just went for it. You got as much short quick stuff as you liked. Or didn't.' His own state of mind is reflected by an occasion when he inquired after Holding's health. 'Survivin' Wiz,' came the baritone reply. Davis heard it as: 'Stay alive.'

Centuries had a new arithmetic. 'You had to set yourself to bat all day,' says Greg Chappell, 'and accept that you weren't going to get any more than 70–80 overs. If you faced half of those, you had also to realise that half of them you wouldn't be able to score off. So you might get a hundred balls a day to score off. And with four fast bowlers, the most any of them will bowl is 20 overs, maybe 15, so they were never going to have a hard day at the office.'

Old rhythms were redundant. 'If you were at the other end for a few overs,' McCosker points out, 'you could go fifteen minutes without a hit. Then you had someone coming at you at ninety-five miles an hour again. There was no continuity. You were switching on and off all the time.'

Rudi Webster and Sydney physiotherapist Dennis Waight were vital additions to the team. Webster, whose use of hypnotherapy on the West Indians inspired his book *Winning Ways*, encouraged self-discipline and self-assertion. Waight's rigid fitness standards were vital in keeping the team's pace attack ticking. 'We'd never had a single person dedicated to us before,' says Holding. 'And in those days we'd never heard of track suits. You played in whites. But Dennis told us that we weren't fit enough. He got us running and stretching and training, and learned what each of us needed.'

The Australians were struck by the character change. 'Lloydy ruled with an iron fist,' Laird recalls. 'He was very strict on their behaviour. There was no partying or drinking after the game and very few verbals on the field.'

Garner was a rare fraterniser, to the irritation of colleagues who preferred subsisting on room-service and Chinese takeaways. 'Some of my teammates disliked me socialising with opposing players,' he wrote, 'but I had my own ideas . . . Often I had to tell a couple of them that no one could tell me who to drink with.'

Webster and Waight came to believe that Garner's predominant need was persuasion. When the fast bowler suddenly succumbed to a strain just before taking the field on a fiercely hot day at Gloucester Park, Webster duly directed him to Royal Perth Hospital.

'Awww, no,' Garner replied. 'I'll just wait for the doc when he gets here.'

'No, Joel,' the manager insisted. 'I want you to get treatment now. It could be serious.'

Vern Stone later quizzed the manager: surely, they could have waited for the doctor? No, Webster replied, Garner was twinge-prone when hard work was in the offing. This strain could be cured by a few hours in a hot casualty-ward queue.

Among doubters the West Indies were silencing was Packer himself. When Webster had warned him two months earlier that the team would be a mettlesome opponent, Packer had laughed: 'That's a joke. You don't know how to win.' His tune changed after West Indian victory in the First Supertest. 'This is dangerous,' he admitted to the manager. 'You've learned how to win, and it'll be difficult to beat you now.'

The team the Australians were about to confront was a stark contrast. There was no need for the whole of the World to exceed the sum of its parts: the parts alone would do nicely.

That every part had its own approach could cause problems. Greig had unsuccessfully wooed England's physiotherapist, Bernie Thomas, and the idea of a collective approach to team fitness lasted one team meeting. When Eddie Barlow mentioned the mountain runs with sacks of sand that he'd decreed at Western Province, the Pakistanis were particularly restive. Asif Iqbal, renowned for his fleet feet between wickets, spoke for the room. 'The day you can get out in the centre and run three as fast as me,' he said, 'I'll start carrying sacks of sand up mountains.' End of subject.

As Greig recalls: 'Barry Richards' idea of practice was to get the best bowlers in his net, and to ask someone like Snowy to imitate Dennis Lillee, because that was who he was going to face. But Snowy didn't like to be told to bowl a certain way at practice. He liked getting away into a net and bowling at a single stump.'

Greig's thoughts of instilling a team ethic with blazers were thwarted by Ian Chappell, who considered them as natural as braces. 'It bugged me that we should travel anonymously, in some cases scruffily, while establishment tour teams invariably dressed in uniform smartness,' Greig remembered. 'But Chappell did not care at all – he would wear what he damn well pleased.'

One could, though, learn a lot. Imran Khan, the rawest World recruit, became a jackdaw, collecting the shiny paraded by Procter and Snow. Cricket education in Pakistan was inhibited by jealousies and rivalries but, among the myriad models, he lengthened an ungainly mincing run, broadened his repertoire and was encouraged to stretch for extra pace.

Greig's brush with commerce in the last year had also affected him profoundly. As Greig's rapport with Packer strengthened, manager Mike Denness became resigned to seeing him only during playing hours, while the South Africans sensed their countryman's ebbing engagement with cricket. 'A World side was never going to be the same as a national side and Tony was working to a different agenda at the time,' Richards recalls. 'Cricket was a passing phase, with the objective of becoming involved in the whole Packer organisation . . . He'd come to practice but, because there were no mobile phones in those days, he was always dashing off again.'

Procter wrote of Greig as an absentee captain more visible in the media than around his team:

> Cricket almost seemed secondary to Greig in Australia, he had so much going commercially. They loved him in the media but I wish he'd been able to do more on the field as World captain . . . I'm sure he regrets getting distracted by the commercial side of the game so soon, because he was a great trier on the field who surpassed his natural abilities by dint of effort, character and temperament.

Yet Procter's judgement says as much about him as Greig. Cricket had little to offer the latter and – after twenty-four consecutive summers round the world and experience of high office – he had little left to give the game. Cricket, by contrast, had denied Procter everything when, as Imran discovered, he still had much to volunteer.

The more retiring Englishmen, by contrast, receded from view, especially when WSC decided to pool the World and West Indian squads for the remaining three Supertests. Lost in the talent avalanche with Woolmer and Snow, Amiss felt a little disused. 'That

wasn't the idea when I signed,' he complained. 'How am I meant
to compete with that?' Pretty soon the Australians were asking the
same question.

Greig liked his bigger pool for the Fourth Supertest at the Sydney
Showground: he hankered to revenge England's 1974–1975 Ashes
tour. His attack was now a solar system of Roberts, Procter, Garner
and Underwood, his batting order of Fredericks, Greenidge, Lloyd,
himself and both Richards almost ugly in its surfeit of skill. The
Australians, denied even Lillee by his ankle injury, had to vest their
new ball in Wayne Prior and Gary Gilmour.

When the original World and West Indian teams were involved in
International Cup games interspersed with the Supertests, however,
the merger was a peculiarly dim promotional ploy. There was an
arrogance like that of a body-builder flexing his pectorals in rele-
gating Procter, joint first-class record-holder for six consecutive
centuries, to number eight.

The sunny Sydney Saturday, 14 January 1978, was good news for
WSC. A record crowd of 14,833 spilling onto the arena behind roped-
off square boundaries when Ian Chappell won the toss reflected the
fact that, for the only occasion that summer, there was no official
Test match in another town to tie people to television sets. Australia's
Test team had lost to India across the road at the Sydney Cricket
Ground two days earlier, while its Supertest men were coming off
a strong victory. WSC crowds in Perth, moreover, had been prime-
time Sydney viewing.

After the premature loss of McCosker to Procter's back-break,
Laird's century stand with Ian Chappell escorted the Australians
past lunch. Watching his Westralian picks, Laird and Langer, add a
spirited 90 in two hours further gratified the captain.

Laird's second consecutive century arrived at the third stroke: a
six swept from Greig was disallowed when a bail proved to have
blown from the stumps, and four leg-glanced became four leg-byes
two balls later. The opener's robust hook from Roberts finally raised
his hundred in four and half hours.

Buoyed by improved sightscreening, the Australians felt more
comfortable against Garner. Screens originally too short had left
Garner's hand in darkness at release, sharpening his menace in

fading light. He didn't need help. 'With Holding and Roberts, say, the ball would reach your midriff off a particular length,' Langer recalls. 'Garner would hit the same spot and it would get up to your throat. Although I'd always been a front-foot player, I began moving slightly back and across to Garner while still trying to come forward whenever I could. Most of the time, I must say, I ended up going further back.' It was Garner who at length tarnished the Australian day, yorking Laird and having Langer caught at the wicket in three balls as the light weakened. The following morning, by having Greg Chappell caught in the covers, he hastened an unruly collapse to 304 all out.

Despite Lillee's absence, the Australians checked the visitors whenever they seemed about to take off. The two Richardses threatened mayhem for half an hour, before Barry was bowled by a perfect Gilmour inswinger. Greg Chappell then proved a point with a bouncer that cracked Viv across the forehead. 'That Showground pitch was frightening,' he says. 'Faster than the WACA wicket at its quickest. Bouncing Viv was probably the most satisfying delivery I ever bowled. If I'd hit someone in the past it'd generally been when they'd got right through the shot. But this time I beat him for pace.'

Chappell watched in satisfaction as Dennis Waight applied icepacks. 'It proved what I'd been saying: that on that pitch all the West Indies had to do was roll their arms over and it would go past head-high.' The batsman, then 74, welcomed stumps a hazy fifteen minutes later.

With the second-day gate of 12,612, WSC was in danger of success, but rain then abridged the following day. Either side of a three-hour hiatus, Richards felt his way for a century with unaccustomed care in conditions suited to Walker and Gilmour. The former, profiting from extravagances by the World's final five, strung together 7–88. What suited him, however, delighted Roberts and Procter for the final half-hour. The wicket had sweated beneath the covers and McCosker and Laird fell in a trice.

At the Commodore that night, Roberts' usual early-evening disappearing act was disturbed by a meeting with John Crilly in the lift. Struggling for a word, the director suggested he join the evening's bar school.

'Don't drink,' said the saturnine fast bowler.

'Come and have an orange juice then.'

The fast bowler declined, polite but firm. 'No, thank you.'

Crilly was surprised soon after to be joined in the saloon by none other than Roberts. The fast bowler wordlessly accepted an orange juice, which he cradled for the next hour while following, if not adding to, conversation. Then he was gone.

Roberts might have heard the coming storm, which scotched play for the first three hours on the Tuesday, and had Langer tugging down his cap to secure it against the gale behind the Antiguan's arm. Recollection of it still brings a chill. 'It was cold front, absolutely howling,' he says. 'And because the wicket had been under the covers in the overcast atmosphere, it was green as green.' For five overs Langer jabbed and jumped, ever later in his strokes. An involuntary boundary ricocheted from his bat to third man as he shouldered arms too slowly. Invisible to the naked eye, the next ball plucked out his off stump.

Knott had moved back some paces, but could still see Greg Chappell's response to the next ball: a perfectly sadistic bouncer crushing the Australian's hand against his glove. 'It was one of the fastest deliveries I have ever seen, and his colour just drained,' wrote the wicketkeeper. Roberts' sequel – a little wider, a little further up – struck from the inside edge of Chappell's withdrawing bat and scattered the stumps crazily.

Brother Ian hooked defiantly, but was in mid-stroke as a bouncer rebounded from his glove to Fredericks in the gully. Marsh was trying to withdraw his bat as he tickled Roberts to Knott, and Gilmour's brief counterblast owed as much to the bowler's pace as the batsman's eye. His two fours and two sixes in an over were acclaimed. 'Snicks,' he says. 'I was getting halfway through the shots, getting a nick, and they were carrying over deep fine leg.' His middle stump then disappeared as though burgled.

The World was just 65 runs from victory with nine wickets standing and Barry Richards entrenched that night when Crilly again met Roberts in the hotel lift.

This time the West Indian broke the silence. 'Will you be having a drink tonight?' he asked.

Crilly didn't much feel like it. 'No, don't think so Andy,' he said. 'Just going to unwind, and have a room service dinner.'

'Good idea,' Roberts replied. 'I'll join you.'

Moments later, Roberts banged on Crilly's door. 'We ordered some food,' the director recalls. 'And he sat there for the whole evening, not saying a word. I switched on the TV and what should come on but the bloody highlights of the day's play. Andy just sat there through the whole thing, smiling to himself, as his wickets were replayed.'

10

'The best bunch of cricketers I've ever seen . . . with one exception'

Nobody worked more willingly at his game than Rick McCosker, but having passed 40 twice in eight Supertest innings, and gathered a dozen runs besides, 'The General' was palpably out of form.

His trait of playing late had been admirable against the moving ball in England, where his Test average was 48, but in WSC it looked almost retroactive. Ian Chappell suggested technical adjustments in a net session. 'He'd noticed that even though my first movement had always been back and across, the extra pace meant that I was still moving sometimes when playing the shot,' says McCosker. 'And he got me to shorten my back swing so that I didn't get so hurried and cramped.'

But charity from bowlers was unforthcoming. 'Rick was a very good cutter and made a lot of runs off his pads,' partner Bruce Laird remembers. 'But Roberts and Garner and Procter gave him nothing for either shot. They'd obviously given him a lot of thought and worked him out beforehand.'

McCosker had even borrowed one of Amiss' helmets, but discovered that his unusually small head wobbled as though within a fish bowl, and its stifling confines on hot days aggravated his sinuses. He needed time, but in this campaign the wounded had to walk.

'That's the reason I think WSC was tougher than Tests,' Ian Chappell says. 'At least when you struggle in Tests you can get back into form with a few Shield runs. How the fuck could you get back into form when you were playing Roberts, Holding, Garner day after day?'

Had he not been at the Showground in the Fourth Supertest between 14 and 19 January 1978, for instance, McCosker might have been at Lismore's Oakes Oval where a second World attack of Holding, Daniel, Julien, Barlow, and King was tattooing bruises all over Trevor Chappell. The youngest of the brothers spent five and a half hours over 56: the Country Cup game's only half-century.

Lismore's turf trampoline was actually the best Ross Edwards' Australians had encountered. Groundsman Neville Clarke, reputed never to have worn a shirt in his life, knew how to dress a pitch. 'It was probably as true and fast a wicket as I've played on,' believes the well-travelled Graham McKenzie. 'Made me feel I was ten years younger.'

When teams reassembled in Sydney on 20 January, McCosker's need of refuge from further public failure was urgent. Ian Chappell rested him with Laird, Langer and Bright for Davis, Edwards, Walters and Malone in an International Cup match.

On another pacy portion of the Showground square, batting was energetically instantaneous. Garner, hooked for two sixes fine by Greg Chappell, retaliated by striking Edwards in the throat. 'Things started to look a bit funny after that,' the batsman recalls. 'I could see two stands, two Joel Garners, two balls, the whole lot.' Queasily conscious as he retired, he was told he had been hit in a carotid artery and lost the blood supply to his brain.

Once again, though, the pitch was also tailored for Caribbean stroke play. Jim Allen turned the sort of party trick Lloyd had been hoping for from him. His 14 fours saved his side seven overs and left its International Cup record at five victories in six attempts.

Mick Malone reviewed his options. They weren't abundant. Line and length, he guessed. The pitch was lifeless, and the dirt-streaked white ball in his hand had long lost its swing 'We'd gone to WSC and said: "These balls are ratshit, they do not swing",' he says. 'But they'd said: "You're wrong, they do".'

No, the only thing swinging would be West Indians. Malone had two deliveries left, and the last West Indian pair – striker Wayne Daniel and partner Joel Garner – needed five runs from them. It was 11.48 p.m. on Tuesday 24 January 1978, and the bowler's isolation seemed all the starker in the floodlit cavern of VFL Park.

He looked to Ian Chappell at cover. 'Any thoughts?' Malone asked.

Knowing that umpire Gary Duperouzel would probably turn a blind eye to a bouncer, the captain suggested one.

'No,' said Malone. 'There's no bounce. I don't think I can get it over him.'

'OK, try to get it on leg stump. Just don't give him any room.'

John Cornell's agony in the VIP lounge was almost exquisite as he watched. Malone's suffering was being shared by a crowd of almost 25,000 people. It had taken the whole season, but at last the alchemy had a golden glow. A bumping pitch, blinding lights, five to make and a last man, record crowd and eight television cameras in.

He and Packer had juggled WSC's schedule for this, the second of an International Cup night triple-header, and Cornell had managed to reach the absent impresario in Honolulu. 'The Boss' was en route home from some coarse golf on the Monterey Peninsula in the Bing Crosby pro-am with partner David Graham, and was delighted to know what he was missing.

Drizzle had been visible at light-up time the night before, and the Australians' truncated game with the World continued where twilight ice-hockey would have been cancelled. But 10,272 people had come, and the apparatus was clearly in order.

Tuesday's half-hour rain delay cost four overs, and Cornell accepted a 3.30 p.m. attendance of less than 5300. But the game turned at tea. Some 18,400 faces were visible in the gloaming at 7 p.m. and the final 24,636 was the second-largest cricket crowd of the summer *anywhere*. Only the first day of the official Third Test at the MCG surpassed it.

The game itself had all the compressed excitement one-day cricket promised. Greg Chappell commandeered 68 in 73 balls, Jim Allen's spontaneous strokes replied, then Ray Bright retrieved the game by bowling him and Collis King in a confused, dramatic over. King stood his ground, ignoring the incriminating stain of the fallen bail and Marsh's pleading. 'Collis didn't want to go but it looked all right from where I was,' Bright recalls. 'And we were pretty glad to see the back of him. We knew he could really hit a ball.'

Julien and Murray conspired, though, and Garner's nerveless hitting in Greg Chappell's final over had deep fielders fumbling away 16 runs. Malone had been in hiding since conceding 25 in his first three overs, but his captain had exhausted his other bowlers' quotas.

As the crowd bubbled, umpire Duperouzel hared to the sight-screen to repel children already storming the playing arena, then reprieved Malone from a palpable leg-side wide to Garner. Garner's swipe to Greg Chappell at long-on finally pitted Malone against Daniel for the penultimate delivery. Cameras swivelled round the ground like prison-yard searchlights, capturing Ian Chappell's urgent dialogue with Malone, a mid-pitch conference of terrified tuition, and a West Indian dressing-room full of curiously camera-shy Australian women.

'I'd probably bowled at Daniel before,' Malone recalls. 'But I just thought: "I'll pitch it up and see what happens". It was a bad ball, it was too short, it was too wide, I gave him too much room.' Seeing the ball veer to leg, Daniel's eyes shut with the effort of connection. So did Malone's. The invading crowd lost sight as the ball vanished over mid wicket. Only Ian Chappell was silent. 'Ian didn't say a word and he didn't need to,' says Malone. 'I didn't need a "bad luck Mick", because I knew it had been a bad ball. And I didn't need "You're a bastard" either. Ian's silence was deafening. But I think I did play the next game somewhere like Toowoomba!'

The West Indians had only one gripe as twelfth-hour victors, although it was to become a common one. Return to the Old Melbourne at 2.30 a.m. meant that, with the cricketing equivalent of a hangover, they were coaxed to their bus at 11 a.m. next day for the afternoon's match against the World. Fredericks and Greenidge fell blearily, and their 20-over total of 3–83 was marked by leg-weary running. It took Richards and a fifty-minute, seventh-wicket thrash by Julien and Murray which added 83 to set the World as many as 239.

After hovering over the 17,923 watching the World reply, Packer bounced from his helicopter. At a contented press conference, he jested about his rusty golf swing and an Australian Cricket Board announcement stating an 'interest' in its own night cricket: 'I seem to remember them saying night cricket was absurd, just a circus act. It seems remarkable they should have discovered it so suddenly.'

Asif Iqbal went out to bat with eyes peeled for the white ball. He'd failed to lay a hand on a chance he'd lost in the crowd while fielding, and bent forward vigilantly to exploit the fatigue of Daniel and Garner. As Imran matched him stroke-for-stroke from 5–81 and as fielders flagged as well, 15 overs from the heroes of the previous evening yielded 125. The Pakistanis piled 158 in 107 minutes.

The cramming of cricket was, in fact, starting to cause ructions. Lloyd was annoyed to learn that Greig – to whom he was to be vice-captain in the merged World at the Fifth Supertest at Gloucester Park on the Friday – apparently wanted to take non-players Bob Woolmer and Dennis Amiss to Perth, rather than sending them to Hamilton for a simultaneous Country Cup game. That meant that Deryck Murray, exhausted by two months' unbroken glovework, would cop another three days' duty. When manager Rudi Webster pressed the point with Mike Denness, Amiss defused the situation by volunteering for Hamilton while Jim Allen offered to keep in Murray's stead. The show had to go on.

Australia Day weekend in Hamilton was a far cry from VFL Park. It was not much of a town, Melville Oval was not much of a ground (one grandstand, classified by the National Trust, and one row of seats inside a mesh fence), and it wasn't going to pull much of a crowd (4000 in three days).

But there was an unusual amount hinging on the game for the Australians. Rick McCosker, after a ten-day net, was searching for form. Mick Malone was hoping for redemption. Doug Walters gave little away, but his solitary fifty for a season's work certainly troubled Ian Chappell. Then there was David Hookes. He'd taken his first steps back to big cricket two weeks after his broken jaw, face still full of wire as he batted in the nets of his West Torrens club. 'They'd really stood by me, wanted to play me, and gave me practice even though we were banned,' he recalls. 'They just said: "If anyone complains about you practising with a broken jaw they'll look a bit churlish".' Removal of the wires freed him to rejoin the tour.

Comebacks have been simpler. From the first delivery on a raw pitch, the ball refused to go straight. Openers McCosker and Kerry O'Keeffe played the thin air as Michael Holding let fly, and even the fast bowler pulled up. 'No way man, this is dangerous,' he said. 'I'm going to slow down for a while.'

The Australians were thankful for the hospitality, until McCosker overstayed it by thick-edging Holding to Allen. O'Keeffe recalls the way Holding's pleasure at taking a wicket so decently turned to disbelief when the umpire's finger stayed down and McCosker customarily stayed put.

'Awww, come on umpire,' drawled Holding. No response. 'Heeeey, Riiick.'

McCosker stood there.

'The mood changed in a ball,' says O'Keeffe. 'Holding went back to his long run, came in at a thousand miles an hour and threw in a bouncer. Rick gloved it off the bridge of his nose and, as it lobbed toward gully, I virtually shouted: "Catch it!"'

As the ball fell just beyond reach and his partner called for a single, O'Keeffe's heart sank. 'I hadn't done a thing,' he recalls. 'I'd been very gallant. You can make up the rest. It cut me in half, slammed into my ribs and they just went through us. Because Rick wasn't a walker.'

Fortunately for Hookes when he arrived at number six, a couple of wickets had restored Holding's humanity. His comeback ball from the Jamaican was a slow full-toss on leg stump, which he pushed gratefully to leg for a single. 'Thanks,' said Hookes arriving at the non-striker's end. 'He just smiled,' the batsman says. 'It was the only freebie I got in two seasons.'

'A bush match,' Holding explains. 'If it had been a Test match I wouldn't have done it. I don't believe in playing that sort of cricket too fiercely. Someone might get hurt.'

Ian Chappell knew he'd lost 'a bastard of a toss'. He had Lillee back for the Fifth Supertest on 27 January, but Gloucester Park was airless and the pitch at its best on the first day. Greig put his feet up, watching the scoreboard and the thermometer: temperatures would hit a city record of 42°C.

Barry Richards occasionally failed in such situations. In recent years at Hampshire, he had seemed a speculator among bats-men, dying to dare. But his roommate Knott had already noticed Richards' immersion in WSC's challenge: 'He practised and trained with 100 per cent dedication, always continuing when others had finished. You were always worried that if you agreed to throw and bowl to him in practice you would be there all day, because he just wanted to bat and bat.'

Richards looked a little overdressed at Gloucester Park in a Vellvic globe, but the helmet he'd worn since Rockhampton reflected his attentiveness. 'If I'd been five years younger I may not have both-ered,' he says. 'But I also didn't know what to expect. I realised that this was going to be cricket designed by marketers and it wasn't clear how competitive it would be and, especially, how the pitches would play.'

At Rockhampton he'd discovered the helmet's main drawback. 'I'd grown a beard as an experiment,' he says. 'But when I started sweating in the helmet, it itched like hell. I can't remember how many I got [it was 93], who got me out, anything about the ground, but I remember shaving the next day.'

Richards' Gloucester Park itch was runs. At Hampshire, Richards had also often happily allowed the rising Gordon Greenidge his head; in Perth he unostentatiously reasserted his seniority. Greenidge had carved 51 from 98 balls at lunch, but Richards had 60 from 87. Where Greenidge sought sixes as early as 29, Richards waited until he was 84. Pipping his partner to a century in the same over of Ian Chappell leg-spin, Richards had faced 30 fewer deliveries. Both were 114 when Greenidge began hobbling, complaining of a sore hamstring as he limped off. 'Gordon,' as Ross Edwards observes, 'had a habit of retir-ing when he felt like a bit of a rest.' Barry Richards didn't need one.

Greenidge's departure brought Viv Richards to challenge his nominal rival as batting's brand-leader. 'We had a big problem there,' says Max Walker. 'The papers were asking who was the best batsman in the world? Richards or Richards? Black or white. Barry already had a 100 when Viv got out there so it was clear we weren't gonna get Viv out for much less than 200.'

The South African enjoyed it. It reminded him of partnering Graeme Pollock. 'The main difference,' he observes, 'was that Graeme was always keen for a single at the end of an over. So Graeme'd try to hit five fours and a single every over, while if Viv could hit all six balls of an over for four he would.'

It was no contest. In their hour and a half straddling tea, Viv could manage just 41 to Barry's 93. Effort was sensed only when Barry caned 16 from three deliveries in Bright's thirteenth over: an on-drive for a fourth and final six looked premeditated. 'Never a dull moment that day,' Bright remembers. 'I reckon a few blokes down the order would have been fast asleep waiting for a bat by then.'

Bright bothered them finally at 4.53 p.m., when a miscue to deep mid-off Greg Chappell ended Barry Richards' innings at 207. 'Only someone with Greg's concentration could have caught that,' says the spinner. 'Everyone was on the boundary and they were thinking more about stopping fours and getting the sixes back.' Some 136 of Richards' total had come in boundaries. He had run just one three. Sixty overs up, 1–369, and that would do. He finally removed his helmet.

There was cause for some regret. The long weekend, and the option of watching the Fifth Test televised from Adelaide had left the South African a gallery of just 3150. Not even Packer was there: he'd stayed in Sydney to visit a WSC coaching clinic instead. Instead of revelling in the skills of a personal hero, West Australian captain John Inverarity was a dissatisfied guest. 'It was obviously cricket of a very high standard being played by some very great players,' he says. 'Richards was a favourite of mine but I maintained that his innings lacked any meaning because the result did not matter. The sort of cricket being played was very hollow and I wasn't moved by the experience. The environment was meaningless.'

Blofeld saw the day epitomising cricket's rift instead, peering across Nelson Crescent at the WACA. 'During the match I was able to look out the windows at the back of the press-box and see a club game in progress,' he wrote. 'It only underlined the strong "them and us" feeling which had grown progressively stronger since the WSC matches had begun.' Richards had deserved better but, to a South African, such sensations were familiar.

Tony Greig enjoyed his moment, batting his full card on Saturday as the World pushed on from the overnight 1–433 to 625. The Australian bowlers participated passively in dismissals, between eighty fours and eight sixes.

Max Walker was the unfortunate impediment when Viv Richards' bullet-like hook at 170 zeroed in on him at deep fine leg. 'It would have been six because I took it right on the fence,' he says. 'I tried to get my little finger out of the way but I couldn't, and I couldn't straighten it out after that.' Only when Lillee struck a recoiling Greig on the back of the helmet did the key change. Lillee pointed to his own head meaningfully, drew a sheepish smile from the World captain, then had him caught at cover by Ross Edwards off a woozy drive.

When Greig then prevailed on Greenidge to resume with himself as runner, Ian Chappell startled umpire Duperouzel with the demand that Greig wear his full batting kit. The mild set-to ensuing was broken by a droll Rod Marsh. 'He can't wear his helmet,' said the wicketkeeper. 'It's at the panel beaters.'

The Australian room was a hot, bothered retreat as Ian Davis and Bruce Laird prepared to open. Greg Chappell was nursing a right arm injured in a run-out attempt, Walker's little finger was broken, and concern was growing of widening cracks in the salt-addled surface. Davis was immediately ill at ease. 'The cracks were an inch wide and they looked terrible, although to be fair it probably played easier than it looked. I thought: "How are we going to play on this?"'

Davis did not last Roberts' first over, and just 20 runs came in the first hour as Laird and Kent fell to Imran while Roberts shattered Ian Chappell's finger with a ball leaping from a crevice. Edwards tried to shield his captain for the remaining eighty minutes, moving stoically into line as he was peppered with short bowling.

Edwards drew the day's final over from Roberts and, striving to cover off stump and keep his bat from harm, twice let the Antiguan strike him on the shoulder. 'Christ they hurt,' Edwards recalls. 'But then Andy gave me the perfect ball. It pitched middle and cut in. I was so far to the off it just got round me and hit the top off leg stump'. One bail dropped mockingly. Australia 4–73, its captain in agony, its best batsman lame, 552 the deficit and the follow-on inevitable.

The invalids gave it their all on the Sunday. Ian Chappell's finger, lashed to a steel splint that drew blood as it stabbed his hand, swept at everything Underwood offered. His brother's sore shoulder made him play straighter, and he exploited Greig's cocky attacking field placings.

The skipper was adeptly caught by a cheeky, stooping Garner behind square leg, but Marsh, Gilmour and Bright remained with Greg Chappell for a total of four hours as the batsman set to rights a Supertest average of 26. Two sixes at the tail of his eight-hour 174 were his only frivolities.

Bright and Walker prolonged the chase into Monday, seeking 58 to elude the follow-on as even Greig's off spinners began springing from the cracks. Two flew past the prodding Walker's nose: 'They went shooting over Knotty's head: the worst bouncers I ever had, and Greigy was a blooming off spinner!' They fell 32 from home, a difference the Australians had still to erase an hour later when Kent was their third second-innings wicket.

Ian Chappell could bat no higher than number nine, and Greig's jollity was galling. Bright broods on his first-ball fall: 'Greigy bowled me one of the lovely little offies that didn't turn. I played for the turn, of course, and he knocked my off stump out. It was just about over, but it made me as irate as any dismissal in my career.'

The Australian captain's playing summer was over as he walked in bested by an innings and 73 runs, but he wouldn't go quietly. Kent, whose meek pair had been completed with a tame prod to short leg from Imran, was buttonholed earnestly. 'Ian had a knack of picking the right moment,' Kent recalls. 'He said I had to do a bit of thinking.' What Kent had done, his captain said, was shirk, protecting himself when his wicket was paramount.

The address marked the Queenslander deeply. 'Ian did it all the time. He was always in the front line. Here I was getting a short one and just sticking my gloves up. If I'd taken it in the ribs or the shoulder I wouldn't have been out. I decided I had to be a lot more cautious about preserving my wicket. I mustn't take the easy option.'

But Chappell's main fury was directed at Greig. He confirmed the World as 'the best bunch of cricketers I've seen – with one exception.' At the Sheraton, he even rounded on Packer to complain of Greig's thickness with the businessman. Packer hadn't enjoyed

Australia Day weekend either – what with 13,652 rolling up to his match – but forbore the tantrum. Perhaps he hoped all behaviour in the west had been aberrant.

Greig himself had taken a telephone call at the Sheraton that he'd long expected: Sussex secretary Stan Allen in Brighton informing him, more in sorrow than anger, of the county committee's unanimous vote sacking him as captain. Though just a month had passed since his reappointment, a kaleidoscope of events in Australia, England, Pakistan and Singapore, and Greig's own temper, had made his fall inevitable.

Since late in 1977, Greig, Knott, Woolmer and Underwood had been keeping a friendly eye on the fortunes of former English teammates in Pakistan. Mike Brearley's team similarly sought news of the Australian summer. Whatever their allegiances, cricketers throughout the period remained – like soldiers on opposite sides of barbed wire swapping cigarettes and family photographs – aware of commonality under the skin.

Bob Willis and John Lever, though two of the more determined anti-Packer ideologues, actually sent Derek Underwood a postcard from the spinner's favourite sub-continental cesspit, Hyderabad's Sainjees Hotel. Their dysenteric greetings had heartened Underwood considerably: 'The fact that they'd taken the trouble to drop a line to Deadly, their old teammate, made me realise that there was no direct animosity against me, more animosity against what WSC stood for.'

Their worlds were about to collide. While playing at Orange against the West Indians in the Country Cup on Wednesday 11 January, Imran Khan, Zaheer Abbas and ultimately Mushtaq Mohammad received invitations via Pakistan's Canberra embassy to play in the Third Test at Karachi in a week's time.

Packer 'excused' the players willingly, flying to Singapore with Cornell and Taylor to broker the deal personally with Omar Kureishi, an emissary of the Board of Cricket Control for Pakistan selection panel. Dividing the International Cricket Conference was the route to its conquest: if one board unilaterally readopted WSC players, others would surely follow. Just days before, the ACB had smartly rejected Packer's symbolic offer of players for the pending West Indies tour.

As Mushtaq, Imran and Zaheer left Sydney on the Friday, however, the plot was complicating. English players were in revolt. Mike Brearley, broken arm in plaster after injury in a one-day match, was about to fly home, but made his last act as captain a statement of solid team opposition to the 'Packerstanis'. His deputy Geoff Boycott then attacked WSC signatories as 'have bat, will travel' mercenaries, and their welcome was chill.

'The attitude of baggage handlers was instructive,' wrote Imran, 'As they examined my luggage as if I was carrying gold bars, I heard remarks like: "I'd play for my country for nothing", and it was no use trying to point out that the same applied to me.'

Players mingled suddenly with politicians. British Prime Minister Jim Callaghan, on a state visit to Pakistan, met manager Ken Barrington at Lahore. Pakistan's cricket-dotty strongman General Zia ul-Haq invited Boycott to tea. Riots were foretold if Mushtaq, Imran and Zaheer did not play but, twelve hours from the Test's starting time in a press conference at the Intercontinental Hotel, BCCP president Chaudhury Mohammed Hussain announced he had overruled his selectors. Future selection was to be restricted 'to those available at all times for Pakistan cricket'.

Greig blamed Boycott, bristling at the Yorkshireman's successful seizure of moral ground. 'I saw red,' he wrote. 'It was a case of someone in a very fragile glass house throwing stones.'

Greig had been reprimanded by the Test and County Cricket Board in July 1977 for publicly disparaging the Old Trafford pitch, and honoured promises to Sussex that he would be guarded in future public remarks, but could no longer restrain himself. In his column in Sydney's *Sun,* Greig called Boycott 'the last man in the world who should comment on who he will play against', having 'steered well clear of the game's best fast bowlers for the past five years'.

'Imran Khan was itching to get a crack at Boycott. He's in the same position as Andy Roberts, who has been chasing Boycott for several seasons. It's an incredible fact, but Boycott has never faced Roberts in county cricket. His ability to be where fast bowlers aren't has long been a talking point among cricketers.' (It was a fact, although it was credible: Hampshire's 1974 fixture with Yorkshire was rained out, Roberts had been injured the following year, absent touring with the West Indies in 1976, and Boycott had been batting in his comeback

Test in 1977. Greig might also have noted that Boycott's highest first-class score was an unbeaten 261 for MCC against a President's XI attack in Bridgetown headed by Roberts in 1973.)

Greig received a two-month suspension to go with his sacking. 'He was a very saddened man when I told him,' Allen reported. 'It's a sad day for me too because I like to think of him as a friend. He has done a lot for Sussex cricket.' What had begun as an effort to build a bridge between WSC and the establishment had actually burned another.

11

'It's gotta be the world's most expensive cricket bat'

Tony Henson's meeting with Rod Marsh in the foyer of Sydney's Chateau Commodore on Saturday 4 February 1978 soon became a committee. C & D's engineer had arrived with his first batch of new-fashioned fibreglass helmets, but he and Marsh were quickly surrounded by cricketers and camp followers milling after the Australians' International Cup semi-final defeat of the World at the Showground.

Prototypes were perused and modelled with interest. There was approval for the aesthetic advance. Marsh too, who'd been trying out his own baseball catcher-type variant, liked the fruit of his visit to C & D with Robertson a month before. A *Truth* journalist sidled up to ask the obvious question: would Marsh wear it in a game?

'Naaah,' said the keeper. 'No way.'

Henson shrank, then his eye caught Marsh's wink. 'That was my introduction to Rodney Marsh,' he recalls.

The space-age Vellvic had become more than protective over the season. For many it was a badge proclaiming World Series Cricket's 'otherness'. Bob Simpson had a head born for green baggy felt, Tony Greig one made seemingly for gridiron.

But critics were more divided than cricketers. Barry Richards' argument that head injury was an occupational hazard of his profession had broad appeal. When John Dyson went for a check-up in December 1977, the twenty-three-year-old opener found even his GP in favour. 'What do you think of these helmets?' the doctor asked. 'Do you think you need one?'

When the New South Welshman replied with shibboleths about safety in secure technique, the doctor shook his head: 'You know, it never ceases to amaze me. You guys will spend $4 or $6 on buying a tin or plastic box to protect your nuts, but you won't consider protecting a far more important part of your anatomy. Do you know how vulnerable the temple is?'

'When he spelt it out,' Dyson recalls, 'I couldn't think of any good reason not to wear one. I couldn't get used to the motorcycle helmets in the nets, so I tried wearing a baseball helmet in a club match.' His decision to trial headgear for Randwick against Gordon, and to adopt it in his Sheffield Shield rig was significant. Dyson had been picked for the Second Test in Perth – where Indians Mohinder Amarnath and Chetan Chauhan were also struck, coincidentally on the same day Hookes was flattened – and was using an alien accessory. 'People would give you strange looks and a few bowlers were interested in knocking it off,' Dyson says. 'Though I found that if you made runs against them that shut them up.'

Vellvics had sprouted after the Second Supertest, with Knott, Zaheer, Mushtaq, McCosker and Davis joining the initial trio of Amiss, Greig and Barry Richards as trialists. Says Davis: 'I thought: "If I'm going to be getting four an over at a hundred miles an hour going past my head then the percentages are that I've a fair chance of being hit".'

Even the International Cup was a danger zone and, when the West Indians met the World in a semi-final at the Showground on Friday 3 February, Andy Roberts showed that one-day attack can be the best defence. In 20 balls yielding six runs, Amiss edged him to second slip, Majid and Asif to Murray, Woolmer onto his stumps and Richards could not avoid a riser that Lloyd levitated to snare at first slip.

David Hookes' helmeted half-hour reintroduction to World Series Cricket at the end of a straightforward six-wicket Australian victory saw the team into Sunday's final. Four from Underwood was cheered, six from Mushtaq acclaimed, and a mishit from the former to the latter forgiven.

Hookes, it seemed, had acquired a new significance. Wrote Adrian McGregor: 'Hookes' martyrdom was the greatest service he could have performed WSC. Any suggestion of sham disappeared.' No one seemed to mind the helmet hiding Hookes' blonde locks if, thanks to its protection, they could see him bat.

Mr and Mrs Tony Henson were among 19,000 at the Showground for the International Cup Final: Greg Chappell's Australians against Clive Lloyd's West Indies. A smorgasbord in the VIP area looked inviting when Australia were set a meagre 125, but at that moment Austin Robertson tapped Henson's shoulder. 'Marshy wants to see you,' he said.

With Bruce Laird's hand broken by Imran, Marsh had volunteered to open the Australian innings. He theorised that keepers just off the field should be ideal openers, their eyes attuned to light, line and pace. So when Henson arrived in the Australian rooms, he discovered Marsh padded up, with a cigarette protruding from between peak and visor of a new C & D helmet. 'I wanna wear this out today,' he said simply.

'No way,' said Henson emphatically. 'You can't. This is only a prototype.' It was barely that: little more than a reinforced fibreglass bucket with a flat sheet of clear polycarbonate bent, rather than prestressed, round the front. If Marsh was struck and injured, Henson thought, C & D's name and the whole helmet concept would be mud. But Marsh wouldn't be swayed. Henson returned to the VIP room, appetite lost.

Passing the commentary box on his way, he met Tony Cozier. 'What's wrong Tony?' the West Indian asked. 'You're white as a sheet.'

The distant Marsh and Davis (in his own Vellvic) were walking out to open. Henson explained and, hearing debate in the box about what Marsh was wearing, consoled himself with the thought that at least his helmet truly looked like a cap. He had now to hope it proved more protective.

The Australians wanted to win as quickly as possible; the pitch did reward strokes and Marsh carved about him. Henson, though, felt rather unpatriotic. 'I'm ashamed to say I sat there hoping every ball that Rod would just get out,' he recalls. 'One ball and a serious injury could have put the idea back years.'

He choked a cheer when Marsh holed out to Garner at deep backward square and felt a more appropriate disappointment when Ross Edwards was run out attempting an unwise second on Jim Allen's arm. Then Hookes' arrival stirred all: twice from successive deliveries he swung Roberts for six, his habitual tug of the cap peak now replaced by an adjustment of his visor. Chappell responded with two upright strokes through midwicket, and their 50-stand in thirty-eight minutes left Australia needing 49 from its remaining seven wickets.

But if Hookes' overeager chip to mid wicket Richards dismayed the crowd, it devastated Henson. 'I'd thought my worries were over,' he remembers, 'but then I saw Rob Langer coming out to bat wearing Rod's helmet.'

Langer had long been a potential helmet consumer. Wary of head injury after a schooldays football injury, he had suffered a worrying series of headaches after being struck in the head by Len Pascoe playing Sheffield Shield. Unfortunately, he had been a little over-keen. 'We'd no idea at this stage that there should be different sizes for different players,' Henson explains. 'And Robbie had this huge bonce. His head was as tight as a pea in a pod and he couldn't get it on properly.'

After trying for a couple of overs to adjust the helmet, Langer jettisoned it. His bareheaded hook at Garner was caught behind. After the bowler also trapped Chappell, and had Walters caught from an elderly self-protecting poke, Wayne Daniel removed the Australian tail with the team still shy of 100. There'd been no poetry to the International Cup Final, but much motion.

Capitulation in Canberra's Country Cup Final the next day meant the WSC Australians had now played for $50,000 in a week and come up with less than nothing. Ian Chappell, Bruce Laird and then Gary Gilmour would be convalescents during the Sixth Supertest, and Marsh's nagging knee meant he would probably play as a batsman alone. Rick McCosker, Richie Robinson and Pascoe were called up.

At the fag end of a punishing season on 9 February 1978, VFL Park's pitch was tame but still tricky. As Davis and McCosker settled, Garner struck the former's helmeted head. His only injury was a stiff neck for a few days thereafter, mostly from bearing the new burden.

Davis found some elusive touch, though McCosker – like Chesty Bond behind a vast abdominal pad – still found form elusive. He searched and snicked, but stayed, and looked more secure when injuries to Roberts and Daniel after their summers of endeavour reduced the World's bowling resources.

Greg Chappell's innings in Perth had revived him and he rolled into his strokes fluently. With Tony Greig and Asif Iqbal having to bowl more than 30 overs, batsmen could finally see a way out.

Garner was the greatest menace, his off cutters skidding into Chappell's pads so regularly that their cane shattered. The exposed bone was permanently dented. 'I had a ball-sized indentation in my shin for years after that,' he recalls. 'The wicket was so dicey that you had to be conscious of getting that second line of defence there.'

But luck was finally siding with the Australians. McCosker grafted longer than all his previous innings in toto for 129. By the time he was caught in the gully, Chappell had passed his score and with a carefree Hookes added 152 in less than an hour and a half. The stand-in captain's declaration an hour from stumps on the Friday suspended his 246 in six hours a teasing run short of his highest Test score.

Marsh had decided that his knee was negotiable for keeping, but Lillee – ankle-strapped and wary of the sandpit surface – found his rhythm even more elusive. Just when he didn't need it, Lillee's captain dropped a straightforward chance from Viv Richards when the batsman was four. Ten fours followed in an hour as the bowler's head sank.

Ross Edwards despaired in the covers as Richards demonstrated the martial art of cricket. Lillee was bowling as badly as he'd ever seen him. 'Fot [Lillee] was all over the place,' he recalls. 'Yards too short. And every time he dropped one in, Viv'd hit him over midwicket or over cover. He'd got into the 90s and I was thinking: "For fuck's sake Fot, don't bowl short".'

Lillee did. 'Halfway down,' Edwards recalls. 'Viv pulled it so hard that he kept spinning round and finished up facing cover. And he just looked straight at me and raised his fist.'

Edwards also remembers Richards' fury when a ball from Bright zipped beneath his bat after four and a half hours and trapped him leg-before for 170. 'Christ was he shitty!' Edwards says. 'It was just a little spinner that kept low and he walked off in a real stink. He'd really set himself to beat Greg's score that day.'

The Australian lead of 104 looked too slender when the ball truly began to tunnel. Garner picked out Chappell's shin again to the first ball of his second innings, and the normally introverted Australian rebelled. 'You big bastard,' he shouted at the West Indian. 'You hit me on the shin again and I'm going to come down and hit you with this bat.' When caught cheaply glancing, he was partly relieved to have escaped further denting.

Hookes, though, was in good heart. Almost too good. 'Greg told me off at lunch when I was 15 or 16, because I was playing the same way as I had in the first innings at 3–360,' Hookes remembers. 'He told me it was another day, and to forget about too many shots.' He sobered up in his second half-century of the match, underpinning the Australians' 167.

The 235 runs separating the World from a clean sweep on the last day looked more difficult when Lillee at last salvaged something from the summer. Viv Richards edged his second delivery, first slip Chappell was awake, and the Antiguan's average tumbled to 95.

Still ill at ease, Lillee notified GTV-9's outside broadcast van: would they film his bowling action front-on? After several overs study at lunch, he finally exclaimed: 'Got it!' His arm had not been coming over straight. Reaching tall in the afternoon, he claimed 5–82, and Walker's fifth scalp for 62 banked $33,333 for the Australians. At last.

The summer of 1977–1978 ended with cricket still profoundly split. As WSC concluded in Melbourne drizzle before a damp 2700, Bob Simpson and his fifteen Australians were boarding their airliner in Sydney for three months in the West Indian sun.

Turning forty-two a fortnight earlier, Simpson had felt half his age. After his season's second century, he had taken the last wicket of a picaresque six-day Test against India in Adelaide to clinch a well-contested series 3–2. Simpson bestowed two birthday cakes sent by Indian manager Polly Umrigar on the local children's hospital, as a *This Is Your Life* crew circulated filming tributes to the Australian. 'On those few days in Adelaide,' Henry Blofeld wrote, 'Test cricket needed no legal advocate. It defended itself in a brilliantly coherent and unanswerable way.'

As well as promoting an echelon of young Australians, summer had rehabilitated a few others. In the preceding year, Gary Cosier's marriage had broken up, he had been left behind by colleagues embracing WSC and, while in England, learned that he had lost his job at home after a change of ownership at radio station 5AA.

Jeff Thomson had helped bring Cosier together with his own patron, Brisbane's 4IP. Its $12,500 contract was a lifeline. 'It wasn't big money or anything, and I'd enjoyed my cricket in Adelaide and didn't really want to go,' he says. 'But a job's a job, especially one where I was going to get time off to play.'

Simpson's side was cheerful and exuberant, although its artificiality was evident. 'There were a lot of new faces, and everyone was trying to make a name for themselves,' says vice-captain Craig Serjeant. 'It was a good feeling, although I don't know there was the comradeship of a really close-knit side. You didn't tend to share in the other blokes' successes all that much, because they were competitors.'

Players were projected into roles. Finding himself a senior player, Cosier felt obliged to entertain: 'I was reasonably aggressive anyway, but I kind of felt that perhaps I should be doing something to get these crowds in to watch. Whack a few round.' Though he batted productively, a faulty pull cost him his wicket four times: 'I made runs, but if I'd been smart about it I would have played more patiently.'

John Dyson could not quite feel a 'Test cricketer'. 'It was my first experience of the interstate media and you couldn't help reading what they wrote,' he says. 'People were searching for solutions that summer and all the papers felt that their own state players should be in the team. So I felt every time I went in: "This time I've just got to get a score".'

Unable to break the Indian spinners' line, he batted starchily. 'They bowled well to their close fielders and you got very little loose stuff,' says Dyson. 'Because I couldn't sweep I tended to drive everything on middle and leg to either mid on or mid wicket, and they got wise to that.'

Serjeant traces his pair at the Gabba to idle perusal between innings of a newspaper that unkindly referred to the duck in his last English innings. Trouble duly came in threes. 'I hit my second ball in the middle,' he recalls. 'But, because I was so tentative, it came down on my foot and just rolled back onto leg stump.'

Closer in age to the selectors than to his side, Simpson was a somewhat remote figure, most at home among the young New South Welshmen he'd coached. On the field he was a director rather than a chairman, and disappointed Serjeant by rarely including him in decision-making. 'Obviously there wasn't a lot of need to consult me because we were all pretty young,' he says. 'But you can only learn so much by watching. You can learn a lot knowing what's in a bloke's mind when he's making a decision.'

Nor was Simpson a pacifist. He gave nothing away of his feelings towards the Chappells, and spoke as though they'd been written out of history altogether. When he finally declared his availability for the West Indies on 14 January, Simpson looked forward. 'They need me,' he said. 'There is a need for me to lead this team and to try and achieve what we set out to do – rebuild the Australian team.'

As he thoughtfully ate an ice-cream beneath a WSC sunhat at VFL Park on its season's last day, Packer was aware that he was still building. There were fewer around him than had attended his opening day three months earlier. His six Supertests had attracted an average 5311 people per day to their improvised grounds, compared to the 11,540 drawn daily by Tests ordinaire.

While it had started from scratch, WSC's $3 million loss had been exacerbated by abrupt changes of plan and a schizophrenic attitude to costs. The cricket enthusiasts and Consolidated Press executives running WSC had never been in sympathy. The former, loose in cricket heaven, regarded the latter as dim-witted yes-men. The latter moaned of the former spending all their time watching games rather than running them.

Publicist Chris Forsyth in his contemporaneous *The Great Cricket Hijack* ended up lampooning general manager Vern Stone for 'hard-nosing his way out of tight corners' in 'near total ignorance': 'Little wonder that people involved in planning, administering, conducting and promoting a twelve-week cricket series could scarcely hide their dismay.' But, as Stone found, cricket is rich in coaching texts and poor in accounting manuals. Because of Consolidated Press reservations about WSC, spasms of spending were followed by periods of penitent austerity. Packer would allow John Cornell to spend $49,000 on each WSC advertisement – eight times a standard cost – while Stone was plied with memos from Consolidated Press deputy chairman Harry Chester demanding vigilance and discipline.

Stone couldn't win. When the VIP area cost $17,000 to feed at the First Supertest, Stone and Chester agreed to limit fare at the Second Supertest to open sandwiches. Without warning Packer walked in there with an eight-person entourage including Neville Wran, and enquired when the buffet followed. He was not a happy magnate. Raiding a downstairs wedding reception, Stone's offsider Ern Steet produced the buffet within forty-five minutes. Packer had gone.

WSC had also failed to explain itself promotionally. Accustomed to a century of green-and-gold tradition, cricket fans were unconvinced by the premise that better money improved standards. A widespread sentiment was that Dennis Lillee had bowled for Australia in Tests, but bowled for himself in Supertests.

Some of Forsyth's news releases were almost deliberate baits. His infamous boundary-count after the First Supertest – where he cited the eighty-seven fours and three sixes struck in the game as proof it had been 'memorable and far superior to what went on in Brisbane' – was loudly heckled. Jack Fingleton retorted: 'Chris old chap, fours have not a single thing to do with it, but the fact that the Packer outfit had to put out this particular piece of propaganda is indicative to me.' Because Forsyth was known at Consolidated Press to be writing *Hijack,* however, his eccentricities were indulged.

In the context of the Consolidated Press organisation, however, WSC had been counted out rather wishfully. While ratings figures had been merely respectable and its commentary box had sounded strained in striving to acclaim the talent on display, Packer had enjoyed a harvest of budget local television. Even the equivocation of sponsors and advertisers was not entirely a setback. While critics scoffed at the high proportion of 'in-house ads' for Consolidated Press products like *Women's Weekly* and other television attractions, Packer was actually replicating the strategy of American Broadcasting Corporation's Roone Arledge in the US: after coarsing its coverage of the 1976 Montreal Olympics with program promos, ABC had enjoyed an enormous ratings pay-off.

Indeed, if cricket 'revolution' had not quite occurred, there was patently a television uprising in progress. Producer David Hill, red phone at his side connecting him to a superintending Packer, had spent his $1.4 million adroitly. With eight cameras and rich replay resources, he had shocked, irritated and eventually intrigued viewers used to a reverent distance.

John Crilly and Brian Morelli had spent hours explaining to rookie cricket cameramen that a call for 'umpire' did not mean the one at square leg, and that 'batsman' meant the man on strike. Videodisc jockeys needed to know that replaying dismissals demanded only the frames either side of a disintegrating wicket, catch or lbw shout, not the tale from the top of the bowler's run to the arrival of the new batsman. Although they had resisted David Grant's boundary interviews, the players had adapted to pitch microphones. On one occasion, Gary Gilmour had even used them to communicate with twelfth man Ray Bright. When Bright's attention proved hard to attract one cold day early in the season, Gilmour had leant to the bottom of the stumps to advise: 'Brighty, do you think you could send a jumper out before a man freezes to death?'

Snug in condoms for protection, the microphones had given a new, sometimes blue, perspective on the game. 'The count for the first season was something like 13 shits, 14 you bastards, three fucks and one cunt that got on the air,' Crilly recalls. 'We were still learning and a few people were a bit slow with the faders.'

WSC's techniques gingered even the ABC. The national broadcaster began filming tosses and roving with a backpack cameraman, for whom it unsuccessfully sought permission to accompany twelfth men onto the field for drinks breaks.

WSC did need the crowds. While gate takings had a lesser role for corporate cricket, people meant popularity and share of public imagination. Crowds would ratchet up ratings, and finally dictate advertising support. But while Tests had bested Supertests at the gate, comparisons tended to distort the relative strength of the Australian Cricket Board. WSC had been at the obvious handicap of exile to non-cricket grounds, and it was already apparent that this was temporary. Among Packer's guests at the Sixth Supertest was Queensland's Sports Minister: the Gabba's arms had been opened.

Packer knew that WSC could never reproduce Test tradition. In fact, he resisted efforts to try. Stone recalls his employer's scandalised response to the idea of green WSC caps resembling the official lid: 'Listen son, you've gotta earn those.' Absence of antiquity, however, held an advantage. WSC's only loyalty was to itself. There was, in the end, no need to stage any match in Adelaide if it lost money. Even Supertests were dispensable if uneconomic. WSC could concentrate on venues and variants of the game that had greatest commercial logic.

Almost 60,000 had attended four mid-week night matches, which cohered with leisure statistics showing rising attendances at after-hours entertainments like trotting and greyhound racing, and crowds shrinking at football and horse racing. As sports historian Shayne Quick concluded: 'By the end of WSC's first domestic season, it was obvious where its future success lay; with a different style of cricket and a different breed of fan.'

The ACB's outlook was therefore bleaker than was recognised. Neither WSC nor the ACB was going to make serious money from a single-product market now split by competition. The new domestic duopoly had slashed ACB takings for five Tests to less than $400,000, compared to $1.13 million from six in 1975–1976. And on that money, plus the largesse of Benson and Hedges and the ABC, the board had to subsidise Australian cricket root and branch. WSC's losses were offset by its television value, and it was not obliged to sustain money-burners like a Sheffield Shield. The true toll of the International Cricket Conference's High Court misadventures also emerged when chairman David Clark and secretary Jack Bailey visited Australia on a global jaunt in January. They advised the ACB and brother boards that they were already saddled with $350,000 in legal costs and faced finding more if they decided to appeal. Nobody felt litigious.

The ACB's Test match summer had ended in Adelaide on an apparent upswing. It had done everything right and WSC had done a lot wrong. But that was the problem. The board could not afford to falter, and WSC had a whole winter to prepare itself for the 1978–1979 season.

Packer was not about to blink. As he told the 170 players and guests at WSC's break-up bash at Lazar's in Melbourne, their organisation was planning to grow. 'There will never be a shortfall of cash,' he said. 'The only thing that will stop us is a lowering of the standard of cricket . . . We were amateurs this year. Next year we're going to do it properly.'

The players had been well paid for their loyalty. In addition to the $1.3 million in salaries distributed, winner-take-all prize money of more than $200,000 ($78,375 to the West Indies, $61,700 to the Australians and $61,425 to the World) had been deposited in a trust for tax-efficient dispersal after three years.

Touring life could also be a money-spinner. Meal allowance was based on three square Old Melbourne feeds – a $7.15 breakfast (juice, cornflakes, omelette, toast, coffee), a $9.70 lunch (seafood cocktail, soup, steak, apple pie, coffee) and identical dinner – and distributed on all days. Dressing-room lunches during playing days put $10 in your pocket. Patronise the regular cocktail evenings and receptions, and one could bank a tad more.

But loyalty towards 'The Boss' was not entirely a bought one. A curious fondness and mutual awe had evolved, born of Packer's affinity for sporting champions and the cricketers' rudimentary understanding of business.

Packer had been everywhere, joining practices, mowing outfields, opening his house to players who made use of his tennis court and swimming pool. He even tolerated Hookes' jibe when he visited: 'Here comes the big capitalist.' One of Packer's few role models – aside from his father and Genghis Khan – was William John Smith alias Gunboat. A Sydney trade unionist turned financier and industrialist – the architect of Australian Consolidated Industries – he wrote at his plutocratic peak: 'The world goes well with me. I direct industry on a vast scale . . . I have no trouble with labour. Men who have grown up with me in the industry call me "Bill" and I call them by their Christian names. I know every man in our works.' Packer's works were screens and fields, but he sought the same satisfaction.

It was an odd rapport. Packer's teetotalism caused him some discomfiture and – placing Jack Nicklaus on a professional pedestal – he could never completely come to terms with his cricketers' eccentric, superstitious ways. But his familiarity was far removed from the ACB's slightly patronising paternalism. Packer was younger than Bob Simpson. A 1970s man. 'I thought he was a great guy,' says Gilmour. 'He'd eat with us, drink with us, come to practice and bowl to you and dive round the field. He was a sportsman really, a competitor. If he'd played marbles, he would've had World Series Marbles.' And while he swore round his players, he was unaffectedly sweet with their partners. Ross Edwards' wife Lyndall remembers Packer crossing the floor at a Perth dinner to introduce himself. 'I should just like to tell you,' he said, 'how well your husband acquitted himself in court in London.'

Appreciative Australians had wondered what to offer The Boss' at Lazar's in farewell. 'What do you give the guy who's got everything?' recalls Max Walker. 'You can't give him a silver cigarette case. He's probably got a gold one. So we went for the old autographed cricket bat.' Packer seemed genuinely moved. 'You probably don't understand how much I'm going to treasure this,' he said. 'It's gotta be the world's most expensive cricket bat. I've put $2.9 million into this bat and you guys, so far, and I want to thank every one of you. It'll never leave my side.'

On behalf of the West Indies, Rudi Webster presented Packer with a premonitory gift: an elaborate voodoo doll. For Packer had always wanted to see some cricket in the islands of the Caribbean.

12

'Simmo bring down a shit side'

Some hex was on Craig Serjeant on the gloomy Friday morning of 3 March 1978. Expecting to spend the First Test at Queen's Park on substitute duties, he learned at the Trinidad Hilton that he would be replacing Rick Darling as Graeme Wood's opening partner. Darling was a nervous kid, who often walked to the centre from a pavilion toilet. But his retching ritual had begun the night before and he was unfit to play.

Dismay filled the team when it arrived at the ground. Their unlockable dressing-room had been ransacked. Serjeant's missing Gray-Nicolls bat was discovered half-way down a toilet. 'Hey Serj,' came a voice. 'Your bat's in the dunny.'

His captain, meanwhile, had returned from the centre cursing. Aware of the eccentricities of Caribbean curation, Simpson had been unconcerned the day before when told by the *Australian*'s Phil Wilkins that the Queen's Park groundsman was hosing his pitch. But the combination of watering with an inclement morning had now made mud of the pitch square.

Respectful of Trinidad's tradition of turn, Australia had included spinners Jim Higgs and Bruce Yardley. But the only spin important that day was the coin. Clive Lloyd won it. The West Indies would bowl.

Hoping for a prolonged delay, Serjeant spent the morning pressing the water from his bat as ground staff mopped up the oval. Surely at worst he would not be batting until late afternoon. But then came the final curse: the umpires wanted one over prior to the 12.30 p.m. lunch. It actually became one over during lunch, for it was 12.32 p.m. by the time the last of the ground staffs tackle was removed and Wood looked up to see Andy Roberts at the end of his run.

The *Sunday Times'* Robin Marlar described the match in his report as 'the one over Test'. Wood barely had time to raise a protective arm as his first ball rebounded from a length, and gladly scuttled a single as the ball glanced fine. Serjeant's first ball struck the same length, took a piece from the pitch and clipped his bat's shoulder en route over keeper Deryck Murray's head. Murray was again a spectator as the fourth ball soared over Wood, bounced again and eluded capture. Serjeant sat down at the break with the score 0–6 feeling far older than twenty-six.

The misfortunes of Bob Simpson's team began, literally, on the runway. Landing in New York after a San Francisco stopover, manager Fred Bennett discovered that direct flight to St John's in Antigua was impossible because of a pilots' strike at Caribbean carrier BWIA. Squeezing aboard the only available transport, a chartered nineteen-seat Primair Heron, the Australians fidgeted for half an hour on the tarmac while the pilot tried to start the aircraft with jumper leads.

Five hundred steel bandsmen helped the airsick Australians attune to the local vibrations, as did their tour opener against the Leeward Islands. There were no practice wickets, an unusable centre wicket and an impossible outfield. Simpson then noticed that local boy Jim Allen was ingenuously wearing his World Series Cricket outfit. Coalitions of environment and allegiance would haunt his team for the next three months.

Having abided the International Cricket Conference embargo under protest, the West Indies Cricket Board of Control had welcomed the High Court mandate of free selection. Public sympathy, it had discovered, was firmly with WSC. As the schools blended, though, there was genuine debate about which played the superior cricket. Strangely, considering they had dominated the elite WSC,

Lloyd's team had as much to prove as Simpson's youngsters. After all, England had embarrassed a mostly WSC Australian team, while Simpson's combination had a fine series victory to their credit. Tony Cozier recalls:

> The English press was in such a state of confusion that they were actually writing that Australia was better now that Chappell and his players were out of it. And, because people were going to such extremes to rubbish WSC, there would have been strong reaction if Simpson did even reasonably well. Lloyd's team wanted to win as convincingly as they could to settle the argument.

Relations between the WICBC and its WSC players, however, were strained. The board was embarrassed that it was powerless to prevent WSC signatories wearing their Packer kit. Snarled communications showed from the first one-day international: Collis King was picked though still in Australia, Alvin Kallicharran omitted when thought to be in Australia but actually in Guyana. It happened that no one shone in the game more brightly than a spunky twenty-two-year-old Bajan called Desmond Haynes, whose breakneck 148 contained a century in boundaries. His eagle eye had Wilkins calling him 'just about the most beautiful piece of batting merchandise not signed by Kerry Packer'.

The Australians also clapped bats for the first time on the now-feted Joel Garner and the less-heralded Guyanese fast bowler Colin Everton Hunte Croft, each of whom took three cheap wickets. Garner they'd seen from afar in Australia, but Croft was something else again: a crazy contraption of arms unwinding from the extremities of the popping crease and following through with a homicidal glare. Two sixes from Cosier in a brave 84 saved some face, but the game proved a mismatch.

As the beaten Australians warmed up for the First Test at Port-of-Spain with a game against Trinidad, a third factor got on Simpson's nerves. Four Australians were left wondering how they'd been given out, a scoreless Serjeant so far down the wicket when adjudged lbw that he was almost run out by short leg. 'As I passed Graham Yallop he was laughing his head off,' he says. 'It was easy for him. He had 60-odd.'

As far as Simpson was concerned, it would also have been fitting had Douglas Sang Hue – an umpire in Australia for WSC – been wearing its badge during the game. Having thought highly of the umpire in 1965, Simpson would write: 'In this match he revealed a different temperament and seemed to be trying to exert his authority in matters which were not his concern.'

Kim Hughes then succumbed to appendicitis, and only Wayne Clark's iron constitution proved immune to local food and water. At least Australia's win against the locals suggested that Queen's Park *would* be a 'Port-of-Spin', and the West Indies selected their own novice off-breaker for the rubber's first match. But the twenty-three-year-old from the speck of Nevis, Derick Parry, would not relieve Roberts, Garner and Croft until Australia's second innings was well under way.

Serjeant's bat could have stayed down the toilet for all its industry at the crease. 'I batted sixty-three minutes for three singles,' he recalls. 'I was just concentrating on playing down the line and protecting my stumps so it didn't matter how much I played and missed.' When he finally did touch Croft to Murray, Australia had added 10 to its lunch score in 13 overs for the loss of Wood and Yallop, and Australia was 4–23 when Simpson was late on Garner's inswinger. Peter Toohey and Gary Cosier interjected, but the former's willingness to hook aroused the lurking Roberts.

'I liked the hook,' Toohey says. 'But I didn't play it particularly well. My footwork wasn't good enough and I didn't stay side-on.' That was sufficient to dispatch Roberts' 'sucker ball' safely, but its sinister sequel went straight into Toohey's forehead. Patrick Eagar's famous photograph catches the kneeling batsman trying to wipe the blood from his face with a handkerchief, while an attendant Vivian Richards stands, hand aloft, signalling the dressing-room like a para-medic signalling 'man down'. The batsman's bloody hand prints stained twelfth man Trevor Laughlin's shirt as he was assisted off.

Toohey remembers the tableau. 'I was conscious the whole way through,' he says. 'Although I was in a bit of state of shock I can remember being propped on the dressing-room table while this local doctor stuck three stitches in my head without an anaes-thetic.' Watching Cosier's lone hand – ninety minutes of back-foot slashing – Toohey resolved to resume if the batsman was still there when the eighth wicket fell.

Cosier was surprised by Toohey's reappearance at 84. 'They'd patched him up, poor bloke,' he says. 'It was like sending a wounded man back to the battle front.' Toohey struck a defiant three and a two but Garner yorked him, and next over Cosier slashed his last. He'd sensed Gordon Greenidge slipping back behind point as Croft approached, but gambled he would clear the fielder and only just failed. That was the way of it. Greenidge and Haynes had the West Indies within a dozen runs of Australia's 90 by stumps, the beamish boy pulling Thomson and Higgs for sixes in his 53.

Toohey had almost forgotten a miscellaneous blow on his thumb but, back at the Hilton, it wouldn't stop aching. 'It gave me hell that night,' he recalls. 'When I woke up the next morning it was blue and I knew it was broken.'

Down to nine of its original eleven, Australia needed greater dividend from Jeff Thomson's testing spell than umpire Sang Hue granted. Then Lloyd seemed to have snicked Wayne Clark to Steve Rixon, but Sang Hue again was unmoved. 'Lloydy had got his gloves off and was about three or four paces away from the wicket,' says Cosier. 'He must have seen us coming from slip, saying Sang Hue had to be joking, because he turned around and just walked back as though nothing had happened.'

Lloyd added 164 with Kallicharran, milking the leg spin of Higgs and Simpson, who bowled long spells in curious preference to off spinner Bruce Yardley. Lloyd flogged his rival captain over long-on for six in a run-a-minute romp on the second afternoon. Thomson finally broke the stand with the first ball after tea, and the Australians worked hard to restrict their eventual deficit to 315.

With five batsmen to last the best part of three days, though, Simpson received further bad news. Clark had been carrying a back injury since Adelaide and picked up an involuntary jerk in his quicker ball that Sang Hue suspected was a throw. Sang Hue also disliked Yardley's bent elbow. He told WICBC president Jeff Stollmeyer that he would no-ball both if he found himself at square leg when they were bowling.

For Simpson, this was the 'dizzy limit'. Clark and Yardley would have to bowl from Sang Hue's end for the rest of the tour. The captain and manager Bennett refrained from telling the team. Morale was already frail. Toohey had wanted to bat on during the first day, but now he had to be talked out of wanting to go home. Kim Hughes was staying only because he was too ill to travel. As Phil Wilkins summarised: 'The boys are growing up fast in the West Indies. It is that sort of cricketing hotbed where international newcomers, wet behind the ears on arrival, grow old and a little grey overnight.'

Batting on the third day had a martyred air. Wood was concaved by a blow in the groin, and Serjeant's ribs buffeted as the pair fought their way to 59 within sight of lunch. Then Wood was obviously lbw to Roberts, and Serjeant less obviously to Garner.

Having begun the match in a toilet, Serjeant's bat ended it in a door. Silence fell and Simpson's admonitory look told all. Bennett told Serjeant he would have to apologise to the ground authorities . . . after his aching ribs were X-rayed.

Yallop, his father Aub watching in the pavilion, negotiated most of the afternoon with Cosier and an hour after tea with Simpson. But the West Indies lowered the boom after the Victorian's defeatist drive at 194 and the last seven sold themselves for a feeble 15. Wilkins picked up the Mighty Sparrow's jeering calypso: 'Oh dear, what can the matter be, Simmo bring down a shit side.'

The barbs hurt Simpson, who prescribed hard graft for Bridgetown. His disenchantment turned to anger when he returned with Cosier and Thomson from a wreath-laying pilgrimage to the Cave Hill grave of Sir Frank Worrell: his young team were discovered skylarking in their Kensington Oval dressing-room instead of practising.

Simpson exploded. 'They were still in the dressing-room pissing about and they should have been out there,' Cosier recalls. 'But I'd never heard an Australian team given a rocket like this one. Greg had got up us once in Christchurch about our fielding in a Test match, and we went out and played really well after it. But Simmo blasted the shit out of them, called 'em every name he could think of.'

Heads fell. Yallop recalls: 'I think the only reason we were in the rooms was that the practice facilities were so bad. We would have had some fielding practice, hit the ball against the fence like we usually did, and then gone back to the rooms. He just came back at the wrong time. It was crazy going on the way he did. It got a few backs up.'

A requested reinforcement, Queenslander David Ogilvie, arrived after a thirty-five-hour flight and was rushed straight into the tour match against Barbados. But his presence in Bridgetown would not prove as influential as those of two other Australians: Austin Robertson and Consolidated Press lawyer Malcolm Turnbull.

World Series Cricket's agents had come at the behest of Deryck Murray. He and Lloyd had noticed the tension of their dealings with the WICBC and, after the First Test, had received an ultimatum: the WSC West Indians had a fortnight to announce availability for the country's tour of India in November. Stollmeyer had immediately denied that WSC players would be sacked from the Test side, although Lloyd just as swiftly explained his men's loyalties: they would forfeit their Test places if necessary to honour their Australian contracts.

Robertson's presence in dressing-rooms no longer passed unremarked. Stollmeyer extracted verbal undertakings from Haynes, Kallicharran, Croft, Parry and Richard Austin – the five at Kensington Oval not in Packer pay – that they would not sign anything with WSC's name on it. The Test match proceeded with disquiet in both teams: the Australians on trial, the West Indies on guard.

WSC Supertests began as imitation Test matches, but the first day at Bridgetown showed that currents were flowing both ways. Graham Yallop became the first Test batsman to adopt a helmet – one of two flown in before the Test – as waves of fast bowling swept in with tidal inevitability. Batting conditions were good, but the end of Yallop's composed 92-run stand with Wood seemed to rob the rest of the order of its resolve. Five wickets fell in 44 runs, and Bruce Yardley was left to rebuild.

Yardley, a thirty-year-old off spinner, had crawled from the crack in the cricket world. A West Australian medium pacer who'd played just one 1966 Sheffield Shield game, Yardley had gradually reinvented himself as a spinner-batsman. Giving the ball more overspin than side-spin with an unconventional grip, he relied on bounce and trajectory for his wickets. A customised batting technique meant he rarely avoided arrest too long but almost never came quietly. Success in the Sheffield Shield and the absenteeism of rivals turned him, in eighteen months, into a Test player.

Kensington Oval reminded him of home at the WACA, where anything short tended to clear the stumps and rewarded the slasher. A square cut soared over a disbelieving deep point for six, a reflex pull off the bridge of the nose flew for another. The crowd were enchanted when Yardley drove fearlessly as Garner overpitched, and even happier when the bowler hit the retreating batsman on the elbow, then the throat, then the toe.

Fair enough, Yardley thought. 'They were young, they were keen and I was going for them. But when I got hit in the elbow I thought my whole arm was gone . . . and I can't have been thinking too straight because the next ball I tried to hook. It hit me in the throat.'

Colin Croft's beamer brought an apology from Lloyd at slip, but no other pardons were begged. Yardley's half-century came in fifty-one minutes. Next ball he was dropped by Croft at third man. 'I did think about retiring,' he says. 'I thought: "You know, I've improved my average here, maybe it's time to get out of the way".' But he didn't for an hour and a half and his 74 came out of 89 before Garner produced a yorker to end the Australian innings at 250.

The crowd's buzz had not faded when Jeff Thomson took the new ball for a spell straight from his salad days. While he was a reluctant tourist who seemed to spend most of his spare time on the phone to wife Cheryl, a blow in the ribs from Roberts seemed to spur him. For the first time in the fifteen months since his shoulder injury, he rediscovered his old, lethal geometry.

When his third ball cracked across Greenidge's knuckles and rebounded to Serjeant at gully, the Australians seemed to have the break they needed. But Greenidge stood his ground and umpire Steve Parris was silent. Disgust deepened as the batsman requested ice for his bruised and shaking hand. Thomson would not be denied, however, and had the opener caught at slip by Cosier in his next over via glove and chest.

Viv Richards' magisterial entrance raised the tempo further. Thomson's yorker had surely to be lbw, but Parris shook his head again as Richards hobbled to one side. A spiteful bouncer top-edged must be a catch, but substitute Trevor Laughlin dropped the waist-high chance on the run. When a riser hit his shoulder, Richards almost rubbed it. 'I've been fortunate enough to see some fast bowling in my time, but that was incredible,' Cosier says. 'There was no way Viv was going to stick around while that was going on.'

Richards' response was a form of West Indian roulette. As Thomson no-balled stretching further, the Antiguan essayed a pull shot, off-balance, but four. A hook, full-blooded, and six into the stand behind square leg followed, then a hairy back-foot drive over the bowler's head. At last came a priceless second glimpse of the Antiguan's wicket. The miscued hook hung over Laughlin forward of square and Clark behind as the crowd stomped and whistled.

'Thommo had taken a bit of tap but he'd really taken Viv on,' recalls Clark. 'When the catch came I wasn't sure whether Trevor should go for it or me because he was quite close. In the end I made a late decision and had to dive.' He hit the ground as the ball hit his hands, but the catch stuck. Richards had been dethroned, and Thomson completed the coup with the day's final ball. Kallicharran edged a ball into his thigh pad that, as verification of its pace, rebounded all the way to a tumbling Yardley at backward square leg. The fast bowler sagged exhausted into his corner of a dressing-room that, for the first time, felt like celebrating.

It was too good to last. Thomson's calf muscle played up after three overs next morning, and Haynes, Lloyd and Murray thrived in his absence. By the time Thomson had returned and served a sentence passed by umpire Ralph Gosein for time off the ground, the West Indies were 13 ahead with four wickets in hand. Thomson crankily kicked the stumps when Yardley's slack return cost a run-out, and he flung a V-sign at the hooting 14,000.

While Thomson was able to limit Australia's deficit to 38 with three further wickets, the Australians were in distress by day's end. Wood alone, with a second half-century, passed 20 in their 5–96 and three-day defeat loomed. Simpson, what's more, had apparently ducked the issue by dropping to number seven. Mutters at his 'stand back and slice' methods on the first day grew when first Cosier then Rixon were sent out ahead of their captain.

Simpson's poise against India's spinners had been universally admired, but his decision to tour the West Indies was a brave one.

Reflexes did not return. 'At home he'd been a great enough player to get away with batting against India,' says Cosier. 'Kicking them away with his pad, flicking 'em round the corner. But while he'd faced Hall and Griffith in the West Indies in 1965, there hadn't been another Hall and Griffith coming after them.' As Rixon emerged as night-watchman a full half-hour before stumps, sections of the crowd seethed: 'Come on Simmo, come on and have a bat, man. They kill you man, they kill you.'

The Australian rooms were tense, especially the West Australians. 'He was a recognised batsman, certainly more competent than Rixon,' Serjeant says. 'What he did was wrong. There was no justification.' Adds Clark: 'It didn't help the relationship. Someone needed to set an example and that was a case where the captain could have done it. That had an effect on the long-term thinking of a few of the guys and it wasn't positive.'

Even the loyal Toohey noticed the fallout. 'It cost Simmo a bit of esteem in the team and he really hadn't been getting on with some in the side already,' he says. 'The guys from WA were pretty cliquey over there, and I think they felt that Simmo favoured the eastern staters in the team.'

Rixon, however, bought Simpson just ten minutes. The captain came out – in the words of John Benaud in the *Age* – as 'a victim of his own tactical ploy'. 'Simpson,' he wrote, 'is simply unable to cope with the pace, and his dithering, especially in the first innings, is diluting the other batsmen's confidence and stroke play.' Benaud refrained from asking if Simpson merited his place in the team but, when he fanned at Roberts' leg cutter the next morning, the captain's series contribution was 40 runs and 1–95.

Only Yardley, Wood and Thomson could salvage much from the West Indies' nine-wicket win. At his post-match press conference, Simpson pleaded for the Australian public to be 'tolerant for a while, because we are going through a new era'.

Robertson and Turnbull, meanwhile, had completed a quiet Test hat-trick: the signatures of Desmond Haynes, Colin Croft and the twenty-three-year-old all-rounder Richard Austin. Robertson even partook of the West Indies' champagne for another win inside three days. Jeff Stollmeyer was dismayed, given both the promises of the new defectors and Test pay rises to which the WICBC had agreed in Trinidad. Unlike Robertson, he now felt 'like a stranger in the West Indies' dressing-room'.

Deryck Murray's request for deferral of the WICBC availability deadline so as to discuss some Pax Packerana freeing players for India sounded like hubris. When 23 March 1978 brought silence, the WICBC realised that its bluff was being called: did they dare sack WSC men?

The answer Lloyd received on Easter Sunday evening at Georgetown's Pegasus Hotel, when he joined selectors Joey Carew, Jackie Holt and Clyde Walcott to pick the team for the Third Test at Bourda, took him unawares. The West Indian captain was optimistic when he met a friend in the lobby wondering if he'd be free later, and surprised when Carew chimed in: 'No, this could be a long session.'

In a rather messy equivocation, Lloyd's co-selectors had resolved to drop Haynes, Austin and Murray. Lloyd went hoarse with protest and, as he left the meeting at 3 a.m., gave in his resignation. Given that his team would almost certainly follow en bloc, the WICBC now faced going into a Test match nine men short. It was a double bluff.

'The public was overwhelmingly in favour of Packer,' comments Tony Cozier. 'But the board had a pretty sound case for what it was doing. In fact they should probably have sacked the whole side straight out.'

The Australians were unaware of events as they recuperated at the Pegasus themselves that evening, after the second day of a warm-up game against Guyana at Bourda. Concern was for Yallop, nursing a jaw broken in the match by Croft, who would now be missing from the Test as well as Toohey and Hughes.

And Croft kept them occupied next day, knocking Yardley cold when the off spinner danced into a leg-stump bouncer after a feisty 37. 'Bruce must have been crazy,' recalls partner Cosier. 'He got Croft away and walked down the pitch calling him a chucker: "Keep your arm straight, Crofty, keep your arm straight". Bruce was virtually on the uncut grass when he got hit in the back of the head, and Crofty actually did pretty well to find him.' Unable when he regained consciousness to remember how he'd needled Croft so

effectively, Yardley asked Alvin Kallicharran. But the little lefthander
just laughed: 'Bruce, you got what you deserved.'

Off-field events were about to envelope both. A resignation statement from Lloyd that he'd drafted with Guyana's sports minister
Shirley Field Ridley was circulating at the Pegasus. Yardley was
addressing the new West Indian captain.

At 11 p.m. on Wednesday 29 March, the famous Guyanese advocate
Sir Lionel Luckhoo asked his distinguished Australian dinner guests
if they could take to their carriages. Having beaten the BWIA strike
and arrived in Georgetown, Stollmeyer and WICBC secretary Peter
Short were on their way to his home for a private meeting.

When Simpson arrived back at the Pegasus with Fred Bennett and
the ABC broadcaster Alan McGilvray, he learned why: the other five
WSC players – Greenidge, Richards, Roberts, Garner and Croft –
had boycotted the Test. 'I knew,' he wrote, 'that all hell was about to
break loose.'

That was the WICBC's fear, and Stollmeyer wanted Luckhoo's
reassurance that Guyana, the poorest quarter of the West Indies
and Lloyd's birthplace, would accept his board's firm anti-Packer
front. Reservists for Kallicharran to lead were being spirited into
Georgetown independently to avoid problems with the air strike.
How would the Guyanese take to two virtual second XIs playing in
Friday's Test?

Gnawing at their nerves was news that Packer himself was
Georgetown-bound by private jet with WSC's West Indian manager
Rudi Webster. Luckhoo advised them that it was a case that *alea
jacta est:* to cancel the Test would be riskier than proceeding. When
Packer finally held a press conference at the Pegasus the following
evening, it was an epilogue to Stollmeyer's announcement of a new
West Indian side. The Australian painted the WICBC as intransi-
gent, while Lloyd complained of the clandestine arrangements for
the reserve side. But as Cozier observes: 'Lloyd and the WSC players
were really the last people who should have complained about sharp
practice. They had simply been trumped.'

Packer in fact was in transit. He had organised a weekend at
Bridgetown's opulent Sandy Lane Hotel for the whole WSC West
Indian family: Lloyd, Webster, players, wives and girlfriends, the

Sobers, plus Lloyd's cousin Lance Gibbs. Keen to colonise the Caribbean with a WSC tour, he gladhanded in Barbados and Jamaica, appearing on television and talking to newspapers. He even autographed dollar notes: a local custom suggesting that WSC would not be unwelcome.

Although a virtual armoured division of riot police shepherded team buses to Bourda on Friday, their presence was needless. A spectator boycott of the Test urged by WSC sympathisers meant that patrons were almost outnumbered by paramilitaries.

As an even Test match unfolded, the Australians glimpsed how the overwhelming majority of West Indian cricketers lived. There was a dangerous opener schooled on Jamaica's sugar cane fields, Basil Williams, nicknamed 'Shotgun' for his arsenal of off-side strokes. The Australians called him the 'death or glory man'. A slight twenty-four-year-old left-hander in ageing, buckskin pads from Port-of-Spain, Larry Gomes, was just as hard to bowl to. 'Pitch it up anywhere near straight and he would hit you through mid wicket,' recalls Serjeant. 'Any width outside off and he'd cut. The margin for error was minuscule and he was so disciplined. We used to say: "This bastard doesn't play like a West Indian".'

Both made centuries, and a brace of half-centuries came from local off spinner Sew Shivnarine, known as 'Blackjack' for his pigment and personal drapery in gold. Pitched into Tests after four matches for Barbados, muscle-bound twenty-three-year-old Sylvester Clarke honoured the traditions of Caribbean speed. The weird windmills of Dominican Norbert Phillip were a useful complement.

At the end of the third day, in fact, Kallicharran's men were in charge: the Australians needed 359 to win in the remaining two days, and were ailing. Strikes in Georgetown had reduced the Pegasus to a ghetto, without electricity, without lifts and with water available only by bucket from wagons. Players stumbled round its stifling sixteenth floor – known as the 'casualty ward' for its occupation by the ill and injured – bent double with dysentery. A dip in the pool with its inoperative chlorinator risked cholera. 'You couldn't flush the toilets,' remembers Cosier, 'the pool was green, there was no ice in the bar, all you had was warm Coke. The only thing that worked was McGilvray's scotch bottle. That worked pretty well. Killed a few germs.'

That the phones also worked was a blessing for Clark, whose wife was expecting a child any day. Roommate Serjeant, facing a pair on the Tuesday, had a sleepless preparation while the fast bowler kept a hotline open to Perth.

Rick Darling, David Ogilvie and Simpson had been undone by Clarke's bounce for 22 when Serjeant joined the obdurate Wood in the ninth over, and he also popped his second ball to short leg's right. It did not go to hand. 'Although I hadn't made runs in the Tests,' he says, 'I hadn't really felt out of form. All I needed was one break. That half-chance might have been it, because I could see the conditions were good. It was getting hotter and, if you got one through, the outfield was like lightning. I batted an hour before lunch and got 17 and I thought: "Strike. This is it, I've got a real chance here".'

Fielders flapped as he and Wood flitted eighty singles. The flux of left and right-hander upset inexperienced bowlers. Wood passed his fourth consecutive no-frills Test half-century, and at the tea score of 3–199 was nine from a maiden Test hundred. Serjeant cooled his heels on 80.

Serjeant left his partner standing after tea: three consecutive boundaries brought up the right-hander's century in three and a half hours. After three overs on 99, Wood finally cut Holder to the fence. It took the second new ball and a brilliant catch of Serjeant on the deep fine leg fence to end their 268-minute, 251-run partnership.

But two wickets fell in the last twenty minutes after a break for bad light, and Cosier – wearing one of the Vellvic helmets for the first time – discovered why Yallop kept custody of the other. 'When I pulled the visor down there was a bloody great scratch across where your eyes were. No wonder Graham only used the other one.' A tangle of bat, gloves and pads, he was bowled playing back. And Wood, after a consummate display of running, responded fatally to Rixon's call in the day's last over. The Test debutant Trevor Laughlin faced the next day with Rixon with 69 runs needed. Reclining at the Pegasus, Serjeant tested the Victorian's nerve. 'Well, Larry,' he said, 'the entire future of Australian cricket is in your hands tomorrow.'

'Thanks Serj,' said Laughlin.

Simpson hadn't missed a ball of Australia's 1960–1961 series against the West Indies, but saw nothing bar his team's winning runs the following day. 'I've never known a Test to be so desperate,' he explained. 'We had to win or the tour wasn't worthwhile any more . . . but just as importantly it was vital for the players themselves. Some of them on thresholds of careers were facing the possibility they wouldn't play Test cricket any more.'

Rixon was nerveless. Laughlin failed only in his sober prod of a return catch from Parry's full toss, but Yardley advanced on the target with typically bold strokes. With scores tied, he pulled a gleeful boundary. Wayne Clark became a father. A hex had lifted.

13

'Sweet reason'

Andrew Caro looked around cautiously as he checked in to the Trinidad Hilton on Sunday 16 April 1978. Bob Simpson's Australians were also guests ahead of the ensuing Fourth Test, but the mission of World Series Cricket's new managing director had little to do with them.

He was in Port-of-Spain seeking Jeff Stollmeyer's mandate for a Caribbean Supertest series in a year's time. Caro had no problem with the meeting but Stollmeyer did. Like its brother boards, the West Indies Cricket Board of Control had promised the International Cricket Conference that it would not deal unilaterally with WSC.

Caro was a well-known businessman, managing director of consumer goods giant Reckitt and Colman until a month before. He had known Packer since being sent to Sydney from Reckitt's British parent in 1971, attending SCG Tests on the Consolidated Press advertisers' guest list, and was a familiar face at the ground. With his new job, his presence was liable to turn heads. And that could be embarrassing for the WICBC.

As Caro signed the register, he sensed a nearby presence and heard a familiar voice. 'Hello Andrew,' said the stalwart commentator, Alan McGilvray. 'What are you doing here?'

'Errr, I can't tell you Alan,' Caro replied. 'But I can't stop you guessing.'

Next morning in the breakfast buffet queue, Caro was sandwiched between McGilvray and Bob Simpson. Cheerful good mornings were interrupted by the public address: 'Call for Mr Andrew Caro. Message from Jeff Stollmeyer for Mr Andrew Caro.'

Stollmeyer's message was that the WICBC needed money. A lot of it. Local sympathy for WSC had left previously open-handed sponsors questioning the wisdom of contributing to a cause without popular support. The WICBC was acutely vulnerable to the spectator boycotts provoked by the player strike, and daily crowds at the Fourth Test were running between 3000 and 5000. Swarms of 24,000 had attended days of the First Test at the same ground.

In January, Stollmeyer had also been visited by David Clark and Jack Bailey of the International Cricket Conference looking for money to pay legal dues left by the group's High Court defeat. The WICBC was being asked to fund a folly it had resisted, which Stollmeyer considered 'morally indefensible'. Caro was welcome, and ferried by limousine and speedboat to Stollmeyer's Monos island residence: the WICBC was willing to defer a planned visit by New Zealand in March 1979, freeing for WSC the Test grounds that were the only possible venues for top-level cricket in the West Indies.

Caro offered the tour proceeds, but Stollmeyer insisted on a lump sum: Caribbean cricket trips of any description are rarely profitable. Caro agreed in principle, arranging to meet Stollmeyer in London after the ICC's annual meeting in July to finalise terms, and he deputised Deryck Murray to act as a WSC agent negotiating with sponsors and local boards.

There was just time to look at some of the real estate, and Caro's trip ended with a stroll round Queen's Park Oval in the company of a local official. His visit, while noted in the press, was ultimately overshadowed by what was occurring in playing hours. The following day, 18 April, the West Indies recaptured the Sir Frank Worrell Trophy.

'The worst performance since I've been in charge,' said Simpson, surveying the Fourth Test's ruins. 'A lack of mental application, no dedication, poor concentration, inconsistency and poor mental conditioning.'

All were supportable. Simpson had erred by inserting the home side – misled by the pitch's similarity to the First Test pitch – but the Australians had been beaten by a better team.

Third Test satisfaction had been dispelled quickly by a hair-raising St George's pitch for the game against Windward Islands in Grenada. Gary Cosier, thumb broken first ball, went through the familiar rite of studying the damage with partner Peter Toohey. 'Do you think that's bad enough to get sent home?' asked Cosier.

'Yep' said Toohey. 'Half your luck.'

The team's trip almost concluded at St Lucia where, after a last-ball win in the second one-day international, a crowd faction took out its frustrations on the luckless Stollmeyer. An armed escort guarded the Australian escape. 'I don't know what they didn't like about the guy's speech,' says Toohey. 'But they started shaking our bus and throwing a few things around, so we had to get out in a bit of a hurry.' The tourists arrived for the Fourth Test typically tired and ill-prepared, and died a dusty death in 25 overs on the last day by losing 9–52.

Simpson's one success was political. When the actions of Clark and Yardley were again tut-tutted, he cannily raised his own concerns about West Indian Norbert Phillip. The stand-off seemed to work and, when the Australians flew to Kingston for a tour match against Jamaica at Sabina Park prior to the Fifth Test, the skipper trusted that it would allow him to take the game off.

The reappearance as umpire of Douglas Sang Hue, however, caught him unawares. Lounging by the Kingston Sheraton pool, Simpson learned that Sang Hue had no-balled Yardley for throwing. Worse still, it seemed he was a likely Fifth Test official. Simpson seethed. Clark's action *had* worried him, but Yardley's, he believed, was purity itself. Sang Hue's colleague Wes Malcolm, later seemed to agree. Simpson stood firm with the local board: he would 'not be happy' if Sang Hue stood in the Test.

It was ticklish. Simpson had no veto over umpire selection. And, as elaborate Test security plans implied, Jamaica was the Caribbean's most volatile island. The Australians' last days on duty were tense. A wag bursting a paper bag in the Sheraton bar sent drinkers ducking for cover. West Indian seamer Vanburn Holder prepared Australians for flammable audiences. 'Whatever you do,' he told them, 'don't dispute a decision at Sabina Park. The crowd'll go wild. Just walk off.' It proved an ironic premonition.

Australians used to Alan McGilvray's pro forma Test summaries on breakfast radio heard something quite different the morning of Thursday 4 May 1978. The sounds of riot police coming to grips with a snarling mob could be heard over McGilvray's microphone as he described Simpson's Australians sprinting for the pavilion through a bottle barrage. 'Now bottles are coming and they're running at the double off the ground,' McGilvray reported. 'And they're being rained with bottles, hundreds of bottles and the players are running for shelter under cover . . . this is not funny.'

Umpiring was the cause, but a decision taken *before* the match. Trouble had been invited when Malcolm's appointment as Ralph Gosein's partner was inexplicably attributed to an Australian demand. As the Test unfolded, even the benign McGilvray was abused, and felt regarded as 'an infiltrator from abroad poisoning minds'. Simpson wrote: 'It is a peculiar sensation to be waiting nervously to bat . . . to turn to talk to your companion and find that he is a big, dark man wearing a riot helmet and having a shot-gun, truncheon and tear-gas canister handy.'

Wood went within 10 runs of his second century of the series, Toohey within three runs of two centuries in the match. The spin of Yardley and Higgs, as the West Indies sought 369 to win on the last day, was impeded only by Alvin Kallicharran's dainty footwork and judgement.

Australians bubbled when Yardley struck twice just before the match's final hour and 20 overs began. Then, 10 overs remaining, umpire Malcolm upheld Higgs' lbw appeal against a sweeping Kallicharran to reduce the home side to 8–242. Malcolm, of course, was the perceived 'Aussie stooge', and Jamaicans roared their disap-proval. They hung on every ball of the next four overs as Phillip and Holder held their bats from harm.

The latter was again withdrawing when Higgs's flipper apparently grazed his glove and another Australian appeal gained Malcolm's raised finger. Holder, despite his pre-match warning, paused pregnant seconds before walking off dejectedly. From their celebratory huddle, the Australians noticed the first bottles landing on the outfield and, on a ground that has the world's smallest Test playing area, the infield as well.

With 6.2 overs remaining and the last man on the way to the crease, the Australians held their ground for twenty-five minutes. Bennett and local liaison officer Gerry Alexander joined them within a police cordon, but the bottles continued and police advised them to 'start moving slowly off'.

About twenty metres from safety their path was blocked, as 300 belligerent Jamaicans filled the air with bottles and rocks. 'We stopped moving slowly,' Trevor Laughlin recalls. 'There was a picture of Woody running off the field the next day, but I wasn't in it. I was about fifteen yards in front of him running for my life. I saw this row of wall-to-wall West Indians in front of me and hit 'em at 100mph.' Jeff Thomson and Alexander were struck by bottles running the gauntlet, and players hared for their helmets.

McGilvray tried to sound unconcerned as he maintained his patter amid the first shots ever discharged at a Test match. 'Now there's gunfire,' he said. 'But there's no danger, they are just firing in the air and the crowd have scattered. It was only pistol fire, although there are some rifles out there.' When assured later that police had fired blanks, he wrote: 'I spent enough time in the army to know that blanks don't make the whistling noise I heard that day.'

As a chant of 'We want Sang Hue' was raised, McGilvray finally reported: 'I suggest, ABC, that I will phone you tonight from my bedroom and give you a report. I guess that's the safest place to be right now.'

At the Sheraton, Simpson was adamant the match should be allowed to conclude. Though tour conditions made no provision for six-day Tests, the WICBC was willing.

But the captain had two significant opponents. Thomson told him early next morning that he and several others did not want to return to the ground. Simpson convened a team meeting: they would, he said, be forfeiting a Test match. Majority would rule at a vote, but he would ensure the publication of the names of those responsible.

'Simmo had the rule book out and was going to try every trick in the book to get a sixth day out of the umpires,' Toohey recalls. 'I mean, I wanted to go back but I wondered whether it was the right decision. We'd heard that bullets had been fired during the riot. We didn't know what to expect.'

On a reconnaissance of Sabina Park, Simpson's team found the more important obstacle of umpire Gosein. While Malcolm was prepared at 11 a.m., Gosein was standing by the tour condition allowing extra time only in 'circumstances other than acts of God'. Flushed from the Sheraton by police escort, he was unmoved by an hour of pleading. Nor was a potential substitute John Gayle. Simpson wrote later that he felt Gosein had been 'got at'. Thomson was more fatalistic. 'Fuck 'em,' he shrugged.

McGilvray was already in Miami, advised by an Australian diplomat 'without beating about the bush . . . that they would like me out of Jamaica' and himself 'vowing I would never return to the West Indies'. The sentiment was not uncommon.

Like bad ventriloquists and helplessly clumsy waiters, cricket captains struggling as players elicit an embarrassed sympathy sometimes overwhelming criticism. Simpson deserves that latitude, for his West Indies tour had always been one with little to gain.

But these were Simpson's Tests too far. He tried bowling more to redeem poor batting form, but this meant that Yardley – who struck twice as often at half the cost – went underused. The forty-two-year-old Simpson also seemed resigned to having little in common with his players. 'I think he was more conscious of the age barrier than we were,' Yallop says. 'He seemed to think that the only way he could run things was by having total control, and that was where he fell apart. He didn't allow the team to grow. He certainly wasn't a well-liked captain at the end of the tour. We were so young that someone had to exercise some influence, but at that time he just went over the top.'

The manner of Simpson's 'second retirement', however, did the Australian Cricket Board little credit. Though he declared his candidacy for the captaincy, the ACB sought no tour report from him. Simpson performed ACB public relations duties in winter without knowing if he was wanted as leader and had to train in case he was. In that respect, Simpson's 'new era' eventually had much in common with the old.

The odysseys of Andrew Caro and Lynton Taylor in the winter of 1978 never hit headlines as hard as those of Austin Robertson and John Cornell, but they proved as profound in their impact. Packer, they emphasised, would fight, not fade.

Caro was in Lahore within ten days of his March appointment, a guest of Majid Khan. Pakistan was sticking to its self-denial of Mushtaq, Asif, Imran, Zaheer and Majid by excluding them from its team to tour England from April, but Caro had no difficulty persuading the tyro batsmen Javed Miandad and Haroon Rashid, and the idiosyncratic medium-pacer Sarfraz Nawaz to accept 'options' for joining WSC when the three-Test series finished in July.

Tony Greig briefed Caro and Taylor on English events in London a month later. Counties had reassimilated 'unbanned' WSC players with public reluctance: if Somerset were to play Richards and Garner, could Gloucestershire afford to take a stand and omit Procter and Zaheer?

Kent's readoption of Underwood, Knott, Woolmer and Asif Iqbal had been especially divisive. Not only was Asif its captain, but Knott's return would demote wicket-keeping prodigy Paul Downton whom England had taken on tour in the winter.

Kent's moral contortion was to replace Asif with a loyal county servant in Alan Ealham, and to persuade Knott to spend the summer working at his Herne Bay sports store. Then a fortnight before the season commenced, cricket committee head John Pocock told the WSC men that their contracts would not be renewed at the end of the season.

Asif shrugged, but Derek Underwood and Bob Woolmer felt betrayed. 'They talked about our disloyalty to Kent and we wondered just where their loyalties lay,' Underwood wrote. 'I reckoned, without being conceited, that I had contributed to Kent's post-war success as much as any other bowler, and yet here I was being fired from the club I had served in what I thought was a dedicated way for sixteen seasons.' Woolmer reflected: 'To be accused of not wanting to play for Kent was very wounding. I've always tried to be loyal and honest and it hurt . . . that certain members of the county committee wanted to pay us off.' Knott was glad to miss it all.

Greig convinced Caro and Taylor that trying to coo to the counties was impractical, so the Cricketers' Association was WSC's best hope of keeping its players in the game. Caro became chummy with president John Arlott and England's captain Mike Brearley. At a secret meeting at the Dorchester on the evening of Tuesday 11 April 1978 with the association's David Brown, Jack Bannister and John Lever, Caro and Taylor were granted fifteen minutes of microphone time at its Birmingham convention on the Thursday.

The association hoped that Caro and Taylor would dissuade extremist players from a mooted black-listing of matches involving WSC men that season (effectively blotting three-quarters of it). Whatever their personal feelings toward WSC, Brown, Bannister and Lever knew that such a step would mar ten years' image-building with the counties, with which they were negotiating a minimum wage for the 1979 season.

Caro and Taylor spoke 'sweet reason'. They pledged not to disrupt England's Test summer with further player poaching, and could truthfully deny rumours that Javed, Haroon and Sarfraz had signed WSC contracts (though they intended doing so).

Despite a turbulent meeting, both establishment and disestablishment achieved their aims. Caro flew for Port-of-Spain the next day having finally, to use Richie Benaud's phrase, 'made love, not war'. And as Ric Sissons wrote in his *The Players:* 'Again the Association was seen to be acting responsibly and in general could justly expect to play a more active role in the discussions of cricket's future.'

Pakistan's cricket community had dreaded their country's English tour. Only by making every ditch a last one had the team drawn its home Tests against England, and writer Tarek Fatah lamented: 'With the type of first-class cricket we play here only God could help us out of the low dumps that lie ahead for Pakistan's cricket.' Captain Wasim Bari was a fine wicketkeeper, but even his deputy Wasim Raja publicly doubted his leadership. Before the tour he told *Pakistan Cricketer* candidly: 'Having played under and against him, in my opinion Bari is not the right choice. He lacks maturity. He is easily overawed and gets excited.'

Slapstick ensued. Pakistan's batsmen were helpless in unfamiliar conditions, its attack toothless after Sarfraz decided he had strained his side. Interested mostly in the privileges of office, the four-man tour management organised with blithe individuality. Assistant manager Imtiaz Ahmed was benign at least: the team's main source of amusement was photographing him asleep in the dressing-room. But manager Mahmood Hussain, acting as a quasi-captain via the twelfth man, occasionally almost exchanged blows with players in the dressing-room.

Ritual Pakistan reselections occurred within days. Young all-rounder Hassan Jamal, playing for Middleton in the Lancashire League, was so chuffed at a call-up before the first Prudential one day match that he drove 200 miles to join the team in London. He was left cadging a floor to sleep on when he learned he'd been omitted while in transit

The main additions to the squad were in the executive: when Imtiaz brought his wife on tour in contravention of instructions, Hussain sent for his own. Local loyalists grief-stricken at innings defeats in the first two Tests lay under the team bus at Lord's refusing to let it leave, until police intervened.

It could hardly, in fact, have worked out better for WSC. Disgraced Pakistani administrators resigned en masse. With Javed, Haroon and Sarfraz confirming their WSC contracts, the Board of Cricket Control in Pakistan consented to talks with Taylor in Karachi.

Pakistan was to resume cricket contact with India in a three-Test series running deep into November, nor could it lack its stars on tours of New Zealand and Australia two months later. 'Speaking sweet reason' at meetings in September, Taylor agreed to release the players at the appropriate time.

Although neither New Zealand nor India had any players involved in the circuit, it was necessary they felt WSC's minatory bulk. Their ICC votes would count. Ian Chappell and John Maley reconnoitred the former in April when Auckland promoter Roy Cox expressed interest in organising a brief pre-season visit by two WSC teams for October.

Roy Cox was a likely lad, whose features betrayed a past of amateur boxing, and promised to round up sponsors and local clubs for off-piste games at smaller venues. To Chappell, it didn't look promising: 'You really couldn't tell what the grounds'd be like because the pitches were completely churned up from rugby.' Lights at potential night match venue Lower Hutt were worse: 'You would have been hard-pressed to bowl underarms under them.' Caro pressed on, agreeing to free twenty-five players for an exhibition series, when he flew to Auckland in September.

The slim-line seamer Richard Hadlee was sounded out about joining WSC, if only as local content when its retinue toured. He had excited rave reviews during a half-season with Nottinghamshire that year and accepted its long-term contract with the observation: 'I learned more in six weeks in English county cricket than in six years in New Zealand.' Hadlee's father Walter was New Zealand Cricket Council chairman and the player had binding sponsorship and coaching deals, but wanted his learning curve to continue: he would play if the NZCC consented.

NZCC secretary Bob Vance was horrified at the prospect. Hadlee was the closest New Zealand had come to a fast bowler since the Maori Wars. A 'sweetly reasonable' Caro promised to hang fire offering Hadlee a full contract if the NZCC consented to his 'guest' appearance for the World in New Zealand. Vance agreed.

Taylor's Karachi visit coincided with commencement of India's peace-making tour so it was no real surprise when, on the eve of the First Test at Faisalabad, pressmen confronted Indian manager Fatehsinghrao Gaekwad with talk that seven of his team had signed WSC contracts, including captain Bishan Bedi and vice-captain Sunil Gavaskar.

Both were known to have been informally approached in Australia: Bedi was a close friend of Mushtaq. Attendance by Ian Chappell and David Hookes of games benefiting Indian great Abbas Ali Baig at Delhi's Feroz Shah Kotla Stadium in April had been noted.

Gaekwad denied the defections, although Gavaskar and wick-etkeeper Syed Kirmani were apparently 'optioned'. Mihir Bose comments in his *A History of Indian Cricket*: 'Gavaskar's flirtation with Packer – it was little more – remains the most obscure subject in Indian cricket.' There certainly appeared a sequel when India toured England in 1979: Gavaskar, having led India against West Indies, was demoted, and Kirmani omitted altogether.

No country, it was clear, could feel invulnerable to WSC's threat. As Asif Iqbal told *Pakistan Cricketer*: 'I would not be surprised if tomorrow a keen youngster approached a top cricketer for the latter's autograph and got a quick reply: "Talk to my manager first".'

Caro did make a token effort to talk to the ICC's Jack Bailey and David Clark, tabling a WSC ambit claim for rights to organise a grand tournament of Australian, English, Pakistani, West Indian and World teams in Australia in 1978–1979. There was some mischief in the proposal, and in Caro's insistence that the ICC pair come to New York's Upper East Side Hotel Pierre to guarantee untapped phones.

The ICC inevitably rejected the plan at Lord's annual meeting on Tuesday 25 July. 'These proposals,' Gordon Ross would write in *Wisden*, 'are so ludicrous as to evoke intense speculation as to what WSC hoped to achieve by them. Was it that Packer had no wish for an agreement and was confident of his own future without any need to placate anyone in cricket?'

Indeed, WSC was having enough success placating individuals without having to deal with the ICC. While in London ostensibly for the ICC's arbitration, Caro met Stollmeyer in the Barclays Bank flat in Mayfair of which the WICBC president – in civilian life a senior West Indian bank executive – had use when visiting the UK.

The WICBC now needed WSC as much as vice versa. Accounts after the Australian tour showed it as basically insolvent, and it wanted an ex-gratia £35,000 in return for blessing Supertests in the Caribbean. Caro could hardly believe that approval was available so cheaply.

He called Packer. 'This is it,' he said. 'It's peanuts.' As Caro says: 'I'd been staying at the Dorchester for two weeks and the bill was £15,000.' It might be that Stollmeyer could bring himself only to accept WSC money to redress the 'morally indefensible': the £35,000 equates with the WICBC's High Court burden.

But cricket's authorities in general had poor grasp of WSC's wherewithal, as Caro realised when he lingered in London a week to attend the Oval Test between England and New Zealand. Approached there by Ted Dexter, then a newspaper columnist in *People*, Caro readily consented to an interview by a boyhood hero.

'Could you tell me,' Dexter inquired languidly, 'why is Mr Packer not bidding for the TV rights for the 1979 World Cup? Is it because he's run out of money?'

'Actually no,' Caro replied. 'It's because he doesn't believe your BBC coverage is up to the standard Channel Nine requires.'

Dexter's jaw dropped. The idea that the BBC did not meet Australian standards was so outrageous it could only be a blind. Next morning Caro read that he had 'confirmed yesterday that the rights were too expensive'.

The only sign of change at Lord's in 1978 was that the BBC had pinched from WSC the idea of a 'cherry-picker' camera mounted on a gantry at the Nursery End for England's Test against New Zealand in August. But as summer realities dawned, county resolve to purge the enemy within weakened. Packer payees eventually filled five of the top ten positions in the season's batting averages and four of the top ten bowling slots.

Kent relented first. As the county prospered and took the season's first crown – the Benson & Hedges Cup on 22 July – Underwood, Woolmer and Asif Iqbal were offered 1979 contracts. Eventually the only stickler was Dennis Amiss's Warwickshire, where the Cricketers' Association's David Brown and captain Bob Willis detested WSC. Visiting his friend, writer Patrick Murphy found Amiss 'on his own writing letters on World Series notepaper, while the rest of the team watched the game at the far end of the viewing area.' Amiss became the only batsman to exceed 2000 runs for the season and, immediately after, the only one sacked by his county. 'A vote to retain Amiss would be a vote for Kerry Packer,' it was explained, although protesting members forced a six-month stay in the hope winter would bring some cricket armistice.

The rhetorical battle persisted. Throughout 1978, Greig's name was as dirty in British newspapers as disgraced politician Jeremy Thorpe or punk rock avatar Sid Vicious. The disclosure in Henry Blofeld's *The Packer Affair* that Greig was an epileptic bordered on the bizarre. Blofeld's conclusion – that epilepsy explained Greig's 'impaired judgement' – was shared by writers of Jim Swanton's credentials. As Greig later told author Murphy: 'That slur was an example of the establishment resorting to anything to discredit me. Everyone else in the cricket media knew about my epilepsy and . . . had the integrity to keep quiet about it.'

Suspended by Sussex, Greig had spent the first eight weeks of his season playing Brighton club cricket, visiting New York to arrange a

promotional game, and replenishing WSC's player stocks with three
new Springboks: Clive Rice, Garth Le Roux and Kepler Wessels.

While considering Greig neither mad nor bad, Rice had discovered he *was* dangerous to know. The twenty-eight-year-old Transvaal
all-rounder had spent three years at Nottinghamshire succeeding
Sobers as the team's foreigner but, at news he had joined WSC just
before a first season as captain, was sacked as a player on the spot.
A flutter of Justice Slade's decision was enough to readmit him to
the dressing room, though the captaincy reverted to previous incum-
bent, Mike Smedley.

Recruitment of Wessels and Le Roux, both at Hove, was duly kept
low-key. Wessels had been just seventeen on straggling into Sussex's
second XI in 1975 but, even amid all his distractions the previous year,
Greig had been impressed by the youth's poise on promotion to the
top team. When Wessels made an unbeaten 138 against Underwood
on a damp Tunbridge Wells pitch, Greig unsuccessfully sought the
batsman's exemption from South African National Service in August
1977 in a letter to Minister Dr Piet Kornhof. Packer was persuaded
to offer Wessels a special limited contract: he would not, after all, be
of age until September 1978.

Packer also accepted Greig's recommendation of Le Roux: a slippery twenty-three-year-old fast bowler who had taken fifty-three
Currie Cup wickets for Eddie Barlow's Western Province in 1977–
1978. Le Roux's 'Pollock-Hobson problem' of not having played
county cricket was resolved when Barlow recommended Le Roux
spend half a season with Sussex second XI. One first-class game
against New Zealand on 24 June and he was politically emancipated.

Just in time, for Greig had a fortnight left of his twelve Sussex
seasons. WSC allegiances had been forgotten at his county reappearance against Hampshire: Greenidge caught him first ball from
Roberts. His eye and nerve seemed gone. In his autobiography,
however, Greig traced his decision to forsake England to unpleas-
antries exchanged at his daughter Samantha's school over a birthday
invitation withheld by a hostile parent:

> I've never been so hurt in my life. I took three strides toward Sam
> who jumped into my arms tears running down her face. I would
> not have minded if that woman had said to my face that she did

not agree with what I had done to cricket, even to the point of
saying she thought it a disgrace. But to take out her feelings on
two little girls was surely unforgivable . . . and from that moment
my life in England was finished.

He consulted the two most important people in his life: wife Donna
and friend Kerry Packer. When the former agreed that their future
lay in Sydney, the latter provided air tickets, and Greig visited Sussex
secretary Stanley Allen at Hove to make it official.

Greig's transit stop proved educational. Approached at Guildford
months earlier by a West Indian wanting to promote a match between
a team of American All-Stars and World All-Stars, he arrived in
New York with Knott and Snow, Greg Chappell and Hookes, Bedi
and Gavaskar, Mushtaq and Majid, Roberts and Fredericks, as a
sampling of cricket's finest. Sir Garfield Sobers, his idol, even agreed
to co-captain.

Among the touring pursuits was a pilgrimage to Yankee Stadium,
to watch World Series titleholders the Yankees play the Seattle
Mariners. A childhood memorising the *Fireside Book of Baseball* had
made Greg Chappell into an absentee baseball enthusiast, and the
American national pastime was undergoing a transition not unlike
cricket's after a period of unprecedented prosperity.

While baseball teams had long been bought and sold, hyperinfla-
tion in the value of 'franchises' had been stoked by exploitation of
television revenue and prodigious increases in spectators. By 1978,
national broadcasting revenue had grown almost fourfold in a decade
while gates (static from 1970–1975) had broken records for the third
consecutive year, with 40.64 million tickets sold.

Player wages – which had grown 1.5 per cent annually since the
turn of the century – had finally caused a revolt culminating in a
twenty-four-day lockout by team owners, and an enshrinement in
the 1976 Basic Agreement of 'free agency rights' for top players.
By 1978 mean salaries had soared to $US100,000; the Philadelphia
Phillies' Mike Schmidt had broken the $US500,000 barrier and, by
1980, Nolan Ryan would be pulling $US1 million a season for the
Houston Astros.

Since 1930, the Yankees had done it bigger and more belligerently
than anyone. That year they paid Babe Ruth more than President

Herbert Hoover, Ruth famously explaining: 'I had a better year than he did'. The team had ushered in the electronic age when purchased by CBS in 1964, and their controlling shareholder since 1973 – George Steinbrenner of the American Ship Building Company – made Kerry Packer seem pusillanimous. 'When you're a shipbuilder, nobody pays attention to you,' he confessed. 'But when you own the New York Yankees, they do, and I love it.' Third baseman Graig Nettles reminisced: 'When I was a kid I wanted to join the circus and play baseball. With the Yankees I got to do both.'

The cricketers at Yankee Stadium had been drawn, though, by the team's self-styled 'straw that stirs the drink'. Reggie Jackson, a supernatural slugger, was the first ball player to twig that 'personality' paid. 'Even the flintiest traditionalists,' wrote Roger Angell, 'must sense we are in . . . the Jacksonian era.' Why was he to be baseball's biggest earner in 1978, Jackson asked himself? Nine batting records in the 1977 World Series? 'Naaaah! It's because I put the asses on the seats!'

The actual venue for the cricketers' game on 3 September 1978, Shea Stadium in the Bronx, was home of the New York Mets: baseball's longest losing streak. And the match itself was reminiscent of the first WSC season. It clashed exactly with American 'establishment cricket' – the annual USA versus Canada game was staged the same day at Staten Island – and publicity was stifled by a New York newspaper strike.

A Brooklyn sports goods firm put up a trophy, but Greig left it behind by leading his team to a diplomatic seven-wicket defeat to the delight of 8000 West Indian expatriates. Helpless on a matting pitch laid over diamond cinders, the World All-Stars were rolled for 124. Hookes' dream of batting with Sobers lasted three deliveries. 'From the non-striker's end I watched him block two balls,' he says. 'Then I got out first ball at the other end. Next over Garry got out himself. So that was my great partnership with Sobers.'

Locals found Roberts and Snow tame from five-metre runs. 'We did the right thing and kept the ball up,' says Chappell. 'But they knew exactly the way to play on their own pitch.' Greig spoke graciously of coming back in a year's time to win.

Getting away, though, became the problem. 'When the promoter started to talk about having to wait for the gate we knew we were in trouble,' Greig recalls. Having conned most of the players into paying their own airfares, he was last seen pocketing their $1000 match fees en route for the Bahamas.

Greg Chappell made about the only wise investment. Visiting the US Open at Flushing Meadow, he recognised Joe DiMaggio in a bar and obtained an autograph, later countersigned by another great slugger in Garry Sobers. Whatever Reggie Jackson's charisma, Greg Chappell knew the noblest Yankee of them all.

14

'Listen, about those helmets'

The World Series Cricket newsletter to players on 10 October 1978 by new publicity director Bill Macartney put a brave and brazen face on it. 'On behalf of all of us ... I welcome Jeff to our field of play and wish him the very best of luck on the track,' it read. 'Jeff has told me that he is tickled pink to be back playing with his old mates – and against his old foes – and believes that with things being equal, he will bowl as fast this year as he has ever bowled.' Unfortunately for Jeff Thomson, things were far from equal.

Len Pascoe had called Andrew Caro in the last week of May. 'I've just had a drink with Thommo, Andrew,' he said. 'Reckons he doesn't like playing under Simmo much. Reckons he'd rather play with us.' And though Thomson had torn up his first contract, he and WSC had no quarrel. John Cornell had dissuaded Packer from hounding Thomson through the courts: fast bowlers had few seasons at the top, every one precious.

Thomson lived to bowl fast, but he also lived to be with mates like Pascoe. He missed them. Nor had Ian Chappell indulged in the lectures and tirades of the fogeyish Simpson. Thomson, moreover, was an undischarged bankrupt beneath debts of $23,000 from his All Sports stores. He'd then been caught and bowled by a $24,000 provisional tax assessment as his 1977–1978 income surged after a cricket-less 1976–1977.

But what Thomson would rather do was distinct from what he could. WSC discovered that a change of ownership at 4IP seemed to have annulled Thomson's contract there, but the Australian Cricket Board had cuffed Thomson three days after the last of the Indian Tests by contracting him for the 1978–1979 Ashes series. There was no way Thomson could play WSC that year. Unless . . .

The proposal of Allen Hemsley lawyer Jim Thynne was for a dubious story in which a jaded Thomson 'retired' officially, and was then spontaneously reanimated by the chance to play WSC. Caro agreed it was worth a try, and a letter was duly forwarded to the ACB on 9 August. Chairman Bob Parish had been chasing Thomson retirement rumours since June. All had been denied. Now he called his lawyers.

On Wednesday 21 September, Thomson's lawyer Frank Gardiner called a Brisbane press conference where the player disclosed his wish to play merely for Queensland and his club Toombul, and to be 'released' from Tests. Reanimation was to begin the following week when Thomson, staying at Pascoe's Bankstown home, was to sign for WSC.

But the closest the hapless Thomson and his mates came was that Sunday, 25 September. He and Lillee paired up again for Ian Chappell at the Drummoyne Oval in the Spastic Centre's annual match. Thomson took a wicket, hit a six, and that was it. That day, in fact, was the specified day from which the ACB had exclusive call on his services.

By the time Macartney was welcoming Thomson to WSC, the ACB was inviting him to a NSW Equity Court witness box. For twelve excruciating hours his testimony was held to the light so its WSC watermark showed. Despite WSC's thundering QC, Tom Hughes, Thomson was a terrible witness. As his biographer David Frith wrote: 'It was an agonised chapter of details forgotten by him, of places and people unfixed chronologically and contracts and schedules and declarations signed without having been read and with no copies left with the signatory.'

Asked if he would sign a letter written for him without reading it, Thomson told the court: 'I have written very few letters on my behalf in my time.' Asked if he'd lied to Parish, he said: 'At that time I'd had a million people bothering me . . . and I was just glad to say yeah, yeah, yeah . . . I'm not quite sure what I said to be absolutely correct, because I was just sick and tired of every Joe Blow ringing me up.' Asked if he'd lied to a journalist, Thomson spat: 'He rings up every blasted day just about. Him and all the rest . . . They get on my goat most times . . . I would've told him anything to get rid of him.'

Caro tried to talk lawyers out of prolonging the ordeal. 'We'd decided we'd try it on and see how far we got,' he says. 'And it wasn't working. In the end I was saying: "This is stupid. Tom Hughes is just costing us a lot of money". That didn't make me very popular.'

Thomson was reading a fishing magazine when, on 3 November, Justice Kearney ruled the cricketer's WSC contract ultra vires, null, void, empty and pointless all along. Destined for a summer of fishing, he even picked up a speeding fine on the Gold Coast road home that night.

WSC had otherwise wintered wisely. Crucially, Packer had relocated its management in Sydney and, where Vern Stone had been a functionary as 'general manager', redefined Caro as managing director.

The first sign that WSC's luck was changing came when it took advantage of hotly disputed Wran government legislation stripping the New South Wales Cricket Association of its dominant rights to the Sydney Cricket Ground by offering $200,000 for its use on seventeen days of 1978–1979. So critical was a 'dinkum cricket ground' to a successful circuit that Packer was also willing to budget $1 million for having the ground floodlit.

Not only was the Sydney Cricket and Sports Ground Trust a willing collaborator but, as Caro discovered on signing the deal in April 1978, it insisted on paying for light towers itself. Caro could hardly wait to phone his employer with the news. 'Kerry,' he chortled. 'I've just saved us $1 million.'

Doors previously closed were suddenly ajar. After WSC closed a deal for use of the Gabba, WSC was even offered the Adelaide Oval by its trust, whose members included Sir Donald Bradman.

The Don and the sporting Packers went back a long way. They had even, in 1932, been aligned against the ACB during one of Australian sport's crazier disputes. On that occasion, the board had threatened to omit Bradman from the Test team because of a writing contract the cricketer had signed with Kerry's grandfather Robert Clyde at Associated Newspapers. A miffed Bradman had threatened to quit in order to honour the deal. It had been Robert Clyde who had prevailed on Bradman to play.

The knight now attended four successive meetings with WSC executives. 'A man with a steel trap mind,' Caro concluded, 'who simply wanted as much as he could get from Kerry Packer.' In fact Caro was uninterested in Adelaide Oval: WSC could use neighbouring Football Park, if it went to Adelaide at all.

The plan was to concentrate on Sydney and Melbourne. Night cricket had been WSC's solitary first season dividend, but market research commissioned in the two cities indicated that sport followers were less implacably opposed than had been suspected. They wanted, at least, to see the 'experiment' continue.

Caro, who at Reckitt had steered its Samuel Taylor division into WSC sponsorship, wooed the promotional dollar with plain speaking. He told a July lunch of the Australian Institute of Management: 'The fact it is cricket is incidental. WSC is a product and over the last two to three years the attempts to market it as such have achieved very little. Our audience will increasingly be one which chooses the Bee Gees instead of ABC concerts.' Past patrons McDonald's, Goulburn Valley Canners and Qantas renewed their support, and new supporters Email, GMH, Goodyear and Waltons liked the Bee Gees market, too.

WSC games would be pitted against an England–Australia Test series in the 1978–1979 season, and promotion would be crucial. Witnessing the success of baseball in selling itself as 'the family day out', Caro and Cornell proposed the concept to Packer in August.

Packer was stonily indifferent. 'No way,' he said. 'I want patriotism. I want people turning up to see Australia win.'

Cornell cringed. 'Are you joking Kerry?' he asked. 'This is an Ashes series we're fighting. It'll never work.'

Packer wasn't listening. His mind was made up. With misgivings, Cornell had to turn the last refuge of a scoundrel into the first refuge of the spectator. He looked up some old friends: brothers Don and Alan Morris, and Allan Johnston who ran the hot-shot creative consultancy Mojo.

In 1973, Johnston had made Paul Hogan's catchline 'Anyhow' into a tobacco endorsement for Winfield. Their latest success was a series of commercials for the brewer Toohey's with the slogan 'I Feel Like a Toohey's or Two' featuring sporting titans. These would include Dennis Lillee, standing tall in the middle of the SCG, to the narration: 'You've been an inspiration to Australia and your mates, and you've written chapter and verse in the cricket book of greats.' Cornell wanted to inspire something similarly anthemic. It became 'C'mon, Aussie, C'mon'.

The press remained a perplexity. The John Fairfax and Herald and Weekly Times newspaper groups would always be nemeses. Cornell hired Bill Macartney, a livewire thirty-year-old journalist from 2UE and another Perth *Daily News* old boy, as a press officer.

Packer at the time was also negotiating with Rupert Murdoch and Robert Sangster to form Lotto Management Services – which won a partnership with the Wran government to run NSW Lotto – and persuaded the former to have the *Australian* dedicate WSC a full-time follower, Phil Wilkins.

From an eleventh floor office at Consolidated Press, Macartney plotted a campaign of 'constant wind-up' and 'wall-to-wall sales-manship'. To help with the former, Caro hired Patricia Daniels from Sydney's Luna Park to put players through promotional hoops. For the latter, he recruited a Reckitt colleague, Margaret Harop, as merchandising designer. WSC products would range from beach towels to blow-up pillows, while nondescript T-shirt slogans like 'Howzat!' were phased out for the likes of 'I'm Into Cricket, Balls and All' and 'Big Boys Play at Night'.

One could read about it: a first season book was published called *Cricket Alive*. One could relive it: David Hill rewound video high-lights for a documentary *The World Series Cricket Story*. One could join it: membership of the children's Cricketeers Club was $10. One could just about play it, or at least roll a dice, in the board game 'Night Cricket'. And WSC had not yet bowled a ball.

The catalyst WSC craved was Australian success, and Lillee espe-cially felt the expectation. Beery self-examination after the Sixth

Supertest in the downstairs 'noise room' at the Old Melbourne had even prompted thoughts of 'retirement'.

'Shake me by the hand,' he had said, solemnly calling Ian Chappell aside.

Sensing the reason for the ceremony, the captain had refused: 'I'm not going to shake your hand. I only shake fast bowlers' hands.'

Lillee had punched him in the stomach, and stuck his hand out insistently. 'Shake me by the hand.'

Chappell had refused, and refused again after another boozy swipe. 'Well you can get fucked,' Lillee had said finally. 'I'll be back next season. Fitter. And I'll take more fucking Supertest wickets than anyone else.'

Stripping his art to basics, Lillee asked Robertson's father, Austin Snr, to 'teach him to run'. The grizzled sprint star, considered 'the fastest man alive' in January 1935 after outpacing English and Scottish champions at a famous Melbourne meet, learned that Lillee had never even been taught to jog. 'In short, as a sprinter,' Robertson wrote, 'Dennis was a great fast bowler.'

After straightening and tightening Lillee's technique, Robertson drilled him in forty-yard sprints. When the fast bowler's time from a flying start was reduced from 4.2 seconds to 3.7, Robertson thought him a Stawell Gift contender.

Lillee bolted from the blocks when all the Australians commenced a three-month pre-season training program that Ian Chappell had decreed. The captain had seen county-fit World and West Indians trample them the previous year, and also memoed players individually to advise them of specific technical flaws he wanted addressed.

Lillee's old University of Western Australia fitness guru Dr Frank Pyke led work in Perth, while St Kilda Football Club coach Ross Smith, Dr Brian Quigley of the University of Queensland, Milperra College trainer Barry Ridge and Graeme Wright from Adelaide College oversaw state programs.

Training did not come naturally to Australian cricketers. Some smoked, all drank, and few ran when they could walk. Masseur Dave McErlane's 'programs' had been individually tailored, even for Lillee. 'I always thought it annoyed him if he couldn't run this old bloke off when we went for a run,' he recalls. 'So when I sprinted with him, I'd just ease off on the last leg so he could feel he was going faster.'

Mandatory fitness targets were hard to face. 'I reckon I worked harder than anyone in the nets,' says Gary Gilmour. 'But I'd never been able to run so I was "unfit". I kept telling them that a Golden Slipper winner never won the Melbourne Cup, that Rob de Castella never took five wickets, but it didn't go down too well.'

Gilmour scraped through WSC's new standards by the skin of his calliper test, only escaping a $1000 suspended fine for failing to improve his fifteen-minute run distance between July and October in a circuit of King's Park in Perth with Rick McCosker's help as pace-maker and Ray Bright pushing from behind every time he stopped. The trio hailed a cab after the quarter-hour and, retracing their route, measured Gilmour's distance on its tachometer. 'It was a pretty rough measure,' he recalls. 'But I'd made it.'

Packer himself issued some personal instructions. Ross Edwards was ordered to take Doug Walters weekly to a Pennant Hills country club. On a rented squash court, Edwards was to bounce tennis balls at his colleague from close-range to improve Walters' technique against short-pitched bowling. Packer would call the club at intervals to make sure the players were following orders, and at one point abruptly scheduled a test at Barry Knight's indoor cricket school in Kent Street.

A pin-striped Packer was waiting when the pair arrived and, as they began their routine, removed his jacket to bowl and advance peculiar ideas on the subject. 'I started arguing with him,' says Edwards. 'Then I figured it maybe wasn't such a good idea to be arguing with the boss, and just said "yes yes yes" and nodded. When he'd gone, Dougie and I just went back to doing it our way.'

Caro hired Lynton Taylor's secretary Irene Cave as a season coordinator. WSC had reproduced the bedrock of first-class cricket for a troupe swelled to sixty by off-season recruiting. The elaborate 'Tour Two' scheduled for rural centres – two dozen games winding a 20,000 kilometre route from Cairns to Devonport – was nick-named 'Packer's Sheffield Shield'. A new team devised for fringe dwellers led by Eddie Barlow was named, with equal nostalgia, the Cavaliers.

The seeds for WSC's next generation were also sewn. On their return from the West Indies, the dashing youngsters Peter Toohey and Graeme Wood were offered WSC places for 1979–1980 after the expiry of their ACB contracts. They proved surprisingly mobile. Toohey visited Consolidated Press at the invitation of Caro and Cornell, and accepted an offer in principle, while Wood signed a five-year offer from Austin Robertson and Rod Marsh in Perth.

'I said no the first time,' Wood recalls. 'But I had a think about it, and I went and spoke to some people in business I respected and, after deliberating a couple of weeks, I signed. Basically I'd had a great tour of the West Indies and I was looking forward to the next challenge.'

The challenge had not been lost on the ACB. It had worked fastidiously to produce an attractive wrap for the gift it planned to present. Its Benson & Hedges 'Battle for the Ashes' brochure was a slender document compared to WSC's propaganda deluge, but its animated television commercial devised by advertising agency J. Walter Thompson proved relatively racy: England's captain Mike Brearley, transfigured as a knight, clashed broadswords with an unidentified Australian. With Bob Simpson having joined the ABC radio commentary panel, Australia had yet to select a captain.

The ACB's commercial awakening had also been reflected in its portioning of cricket telecast rights. The ACB's 6 September 1978 meeting granted exclusive Gillette Cup rights to the 0-10 network. It had even mimicked WSC by agreeing a 50 six-ball over format, improving its commercial television economics by multiplying the available advertising slots.

The decision's implication, with ABC's Test rights expiring at season's end, was that the ACB saw its long-term future with commercial networks, although apparently on its terms. As Shayne Quick observed: 'To provide 0-10 with exclusive coverage of the Gillette Cup, the ACB had to buy back the TV rights from the ABC. An answer to why this was not possible in late 1976 when Packer initially approached the ACB has not been forthcoming.' One explanation is that the ACB had taken stock of the nature of its rights and realised that such a step was possible; another is that it hoped for commercial spirits more kindred than Mr Packer's.

The first day of 0-10 coverage of the Gillette Cup, Saturday 28 October was watched by Mike Brearley's jet-jaded Englishmen in Adelaide. Brearley returned from a luncheon engagement with Bradman to hear that Thomson had taken 6–18 against South Australia at the Gabba. Between the commercials, he then watched the ACB's rising star Rodney Hogg go wicketless. Thanks to the NSW Equity Court they'd see nothing of one and a great deal of the other as the season unfolded.

Politics were detectable when Brearley took an exploratory net at the Adelaide Oval and glimpsed a familiar face. 'Hookes said "hullo" shyly from the corner of the nets as though he did not want to come into the sunlight,' Brearley wrote. 'I asked him how he was, and said: "Shall we be seeing you a bit?" When I looked up again he was gone. It was a most peculiar encounter.'

Indeed, WSC and the ACB would circle one another all summer, like divorced partners trying not to meet. That was no mean feat considering the eighty-eight days of WSC, and the eighty-six days of first-class and one-day cricket involving touring Englishmen and Pakistanis. Not to mention a hundred days of Sheffield Shield cricket.

Both camps were anxious. The threat was of very thin audiences all round. Success for one side would obviously mean abject failure for the other. The five Supertests and eight Test matches, in contrast to the first year, were interspersed rather than simultaneous in an attempt to spread the wear, but the television combat could not be avoided. The ACB had more than fifty days of televised cricket, WSC almost forty, and at least ten would clash. The SCG was destined to resemble a stretch of northern France circa 1916, tramped on by advancing and retreating armies half the days of November through February.

Athletes, rugby players and greyhounds had been the toast of Aucklanders at the Mount Smart Stadium. On the frigid Saturday morning that broke on 4 November, twenty-five jaded WSC emissaries would have been happier had they been left to it.

Arriving at their Logan Park Hotel twelve hours earlier, they'd found half the city discussing the All Blacks' Test against Wales, the rest the World Rowing Championships. No wonder there were 1200 people to watch them fret and strut on a trapdoored stage. Instructions John Maley had left in April for pitch preparation had been read as far as the chapter on bounce. Locals had overlooked those on rolling and mowing.

Half the Australians' runs came from the bat of Greg Chappell, who still cherishes his 74 and 89 in conditions that reminded him of those during his first English Test century five and a half years before. Mount Smart 1978 might even have been harder than Lord's 1972: 'It was not only seaming but swinging, staying down then bouncing. There was no rhyme or reason to it. You might on average expect to see one bloke hit a game, just through an error of judgement, but blokes were getting cleaned up every over.'

It was no use complaining. In a new-generation helmet he'd brought to face Lillee for the first time in two and a half years, Clive Rice resembled a *Star Wars* storm-trooper. He had promptly sustained broken ribs. When partner Alan Knott asked his condition he merely gasped: 'Fine.'

There was at least value for runs if you managed to hit the 400-metre running track that circled the ground. 'You'd come off onto the track and it was like coming off grass onto the dance floor,' says Max Walker. 'The ball'd hit the surface and go dwaaang over your head.'

But dwanging was minimal for the next two and a half days, half the wickets being hewn by Lillee (12–89) and the World's special guest star Richard Hadlee (7–59). By Monday, even batsmen were admiring the Australian's craft. Collis King, bowled by an away swinger that cut back between his bat and pad, applauded it all the way off.

Conditions were even harder at Tauranga, which promised 'the most picturesque ground in the world' and produced a pitch that Ian Davis remembers as 'a mowed front lawn'. He made 30 while ten colleagues scrounged 53 more. 'The bowlers didn't let up,' he says. 'They wanted to get into rhythm more than us. It was probably the best I'd batted in years. Every time the ball pitched it'd take a hunk of wicket with it. I made 30 but I got about sixty-five bruises.'

Promises to Ross Edwards and his WSC co-manager Bruce McDonald of rich incentives and welcoming crowds flocking for Hadlee quickly proved empty. Rapport with promoter Roy Cox disappeared and, when John Cornell arrived in mid-afternoon from Australia with a promotional film crew, he almost had a stand-up fight to film between the organisers and the WSC managers over obligations to the local sponsor.

In a fortnight, in fact, enough mistakes and mishaps occurred to choke a four-month tour of England. 'It was a total disaster,' says Mick Malone. 'Badly organised from start to finish, it rained all the time and no one turned up to watch. But I reckon that if they'd asked us to play from one in the morning to six then sweep the pitch we would have done it. It was all in or all out.'

The peculiar phenomenon that was New Zealand cricket was absorbed. Nobody, for instance, had seen a helicopter being used to dry a pitch before as it was at Pukekura Park. Nor had they seen a batsman wounded like the luckless King, his leg bleeding from a graze administered by the white ball's razor-edge seam. Barry Richards had never had to replace a courtesy car driver behind the wheel before, but did when his female chauffeur fell asleep and drove off the road on a four-hour drive.

A radio breakfast program hosted from the hotel dining-room was also a first. But Radio 2ZB, broadcasting from Lower Hutt's South Pacific Motor Inn on 16 November, did deliver WSC its best crowd of the trip: 4000. 'The trouble with the public is that it's suspicious of something new,' Cox told reporters in Auckland. 'People won't accept it until they've actually seen it.' The minuscule crowds did indeed ensure well-kept secrecy until TV2 broadcast two hours of the final one-day match at Mount Smart on Sunday 19 November.

Scores brought back memories of school days. Davis, Bruce Laird, Ray Bright, Mike Procter and Bob Woolmer averaged less than 12, Tony Greig less than five. 'It really ended up the opposite of what we'd intended,' Ian Chappell concludes. 'It was better if you had a ratshit tour. The longer you batted, the worse your form became.'

One beneficiary was Hadlee, who loved every confidence-building moment shooting out the cream of the world's cricketers. New Zealand's son of the seam took 25 wickets at 8.5 runs, while his 119 runs came at a heady 20. Richards recalls watching his jaw set as the tour went on: 'I shared a room with Richard and he was only just growing aware of what he could do in cricket. I think that's when he started realising he was up to what it took to be a top player.'

Edwards' report on the trip to Caro was trenchant:

> Roy Cox and his organisation were regarded universally by local organisers with suspicion and at times with barely concealed mistrust. These feelings were so general it was hard to believe they did not have some basis in fact. On occasions it was necessary for WSC management to undertake additional commitments and responsibilities. This was necessary in order to maintain WSC's credibility as a result of Cox making ill-considered spontaneous promises . . . without consultation which, if we had not taken action, could have had serious media consequences . . . Most wickets were dangerous.

When the teams touched down in Sydney, they learned that their boss had led a perilous life in their absence. While game-fishing 130 kilometres north of Cairns with Jack Nicklaus, Packer's boat the *Melita* had been wrecked on a coral reef. WSC's overlord had been forced to take to the lifeboats. At times during the preceding fortnight they would gladly have swapped places with him.

Sydney airport's transit lounge on Monday evening, 20 November 1978, was for ten minutes a cricket capsule. As WSC teams hefted themselves from an Air New Zealand flight to an Ansett connection for Perth, they met Brearley's English entourage, booked for Bundaberg after winning their tour match at the SCG.

It was easy to see who was on which side of the barricades. The WSC players were in jet-setting casuals, Brearley's ambassadorial men blazered and necktied. But the divide was cosmetic. Cordial shoptalk broke out. The only wince was when Derek Randall playfully jabbed the tender ribs of his Nottinghamshire colleague Clive Rice. Even Greig, shyly removed with his family and Australian business manager Bruce Francis in the bistro, was included in the extended family affair. Geoff Boycott went conspicuously to shake his hand.

WSC now cast a long shadow in Sydney, with the SCG skyline pierced by its new light towers aka 'Packer's cigars'. Preparation for their first use – the Australians' opening International Cup night match against the West Indies scheduled for Tuesday week – also raised a hell of a racket. Bill Macartney and Patricia Daniels had made Sydney reverberate. Top-rating radio station 2SM – owned by the Catholic Church – played 'C'mon, Aussie' until its needles were blunt. 'They were the number one rock radio people in town,' says Macartney, 'and they really kicked ass for us.'

On the SCG No. 2 as the Englishmen had been playing, Jeff Thomson and Len Pascoe had bowled at a polycarbonate screen to promote the 'Fastest Bowler In The World' competition that Macartney and David Hill were trying to organise. They broke it. 'Thommo hit a screw at the bottom with a full pitch,' Macartney recalls. 'So that was the end of that.'

In lieu thereof he introduced journalists to Kepler Wessels, a new kid on WSC's block. Two days later, Martin Kent walked into the bar at Perth's Sheraton to find the youngster sipping a lemonade. Recognising him from the International Wanderers tour three years earlier, the Queenslander asked: 'So, what brings you here?'

'Don't you know?' Wessels replied. 'I'm playing for you.'

Wessels was not insulted. He had not had the luxury of playing prima donna since arriving in Sydney in October to discover WSC's red carpet rolled up. Lynton Taylor had spelt out his package. He had a hotel room for a week while he found a job and lodgings. Greig had booked him a spot at Waverley, and only runs there would earn him a permanent WSC place.

The sensation that WSC would make the South African army he'd served the year before look like the Salvation Army filled Wessels with despair. 'Already my career had been put back a year through having to do National Service, and I shuddered at the thought of having to play only club cricket for a season,' he wrote. 'On top of this I was suffering a personality crisis. There I was, an immature kid lost in a big city and my whole world was about to collapse.'

He trained with a military discipline: 'There was only one thing I could do: work even harder than before . . . in what had all of a sudden become a cut-throat business.' The kindness of strangers helped. Caro got him a job with Allen Allen & Hemsley, and Wessels accepted a bunk offered by Waverley teammate Peter McKenzie.

Failure in the first round of grade cricket left him nearly suicidal, but the phone call he coveted came after centuries against Penrith and Sydney. Packer said simply: 'You're in.'

Among the Australians, what's more, for their team was short of new blood, especially top-order blood. When Packer offered him Wessels' services, Ian Chappell snapped up the youth who had so impressed him as a South African teenager.

It was still an awe-struck twenty-one-year-old who stepped out at the SCG No. 2 in his new colours. An early visitor was Tony Henson, the C & D helmet-maker, who called in case Wessels was a potential sale. Initial reticence changed as he watched a Thomson bouncer clear the nets still rising. 'Listen,' Wessels paused. 'About those helmets . . .'

Henson's customer base was widening. This season would be rapid. When the WSC players gathered in Perth, David Hill's televised time trial at the WACA even gave them a few figures to work from: special guest Thomson earned a welcome $4000 when he touched 148 kilometres an hour, outpacing a tightly-bunched Holding (141.3), Imran (139.7), Croft (139.2), Roberts (138.6), Lillee (136.4), Le Roux (135.9), Daniel (133.5), Pascoe (131.6), Hadlee (129.8), Procter (128.6) and Sarfraz (121.7).

After the ordeal of New Zealand, the force was with Thomson's kind. For Hookes, in particular, it had been a harrowing two weeks. 'I suppose I'd buried it a bit when I'd come back after Andy hit me the year before,' he recalls. 'But in New Zealand, the pitches were so bad I started to get flashbacks about the ball he'd hit me with. He wasn't even there, and in fact after a while it didn't matter who was bowling. The spinners could be on and I'd see that ball again. And then I'd get out.'

Henson had refined his design over winter with a windscreen manufacturer, Cyklas, and a plastics firm, Cadillac Plastics. It now included a prestressed visor and temple guards. General West Indian disdain of hard headgear was maintained only by Viv Richards. Even Ian Chappell, at a protective Packer's insistence, was among early shoppers.

Leaving a WSC opening bash at entrepreneur Michael Edgley's Swan River mansion early, Wessels packed his new helmet. He was joining Eddie Barlow's trialists in the Cavaliers and Clive Lloyd's

West Indians on an overnight rail journey to Kalgoorlie for the first match of the Country Cup. Five hours after pulling into the gold town on Thursday, 23 November, he was headed for a promising debut half-century as a full-fledged World Series cricketer.

WSC's season took on its own breakneck haste as teams played one-day games for $10,000 staked by Swan Brewery at Gloucester Park while the Cavaliers hit the road and rails. Series co-ordinator Irene Cave and assistants Barbara Loois and Liz Herbert enforced punctuality with fines for laggards. When the Kalgoorlie party returned to Perth at 11 p.m. on Thursday, the Cavaliers joined the World on a midnight flight to Bunbury for a match the next day.

No one was underworked. Playing duties were interwoven with coaching commitments. For Martin Kent, for instance, rain in Bunbury entailed his dispatch back to Perth by car for another train trip to Kalgoorlie where further coaching clinics had been organised. When the clinic ended late, Kent returned to Perth with just enough time to catch an Ansett red-eye that dropped him in Sydney at dawn on Monday.

It was possible there to savour the sense of excitement that Bill Macartney's gang had incubated for WSC's SCG debut. In a deal with Yellow Cabs they had made WSC the first advertiser to use hoardings on the back of taxis. Murdoch's *Australian* featured a four-page advertising supplement on the forthcoming summer, while a balloon carrying the WSC logo floated above the city centre. The Chateau Commodore was festooned with posters, ties, towels, T-shirts, jackets, even soap in the shape of white cricket balls. In case the purpose of it all escaped attention, TCN-9 scrubbed its sched-uled program at 9.30 p.m. on Monday for Hill's *The World Series Cricket Story*.

In his hotel room, Anglo-Australian writer David Frith watched with mingled horror and admiration. 'It amounted to an hour-long commercial,' he wrote, 'some of it hypnotic . . . some of it far-fetched. The montage of dismissals made it seem like the fastest game on earth, not the slowest, as legions of antagonists have always claimed. There seemed little purpose in trying to find a meaning for it all.'

Non-stop action, pulsating soundtrack and John Laws' melodra-matic baritone rammed home the message unceasingly: a cricketing

Krakatoa would erupt the following day. Even the placement of a Benson & Hedges advertisement for the Tests beginning in three days – a mistake caused by the late program change – seemed Macchiavellian to journalist Alan Lee: 'For a moment I wondered if the Packer network had made an unforgivable blunder by plugging the opposition . . . Then I thought again. The Ashes advertisement, though adequate in its way, was totally overshadowed by the World Series commercials. Perhaps Packer wanted the nation to see it that way too?'

15

'These people have found truth'

Bill Macartney leaned back in parodied self-satisfaction as his companions looked down on the sea of faces beneath the SCG's executive chamber. 'So,' he drawled, 'what do you think of my crowd?' It was 8 p.m. on Tuesday, 28 November 1978, and WSC had 50,000 rocking, rollicking converts.

'After all the hype and the publicity,' said ticket manager Bruce McDonald, 'I would have been disappointed with anything less.'

Their frivolity actually caused some offence in the party. 'I really had anticipated a big crowd,' McDonald recalls, 'so I was quite underwhelmed. But it upset a few people when they thought I was pooh-bagging the whole thing.' For many in attendance, WSC had become more than cricket, more than business, an end in itself.

McDonald had called Packer before gates opened to describe lines of spectators twisting down Anzac Parade. The 2.15 p.m. toss was transacted for Ian Chappell and Clive Lloyd by fifteen-year-old Glen Michelic, a WSC coaching find from Fairfield, and the Australians fanned in the field to the strains of 'C'mon, Aussie' hurling give-away white balls into the 5000 early arrivals.

Curious and deferential WSC officers, like an occupying army visiting the deserted bunker of a routed enemy, studied the memora-bilia lining their executive room two floors up in the SCG members' stand. Attentive to the play, they toasted Lillee's third-ball victory over Viv Richards. But, as Australian success filled the afternoon, and the Hill's voice swelled, their celebrations became less of cause than effect.

Packer arrived in mid-afternoon, joining McDonald at the turnstiles in the fashion of a retail chain owner keeping his common touch at the till. Reality dawned at tea when an updated crowd figure of 30,000 was confirmed in expectation of the Australian innings. A glance out the back of the executive room confirmed more to come. WSC was not against the establishment this evening. It was the establishment.

Packer had already taken the venturesome step of admitting ladies to the members' for the first time and, when worried police asked that the gates be opened to ease queues still banked up at turnstiles that had clicked 44,377 times, approval was readily given.

John Cornell, who rarely permitted himself more than a sly smile, was beside Paul Hogan, Austin Robertson, Delvene Delaney and himself. 'These people have found truth,' he muttered mystically. He rushed the attendance figure to the press box personally, and dashed to fetch Lillee when the Australian innings began.

JP Sport's first client, 4–12 in the bag, had never visited the executive room before and admired the view with awe. 'There were hordes of people and cars as far as the eye could see,' he wrote. 'As I looked out in the gloomy light I got a tingling feeling through my body.' Tony Greig, arriving late after a cross-country flight with the Amisses and Woolmers, choked back tears.

Chasing 128, the Australian batsmen never had to touch the heights. Ian Davis, striking Bernard Julien for three smart fours, joined his captain in an even-time stand of 42. When the target narrowed to 34 runs with 20 overs remaining, three cheap wickets stirred the Hill's 'C'mon, Aussie' choir, but robust blows from Davis and Marsh clinched the match by 9.20 p.m.

Match reports were revealing, not so much in what was written but what was not. The local press contingent was three-strong: the *Australian's* Phil Wilkins had only two news agency companions. Packer's Fairfax rivals gave their syndicated copy grudging space, although the organisation's *National Times* a fortnight later carried Adrian McGregor's colourful, intelligent tribute. 'The incongruity of it all,' he wrote. 'That Packer at that moment, so absolutely removed from the hoi polloi, should have . . . achieved the proletarianisation of cricket. He had enticed sports fans out of the pubs . . . transforming the subtleties of traditional cricket into the spectacular that is night cricket.'

English journalists applied their own interpretations. *The Times'* John Woodcock had been repelled by publicity for the Australians: 'The fact that most were discredited when they came back from England 14 months ago has been forgotten. Packer, for the time being, has made them into idols again.'

Others were filled with respect and foreboding. Alan Lee wrote of a 'wild and wonderful experience': 'One thing was certain. Packer had struck gold and found something that would arouse the envy of the traditional cricket authorities.' David Frith, a heartfelt, but not fanatical traditionalist, preferred not to ponder. Personally he could not enjoy night cricket. 'The nausea I felt this evening I put down to fatigue, for the cricket had its moments. If I'm prejudiced at all perhaps it is in favour of cricket in God's sunshine.'

At his moment of triumph, Packer was also reflective, and intently entertained a cross-section of his world: the day-time television favourite Mike Walsh, celebrity sportscaster Mike Gibson, the tele-thinker Bruce Gyngell and agent Harry M. Miller mixed with Lillee and Marsh, Sobers and Lloyd.

Greig found his boss thoughtfully absorbed when he whispered his belief: 'This is it.'

'Yes,' Packer replied, 'I think you're right.' Greig was amazed at Packer's serenity. 'It was almost like he had known it was going to happen all along,' he wrote.

As the ground emptied in the cool of the evening, Packer deflected one journalist with a perfunctory 'it's been an encouraging start' and repaired to the top tier of the stand alone. When Andrew Caro, who had missed the game with commitments in Perth, sought his views next morning, Packer merely muttered: 'No, it wasn't bad. I thought your lot started partying a bit early though.'

Graham Yallop's first pre-Test press conference as Australian captain at Brisbane's Eagle Farm airport next day was an unavoidable chore, and demanded an optimism he didn't feel.

Encircled by cameras, microphones and forty journalists, the question of how Australia would fare floated down the pitch like a welcome long hop. Yallop's flippant expectation of a 'six-nil' series victory was the press equivalent of the bad ball taking a wicket.

Yallop was looking, above all, for the selectors Sam Loxton, Neil Harvey and Phil Ridings, whose decision had skyjacked him leaving Perth the previous week. Just as WSC's caravan had been arriving, Yallop's outbound flight with Victorian teammates had been interrupted by their Ansett pilot's voice: 'The Victorian Sheffield Shield players will please remain on the plane when it lands in Melbourne.'

At Tullamarine, Victorian Cricket Association secretary Dave Richards had boarded to announce the Australian team for the First Test against England in Brisbane ten days later. Colleagues congratulated Yallop, Trevor Laughlin, Alan Hurst and Jim Higgs on their selections as Richards added that Yallop was captain, Australia's third youngest at twenty-six.

So frequent were the calls that Yallop requested a silent number, but the captain hoped vainly for contact from at least one official. And when at last he met his governors in Brisbane, their thoughts were more of Sydney. It was raining there, but another 20,134 were watching the WSC Australians win their second SCG stanza, and Bob Parish was composing a congratulatory announcement for his board's *bête noire* noting the 'excellent' crowd and attractive concept, one that the ACB would replicate 'if changes are demanded by the public'.

Problems had also arisen in trying to update ACB contracts. Wood, who had signed with WSC for 1979–1980, did not want another two years with the board. 'As far as I was concerned, what they were doing was wrong,' Wood says. 'We were part way through a contract as it was and they wanted to tie us up even longer. I got legal advice that they couldn't do what they were trying to do.' He held out, successfully, for a one-year contract.

Elaborate trimmings being planned to counter the potent Packer marketing package – cheap children's tickets, skydivers, a brass band, a commemorative coin toss – contrasted with ramshackle arrangements for the team itself. Although Yallop knew his appointed vice-captain Cosier well, his team had experience of just fifty-five

Tests and were virtual strangers to one another. He had no manager, no advisers, and two days to achieve the magic of unity. 'Boy, it was mind-boggling,' he says. 'No one knew anyone else in the team. The selectors were just stabbing in the dark, guessing. And because they didn't believe in managers in those days either, I had to do everything myself. Tickets, taxis to the ground for the boys, laundry, everything.' For Yallop, who had only left his father's APY Castings business that year and who Ray Robinson remembered as the most introverted Australian captain in his lengthy experience, the cares of office were doubly demanding.

Locals were pessimistic. '"I only watch the best – I'll be at the Packer matches" was the comment I heard more than a few times,' Lee reported, 'once combined with a confession from a broad Australian that he had backed England to win every Test match.'

Yallop finally caught up with his patrons at the Gabba on the Friday, the day before the Test, and examined the pitch with Loxton. 'Looks like a perfect batting wicket to me,' said the selector. 'Looks like whoever wins the toss should bat for three days.' The following morning Yallop was handed his team in batting order, with Cosier inked in at number two and the seam-bowling all-rounder Phil Carlson at number twelve to accommodate two spinners. He pondered fielding when he won the toss, but played safe: 'At the time I was so young, I just thought: "Well they're great men with a huge amount of Test knowledge and experience, they must know". As soon as the first over was bowled I thought: "Oh boy, what have we done?"'

A poignant chant of 'C'mon, Aussie' from schoolchildren on $1 tickets accompanied Cosier and Wood to the centre. Sixteen Tests gave the former twice the experience of any colleague, but he worried that his runs that year for Queensland had been made at number five. And that he and Wood had never run together.

Bob Willis's opening over from the Stanley Street end began with an educative exchange of singles, but Wood's snappy call from the fifth ball and the economical movement of cover point David Gower left Cosier stranded. Exploiting sideways movement and increasingly tentative strokes, Brearley's roster of seamers seized the day in an hour and a half. The only sounds were of appeals and juvenile voices still trilling despite the 6–26 scoreline. As Lee wrote: 'Perhaps they didn't understand what was happening out there in the middle but, in the circumstances, they sounded absurd.'

England passed Australia's 116 with seven wickets standing. Although the unheralded Rodney Hogg and Alan Hurst limited the deficit to 170, the Australian top order proved almost as brittle at the second attempt. One ball sufficed for the hapless Cosier, bowled through a wretched drive by Willis's first delivery. 'It was a bad shot,' he agrees. 'But if you're a conditioned opener you don't try and drive the first ball of an innings, even if it's a full toss. I wasn't. And Bob Willis got one on the stumps first up, which probably never happened with him again.'

Peter Toohey again followed quickly. 'That had a big impact on me, and on England's bowlers as well,' he says. 'I wasn't a new ball player and I certainly wasn't an opening batsman which I virtually was in that Test. My technique wasn't good enough, and they were so good at bowling that nagging off-stump line.'

Four and a half hours' resistance from Yallop and Kim Hughes and a defiant tail finally extended Brearley's men, but they had their expected one-nil lead by 3.15 p.m. on the Thursday. Yallop's 'six-nil' throwaway had taken a week to throw away. Even harsher was the testimony of the ticket sellers. The Brisbane Test had drawn just 43,523 people, fewer than WSC had herded into the SCG in a night even before Packer opened his gates. 'I was fighting wars on two fronts,' Yallop remembers. 'And I couldn't really win either of them.'

Having swaggered into direct competition with official cricket the previous season, WSC was playing its cards more cannily. The Cavaliers began a low-key fortnight in northern Queensland during the Test, wending their way down from Cairns, through Townsville, Mackay, Rockhampton, Gladstone, to the Gold Coast and Toowoomba.

The next Australian face-off with the World at the SCG was fixed for the First Test's rest day. TV broadcasts just after evening news in eastern states caught the new name Garth Le Roux. In three deliveries he removed both Chappells, then upended Laird an over later for figures of 5–2–6–3. Two hours' loitering later Le Roux was recalled to hit Lillee with three consecutive deliveries to Tony Greig's undisguised glee. 'It was stuff that showbiz is made of,' wrote Phil Wilkins. 'And from the VIP room, Kerry chortled and rubbed his hands with glee and counted the cash.'

Greig's pleasure was, however, increasingly vicarious. His average of less than eight from fourteen innings had brought him to the verge of surrender. Meeting his World selectors Asif Iqbal, Mike Procter and manager Mike Denness at the Old Melbourne to select an XI for the floodlit First Supertest against the Australians, he told them he would spend it in the nets instead.

The selectors sympathised, though Procter was struck by the incongruity of Greig's faith in practice. 'I admired his honesty,' he wrote, 'but he really only had himself to blame: as captain he was never with the World side in the nets on the eve of a Supertest – he was always off doing a commercial or a TV interview.' Even Greig's humility was given a theatricality: as Asif's team was inserted by Ian Chappell, there were live crosses to VFL Park's nets where Greig was undergoing bowling-machine therapy under Sir Garfield Sobers' supervision. As the game's best-paid twelfth man, Greig also performed on-field cameos on a motorised drinksmobile.

While 'one-night' cricket worked, packaging 'Test cricket' as four consecutive seven and a half hour days from 1.30 p.m. was a bold move. One consequence was apparent as Lillee released his first white ball of the match at Majid Khan. The film of child spectators could raise just a thin chant of the bowler's name. Night cricket's population pattern meant that barely 600 saw the game commence, although 15,000 were in attendance at the break and an excellent 19,000 saw stumps drawn: the reverse of the long-form game.

Nor did the entertainment grab WSC's new constituency. The rejuvenated Lillee permitted just 51 runs in 33 overs, and on a mud mat of a pitch the World crept to 175 at fewer than two runs an over. 'It was hard-grinding Test-style cricket,' Alan Lee noted, 'and the hordes of converts whom Packer had collected with one-day cricket were probably bored and bewildered.'

At stumps at 10.30 p.m., Lee also noticed metabolic effects. He was ravenous, having worked from mid-morning to midnight without a break. 'It then occurred to me that the WSC players faced something like twenty-five such days in the season.'

The seven and a half hours broken by a half-hour 'tea' and one hour 'dinner' were indeed passing strange. With two and a half hours ahead, most players passed up dinner. 'It was an odd feeling to finish play for the day at 10.30 p.m.,' Knott wrote. 'I would normally have a meal round midnight, unwind by watching a late-night movie and get to bed about 2 a.m.' He felt the format too long, and a threat to standards.

Lillee and Le Roux's one-upmanship was conventional enough. After Lillee's pawing appeal won an lbw appeal against the South African, Le Roux raked the Australian order and had Lillee fending to Majid to give his side a lead of 25 runs.

Majid's six-hour 77 was then orthodoxy itself though, as the white ball turned grey on being forced to serve beyond the usual 50 overs, Ian Chappell missed his flying edge from Lillee in the second day's evening light. Chappell caught Majid's edge of a more pristine second new ball low to his left, but by then Procter had helped the Pakistani set the Australians a target of 283.

The game was the boss. Wessels gouged 46 from the surface in three and a half hours. Then Greg Chappell donned his new helmet for VFL Park's peculiar light configuration, which players had found inferior to that at the SCG, and spent four and a half hours over a meticulous 81. 'I felt that if ever I was going to get cleaned up, it was going to be under lights,' he says. 'It was that much harder to see the ball, your reaction time was that much slower, and at VFL Park in particular the four light pylons cast four shadows on the ball instead of the single shadow you get during daylight. The ball coming toward you, being rimmed by shadow, actually seemed smaller than a normal one.'

Imran found also that he could make the grey marble jackknife by rubbing away its residual lacquer. He induced a final collapse by bowling Marsh as the wicketkeeper shouldered arms, and took 4–8 with his last sixteen deliveries.

Packer had been in good humour throughout, ribbing David Frith about the writer's freebie Benson & Hedges overnight bag from the Gabba: 'Bet it doesn't last until the end of the summer.' But the Australians' 102-run defeat was a setback for WSC. Wessels, expecting modest commendation, received instead a personal chiding. 'I was overoptimistic,' he wrote, 'because he proceeded to tell me in no uncertain terms that he did not import players to score 40s, and that I must get my arse moving.'

Fortunately Packer had found a player on whom such psychology worked. A shaken Wessels decided to make Packer eat his words.

The Australians spent the better part of the next month force-feeding detractors. As crowds followed a sequence of five International Cup games in which the Australians suffered only one narrow defeat, WSC fed from their success.

As important as the turnstile to Packer, of course, was success at the home box-office. And according to the Roy Morgan Research Centre's new 'people meter' computers, only the Melbourne Cup and VFL Grand Final had attracted more viewers than the SCG's opening night spectacular. ABC ratings dwindled as Tests were lost in Brisbane then Perth.

The Australians' waxing fortunes were built around their bowlers. Lillee was running in like the trained sprinter he now was. In a poor summer for pitches all round – only John Maley's VFL Park track favoured batsmen – Len Pascoe, Max Walker and Ray Bright also prospered.

Wessels scrapped hard for reward, a prefabricated disciple of Ian Chappell who revered Greg Chappell, Marsh and Lillee. 'They used to grade people according to whether or not they would like to have them with them "in the trenches",' the South African recalled. 'There are no others I would prefer to have "in the trenches" with me than these four and I hope they would say the same about me.'

David Hookes worked to exorcise his fast bowling demons. Ten trance sessions of positive thought with an Adelaide hypnotherapist, Lindsay Wilkie, smoothed his flow of runs. But Ian Chappell was the only other reliable source of runs. His brother, Ian Davis and Bruce Laird struggled technically in the unremitting cycle of fast bowling.

It so happened that everyone else suffered more. While their batting depth meant they thrived in the longer contest, the World players, older and less mobile in the field, found the sprint of the International Cup a strain.

The West Indians remained athletic and elastic for 50-over stretches, but a run-drought among their batsmen, especially Richards, and injuries to Holding, Garner, Daniel and Fredericks handicapped them over longer distances.

Even wicketkeeper Deryck Murray, injury-free for fifteen years, suffered a dislocated shoulder, and burdened his stand-in Desmond Haynes. The twenty-two-year-old opener could juggle roles over a day: on 19 December he blazed an undefeated 97 against the Australians at VFL Park. But two days later, as the World thrashed the West Indians in the Second Supertest at the SCG, he could hardly hold the bat and failed twice after nine and a half hours behind the stumps.

Packer was furious at the West Indians' sudden frailty. He stormed the SCG rooms after their dismissal for 66 in an International Cup loss to the Australians two days after Christmas. He'd bloody well send them home. In the meantime, they could bloody well play another match that day. West Indians hung their heads and Joel Garner wondered if they weren't suffering delayed reaction to their Test ban. 'Most of us played as if in a daze, and we could not blame the weather, the kind of cricket or the locations,' he wrote. 'I think that what really affected us was a kind of guilt . . . we remained at heart West Indies players. I felt that this meant we should be playing Test cricket. We all began to appreciate more fully what the Australian players had put up with during that first season of WSC when they were out in the cold.'

That WSC's gruelling nature was marketable soon dawned on Bill Macartney. After Christmas he wrote a memo to players and managers:

> It seems we are gaining a substantial number of new fans who traditionally may not have come within the bounds of cricket followers. Women are a significant and important example. So to continue the flow of 'different' information, and give the feature writers something to talk about, I would like to tell them about the injuries gathered by professionals in the 'gentle game' of cricket. For that purpose, could you list the injuries you've suffered during the course of your career, and what sort of incidents in brief caused them?

Five frantic days round the New Year sum up the bruising, brawling, boisterous business of the WSC machine.

A sort of amphetamine cricket of low scores, irresistible fast bowling and slick fielding was played during the first International Cup triple-header at the Gabba, the wretched First Test pitches having gone wild.

Some 5300 attended the 'neutral' West Indians–World game on Saturday 30 December. An attack minus Holding and Croft constrained all but Barry Richards, but loss of Garner to a broken finger in the field deepened West Indian despondency at a 90-run defeat inflicted by Le Roux and Sarfraz.

On the Sunday, some 18,000 hung from the rafters to watch Australia – thanks to an Ian Chappell–Gilmour stand of 75 for the sixth wicket in 51 minutes – set the West Indians 166 to win. Lillee, resenting a first-ball bouncer from Roberts, immediately had Haynes caught at square leg, Richards caught behind first ball and examined umpire Peter Enright's glasses when Lloyd was given not out waving at the next delivery.

The West Indian captain thrashed three sixes from Gilmour onto the dog track, but Lillee returned to dish out consecutive bouncers at Roberts and polish off the innings. The match ended in chaos to the strains of 'C'mon Aussie'. Pascoe ran out Roberts, Gilmour ran out Croft and Ian Chappell upended a child in his haste for the pavilion.

On New Year's Day, the Australians found themselves sent in on the worst pitch of their trip. South Africans Le Roux and Rice took the field to the *Rocky* theme, and worked cruel tricks using the white ball's outsize seam. 'When I caught Greg Chappell at slip off the second ball it was like catching a razor blade at 100mph,' remembers Barry Richards. 'The pitch was a real Clem Jones special.' After a dozen overs, they were 4–9. By noon Le Roux (5–6) and Rice (4–14) had rumbled them for 54.

With Lillee nursing a thigh injury, Richards went out to slap 21 in 21 balls. Javed Miandad took the same time to smack 25. Majid, obstinately correct, managed to connect twice in 23 deliveries. The match's conclusion at 1.11 p.m. entailed a post-lunch exhibition for the 8179, while players performed double duties at Goodyear Autograph Booths: hero-worship made easy.

On comfortably the week's truest surface at Port Macquarie's Oxley Oval the following day, Viv Richards finally prospered. His four sixes, one lodging ten metres up a Norfolk pine, curtailed the game at the adjacent East Port bowls club. The West Indians won by seven wickets, but even then not without cost. The luckless Murray, kneecapped by Collis King's sharp return, was ice-packed all the way back to Sydney's Chateau Commodore that night.

Back on treacherous turf at the SCG on Wednesday 3 January 1979, Croft, Roberts, Daniel and Julien reduced the World to 7–49 . . . odds at last in Greig's favour. Weaving and wearing bouncers during a frenzied 62 at number eight, he won favour from 14,000 with a six into the Noble Stand. To Lee he exhibited the bruising on his left thigh. 'I may not get many more,' Greig said. 'So I'd better show this one off.'

Before Gordon Greenidge's unbeaten 82 made the game safe, Le Roux bowled daggers at Viv Richards, striking him in chest and back and removing his cap with a ball Alan Knott took overhead. The blood-sportsmanship disturbed the humane Tony Lewis. 'The most dangerous act in the entertainment business these days is not balancing on high wire or even putting a head in a lion's mouth,' he wrote. 'It is batting in Kerry Packer's Flying Circus. Fast bowling and repeated bouncers are destroying some of the best batsmen we have ever seen.'

But the bottom line of WSC's tour was significant. It had coincided with Melbourne's Third Test. The pinnacle of the official summer had been attended by 128,758. But WSC's hard sell, on far smaller grounds in three cities and with Australians playing only twice, had still attracted 50,000. Mike Brearley's Englishmen overflew the illuminated SCG that last evening as their Fourth Test appointment at the ground loomed: a reminder that their rival attraction was working the night shift.

16

'Rejected, dejected, we're sorry we're born'

Cairns had not expected night cricket, but when 'Packer's Sheffield Shield' visited on the first two days of December 1978, it turned out that way. As Eddie Barlow's Cavaliers triumphed in tropical twilight, they were already living a remarkable low-life.

Composed largely of those Australians unemployed in the capital cities like McCosker, Walters, Edwards, Robinson, O'Keeffe, Langer, Malone, Prior and Trevor Chappell, the Cavaliers were a convenience. With peripheral internationals like Mushtaq, Haroon, Snow, Amiss and Woolmer, and wandering West Indians in Holford, Allen, Julien and Austin, they were rural ambassadors, country coaches and punching-bags for World, Australian and West Indian teams released from higher profile duties.

At World Series Cricket's selection table they had a stool. Bernard Julien might be a Cavalier against the World one day, a West Indian against the Cavaliers the next. Success, too, was its own punishment. Barlow and manager Graham Ferrett were resigned to losing players as soon as they glimpsed form and to inheriting the lame and the blind.

By Cairns they had already surrendered their promising colt Kepler Wessels to the WSC Australians, and accepted the out-of-touch Martin Kent. The barren Cricket Association Ground pitch favouring Mushtaq and O'Keeffe before Haroon's torchlit swinging with Walters was good for morale. 'I think it helped that they couldn't actually see their opposition,' says Ferrett.

That was no reason though, they discovered, to get uppity. West Indians sharing their evening flight to Townsville did not share the Cavaliers' pleasure at a maiden victory. 'We were pretty carried away after slogging in the dark,' recalls O'Keeffe, 'so we hit the drink pretty hard when we piled into the plane, while they sat up the front, all sullen. We probably overdid it.'

Comeuppance was inevitable. The pitch at Townsville's Endeavour Park was like foliage underfoot. 'We'd stared three days at this flat thing without a blade of grass on it,' O'Keeffe continues. 'Amazingly enough, none of us were terribly keen on batting.'

Though Ferrett demanded that a disbelieving groundsman shave his pride and joy, Roberts and Holding trampled the Cavaliers for 131. West Indian honour was satisfied. Ross Edwards was aggrieved. 'I'd been coaching in Townsville for three days,' he says. 'So I hadn't even played in Cairns.'

Such was the Cavalier lot for the next two months: moments of success, long periods of failure, and changing faces on bat-and-bone-jarring pitches. The sham shield did Kent no good. His week of ducks in Townsville, Cairns and Rockhampton was broken by a single in Mackay.

There were, however, worse lives. Wives and children travelled at discount ticket and room rates. Tour managers blended Ferrett's teenage son Tim, Ian Chappell's wife Kay and ticket manager Vern Toose, a Consolidated Press relic and returned serviceman who relived surviving a Japanese bayonet wound in gruesome detail. Some who found WSC's upper reaches alien came to prefer the small occasion.

Rockhampton was typical. Rain left Ferrett with a restive crowd, and Gordon Greenidge proposed an outfield catching competition with Walters and Haroon, and WSC hats as prizes. Ferrett gave away hundreds. Ten Cavaliers began the game, with a midday airport dash to collect Bob Woolmer seven hours after he'd left Sydney. The

Englishman had barely finished padding up when he was on duty, his unbeaten 69 surprisingly serene.

Two days later on a Gladstone greentop, however, Woolmer was scratched for six weeks with a finger broken by Holding. The player, together with his wife Gillian, accepted Ferrett's offer to join the Cavaliers' management. 'It was a role I gratefully accepted and enjoyed,' Woolmer wrote, 'looking after all the paperwork, marshalling the team onto planes or trains at the right time and the correct place.'

Country crowds of 2000 disenchanted some of the Pakistanis, accustomed to five-star treatment at home. Sarfraz Nawaz seemed to crave a batman more than a bat. 'I think he expected to be treated a bit specially,' says Ferrett. 'Like a full international tour. I had to let him know things like he was expected to carry his own bag up to his room.' Breakfast table debates about the Bhuttos also proved inscrutable to Australians.

Countryman Haroon Rashid, however, proved a revelation with his virile, fearless stroke play. One of Pakistan's most underrated batsmen, he lost nothing by comparison with Viv Richards when the pair made centuries at Rockhampton, in firepower or physique.

'He was the darkest, hairiest bloke I think I ever saw,' Edwards remembers. 'In the dressing-room, he was like a coconut. By crikey, though, he could hit the ball.' Haroon even took it in good part when O'Keeffe slipped him 'unclean' roast beef and horseradish sandwiches.

Peaked-cap players slow to adapt to a helmeted age suffered on the poor pitches. Walters did not reach 30 in a dozen innings after Cairns, and finally joined the 'managers' with a broken finger. McCosker, Amiss, Kent and Redpath all averaged less than 20.

Rob Langer, Test material had he not signed with WSC, found a degree of rationalisation necessary. 'I eased my mind with the thought that, in twenty years' time, could I say I'd earned the privilege of Test cricket? I would have been proud, but I think there would have been sniggers if I put my green cap on the trophy shelf.'

While the likes of Snow, Julien and Malone could prove lethal, spinners Mushtaq, Holford, Padmore and O'Keeffe were all but paid spectators. O'Keeffe, thoughtful and serious about his leg-spinning art, drifted. 'I basically kept to myself a lot,' he says. 'You got frustrated because the scorecards never told the full stories about the degree of luck involved. The bush telegraph wasn't strong. To come under consideration you had to win a match, and leg spinners didn't do it. I was a stayer being run over sprint distances. Sometimes I'd catch them up but most of the time I'd tail off and if I was lucky pass a few tired runners.'

At least he knew he was in good company: 'Players were playing and failing in up-country games that meant nothing, who could have been plundering some Test attacks round at the time . . . The saviour for me was that there were so many people to like. I got as much pleasure dining with Mushtaq and John Snow as I did from dining with the Chappells.'

Indeed, the resolve of most players was remarkable. The enthusiastic Barlow enforced fitness drills with scoutmasterly verve, glasses fogging at his own exertion. As injuries and promotions raked the Cavaliers ranks, journeymen like Rohan Kanhai, Lance Gibbs, the Pakistani wicketkeeper-batsman Taslim Arif (who the following year would make the highest Test score by a keeper) joined up. When the Cavaliers first played the Australians at Maitland even Tim Ferrett appeared, attired by Ian Davis and Trevor Chappell, ferrying drinks with John Snow's three-year-old daughter.

The Australians – star-struck by the growing capital city success of WSC – proved the Cavaliers' meanest opponents. 'The top side had an attitude that we didn't,' Edwards says. 'They were media darlings and they expected to get what they wanted all the time. Some of them got a bit cocky.'

Competition immediately went up a notch at Maitland Sports Ground when Wayne Prior broke Wessels' ribs before he'd scored, though the South African made his cussed way to 92. The Cavaliers could manage only one more between them.

Animosity, though, was then replaced by fear. When an air strike grounded all aircraft, players looked askance at a DC-3 chartered to fly the team from Williamtown to Melbourne. But the alternative of thirty-two hours on a bus was not an option for those in a VFL Park International Cup game next evening.

Sick bags were located when the aircraft backed off the tarmac to raise take-off speed, gunned its engines and made a lurching dash into the air. There was then the obligatory storm. 'It was,' recalls

Davis, 'like one of those old movies where the little biplane flies through the thunder and lightning and you're hoping the hero won't crash.'

'The pilot said he was going to try and fly round it,' Langer recalls. 'We reckoned he went through the middle. I mean, the plane was absolutely chocka. Bodies, equipment, hostesses, wives and kids everywhere. My dad and I were sitting up the back, my son and Ian Chappell's little daughter were so scared they fell asleep next to each other.'

Langer rivalled Rick McCosker as the team's worst flier. On Hercules transports during his national service, comrades had kept a book on how quickly Langer would be sick. Neither, though, went worse than a whiter shade of pale – even when the DC-3's captain insisted on a scenic lap of VFL Park to admire its lights – before the plane touched down. McCosker promptly threw up with relief.

The trip was immortalised in the 'Song of the Cavaliers', to the tune of 'Mull of Kintyre': 'Far have I travelled and much have I seen . . . By coach, train and Cessna and a DC-3.' It was with some pleasure that librettist Edwards inked in the last verse at Morwell on Christmas Eve, when the Cavaliers rolled Greg Chappell's Australian XI: 'We're aged and injured or just out of form/Rejected dejected we're sorry we're born/When other teams play us they think it's a farce/But we wipe off their smiles when we give them the arse.'

Martin Kent's hopes had been sustained by Ferrett's advice that Ian Chappell was watching from afar. 'Bertie'd really like you to get a few today, Super,' the manager would say. 'Get stuck in.'

Leaving Lismore in the New Year with a single-figure average, Kent knew that attention wouldn't last. There was nothing for it. He would slog. Three days and 1600 kilometres later in a heat-haze at Mildura's City Oval, Kent entered at 3–13, and watched Le Roux break Walters' hand.

Between a dust-storm and a thunderstorm, the Queenslander scored a cyclonic 114 out of 141. 'Le Roux and Imran were bowling, and they were just trying to knock my head off,' says Kent. 'And when they weren't doing that they were trying to york me. But it was a pretty slow track, a bit like the Gabba, so I just kept smashing them.' A half-century at Bendigo's Queen Elizabeth Oval three days later, and Bertie was briefed that his headstrong hopeful had finally 'got a few'.

Bendigo was a watershed. The World swiped Haroon and Amiss and, with Walters and Woolmer still mending as managers, Kay Chappell was asked about her match fitness. Kanhai and Graham McKenzie were fetched, and O'Keeffe recalls opening the bowling at Barry Richards: 'Sometimes Eddie Barlow had some strange ideas.'

'Bunter awakes with a recurring dream/Concerning selections and picking a team,' runs the salient verse of the team song. 'One day it will happen but we don't know when/That we'll walk on the field with more than ten men.'

Barlow himself was then out of action at Tamworth two days later, and his stand-in David Holford saw even Snow and Kanhai recruited. Overwhelming defeat provoked a long team meeting, Ferrett agreeing that the Cavaliers' pride in being the 'no fuss' team was being abused. 'Support and co-operation from the three main sides in regard to players being released for country matches has been completely inadequate,' Ferrett noted in his minutes. 'Furthermore, the morale of the Cavaliers was dented due to the imbalance of the sides and were therefore incapable of making the match of high standard.'

Having to rely on newspapers for information was also not fair. 'It was resolved that the Cavaliers desire a meeting with the executive regarding their future as individual members of WSC,' he wrote. 'At the moment they feel left out and ill-informed of the future of WSC.' Protest registered, the team boarded a coach for Armidale with a week in Orange, Wagga and Albury to look forward to.

Drain on the Cavaliers could be traced straight to the top. Sounds of success there mingled with those of splintering bone. When the Australians and West Indians played a meaningless $3000 stake game at Football Park on the first Saturday of the new year – largely to appease South Australian Premier Des Corcoran – some 22,068 people watched teams of crocks. Max Walker had joined Lillee on the injured list, and Davis was playing in spite of a broken finger. Murray, Rowe, Fredericks, Roberts and Holding were scratchings, and an inconvenient hat-trick by Gilmour (Haynes, Lloyd and Allen) forced Garner to bat with his broken finger to ensure a two-wicket win in the last over with Holford.

Garner soldiered on to VFL Park two days later, where a refreshed Andy Roberts began an arduous match by fracturing Majid's cheek-bone. As Tony Greig and Mike Procter shared the day's highest partnership of 24 in a total of 103, they were humiliated regularly by steepling bounce.

Procter's warning to Garner between innings that the ball tends to follow a broken digit proved good. A very reluctant last man at 9–67, Garner had his middle finger picked out by Clive Rice's tailored bouncer. Hurling his glove to the ground, the West Indian reeled from the field. The West Indians buckled again against the Australians before a teeming 39,252 at VFL Park the following day. Chasing 174, the side's last eight wickets dissolved in 38 runs.

England's tour had also been bloodstained, and Queensland's David Ogilvie sold a hamper of C & D helmets to the tourists at the Crest Hotel just before the First Test. 'If great batsmen like Ian Chappell feel they should be worn then it makes sense for me to wear one,' diarised the young David Gower. 'If it helps my confidence, what have I got to lose?' While the technician Boycott did not 'feel the need' personally, he recognised it. '£15 is not a very high price to put on a skull,' he wrote.

'The reasons behind the outbreak of such injuries were not easy to define,' Alan Lee wrote, 'although the further we went . . . the more disturbing standard of pitches became. Gone were the hard and even-bounced wickets for which the country has long been known; in their place a motley assortment including seamer's delights and raging turners.'

It was no coincidence that Wessels, the summer's most consistent scorer, frequently made others look nude in his protective array. A front-foot player, he needed all his armour for a century in the Third Supertest at VFL Park on Friday 12 January 1979.

Left with a splitting headache by Croft at 17, and hit in the groin as his century approached, he passed out at tea and had to be revived by masseur Dave McErlane so he could stagger the necessary runs. Wessels savoured Packer's habitual stumps visit, as

Ian Chappell reminded 'the Boss' of his swipe at the Springbok a month earlier. 'You reckon that's worthy of an import?' said the Australian captain acidly.

'For once Packer was lost for words,' Wessels wrote. 'And I thoroughly enjoyed watching his reaction.'

The Supertest became, however, a relative frolic on an even-tempered Maley pitch. Wessels' introspection helped Hookes complete his return to batting health during their largely wordless partnership of 145. 'He didn't talk much, which suited me at that stage,' Hookes says. 'Batting conditions were good, and I could just concentrate on my own game.' Hookes proceeded to what he felt was a 'maiden Test century' with fourteen fours.

Lawrence Rowe's reputation, meantime, had always puzzled younger Australians. 'We were always hearing what a good batsman he was,' Mick Malone recalls. 'And he was always disappointing. I'd never seen him make a run.' With new, soft contact lenses, however, Rowe's touch had been returning, and Malone was among the helpless bowling witnesses.

'You always made the mistake of chasing Lawrence's shots,' says Ian Chappell. 'They'd be timed well-enough just to reach the boundary. With Viv you just waited for someone to throw the ball back, but Lawrence probably tired you more because you always felt you could catch them up. But you never did.'

Rowe taunted fielders two dozen times in the next six and a half hours, teasing also with his unbridled driving. 'You'd think he was short,' says Ray Bright. 'But his top hand would always get forward of the ball and he'd be hitting you along the ground through covers again.' With his last scoring shot of the second day, Rowe reached 150.

Even Lillee patted Rowe on the back when he sauntered off with 175 the next morning. The match was the one international attraction – Supertest or Ashes Test – to aggregate more than 1000 runs that summer: quality batsmanship, no one brained and even 53 overs of Richard Austin's becalming off-spin. Normal abnormal service, however, would resume in just forty-eight hours.

For some weeks, WSC's Barbara Loois had been foraging in curtain shops and department stores for pastel fabrics. Plans to breach cricket's colour bar were reaching fruition. Her only difficulty was that strawberry dye matching the West Indian mousse would not take to the synthetic surfaces of normal leg guards. Leather pads were imported.

The wattle Wessels and Davis opening the Australian innings in a reef of coral pink fielders on 17 January had 45,523 at the SCG blinking and television viewers fiddling with sets. The Australians acclimatised fitfully in their 9–149. Hookes holed out to Rowe as he lost a bouncer against the pale pitch and Marsh swayed sightlessly into another Daniel lifter that removed his helmet as it cut his eye.

The game was significant in WSC's progress, for West Indian victory would see the team graduate to the International Cup Finals against the Australians: the optimum arrangement. Among on-lookers was England's captain Mike Brearley, whose American companion Dudley Doust was reminded of baseball as they studied the curious kaleidoscope.

Even moments of pandemonium seemed impressive, as when Lillee made an unsuccessful lbw appeal against Austin that became an attempt to run Rowe out. 'All the fielders were converging while Austin was still running for his life toward the bowler's end,' Brearley wrote. 'He had no idea what was happening at the other end, where Rowe was running back down the wicket shouting to attract Austin's attention . . . As a piece of cricket it was a mess but, with the yellow and strawberry colours, the game was more dramatic because one could see who was on which side.'

They left before rain made the match truly bizarre. WSC managing director Andrew Caro bustled to the centre to remind umpires Douglas Sang Hue and Gary Duperouzel of their responsibilities, and the game recommenced with the pinks apparently pursuing 48 in 16 overs.

The plot thickened when the West Indians reached their target in nine overs and players began filing off. The umpires reasserted themselves by insisting that the required minimum of 15 overs be played, an impossibility when the SCG lights had to be extinguished by 10.30 p.m. to meet Randwick council by-laws. The West Indians were 4–66 as the black-out fell, and some newspapers were baffled by the possibility of a draw. The *Age* guessed correctly, its story blessed with a Walkley Award-winning headline by subeditor Bob Parsonage: 'Pink bats beat the weather!'

Argument smouldered the next day as players attended a pre-arranged 'At Home' at the Packer residence, 76 Victoria Road, Bellevue Hill. Ian Chappell was adamant about the match's invalidity. He was also furious at the brawling, sprawling crowd behaviour leading to twenty-five arrests.

The Packers soothed ruffled feathers, and Ross Edwards was floored to hear Ros Packer greet his wife by name: 'You must be Lyndall, I've heard so much about you.' 'That really impressed me,' Edwards says. 'She'd really done her homework.'

The guests had other questions. An International Cricket Conference delegation – chairman Charles Palmer, past-chairman David Clark and secretary Jack Bailey – had now spent a fortnight in Australia since meeting the Australian Cricket Board in Melbourne. Columnists wondered if a healing of world cricket's WSC wound was near.

English attitude to Packer was still summed up by comic Warren Mitchell, whose Sydney season of Johnny Speight's *The Thoughts of Chairman Alf* featured a routine griping about 'that bloody Kerry Packer'. But Brearley's team had performed as unpaid WSC servants a week earlier by securing the Ashes with a fine Fourth Test victory at the SCG. Now the ACB had two 'dead' Tests to promote, and more than two months of cricket in which to sustain interest. The ICC also had a World Cup in England that year to think about, and peace was paramount. When word leaked that Palmer and Bailey had met Caro and Taylor at Consolidated Press on Wednesday 10 January 1979, imminence of a truce was hailed.

It wouldn't be that simple. Packer had no love for the global body, or indeed for any nosy pom sticking his oar into Australian waters. A follow-up discussion the next Tuesday attended by Packer, Caro, Taylor and Consolidated Press deputy chairman Harry Chester was civilised, but abbreviated when Packer told the blow-ins: 'I can't understand why I've got members of the MCC in my office discussing what is basically an Australian problem. If I'm going to speak to anyone, I want to speak to Parish and Steele.' At their Royal Sydney

Golf Club lodgings, the Englishmen realised that the ACB would have to act on the ICC's behalf.

Packer would tell his players little at dinner. There was still little to tell. But he knew at last that, with the ABC's television rights finished at season's end, he had never been closer to his original goal.

Giving up was hard. Some felt Packer could still be thwarted. 'I'd have been inclined to go on and fight it out for another year,' says ACB treasurer Ray Steele. 'Because I could see he was losing an awful lot of money. Everybody that worked for Packer was paid and paid big money, and cricket had thousands working in an honorary capacity. We had players under contract so he couldn't recruit, while his players had a limited life and couldn't go on forever.' He recognised, however, that a fight to the finish might prove just that.

Chairman Bob Parish ensured that he had the ICC's explicit mandate. Dated 17 January on the golf club's notepaper, Charles Palmer's four-page handwritten letter arrived with the key paragraph: 'I confirm that, as chairman of the ICC, I hereby authorise you to hold unilateral talks with WSC on the lines above, and I also confirm that talks only be accepted on condition that Mr Packer is present himself.'

The ACB's first 1979 meeting in Adelaide nine days later, on the eve of the Fifth Test, was briefed. The ICC advice was read out. Steele faced a bleak financial picture. 'When you have two bodies promoting cricket, you automatically divide sponsorship available, crowds, public interest, TV and radio income,' says Steele. 'We'd already lost a lot. The QCA told us it was on the verge of going through. At the VCA we were a bit better off because we'd built up some assets and owned our own building, but we were also in trouble.'

Secretary Alan Barnes reported an unusual volume of mail urging rapprochement, and the meeting officially attributed the burned-out Ashes summer to the divided cricket market and the weakness and anonymity of local players. But the ACB had also been outsold in a battle for public imagination. When Test selector Phil Ridings handed Mike Brearley his Fifth Test winner's cheque in Adelaide on Thursday 1 February, and proposed that differences between the English and Australian sides were not as profound as the 4–1 score-line suggested, a derisory voice sang: 'What series have you been watching?'

Permitted by the meeting to negotiate exclusive commercial television rights, the ACB chairman wrote to Consolidated Press indicating its peaceful mood. He met formal but sympathetic response. 'Parish and the board were the losers that summer,' Caro recalls. 'I mean, we outmarketed the bastards. But the poms were absolutely pusillanimous and they delivered Bob Parish's head on an absolute platter, like John the Baptist.'

17

'I feel very sorry for the Australians'

'C'mon, Aussie, C'mon' surged from speakers a night early at Sydney's Entertainment Centre. World Series Cricket's Australians, guests of American pop group Chicago, were invited on stage for an encore of their anthem. Chicago's vocalist Peter Cetera had been lured to the SCG as part of the Fourth Supertest pre-publicity that day, shaped as a southpaw in coloured pads and helmet, and left a fistful of concert tickets.

The tune anticipated rout at the SCG and, spinning into a stiff breeze at the Paddington end, Ray Bright reaped six West Indian wickets in a session. 'I'd got used to bowling with the white ball, too, and I found it unusually easy to grip,' he adds. 'Unlike the red one I could get it to curve in with the arm before spinning it away.'

Roberts and Croft swept away the Australian top order, but Hookes found Ian Redpath a tenacious ally. The South Australian admired his thirty-seven-year-old partner's masochistic pleasure at being a full-fledged 'Aussie' again, teasing him as he accepted body blows without shrinking: 'You old goat, go back to your antique shop, you shouldn't be out here.'

Despite Bright's success, Lloyd ignored his token spinner, Albert Padmore, to keep the Australians in check. 'I don't think Clive would have played a top-class spinner at the SCG even if he'd had one,' says Greg Chappell. 'The bounce was up and down so it gave fast bowlers as much help as slow. If he'd played a spinner, too, he would have increased the number of balls per hour, which could have been crucial in a low-scoring game. The West Indies approach was like the Chinese water torture. If you just kept at 'em and at 'em and at 'em, they'd break mentally if not physically.' Redpath's nine runs lasted 143 minutes but he did not break, or even bend. The 71 he added with Hookes was the basis of a useful Australian lead of 22.

Lillee had been conserving his energies, coaxing a complaining hamstring to greater and greater extensions under Doc McErlane's supervision, until stung by Colin Croft's bouncers at the Australian tail. The West Indians were left two and a quarter hours' flood-lit batting on the third evening, and he neutralised five of their first seven, including an inert and apprehensive Viv Richards. The Australians' ten-wicket win brought $10,000, and Ian Chappell pondered pay-off time.

Almost $100,000 rode on the Australians' last fortnight. The $35,000 best-of-five International Cup Finals against the West Indies beginning on Saturday 27 January at VFL Park were followed by the $61,000 Supertest Final against the World scheduled the Friday following.

Those Ian Chappell considered his one-day specialists were called on. Martin Kent in Wagga had been planning a journey north to be best man at a friend's wedding when his call-up came. Mick Malone felt his faith in Chappell vindicated. 'Ian was always watching you, even when he wasn't actually around,' he says. 'You'd go four or five matches without seeing him and the first thing he'd say when you saw him would be: "Saw you got 4–26 and 3–19 at Toowoomba. Keep that up and we'll be needing you." Ian could make me feel like Dennis Lillee when he threw me the ball.'

Ian Davis was also recalled, and with Wessels launched the first final with crisp strokes. Accompanied by a chant of 'C'mon, Kepler, C'mon', Wessels then added 116 in less than an hour and a half with Greg Chappell and was unstoppable until bowled for 136 from the innings' final ball. The West Indian top order were a negligent contrast, top-scorer Gordon Greenidge run out by Rod Marsh in an evening daze as he wandered from his ground.

Wessels continued his rich vein of form in the second final, although Davis's enjoyment was seasoned with annoyance. 'If Kepler felt he was playing well he'd drop singles and make sure he got five or six balls an over,' he recalls. 'After an hour I was facing one ball an over, and I felt like I'd just been hung out to dry.'

Wessels, though, called one too many: Richards pounced on what seemed a perfectly realisable single wide of cover and threw down the non-striker's stumps in the one movement. Losing impetus, the Australians seemed short-changed by their 8–189.

Victory still appeared likely when mistiming and misfortune dogged the West Indians on the slow surface. Rowe and Richards added 57 with the day's surest strokes, but the former's mishit to leg from Greg Chappell was extraordinarily caught by Marsh. The keeper covered the thirty metres from his crouch to square leg when the ball bisected converging fielders. 'It was one of the greatest catches I've seen,' wrote an expert watcher in Alan Knott. 'Chasing a skier, overrunning it and then diving back parallel to the ground about three feet above it, catching the ball with arms at full stretch. How he held onto it when he hit the ground I cannot imagine.'

Collis King's pinch-hitting, however, levelled the series with two overs of daring against Malone and Lillee. The last ball of the penultimate over, joyfully back-foot driven to the long off boundary, completed the rescue.

The West Indians had found their form at last and Wessels' 70 on the Australia Day Monday in 6–200 was insufficient when Greenidge made a smart 81 in two-and-a-half hours and confirmed the Australians' lingering regard. A mid-season poll of their ranks had discovered that he was the opponent most Australians' wished was a countryman. Some, like Malone, preferred bowling at Richards: 'You could keep Gordon quiet with five balls, but if the sixth was a half-volley he'd hit it for four. You'd been looking at a maiden and suddenly you were thinking: "There's my over ruined".' The Australians' season of self-disciplined adaptation to one-day cricket now hinged on the fourth final on Tuesday 30 January.

'Fix it,' said Packer.

Andrew Caro was in no doubt of his duty. WSC had been spared timing problems the night before only by the West Indians' three spare overs at the finish. Now this fourth final was going to run past 10.30 p.m. if played to a finish, which Packer and John Cornell could see was unsatisfactory in a decisive match. Packer wanted the overs played out. And that was Caro's job.

Caro groaned. Once again it was down to him. For a year he'd been WSC front and back, from trials to turnstiles, and now he was worn out. 'Basically I should have told him to piss off,' Caro says. 'In fact he probably would have accepted that. There was no way he could go on interfering with playing conditions as he pleased.

'But I was basically exhausted. I'd been round the world umpteen times, and I was traumatised from dealing with Packer all the time. Most of my staff were terrified of him, so I was always the one who took him on. Kerry can be a great man when things are against him, but in success he can be insufferable and overbearing.'

Chasing 241, the West Indians had receded as far as 6–132, been revived by a partnership of 40 between Lloyd and Bernard Julien, then stalled by injury to the former requiring a runner, Richard Austin. As bats flailed and fielders dived, Caro went in search of an extra fifteen minutes. A staffer went to slow VFL Park's clock as he sought ground officials to brief. Then he tried to raise the Waverley Council for permission to keep the lights on.

The players were still in the dark, and Caro dashed at last to the Australian dressing-room. Kerry O'Keeffe was parking the drinks-mobile, so he told Wayne Prior to tell the umpires that the match was now to be played to finish. Prior headed for the centre. He told Ian Chappell.

The captain moaned. He would now have to find fill-in bowlers in order to conserve two overs from Lillee for the final follies. But WSC's problem was deeper: umpires and West Indians were still playing to time and a revised target based on run rates.

Hookes was jeered as he took the ball at the commentary-box end, but Julien promptly shelled him to mid on in his first over. In his fourth over, Andy Roberts lofted to long off where Lillee took a gymnastic catch perilously near the boundary rope. Roberts, blind to the catch because of the ground's sloping contour, did not see

Lillee's back-flip beyond the boundary. Nor did umpires invoke the experimental English law that would have ruled the catch a six. With the benefit of GTV-9's all-seeing eye, however, the West Indians were brooding when Roberts returned.

They were also punching calculators. At 10.19 p.m. (real time kept by scorer Irving Rosenwater), Lloyd and Garner tugged seven from Malone's forty-fourth over to drag the West Indians to 8–197. At 10.23 p.m., Hookes was recalled. His four gentle overs had cost just 18, but Lloyd now swung a boundary and Garner a six beyond mid wicket. Julien sprang from the dug-out at 10.27 p.m. to deliver the final account: at 8–210, 17 were needed from what would now be the game's last over to eclipse the Australians' run-rate of 4.8. The umpires were also informed. But not Ian Chappell.

One more over, from someone, and Chappell felt he could recall Lillee. Malone was bowled out. So was Gilmour. Walker had conceded 32 from seven overs, but it would have to be the Victorian. In Rosenwater's precise hand, the over reads: 10.28 p.m. Walker: Lloyd 6 4 1 – Garner 1 – Lloyd 4 2. The score: 8–228. The West Indian run rate for 46 overs: 4.95. Lloyd, Garner and Austin raised their arms, the umpires lifted the bails. The time was 10.34 p.m., but the Australians felt they had just seen four overs and $35,000 vanish. In disbelieving disorder, they traipsed off.

In the dressing-room, Ian Chappell sought answers. Marsh scattered his gear, and disgust seethed among their juniors. 'We'd been told the game would finish when it finished and they were playing under a different set of rules,' says Kent. 'We felt cheated, and cheated out of a fair amount of brass.'

WSC officials were incriminated by their silence, until Packer himself appeared. He would make it up: the Australians would receive parity of prize money. 'You can take your money,' bellowed Chappell. 'And stick it right up your arse.'

Silence fell. 'I thought we'd all been sacked,' says Ross Edwards. The players piled aboard their bus for the Old Melbourne, variously dejected and demented. Marsh finally told the team as they arrived that they'd 'taken it like Australians'. He organised a wake, charged to WSC.

Caro took the rap and resigned. 'It was my fault and I accept that,' he says. 'All I can say is that, after a year of dealing with Kerry, I was

worn out and my judgement was impaired,' he says. The freedom
Packer and Cornell felt tampering with official match rules, however,
left them equally culpable.

The findings of a VFL Park inquest were laid before journalists at a midnight press conference. Packer told pressmen he had
apologised: 'Obviously I had to apologise to them because of the
breakdown in communication. We've had a mistake made. I feel very
sorry for the Australians.'

So sorry he then made for the Old Melbourne and knocked at the
door of Marsh's wake. Ian Chappell was not around but, when the
teetotal Packer accepted a beer that Marsh wickedly forced on him,
'the Boss' achieved at least partial forgiveness.

Like many similar columns, Tony Greig's involvement in his Sunday
newspaper scribbling was mostly confined to signing his name,
but its rich rhetoric had Ian Chappell handing out photocopies as
the Australians arrived in Sydney the next day for the Supertest
final. Greig had tipped a comfortable World victory, enriched by a
personal century: 'If I'm good in any situation it's the big one, and
the more they hoot me, the more the bowlers throw at me, the better
I'll like it.'

Greig's willingness to offer himself as a hate-object was readily
accepted. 'We were working so hard to show it would work,'
Edwards says, 'that to have someone swanning round and pretend-
ing to be a superheavy when his performances didn't justify it we
found offensive.' The dangerous direction the match seemed to be
taking convinced Eddie Barlow – replacing the injured Majid as Barry
Richards' opening partner – that he should finally *get* that helmet.

Greg Chappell was out before he was in. An irritated eye he had
noticed lunching with his wife Judy in King's Cross proved to be
Bell's palsy on the right side of his face. Packer had been a fellow
sufferer and, on collecting the batsman from a series of X-rays at
Sydney hospital, took Chappell to his own Macquarie Street neuro-
surgeon. Not only would Chappell be confined to Supertest Final
commentaries in dark glasses, but his West Indies trip might be in
jeopardy.

When Garth Le Roux and the SCG surface began taking their
toll, it seemed a good match to be missing. Within half an hour of

the 3.30 p.m. intermission, Le Roux and countrymen Mike Procter and Clive Rice had reduced the home team to 7–80. Ian Chappell's imprudent hook at his ninth ball had been the sole gesture of defiance. Bright, Gilmour and Pascoe more than doubled the score, but two more Springboks, Richards and Barlow, were walking to the centre by the time the ground's lights were on.

Though Richards swung Lillee's third ball over square leg for six to strike a blow for batsmanship, Barlow was pegged to his stumps two balls later and Gilmour bowled an inspired spell. Despite his constant complaints of an inability to run, he shuttled 19 consecutive overs from the Randwick end that evening and had picked off Rice, Zaheer and Asif Iqbal for 42 when finally relieved at 10.15 p.m.

Greig lasted just five panicky deliveries. Lillee drew jerks and twitches and hazy swings from him, then induced a touch to Marsh that was celebrated like a ritual slaughter. The game's most important batting, amid all the talent on tap, came from Le Roux and Derek Underwood. Resolute in their helmets for 81 minutes on Saturday, they turned 9–104 into 168 and narrowed the Australians' lead to just four runs.

Hookes and Laird battled the elements for much of the rest of the day. Hookes was assured, Laird coming from a beggarly 58 in seven Supertest innings that season. Imran's cutters darted about in the evening but, at 9.20 p.m., Hookes heard Greig tell the Pakistani he could have just one further over. Laird snicked the second ball to Alan Knott. Imran kept the ball. Hookes cursed.

Asif Iqbal's dash at deep square leg then cost Kent dearly. 'I could see it was Asif and I knew he was one of the best around,' says Kent. 'But I was running to the end further away, so I took my time over the first and only realised I was in trouble on the way back.' As the ball soared beyond him to the non-striker's stumps, Kent stuck his bat out in attempted interception. 'It came down my backhand side and I missed the bloody thing. Goodnight Dick.'

When Marsh followed before stumps, the Australians needed Hookes to extend his overnight 93 on Sunday. Never dismissed in the 90s before, he pondered 150. But he had added only three when he overanxiously dragged a Le Roux half-volley onto his stumps.

The World's target of 226, though, should still have been beyond its reach. It was the match's highest score. The Australian bowlers were at their hungriest and the pitch was crumbling underfoot. Barlow, double-glazed behind his new helmet and old glasses, lasted ten scoreless deliveries before following Lillee's leg cutter to Gilmour in the gully. Even Richards looked vulnerable. Greig stalked the dressing-room chain-smoking.

Zaheer played a flurry of shots, Rice and Asif failed, but Richards grafted unrecognisably. His first 40 took almost two and a half hours and thirty-six overs, and partners found him anxious for reassurance. As critic rather than cricketer, Greg Chappell watched his toil. 'Without the build-up of Test cricket I wouldn't have been happy playing World Series,' he says. 'That was what Barry had done all along. I don't think he batted particularly well, but it was just sheer effort of will that allowed him to do it. He called on those great reserves of determination and experience and willpower that we always knew he had.'

Richards' application was an education for the Australians. 'Usually he did it so easy,' says Bright. 'But he earned his stripes that day. Dennis was beating him over and over but we couldn't break Barry's concentration.'

Procter took up the scoring slack with a six over extra cover from Bright and hooks and square-cuts from Pascoe. When Bright parted them with 50 still required, Richards finally seized the night. Gilmour disappeared for four and six over mid wicket, then was driven straight with a sting like a headmaster's strap. An over later Gilmour was driven and stroked through mid wicket for boundaries. Three from Lillee turned Richards' five-hour vigil into a match-winning century.

The Australians sank sullenly. With two runs needed and Richards on strike, Ian Chappell took the ball and hurled it for four leg-side wides. His team had returned penniless from its $100,000 week, although the greatest rub was losing to Greig. Chappell smoked a cigar at the post-match presentations, and refused his rival's handshake. 'Great contribution from you again,' he snapped instead.

It completed a year of estrangement between two pillars of WSC. Three years before, Chappell had described Greig as 'almost an Australian' in fair-minded competitiveness. In WSC's mid-season questionnaire, Greig had classed Chappell the Australian he most respected. Now they were irreconcilable. 'It's the sort of thing I have come to expect from him,' Greig told journalists. 'But I'm happy when Chappell does something like that because then I know he is hurt – and I like to see him hurt.' Chappell retorted: 'I didn't shake hands with Greig because I have no respect for him as a cricketer or a captain. I used to have but it's all gone.'

Procter delightedly tallied South Africa's contribution to the World's win – two-thirds of its runs, 16 wickets, five catches – and chirped to Chappell that the game would have ended a day earlier had there been more Springboks assembled. 'That went down really well,' he wrote.

The World's twelfth man Bob Woolmer recorded: 'I shall never forget . . . the faces of the Australians as they trudged off the field, realising they had lost the match and seventy thousand in bonus money . . . That match was labelled a fix by the media. Nothing could have been further from the truth: it was pure and great Test cricket with both sides keyed up to do well and performing at a very high level.' It had certainly been a test.

Test cricket proper returned to the SCG a week later, but a sorry series for Australia was given a pauper's funeral. After WSC had drawn almost 40,000 in its three days, the Australian Cricket Board could find only 22,000 in four willing to attend Australia's fifth defeat.

England had prevailed with maximum efficiency and minimum aesthetic effect. 'We wanted larger crowds,' recorded David Gower, 'and we were conscious of the success of WSC, but felt our priority was a convincing win. It wasn't our fault the crowds stayed away towards the end – are we to blame because the Aussies don't like a losing side?'

Of the seventeen leaderless and directionless Australians called on, five alone had lasted more than four consecutive Tests. Vice-captain Gary Cosier lasted two, his axing passed on – in time-honoured fash-ion – by journalist Dick Tucker after the Second Test in Perth.

'Has the team been announced?' Cosier asked.

'No, not yet,' Tucker replied. 'But you're not in it.'

Peter Toohey and Bruce Yardley, successes against India and the West Indies, grappled uneasily with failure. 'I got theories left, right and centre and in a short time my confidence was absolutely shot,' says Toohey. 'You could have taken me to Blayney against the worst bowler in the world and he would have got me out. They had the choice in the Fifth Test of dropping me completely or making me twelfth man. Frankly I wish they'd dropped me.' Yardley had been easily read by players fluent in off spin: 'The way the Indians and West Indians played had really suited me. The English players sat on you, never took a chance.'

Taking two-thirds of the English wickets in 40 per cent of the overs, Rodney Hogg and Alan Hurst had saved Australian faces. But Graham Yallop, a tongue-tied contrast with Brearley, had been perplexed by Hogg's various humours. Recalls Hurst:

These two would be talking about resolving things face to face behind the pavilion, and it was a downer in a team that needed all the positives it could get. For young guys like Wood and Darling there was nothing worse than seeing their captain was not getting respect. Simpson had been well above the rest of his team obviously in experience and age. But Yallop was really just on the same level as the rest of the players. You couldn't look up to him. Basically he didn't want the job, and he didn't have the experience or the personal manner for the role.

For twenty-two-year-old Andrew Hilditch, his Test debut in Sydney, it was a dizzying turn in an already disorienting career. Named New South Wales' captain after just two matches the previous year, he was run out unluckily and caught behind very unconvincingly for three and one. 'The second innings will always stand out,' he says. 'The ball came off so slowly that, when I touched it, I was absolutely confident it wouldn't carry. I could turn round and watch it bounce. It's amazing there wasn't a scene, but I guess it was my first Test and I was a bit timid.' In fairness to wicketkeeper Bob Taylor, he did not appeal and relied on assurances of his slipsmen. But it is intriguing to imagine what might have been the upshot had TCN-9's omniscient cameras and replays been telecasting the Test rather than the static and myopic ABC. To cleanse his mind of the memory, Hilditch went next door to the Sydney Showground to see the Rod Stewart concert, whose soundchecks had deafened fielders for the duration of Australia's nine-wicket defeat.

The irony of the nadir of Yallop's summer is that the match was a personal landmark. His 121 from Australia's first-innings 198 was touched by genius, though in his own mind is recalled with some bafflement. 'I just couldn't believe it because on the first day it was a very good wicket,' he says. 'I felt everything was falling apart round me, and I just had to make as many as I could as quickly as possible.'

Though their caps carried the Pakistani pentangle when they arrived from New Zealand for two Tests against Australia on 26 February 1979, Asif Iqbal, Majid, Javed, Sarfraz, Imran, Haroon and captain Mushtaq did little to hide their other allegiance. Warming up at Manuka Oval against NSW, Mushtaq, Majid and Javed all wore WSC shirts, albeit with insignias obscured at the request of manager Ebbu Ghazali.

Ghazali's own position, too, appeared nominal. When the team visited Adelaide, Mushtaq accepted a dinner invitation from his old Cavaliers squire Graham Ferrett for his entire entourage. 'What time for dinner, manager?' Mushtaq asked.

'Oh, 8 p.m?' said Ferrett.

'Very good, manager.'

Fifteen players, wives, management and press arrived at the tick of the clock. 'Suddenly we were hunting for takeaway restaurants,' Ferrett recalls. 'And my wife and Kay Chappell were learning how to make Pakistani breads for thirty.'

Packer himself visited his men at the MCG during Pakistan's First Test, where he bumped into Ray Steele. In conciliatory spirit, the ACB treasurer invited the businessman to lunch in the VCA Delegates Room, though some gaps remained unbridged.

As they walked to lunch Steele remarked on Packer's Pakistan tie. 'That's because I don't have an Australian one,' came the tart reply. A polite lunch ensued, but Steele did not offer one.

The young Australians' Test initiation was a bracing bolt of WSC. While five of the Australians at Melbourne had seven Tests between them (including the promising NSW left-hander Allan Border), Pakistan was a gilt-edged combination.

Imran had Hilditch caught from a fierce lifter, bowled Border and Yallop, and shortened Peter Sleep's Test debut with a leg cutter. 'There were very few occasions I walked off feeling as though I've really been bowled,' says Hilditch, 'that the bowler was much too good. The ball from Imran just exploded off a length. I couldn't help feeling I was learning a lot about the part luck plays in cricket in a very short time.'

The Pakistanis played very hard ball, Javed running out Hogg from a no-ball as the tailender went pitch-prodding. 'We took an instant dislike to some of them,' says Hurst. 'We'd got used to the very sportsmanlike approach of the English players, but the Pakistanis seemed a very arrogant bunch.'

Hilditch was more accepting. 'I don't think there was any co-ordinated antagonism,' he says. 'In fact I found the Pakistanis on the whole behaved in quite a gentlemanly manner on the field. What incidents there were, and there were a few I suppose, probably owed more to a few volatile characters.'

There were none more volatile than Sarfraz. Border, Hilditch and Kim Hughes had ushered Australia to within 77 of a towering last day target of 382 when Sarfraz moodily removed their seven remaining wickets for the cost of a single in 33 deliveries. Border's maiden Test century was misspent on Australia's eleventh defeat in fifteen Tests.

Andrew Hilditch explains it still with a faint incomprehension: 'It is very hard to understand. People asking me about it now assume there must have been more to it than what happened. The impression they have is that there was incredible heat against us when we went out, but I would never have picked the ball up in those circumstances. It seemed just ridiculously hostile not to pick up the ball and throw it to him.' Sarfraz's ridiculously hostile response to Hilditch's politeness now towers over not only Perth's Second Test, but the batsman's entire Test career.

Hilditch had arrived ready for a memorable match whatever occurred. With Yallop's sorry season ending on crutches after a grade match, Kim Hughes would be leading Australia in his tenth Test. Hilditch had been appointed his vice-captain, Australia's fourth of the summer, in his third. Their first day in charge proved profitable. Only Javed resisted the rapid right-arm Hurst and the workmanlike left-arm Geoff Dymock.

In December 1977, Andrew Hilditch had captained NSW Colts. Two months later, he had led NSW. And on the morning of Sunday,

25 March 1979 he became de facto captain of Australia. Hilditch was taking his habitual daily dose of batting practice when Hughes turned an ankle standing on a ball in an adjacent net.

It didn't actually 'feel' daunting. Events slipped into place as soon as Hilditch led the team out on the third day with a lead of 50. In Hogg's first over, Majid was expertly caught in the gully by substitute Trevor Laughlin, a specialist who had gone there unbidden.

Laughlin exerted a final influence when Asif Iqbal prolonged Pakistan's innings on the final morning with last man Sikander Bakht. Australians gathered at drinks to discuss the ease with which Asif was farming the bowling: in thirty-five minutes, Sikander had faced just three balls. Word passed: Laughlin was asked to watch Sikander backing-up.

'I took a look at the next few balls and he was, you know, three or four metres out of his ground,' says Laughlin. He crossed to Hurst: 'If you want him, you got him.'

Hurst wanted him, and Sikander was got. Hurst trimmed the bails matter-of-factly as he ran through the crease. 'It was very funny to look at,' Laughlin recalls. 'Hurstie just ran through and Sikander was off looking the other way, metres down running full tilt for the other end.' It was the classic 'Mankad': premeditated, improvised and leaving all heaven in a rage. Asif swiped at his stumps. Sikander gesticulated. 'You've cheated,' Hurst told him. 'So you're out.'

Hilditch had spent a cool two and a half hours with Rick Darling adding 87 when he entered *Wisden's* chamber of handled-the-ball horrors. Mid off fielded Darling's drive, but Sarfraz's fumble of the return rolled to a halt five metres away. Hilditch picked it up and threw it back. He recalls:

I don't think he even stopped to catch it. He just turned round and started to scream. I thought: 'No-one can listen to this madman.' Even as I was going off I expected all the time that the captain would intervene at any moment and I'd get a tap on the shoulder and be asked to go back . . . My second reaction was that 29 was such a disappointment. Rick and I had been going so well. There'd been problems with the opening positions and we seemed to have resolved them, and I'd been telling myself that this was the real start of my Australian career . . . Then I gradually started thinking: 'This could not be happening. Is this going to cost us the Test?'

Australia's rooms were silent. 'You could see the anger well up in Andrew when he got back,' says Hurst. 'He just said: "I don't believe that. I don't believe that just happened". None of us could. Before the game hardly any of us had seen a "Mankad". We'd certainly never seen a handled the ball. It was like a dream.'

Allan Border, three months after scoring his maiden first-class century on the same ground against Western Australia, now proceeded to win his first Test for Australia. Though rain clouds skirted the arena, Border's concentration was watertight. Thirty-one-year-old Victorian Jeff Moss, Yallop's replacement playing in his first Test, looted 20 from two overs by Imran as the match entered its final hour and noise returned to the Australians' rooms. 'One reason I remember the game so fondly is the feeling in the dressing-room that afternoon,' says Hilditch. 'We were playing an unbelievably talented side and beating them. Players like Allan Border were emerging as the future of Australian cricket.' Mushtaq capitulated in the fourth last over: he called up opening batsman Mudassar, whose second ball Moss flicked to leg for the winning runs.

A fraternal trip to Pakistan's dressing-room proved pointless. 'It wasn't so often we won Tests at the time, and it was the end of our summer,' says Hurst. 'So we were keen on a drink. We were just disdained. I sat next to Imran and tried to say a few things to get him talking, but got no response.' Nor did the WACA echo with 'C'mon, Aussie, C'mon', though it was as meaningful that day as any other in the cricket cascade of the preceding four months.

18

'I think this Lennie want to kill you man'

There was a palpable end-of-term feeling among Ian Chappell's Australians as they practised at Sabina Park on Sunday 18 February 1979. Two months' hard Caribbean labour lay ahead but two years' toil was astern. Plied with rum even before boarding their airliner, they'd shed their flash red and white tour jackets en route for jeans and T-shirts.

Ian Chappell, however, was typically earnest. This might be his last leadership assignment, and it had been on an almost identical tour six years earlier that he had won his first overseas series. Port-of-Spain 1973 was writ large in memory: with Rohan Kanhai's team 3–219 chasing 333 at lunch on the last day, Chappell's entreaties had wrung a 44-run win.

Five companions were retracing their 1973 steps: brother Greg, Lillee, Marsh, Max Walker and Kerry O'Keeffe. Passed fit a day before departure, Greg batted behind sunglasses prescribed for the tour's first week to neutralise his palsy. 'I needn't have gone,' he says. 'But I had something to prove to myself: that I could make large numbers of runs against their attack. And when I was told there was no reason I couldn't recover fully, there seemed no point missing out for the sake of a week.'

Lillee's 1973 trip had been his blackest two months. Breakdown with spinal stress fractures in Antigua had left him a spectator. Eighteen months as a chiropractic experiment had followed. His mate Marsh coveted runs that had eluded him for two years, Walker and O'Keeffe regular team places that latterly had escaped them.

Thanks to cricket's peace talks, the team had been strengthened three days before by Thomson's sudden release from his Australian Cricket Board contract. He had been a familiar non-playing face at games during the summer, but his could be little more than psychological presence. He could hardly be fully fit after nine idle months.

Loose talk of truces irritated Chappell, too. In a fifty-two day period, the Australians faced thirty-seven days' international cricket: five five-day Supertests and a dozen one-day internationals. Passengers could not be carried. Ian Davis had already encountered the ethic, after telling Chappell a week before departure that the Commonwealth Bank was reluctant to grant him leave for the tour. Distressed also by hepatitis, thinking about a young wife, Davis was agonising. 'I um'd and ah'd,' Davis recalls. 'I thought: "Jeez, if I quit I'll have nothing to come back to" . . . I was dumb really, but marriage does change you. When I was in Nowra, I used to eat, sleep, shower and shit cricket. But when I got married I did realise that there was more in life than cricket, and that there was no point dying for it.'

Although Kepler Wessels' South African passport had already denied the captain one opening batsman, Chappell had not urged Davis to reconsider. He'd turned instead to Rick McCosker, a dedicated disciple who'd previously put bat before bank.

Davis had felt a little like a soldier drummed from the corps: 'Ian always emphasised how you had to devote yourself to cricket. He once said: "If you want to play Tests, don't get married until you're thirty." He didn't talk to me much about it, didn't try to talk me out of it. I guess he thought: "Here's a young bloke, reckons he wants to play first-class cricket, and he's knocking back a cricket trip."'

Similarly at Sabina Park, the captain noted Pascoe's detachment. With his soulmate Thomson handy, Pascoe chatted cheerily with Jamaicans while loafing through the net session. At a cocktail party later, Chappell decided to get in his ear. 'So Lenny,' he said, 'who booked your tour then? Jetset or Qantas? You're obviously here for a holiday.'

Pascoe pouted. 'What do you fucking mean?'

'Well everyone's bowling their guts out, and you're down at fine leg talking to the locals. There's a third pace spot in this side and I haven't decided who's going to fill it.' When Pascoe seemed to sulk, Chappell thought he'd best try and lighten the exchange: 'C'mon Lenny. Where's your sense of humour anyway?'

Pascoe's paw was on Chappell's collar in a trice, lifting the captain off the ground, his expression such as hijack victims see on terrorists. 'I fucking haven't got one,' Pascoe told him.

Bruce Laird moved to separate them, but as quickly as Pascoe's hand had extended it was retracted with a laugh and the captain dropped to the ground. 'See?' he guffawed. 'I *have* got a fucking sense of humour after all.' As Pascoe moved off, Chappell couldn't be sure whether his message had been received.

Translating World Series Cricket into West Indian patois had fashioned a tour unlike any other. In 1973, Australia's schedule had featured twenty-five days' Test cricket and twenty-one of first-class cricket threaded over three months. The Australians would work to rule in 1979: seventeen international engagements compressed into eight weeks.

The profit-conscious schedule organised by the Jamaican businessmen on WSC Caribbean – Patrick Terrelonge, Franz Botek and Conrad Pine – meant that batsmen would have precious little opportunity to relocate lost form, bowlers faint hope of attaining match fitness.

The prize pot, though, was without local precedent. The region's bellwether agricultural trading company, Neal and Massy, had stumped up $US250,000 in sponsorship: their banner draped the Kingston Sheraton proudly as the Australians arrived. West Indian Tobacco had staked each Supertest and one-day match. With match and individual awards from WOT Sports, Heineken, Red Stripe and Ovaltine, some $US55,550 hinged on the series. If this tour did not make money, no cricket trip would. Given the purses closed on Jeff Stollmeyer a year before, and Caribbean cricket's years of financial hardship, it is little wonder that the West Indian Cricket Board of Control president could not bring himself to attend any of the matches he had helped broker.

WSC's entourage was small. Austin Robertson was tour leader with Barbara Loois travelling ahead to arrange accommodation. Manager Richie Robinson was intended to allow Marsh a few days ungloved. The loyal Dave McErlane was along to massage the cricketers, Bruce McDonald to massage finances and carry scorebooks, while Walker, with forty rolls of WSC film, doubled as tour photographer.

Television coverage was one reporter and one backpack cameraman: GTV-9's Mike Lester and Greg Cameron. John Maley, part of whose cricket odyssey had been five months at Trinidad's Crompton club, also strung along for part of the tour. The *Australian's* Phil Wilkins continued his devotionals with Reuters reporter Terry Williams, but there was no chorus of publicists, no coloured carnival and – in particular – no 'C'mon, Aussie, C'mon'.

It was Wilkins who discovered Ian Chappell a week later by the Sheraton's pool. Ten days in Jamaica and Chappell wore a heavy beard, guarding against the equatorial sun, that made him resemble an escaped convict. Wilkins shuffled up to ask a question about the just completed Supertest. 'Fuck off, you prick,' came the response.

Wilkins could make it up himself. Three days after arrival, the Australians had wandered into a one-day international before 8000. The chase for 175 soon turned academic and they had barely survived their allotment. On duty in the second over, Chappell had been left gasping by a blow in the chest from Michael Holding. McErlane had sent him for X-rays when he saw the soup-plate bruise. The match's only positive had been Hookes' continued command – he'd hooked Garner over the sightscreen – and brother Greg's squinting 23 with the naked eye.

Greg had captained the Australians the next day to a one-wicket win in the twilight, Thomson and Walker adding a hair-raising dozen. But the second ball of the innings from Holding had maimed McCosker's finger, spelling him for a month and turning Trevor Chappell into Laird's ersatz partner.

Ian Chappell's week had truly gone awry, after a lay-day, in the First Supertest. Though Lillee, Gary Gilmour and Ray Bright felled the final West Indian at 188, in the remaining hour and a quarter the Australians had discovered the trickery of the improvised sightboard at Sabina Park's southern end. Emerging from a background of building works in a half-completed stand, Roberts had stung Laird's shoulder, glanced his helmet, and opened Trevor Chappell's chin as the batsman arched back from a bouncer. Six stitches were needed to close the wound.

Ian Chappell and Laird were swept aside when Holding moved south, while Greg Chappell's half-hour before stumps proved figuratively eye-opening. 'Although they produce so many fast bowlers, West Indian pitches aren't often as fast as people expect,' he comments. 'But that Sabina Park wicket was as fast as any I'd seen. They took us by storm, they were very aggressive, probably thinking that if they got on top of us early we might fall in a heap.'

The Australians fell dishevelled in 100 minutes next morning. Greg feathered his hook at the fifth ball to Murray, Hookes was yorked, and Trevor Chappell's return proved no more than a courageous cameo. 'I'd thought: "Shit we've got a real chance here, they've only made 188",' Ian Chappell recalls. 'But they'd just steamrolled us.'

Lillee led a rally from the southern end camouflage, deceiving Lawrence Rowe horribly second ball. The sound of his ear guard concaving as the ball broke his cheekbone silenced his home town. But Lloyd reversed the steamroller over the Australians as soon as the fast bowler rested.

He and Andy Roberts ruled the third day. Lloyd's bravura back swing made a contrast with Roberts, whose bat rose grudgingly, as 108 came before lunch. Enjoying the second new ball after lunch, the pair went run-for-run drumming 117 in eighty-five minutes. Fielders fell back until they could go no further: Sabina Park's straight boundaries are just sixty metres from the pitch. The thirty-five fours and two sixes had stand-in scorer McDonald scrawling to keep up. How did you bowl to Lloyd in this mood? 'With a helmet,' Gilmour commented.

At Lloyd's every pendulous swing, Jamaicans grew more vocal. Only Martin Kent could raise a cheer as he patrolled the wire fence at long-on that jacketed the crowd. 'Kent?' came a voice. 'You bin to South Africa?'

'Yeah,' the Australian croaked.

The voice continued: 'You not goin' again maaan?'

'No,' Kent said. 'No way. Finished there.' Kent's section of the crowd bayed delightedly.

They continued as Holding first removed Laird's helmet with a bouncer, then his off stump with a yorker. The local was bowling with beach cricket glee after a truncated Australian summer. 'My fitness in those days was very poor,' Holding explains. 'I used to do my own athletics and weight training, but I was still learning about stretching. I suffered badly with pulled muscles and anteriors, because there was no match against a county or state team where I could relax. I was very pleased to be home and relax and feel fit again.' And also to get all three Chappells. Bright was taking his second nightwatch at stumps with the tourists' 4–91 in vain pursuit of a further 473 in two days.

Ian Chappell was a remote figure watching the last six Australians muster 103 on the fourth day. He brooded as much over the manner of the defeat as its margin: 'We were starting to whinge: "Aww, the nicks aren't carrying and they're playing and missing. And how many bouncers an over can they bowl?" Which was very unusual for us. Generally we took our punishment. But, once you hear that, you know you're on the slippery dip. So I thought: "I'd better do something about this".'

He could not remember having to lecture an Australian team since that landmark 1973 tour, but the anniversary was worth honouring. 'This whingeing isn't the way we work,' he told his charges. 'And if you're looking to the umpires for protection, forget it. If you think Douglas (Sang Hue) and Ralph (Gosein) are going to stop them bowling bouncers over here, think again.' The captain, they learned, would be leading from the front. Ian Chappell had decided to open.

'Ian rarely addressed us,' says Bright. 'He didn't really get into us, so much as say we had it in us to come back.' The captain's final entreaty recurred again and again in the coming two months. 'Whatever we do, let's make 'em respect us.'

Victoria Park in Castries on the island of Saint Lucia was a proving ground five days later on 3 March, when the Australians almost wrested a one-day game from the West Indies in dying light. Laird hit five forthright fours in 56 over two and a half hours, and was caught deep flinging out an uncharacteristic hook. Lillee and Gilmour slapped 29 in ten minutes, but Lillee was bowled by Holding attempting a third six that would have tied the match.

Ian Chappell was happier. Rain next day allowed an early exit for Bridgetown, and a group of players joined retired West Indian fast bowler Richard Edwards on a fishing trip. Though they returned only with seasickness, Thomson and Pascoe had taken precautions at the local fishmarkets and their barbeque relaxed the ensuing team meeting.

But Chappell still felt that his message needed selected amplification. When Pascoe left the team bus idling next morning ducking a net session at Kensington Oval, Chappell decided that the cab fare might work on the fast bowler where words had failed. Thomson was told to fetch him, the bus driver told to drive.

Chappell said nothing when Pascoe arrived, and nothing when the late-comer malingered off two paces. Instead he padded up and, conspicuously leaving his helmet aside, walked into Pascoe's net. The fast-bowler's run-up lengthened.

Phil Wilkins calls the next twenty minutes 'the finest exhibition of net batting I've ever seen'. Bouncers hummed round Chappell's ears like hornets as Pascoe homed in on him from twenty yards and less. 'Oh skipper, he's trying to knock your block off,' chortled locals behind the nets. 'I think this Lennie want to kill you, man.'

Chappell took his standard twenty-minute session and, as was his custom, thanked bowlers as he left. With heavy emphasis he turned to Pascoe: 'Thanks, Lennie. Best work-out I've had in a long time.'

Still snorting as he gathered his breath, Pascoe could only grunt: 'Thought you'd fucking say that.'

That evening, Chappell picked Pascoe for his first game on tour. In the next day's international, it was Pascoe who made the crucial breaches with the new ball, curbing the in-form Gordon Greenidge and Roy Fredericks. The Australians celebrated a 42-run win when Lillee and Walker gathered in the last seven wickets for just nine runs.

The face missing was a number three to stand in for the skipper. 'I didn't want Greg to have to bat there,' he says. 'Because I always reckoned that if the West Indies were able to pick me up quickly and then get Greg as well they got a bit of a boost and we lost a bit of our edge.' Kerry O'Keeffe was pondered as a stop-gap, but Greg urged his brother to elevate Kent from the number seven slot that the twenty-five-year-old Queenslander had filled at Sabina Park.

Kent was confident despite the score of 2–13 as Australia pursued 241 the next day. With Roberts and Holding resting, only Joel Garner, he felt, needed constant vigilance. Kent recalls:

> I got to know that there were a few blokes who'd always give you something. Andy wouldn't. He was always just short, preservation was the name of the game. Michael was always up there, too, and Garner. But Crofty and Mandingo [Daniel], they'd slip you one in the slot occasionally. If they weren't bouncing you they were trying yorkers, which could become half-volleys. They were quick, and a good challenge, but Daniel didn't do much with the ball and Crofty was bowling mostly in-swingers, so you didn't have to worry much about late movement.

Batting with Greg then Trevor Chappell, his erect driving swung the game. When Lloyd sought a few cheap overs from Richard Austin, Kent flipped him expertly over the inner ring then pulled him over mid wicket for six. Despite his 109, he cursed as he slapped Daniel to cover-point Collis King: 'It was there and I went for it, and I shouldn't have got out. It'd been my day but it was that old syndrome. I'd done the work. I'd made 100 and nobody should have got me.'

Lillee hit a six in the last over from Colin Croft, but was caught next ball by Richards, and Kent was still cursing defeat when his captain sat down beside him in the dressing-room. 'What d'you think of yourself as a cricketer, Super?' Chappell asked. 'Where d'you think you've got to?'

Due modesty and the day's lessons in mind, Kent thought before replying. 'Oh, I'm not bad,' he said. 'But I've got a lot to learn.'

Chappell's response came short and sharp. 'It's okay to say that, but listen: the sooner you believe in yourself, the better you're going to be. Back yourself. You're in this company, so you can play. Believe it. Don't think you're always just starting.' He moved off again.

Kent looked round him. Yes, here he was, batting number three between Ian and Greg Chappell. He could play. 'That was a turning point for me. Realising I'd gained acceptance. I'd probably done it when I'd played my first Supertest, but it just took a while to realise I had respect.' If he and his colleagues could widen that respectful group to include West Indians, then a 369-run Supertest defeat could still be redeemed.

Kent's next heart-to-heart with his captain came two days later, forty minutes into the Second Supertest after Lloyd had inserted the Australians on what flattened into a good batting wicket. With Roberts resting a sprained back, Kent struck off Ian Chappell's flint. 'Batting with Ian was career-building and character-building,' Kent recalls. 'When I'd batted with Greg in Queensland the partnership had always got me going, the rivalry of going at it with a partner I admired. I found that Ian was the same.'

He flagged, in fact, the moment their 104-run stand was ended by his captain's dismissal, caught by a diving Lloyd at slip from King. Abruptly, the cares of the innings became his. When his next fifty minutes produced another four stuttering singles, he slashed to point for 78. Kent hung his head again: he had always told himself 80s were centuries. 'In the 70s I always reckoned you only needed 10 to get a hundred,' he says. 'Eighty and you were there, you were a bee's dick away, you'd make it. I was two short of a hundred that day as far as I was concerned.'

When middle-order subsidence was staunched by Bright and Marsh to allow the Australians a certain comfort at 311, Lillee and Thomson bounced the first three West Indians for 15. Fredericks spun into his hooks as the Australians remembered from Perth three years before, adding 73 with Richards inside an hour, but the Australians had salted a lead of 120 by stumps on the third day.

Ian and Greg Chappell, shovel and pick, displayed fraternal compatibility. Holding felt the former one of very few batsmen who could 'embarrass' him. 'Ian had won the 1975–1976 series in my opinion,' the fast bowler says. 'He had always got on top of the bowlers, and others like Greg got the benefit: the same role Viv later fulfilled for us. Other batsmen could get on top of you, but Ian would embarrass you.'

The Australian captain did just that for three controlled hours. 'He hooked me and pulled me through mid wicket over and over,' Holding remembers. 'I would not mind a batsman hooking or pulling me generally, I would feel that he was taking a risk, but Ian was doing it without semblance of error, without any risk whatever.'

Now that he could leave his sunglasses by the pool, Greg's powers were returning daily. His 90 was flawless until he edged Croft low to Murray. Holding had to settle for bowling Trevor Chappell off his pads for 22. Defending 366 on the final day, the Australians felt close to parity in the series. They knew, too, that King was nursing a broken hand, and that Roberts would not be stalking the lower order with his broad, blunting bat.

Greenidge's leg-side edge left the West Indians' 2–41, but there were worrisome catcalls from his home crowd when the batsman queried Douglas Sang Hue's decision. Bottles had bounced from the double-decker stand during rain breaks on the second day, and radio news bulletins were that very morning reporting a military coup in Grenada. As Tony Cozier says: 'It would have been easy for people to decide that: "They're overthrowing authority there, why don't we do it here"?' Sang Hue's partner Gosein looked especially concerned: he had been star of Sabina Park's fiasco ten months earlier, when the riot following Van Holder's theatrics had cost Bob Simpson's team victory.

Richards and Fredericks again stirred a frenzy in the stands in the next hour. Steel band kettledrums resounded at the Antiguan's three sub-orbital sixes. Fredericks stormed past his half-century with five fours off the reel, then stormed from the ground as Gosein judged him lbw to Pascoe. He had barely made it to the fence when bottles began raining from stands square of the wicket. Instead of contemplating the West Indians' last accredited pair and their 234-run distance from home, the Australians were heading for cover contemplating their own safety.

Riot police stared down the crowd but, when play recommenced fifty minutes later, the chant of 'We want Fredericks' accompanied the entrance of Richards and Lloyd. Spectators, rearmed in the hiatus, again pelted the outfield. Back in the dressing-room, where the Australians were told that the atmosphere had grown too dangerous to continue, Lillee was 'heartbroken': 'It seemed to me there was something suicidal about visiting teams doing well in the Caribbean. We were playing our hearts out . . . but as soon as we looked like winning we'd put ourselves in danger with the irate crowds.'

As it happened, the Australians' worst injury occurred between ground and hotel. O'Keeffe, on tour expressly to play as second

spinner on the traditional turning pitch in Trinidad, was jogging with
Mick Malone to stay fit for the big moment.

'We'd just got to the racecourse and there was a designated stop
sign,' he says. 'And I ran out from the left as this woman was looking to the right. I saw her coming and thought she'd stop but, as you
sometimes do when you're looking to turn, she didn't.'

O'Keeffe was shovelled onto the car's bonnet and deposited dazed
on the pavement, where Malone tried to figure the extent of injury.
'Try and run it out,' the West Australian urged.

'It was broken in three places and all the medial ligaments were
shredded,' O'Keeffe recalls. 'So I crumpled in a few paces. Run it
out! Mick's career option was not physiotherapy.'

Next time teammates saw him was in hospital, his tibia fractured
close to the right knee. Austin Robertson was organising passage
home. O'Keeffe rolled his eyes at their parting gift of a warm bottle
of Coke: 'You extravagant fools.'

His only chuckle came when island police returned with a tran-
script of the statement he had given, containing O'Keeffe's account
of the accident translated into local Bajan. It all came back to him as
he read: 'I got up from de road, and my leg did pain me awful bad.'

Witnessing twin West Indian wins in 1978, Trinidadians in Port-of-
Spain had behaved irreproachably. And WSC Caribbean wanted to
keep it that way: Queen's Park Oval is the region's biggest and the
eight days' cricket scheduled there were the trip's cash cornerstone.
A steel band played and thousands of balloons were released as each
player was announced individually and introduced to the president
of Trinidad and Tobago, Ellis Innocent Clarke.

Ian Chappell was without O'Keeffe, but his belief in Trinidad's
turn was profound. Despite the pitch's dampness, his priority on
winning the toss was to avoid batting on the last day.

If the match made it that far. It seemed over in an hour and a
half of Holding. Long spells had seemed unattainable in Australia,
yet here he had spring for nine opening overs and ran the gamut
of Chappells with Hookes caught down leg side for good measure.
Only Laird and Marsh stood between the West Indians and the
Australian tail, and the opener had six single-digit scores in nine
innings behind him.

'Maybe facing those guys two years in a row had worn me down a bit,' he says. 'And once you were out of form in WSC you were stuck.' Stuck on this pitch, he watched his partners come and go helplessly. 'They soak it at Trinidad for the first day to hold the pitch together,' he recalls. 'And that morning the Windies were just putting it there and it was taking off.'

Laird had gathered a dozen of Australia's first 40 just before lunch when granted a critical reprieve by Lloyd at first slip from Croft. As first Marsh then Bright managed to settle, his fluency began to return. Croft allowed him room for his pet cut, and a marble outfield rewarded every stroke.

His half-century arrived just after tea, and Laird prospered further with Lillee at the expense of a tiring attack. As his unbeaten 112 from 204 was toasted at stumps, McErlane ice-packed him gently. 'Poor old Bruce,' says the masseur. 'He just couldn't get out of the way.'

Solemn handshakes from Fredericks, Greg Chappell and Viv Richards were accepted, and Ian Chappell still puts the innings on a pedestal. '"Stumpy" never made a Test hundred, but he made three WSC hundreds that rank up there with the best I've seen,' he says. 'You're always told about Stan McCabe's three great innings, and when the players get together now "Stumpy's" are innings mentioned the same way.'

Lillee was a steely partner when play resumed, unmoved by Holding's prompt acceptance of a second new ball. 'The Windies were pretty cocky when they were on top by this time in World Series,' Laird recalls. 'When I met Dennis in the middle we decided we'd just stick around and try and guts it out. So Michael comes in, bowls a bouncer first up, and Dennis hooks him into the stand for six. Just stick around, eh? Dennis looked down the wicket at me and sort of smiled, but I don't think he'd intended to do it.'

Laird misread Roberts' line and allowed a ball to hit his off stump twenty minutes later, but had seen 200 added for the last three wickets. The Australians' 246 grew more defensible when Thomson had Fredericks caught on the fence hooking and plucked out Rowe's off stump after the Jamaican twice edged him through slip. Richards, Lloyd, Greenidge and King were shifted when set, and only Roberts' two-hour half-century on the third day shoved the West Indians to within 16 of the Australian total.

Their advantage was lost, with both openers, in the first over. Ian Chappell's miscued hook looped back to Holding, then Kent's edgy call for a single to mid-on Greenidge next ball sacrificed Laird.

The Queenslander concentrated contritely, and drew much of the bowling as Greg Chappell settled. Chappell watched his protege closely. 'The West Indians gave him little to drive and Martin wasn't a hooker or cutter,' says Chappell. 'But he'd worked out ways to keep up the scoring rate. Every time Andy'd overpitch, trying to bowl a yorker, Martin'd belt them into the ground and bounce them over the bowlers' head. Andy didn't like it.'

Albert Padmore's off spin posed most problems. Three of four wickets clustered round tea on the third day came his way, although Chappell and Bright had steered the Australians to a lead of 171 by stumps.

Chappell conserved and husbanded his energies by conceiving three levels of concentration – one prior to batting, one between balls, one facing – and now was moving smoothly between gears. When Lillee joined him, he felt relaxed and detached enough as non-striker to let his eyes wander through the crowd. 'I could always spot particular people arriving,' he said. 'It used to amaze some friends that after play I could usually say: "Oh you came in at 11.30 a.m. and went and sat in the fifth row of the members".'

A factor in Greg Chappell's favour in the Caribbean was that very clarity of eye. He picked up the red ball being used more quickly than the white employed throughout 1978–1979 in Australia. He later recalled with West Indian manager Rudi Webster the experience of facing Max Walker at practice with red balls after a session using white: 'The difference was amazing! I saw it so much quicker and easier . . . I know that other people see the white ball quicker but in my case the reverse is true. Perhaps I have been conditioned to see the red ball.'

After watching videos of his cricket with Richie Benaud at home, Chappell had also decided to eliminate technical adjustments he'd dabbled with. Returning to the unadorned methods of his decade of first-class cricket, he played well forward to Padmore, surely back to pace, and drew special pleasure from sweet strokes against the second new ball. Chappell's eight self-absorbed hours at the crease did not end until he sought to poach a few runs upon Lillee's fall at 256. Having gathered 150 while six partners had scraped 92, he tugged Fredericks to midwicket.

The turn Padmore had evinced was now the sole cause for West Indian concern, and they hared for their 299 target. With tutorial correctness, Greenidge smacked three fours in Lillee's first over. Fredericks demonstrated the pitch's lifelessness to Thomson, then pounced on Bright after tea to prevent him settling into a groove.

The West Indians had gone a third of the way to their target in even time without as much as the rumour of a wicket when Lillee devoted his second spell to the cutters that would, in time, prolong his career. Ian Chappell at once scooped up Greenidge at first slip. But the West Indians would still begin the final day 180 runs from an invincible two-nil series lead.

An airless stadium greeted the Australians, and a pitch as plumb as the one the Chappells and Marsh recalled from six years before. Many of their rivals were also common to that contest – Lloyd, Murray, Fredericks, Rowe – and amid the symmetry Ian Chappell drew comfort from a conviction: sides never chased 300 successfully.

His resources, though, were thin. He asked Thomson if he'd considered Lillee-like cutters, but understood the expressman's reluctance. Bright's tweak was insufficient to worry batsmen well-set, and Chappell pondered his own wrist spin. It had bothered a West Indian tail on a similar pitch at VFL Park two months earlier.

It would just be a matter of plugging away. After twenty minutes, the Australians turned lucky: Bright snuck beneath Rowe's back-stroke. Next over, Fredericks dragged Lillee on. Richards threatened destruction, but Pascoe's disciplined line frustrated Lloyd into an indiscreet cut. With 100 runs to protect, Chappell gambled on Richards' impatience and introduced himself in Bright's stead.

'I was disappointed to have only picked up one,' Bright says. 'But Ian's leg spinners had a bit more bounce and were more danger-ous on that wicket on the last day. I'd found out that, for all the talk about Trinidad spinning, the important thing is that it doesn't bounce and it's the one keeping low which worries batsmen. Ian also reckoned that the West Indians were tending just to play me out, but might take more risks against him.' Richards needed no excuse to take risks. At times that year, in fact, they'd seemed a fatal attraction.

At once he struck Chappell high towards long-on. Bright judged the catch to a nicety.

Lillee's back had begun to ache during the match and, as his spell continued after lunch, Chappell dreaded him breaking down. He needed just a few more overs but, as he sauntered toward Lillee to ask, could see his mate was history. 'The dust was everywhere,' Chappell remembers. 'Getting in your throat, in your hair, and it was fucking hot and I was thinking: "Shit, I'm going to have to take Dennis off soon. Who do I go to then? Everyone else is just cannon fodder".'

He asked anyway. Could Lillee continue? Lillee's mouth opened, but Chappell heard nothing. 'He couldn't even speak,' Chappell says. 'Nothing came out of his mouth. He signalled that he was okay to go on instead.' With a final fling, Lillee produced a lifter that King steered to Laird at short leg: 6–222.

Laird was standing over the stumps four runs later to accept Marsh's throw as Murray called Roberts for a bye on the keeper's fumble. The local hero's misjudgement was greeted with horror, then bottles, but the Australians decided to try and return to their positions. It might be impossible to return if they left. Bright returned to long-on and Trevor Chappell volunteered for fine leg.

'I was okay actually,' Bright recalls. 'Because I was under the stand's shadow, and the guys throwing bottles from behind the mesh were clearing the top of my head. But eventually a little West Indian came up and said I'd be better off clearing out because things could get ugly and they might start on me.' While his players gathered with the umpires in the centre, their captain ran for the West Indian dressing-room. 'There was no way we were going to lose that match to mob rule,' he says.

Chappell implored Lloyd to appeal to fans. The West Indian had reasoned successfully with his Georgetown home crowd in a Test against New Zealand in 1972, but now was not so keen. Chappell turned to Murray. If the local would tell his own people on the public address system that he'd been fairly dismissed, they might be placated. 'Yeah, I was out,' said Murray. 'I'll do it.'

Murray's words worked. Only twenty-five minutes were wasted bottle-sweeping. Ample time remained, in fact, for the West Indians to bridge the 73-run gap, and Lillee was prone and semi-conscious on McErlane's treatment table when play resumed. Holding sampled Chappell's spin confidently. Roberts pushed stolidly down Pascoe's line.

Forty-one runs ticked, and Holding hoisted Chappell over midwicket for six as the spinner's toss tempted. The Australian threw the ball higher. 'I was trying to score at every opportunity because runs were not easy to get,' says Holding. 'In the air it looked a full toss, but it was one of those balls that dip more quickly than you expect.' It dropped, spun and scuttled past Holding's bat. Three balls later and Laird caught Croft's nervous nudge.

McErlane's crazed cries roused Lillee as Pascoe beat a path through Padmore. With a session to spare, but only 25 runs, Australia had levelled. The tourists unbottled rum to dilute their pineapple juice. A rock flew through the adjacent local dressing-room window, showering Lloyd's kit with glass. In the next two weeks, the potency of rum and rocks combined would be underscored.

19

'One to the eye, one to the bollocks'

The Western Australian Cricket Association members' bar, which had been an establishment snug in December 1978, seemed to be admitting all manner of riff-raff during Australia's Second Test with Pakistan three months later. *Sun* journalist Tom Prior was particularly wounded to find Graham Ferrett among guests.

'What are you doing here?' said the veteran journalist. 'You and your kind, you've got no right to be here.'

Prior, though, had failed to notice Ferrett's host: Australian Cricket Board selector Neil Harvey. Though Ferrett had been managing World Series Cricket's Cavaliers, Harvey had known him since the car-dealer had provided courtesy Chryslers to Richie Benaud's Australian sides. And the truth was that Australia's cricket scar was closing, if not quite healing.

The reason was visible in the public impact of a season's cricket fatigue: daily crowds in Perth averaged 4500, compared with 18,250 at a 1974 victory, and 16,750 for a 1975 defeat. It was the ACB's last financial foozle.

Pace of the thaw had taken the likes of Prior by surprise, but the field had skewed drastically. The Ashes tour profit of $126,634 was quarter of the $501,652 four years before. With less for distribution to the states, associations in New South Wales and Victoria had lost more than $500,000 between them over the two seasons of split. The NSWCA would have to sell Cricket House, its home for forty-seven years, before year's end.

Most melancholy was the Sheffield Shield. Had quorums been required, many matches would hardly have begun. Where more than 350,000 had attended the competition's twenty games in 1974–1975, there were a motley 137,000 for twenty-five in 1978–1979.

Searching for a summer profit, the ACB had evolved a preliminary 1979–1980 program mimicking elements of WSC's schedule: a triangular tournament involving India and England, the two nations least affected by defections.

The program showed the handiwork of the VCA's able Dave Richards. A year before, at the ACB's annual meeting in Adelaide, he had reflected on the one-day game's growing popularity and that 'a new audience had developed through television exposure of cricket and that this audience would look at cricket whether it was played in one-day matches or at night.'

Nine one-day internationals were envisaged, and just three Australia–India Tests at the populous MCG, SCG and Adelaide Oval. Running six weeks and entailing only twenty-four international playing days – half the dimensions of the 1978–1979 sprawl – the schedule was a budget-balancer.

It was also a sign to WSC. Australian cricket's parlousness bothered Packer almost as much as the ACB. Though he'd suggested in May 1977 that an obstinate ACB would 'walk into a meat-mangler', mince would not televise. As sport historian Shayne Quick put it: 'Packer's foray into cricket, and televised sport, could only grow and prosper with a healthy and solvent ACB . . . The downfall of the ACB would result in the demise of WSC and Australian cricket in general.'

WSC's lifespan, moreover, was limited. While it was financially hale, and bordering on substantial profitability, its assets were undergoing accelerated depreciation. Ten of twenty-three Australians, five of eighteen West Indians and no fewer than fourteen of nineteen World players were past thirty. Although they kept such thoughts private, some had also become listless. 'For all the excitement of WSC

I really missed the tension and commitment of real Test cricket,'
Imran Khan would write. 'Had WSC gone on for another season, as
originally planned, I think a number of players including me would
have dropped out.' As Ross Edwards observes: 'We would have had
one great summer, the ACB would have had one disastrous summer,
and there would have been nothing left for any of us.'

Packer's declaration of intent came on 8 February 1979. Andrew
Caro's successor as WSC managing director was Lynton Taylor,
a former West Torrens cricketer but foremost Packer's senior
programming executive. ACB chairman Bob Parish's Sydney trip to
meet Packer the following week talked television, specifically expiry
of the ABC's rights on 26 March. Tenders for rights, Consolidated
Press was informed, closed a week later. It was ACB treasurer Ray
Steele who flew to Consolidated Press to meet Packer, Taylor and
Chester for discussion of the Nine 'offer': Packer and Chester were
pleasant, Taylor noticeably efficient. 'A tough little cookie, Taylor,'
says Steele. 'Very capable.'

Packer's attitude suited the board. All it craved was the return
of its monopoly. Although the board maintained pretence of
strong competition, Packer had only one serious rival: the ABC.
Realising that its best offer of $200,000 a season was a fraction
of the $500,000 annuity Packer renewed, ABC general manager
Talbot Duckmanton tried a last appeal to loyalty in a letter to
Parish reminding him of the national broadcaster's twenty-three
years' steadfastness.

But if the ACB was to replenish its coffers, it could not also afford
to go on subsidising the ABC. Duckmanton would lament in an
internal ABC memo:

> In the letter I sent to the board making our offer, I reminded the
> board of the extensive coverage we have long provided of Sheffield
> Shield and international matches – the exciting matches and the
> dull matches – on both radio and TV: coverage which I believe has
> done a great deal to develop and maintain the public's interest in
> cricket over the years. I asked for the opportunity to discuss our
> proposals further with the board before a final decision was made
> to accept an offer from a commercial network. We were not given
> that opportunity.

Gary Gilmour did not like Guyana. 'I'd had this rivalry with Colin Croft all summer,' he says. 'And at the end he told me that his mum was a witchdoctor and she'd be sticking pins in her dolls when we got there.' Gilmour thought more about it when the Australians began loitering in airports awaiting flights mysteriously delayed: 'I knew Colin was an air traffic controller, so I told the boys he was behind it.'

Croft's Georgetown home was certainly a poisoned patch of the Third World. Four months earlier, at neighbouring Jonestown, Reverend Jim Jones' followers had staged their grisly mass suicide. Arriving with WSC's advance ambassadors Lance Gibbs, Sir Garfield Sobers and Wes Hall a week before the Fourth Supertest, Mick Malone was told it had been raining for a week. It did nothing but rain all the next.

Idling Australians contemplated the workings of their schedule. Despite four single-figure innings since Jamaica, David Hookes felt shorter of luck than runs. 'I was never really out of form,' he says. 'I got run-out, got a couple of good catches, I just couldn't get started.'

Max Walker was an aggrieved 'perpetual twelfth man'. The lynch-pin of 1973 had not bowled an over in the three weeks since Richards had caned 74 from his nine overs in a Bridgetown one-day match, nor would he again. Walker recalls:

> You had to believe in yourself, that you'd got the contract for a reason. I think I'd accepted that the one-day stuff was the way it was going to be for me, but after a while I couldn't even get in there. I probably did put on a few pounds and weighed a bit more than I would have if I'd been playing day in, day out. Eventually, I guess, I could probably see the finish line. I was almost looking forward to a time when my livelihood didn't depend on me need-ing to get a century or take five wickets every day.

Designated drink-mixer again for the Fourth Supertest, Walker decided he'd best take his camera to Bourda the next day to amuse himself.

There was plenty of local colour. Deprived of their heroes for two years and enticed by a newspaper's forecasting that the game would start despite the rain 'and start on time at that', Guyanans surged through gates that opened at 8 a.m. on Sunday, 25 March. Bourda brimmed with 13,000 as players breakfasted.

The wait was interminable. Players strolled and umpires inspected amid confident announcements that a start was imminent. By 2.30 p.m., when play was finally stated an hour away, many watchers had been at the ground ten hours and seen only a steel band's endless encores. 'They'd been told to expect something more than Test cricket,' says Cozier. 'And it was all there to wind them up. Players came out in civvies prodding the pitch and went off again. The sun was out, and there were marching bands on the outfield that they were being told was too wet to play on.'

'It's gonna blow, man,' averred Wes Hall to WSC's Bruce McDonald as they stood atop the members' stand. 'It's gonna blow.'

'Don't tell me,' McDonald replied. 'Tell the umpires, and the players.'

It seemed routine almost when the Australians gathered at their window to watch fences bend and chairs, rocks and bottles fly. Walker shot a few rolls. Lillee walked round banging a pair of wooden thongs together to simulate gunfire. But, as the pavilion cleared of all but a handful of officials and the players themselves, nervous glances were cast toward the security presence in the ground. Such as it was.

'We were shitting ourselves,' says Martin Kent. 'You expect the security to arrive and say: "It's the police, it's all okay". This armed sergeant dived into our changing room for his safety. He was shaking, physically shaking, and he went white. This guy had a black wetsuit and he went white.'

Two other guards dived in, and umpires Douglas Sang Hue and Ralph Gosein took shelter, before Jeff Thomson shut, barred and bolted the door. Bags were heaped against the mob's weight. Helmets were donned and bats picked up. Hoping that a measure of communist solidarity might help his cause, the sergeant shouted: 'Don't hurt me, comrades, I'm one of you.'

'You're the only guy who's been in a war, Doc,' shouted Ian Chappell to masseur Dave McErlane. 'You're the general. What do we do if they get in?'

McErlane shouted back. They should all grab chairs and tilt them upwards, one leg high, another low: 'One to the eyes. One to the bollocks.'

The advice held until Thomson found himself fighting for a steel chair with the sergeant. He turned to Pascoe: 'Listen Len, when the mob starts coming through that door, I reckon I'll make like I'm one of them and start smashing things.'

Lillee felt for Gosein and Sang Hue. 'Had the mob broken in,' he wrote, 'which I felt could happen any moment, and caught them in there with the players, anything could have happened to them. I have no doubt whatsoever that they were really fearing for their lives. Mind you, so was I.'

Walker was, sort of, delighted. 'I wasn't sure if a thirtieth of a second hand-held would work,' he says. 'Because everyone was shaking like hell and ramming cigarettes through the holes in the helmet visors.' But it was a great 'photo opportunity'. Walker shot reels, then headed for the toilet.

The West Indians' toilet was booked solid, as bottles flew through their windows. The moat round Bourda seemed a sanctuary and Rowe picked up a favourite bat to beat an escape route through the boarded windows. They wouldn't budge. But the massage table, hurled against the door, *was* budging. Garner felt 'a bit like I imagine Americans felt at the Alamo.'

While players were the focus of ire, followers were not spared. GTV-9's Mike Lester and Greg Cameron were ambushed up a ladder as the commentary box was attacked, and their $3000 camera smashed. The *Australian's* Phil Wilkins and two security guards hid in the ladies' toilet.

Wilkins says the crowd only hesitated when it came to ransacking the venerable members' stand: 'They seemed to be aware suddenly that they were trespassing, and trampling the flag of the British Empire.' Riot police arrived with rifles and teargas in time to see the mob disperse, though baton charges were needed to clear the arena. The sergeant and his aides cheered up, especially after they found the Australian team fridge stocked with chicken and beer.

An escort van had joined the team buses at a secret exit on the far side of the ground although, in keeping with the day, the Pakistani bus driver decided that the escort was moving too slowly and over-took it on the way back to the Pegasus Hotel.

Ian Chappell's team meeting weighed whether to return to Bourda or Australia. 'We were told West Indians are "just great cricket lovers" and they are,' says Hookes. 'But they're also very physical, very aggressive and very pissed. You would never feel the same way about an Indian crowd as you would in the West Indies, because Indians aren't so overpowering. Indians've got the same inclination to throw a bottle, but their arms aren't as good.'

'I suppose I'd have been happy enough to go home,' says Kent. 'And there were a few who wanted to take the first flight back to Australia. But it was decided that in retrospect the riot hadn't been personal and that we should go on.' Thomson notably, having resisted returning to Sabina Park under Bob Simpson in May 1978, wanted to play. And the captain said that henceforth he would personally check each venue's security arrangements. Georgetown Cricket Club, after a frantic night shift, had patched the ground remarkably. Play actually commenced on time on Monday morning. Clive Lloyd inserted the Australians, what's more, under an azure sky before a good-natured crowd.

Cricket safety was now the priority. Spurred again by an early wicket, Kent hit seven punitive shots in his half-century. He left the stage to Greg Chappell, who was all smooth command as he closed on a century in less than five hours.

The tourists conceded a meaningless lead of 135 on the first innings after Collis King filled the final morning of the empty contest with a cascade of boundaries. But, as he turned his overnight 40 into 110 within an hour, he was least of Ian Chappell's concerns.

The captain had been returning from the centre of Bourda on the second morning when he had bumped into WSC Caribbean's diminutive public relations manager Vic Insanally, whose voice he recognised as the announcer who'd promised play on Sunday at any tick of the pavilion clock. Chappell had the last word of their contretemps over culpability for the riot by punching Insanally in the stomach.

Presence of the local police chief, Bairam Raghubir, made this one of Chappell's most impetuous hooks: he became WSC's first criminal charge. His team's passports were confiscated. Lawyer Rex McKay joined them to broker a formal apology.

What was worse was that the Australians were committed to a one-day international the day after the Supertest at the Rose Hall ground, a helicopter journey east in malarial Berbice. Ian Chappell's legal obligations had reduced them to ten fit men: Lillee and Marsh were in dire need of a rest, while Walker had been granted early release to attend the birth of his second son Keegan in Melbourne.

Fortuitously, Rick McCosker's thumb had healed after five weeks, while Richie Robinson rediscovered his wicket-keeping roots. McCosker batted well, too, making 89, but Greenidge and Richards ransacked an attack of Mick Malone, Gary Gilmour, Greg Chappell, Hookes, Thomson, and Pascoe. When their helicopter returned to Georgetown on Thursday evening, the Pegasus foyer was a blur. Bruce McDonald had been at Georgetown's taxation department all day pleading for the team's clearance to leave the next morning. The Australians had one-day matches in Trinidad on Saturday, Sunday and Monday. Chappell's guilty plea to assault charges was being organised by McKay – the captain had agreed to shake Insanally's hand for the press – and Robinson as manager collected the $44 fine to appease the local magistrate's court. Walker was telephoning consulates in an effort to retrieve his passport in time for his Melbourne trip.

Colin Croft's mother, it would seem, finally stowed her dolls: the team's short hop from the mainland to Trinidad was negotiated as Walker settled in for his thirty-eight-hour flight home.

As the tour's final fortnight began, its undertow finally snagged the Australians. They were mauled four times in five days by the West Indians. 'They knew they were 15–20 runs better than any other team in their fielding alone,' says Greg Chappell. 'So they had the confidence and arrogance of knowing that, whatever we made, they could make more. It took a lot to get up knowing they could always raise themselves a cog no matter how we played.'

Lillee's back seized at last after a single over on the Saturday. A doctor prescribed three weeks' suspended animation. Thomson felt back spasms too, and would need nursing. On the Sunday, Greg

Chappell strained his own back. Gilmour slipped on a boundary rope next day, pulling a hamstring.

Lillee and Greg Chappell flew on Wednesday to Antigua – the scene of the Fifth Supertest – while the Australians played their eleventh one-day match at Roseau in Dominica. Local dignitaries looked on severely as Marsh directed Australian bowlers including Richie Robinson and Trevor Chappell, and Bruce McDonald was grilled at lunch. 'I got a real lambasting from the President,' the WSC man recalls. 'He reckoned we'd let down the whole of Dominica by letting Dennis and Greg go to Antigua.'

In the evening, Ian Chappell disappeared for the beach. A solitary figure sitting in the water, he tried to divorce himself from the tour and to consider his own game. It was a luxury he'd had little time for. 'No one has ever known the pressure Ian was under on that tour,' says Phil Wilkins. 'He was fighting the world's strongest team, his blokes were being bottled and barracked and bashed. And he was fighting the whole cricket world to establish something he thought would be worthwhile.'

Chappell was also fighting back the years. He was thirty-five, and had developed during WSC the first symptoms of arthritis in his right heel. He now ran on his toe to prevent his heel hitting the ground.

But the more Chappell felt change, the more he tended to resist it. What he must not do was fight nature. He'd been trying not to hook. At Antigua, Chappell decided, he'd hook like hell.

A head stood out as the captain counted those boarding the team bus leaving for Antigua's Recreation Ground in St John's on Friday 6 April. A week earlier, he'd forced an air ticket on Lillee at a farewell drink for the fast bowler. But the invalid had tagged along to Antigua, poignantly the island on which he'd broken down six years earlier. After a beach run and net-bowling to McErlane, he had convinced himself he could survive five days.

Despite Greg Chappell's peerless 104, however, the Australians could eke just 234 after losing 5–41 in an hour either side of tea. Holding again began the decline by breaking David Hookes' ribs second ball, then having him caught fending, and the Jamaican's follow-up for Bright was perfect. 'Mike either bowled one really full to me first up or one really short,' says the spinner. 'I was expecting the short one that day and I got a very handy yorker instead, right on the toe.'

Lillee in Antigua was unrecognisable from the Lillee who had bowled until his back was numb in 1973, or even the Lillee of the Centenary Test two years earlier. WSC had made him energy-conscious. His short, sagacious spells were at strict medium-pace. His only handicap proved a severely hung-over keeper: the first few overs of the second day were a mystery to Marsh. Lillee leapt when Douglas Sang Hue raised his finger confirming Lawrence Rowe's snicked hook, but the appeal died and Sang Hue had to rescind his decision when Marsh was seen studying the ball at his feet with dizzy disgust.

Rowe was an edgy eight, his usual skittish start. 'Lawrence suffered because he was orthodox in an unorthodox line-up,' says Ian Chappell. 'We always said that he was such a good player that he nicked ones early that others missed, and because he was orthodox his nicks always carried.'

Rowe stowed his hook. He cut and drove clinically instead, closing on his first Caribbean century in five years. Three and a half hours and 127 runs after his first attempt, Marsh caught him down the leg side from Lillee. Lillee, too, finally limited the Australian deficit to 204 by leaving Deryck Murray with a gashed eye from a mistimed hook.

Although a day's rain eased the Australian plight, almost nine hours' orderly retreat loomed. And at 3–92, with an hour left of the fourth day, the Chappells were for the last time the Australians' retaining wall. Greg's mastery was now monumental: his last seventeen hours' batting in the West Indies yielded 452 runs at 113. And Ian hooked with abandon to clear the West Indian lead and draw their pacemen's sting.

The Australians were still less than 50 in credit when Holding ended Hookes' pained cameo. Safekeeping of a drawn series was left in the custody of Marsh and Bright, with two sessions stretching ahead. 'Every run, every minute was valuable,' says Bright. 'They were attacking, slips and bat-pads, so you could get runs. But we had to use up lots of time: at 6–250 a bit of the sting was out of them and, if we could stick around, things might get easier.'

Turning the corner of tea, the work did ease. Marsh and Bright prospered against Padmore, and eventually Richards and Fredericks. Lloyd threw the ball to his Guyanan colleague Fredericks when Bright passed his half-century, and Marsh stood on 86. With four consecutive boundaries, the wicketkeeper became WSC's last centurion. 'Yeah, that was good,' Marsh told Ian Chappell. 'We made 'em respect us, didn't we?'

Two golf trips pended as April began, and the Chappells were able to take theirs first. The only white ball Ian and Greg Chappell felt like hitting as they left the West Indies on Black Friday was dimpled. With Hookes they headed for Pebble Beach. They made a foursome on the famous Pacific course with tennis coach Ray Ruffels.

Kerry Packer's golfing holiday in the US with Jack Nicklaus was the other booked. Consolidated Press's Lynton Taylor and Harry Chester were at that moment with ACB solicitors from Hedderwicks finalising an 'in principle' agreement to Nine's television rights bid. The well-informed Tony Greig told an Adelaide luncheon of South Australia's Epilepsy Association on Wednesday 19 April: 'A compromise is imminent. I will only be happy when it is all solved.'

After a board meeting in Sydney on the Sunday and Monday, the ACB turned Anzac Day into Armistice Day. Calling ABC general manager Talbot Duckmanton to formally end their 'special relationship', Bob Parish announced the Nine agreement in a two-paragraph press statement in late afternoon. 'I'm hopeful the decision taken is in the best interests of Australian cricket,' he said haltingly. 'I believe that it is.'

Packer, clubs stowed, now saw to it that 'the best interests of Australian cricket' were congruent with the best interests of his television network. Not only was Nine to receive the rights, but also the cricket it wanted. In Australian cricket's new hierarchy, PBL Sports – a subsidiary of Consolidated Press's television holding company Publishing and Broadcasting Ltd which cradled WSC player contracts – was to be the ACB's partner. It would effectively lease the Australian cricketers back to their board.

PBL would receive exclusive promotional rights to the Australian game. WSC's logo would endure, adorning a tricornered World Series

Cup to be sponsored by Benson & Hedges. The cricket Packer sought was broadly similar to his original conception of WSC: Australia, the West Indies and England in Test and one-day competition, spinning off at least 300 hours of cheap, cheerful television.

Parish contacted the Indian Cricket Board to defer the cut-rate Indian summer for the sake of 'global cricket harmony'. In return he committed Australia to a planned September 1979 tour of India, and invited India to tour Australia a year later. Taylor and Parish began plotting a golden triangle featuring Australia, the West Indies and 'one other' for 1979–1980: as the Test and County Cricket Board might baulk at coloured clothing and field restriction circles, Pakistan was seen as a potential substitute.

Phobias were fought as the ACB executive committee ticked off demands, with eyes on Sir Donald Bradman's responses. Parish paused over the coloured clothing clause, but the knight skipped to the next page. 'Aren't you going to say anything?' Parish asked.

'Why should I?' Bradman replied. 'The Pinks played the Blues in Sydney in 1822. Coloured clothing means nothing.'

The zeal with which the Australians were taking to their task startled the International Cricket Conference, but its priority was a trouble-free World Cup in June. As ACB treasurer Steele recalls: 'They reckoned they were going broke . . . because they were only getting second-grade teams on their tours. And Packer suddenly seemed to have Indians under option, as well as all the West Indians and most of the Pakistanis. We had it in writing they wanted us to solve it, though, so they had to give something.'

The Hedderwicks lawyers had one reservation. Exclusive broadcasting rights granted for Queensland Rugby League had already been struck down by the Trade Practices Commission. An ABC challenge based on 'deprivation of national coverage' could probably be subverted by offering it relay rights, but the ACB had a dread of further expensive legal action. Consolidated Press agreed to underwrite legal costs. With the agreement reduced at last to fine print, Packer made his golf swing from Sydney.

Chairman Parish was the figure in the frame when on Wednesday 30 May, newspapers and television stations gathered for a press conference in the VCA House board room at 3.30 p.m. Journalists, photographers and television cameramen jockeyed round the table as

Parish read from a statement with customary gravity. 'I am making this statement on behalf of the Australian Cricket Board,' he said. 'I am pleased to announce that the agreement between the ACB and PBL Sports Pty Ltd has been signed and will be lodged with the Trade Practices Commissioner.'

Parish was flanked by Taylor and Len Maddocks, with Steele further to his right looking slightly strained. The ACB chairman spoke for five minutes. He then invited questions, with the obvious inquiry about who had won deflected by Taylor: 'I don't think either side won. I think the game of cricket has won. It is peace with honour.'

Melbourne 30 May 1979 became official cricket history's equivalent of Munich 30 September 1938, with Parish as Neville Chamberlain. Jim Swanton's compendious *World of Cricket* rarely mentions it, and him, without slur. In its entry on WSC, West Indian Trevor McDonald summarises the settlement as follows:

> Always with an eye to their own interests, the Australians had agreed to put off the Indian invitation. The agreement gave the Australian board an unspecified amount of Packer money and it gave Mr Packer a strong voice in the running as well as the televising of the cricket in that country. In view of what had always been regarded as Australian intransigence . . . their capitulation was more than a little surprising. The sight of Mr Packer and the ACB chairman Bob Parrish [sic] cooing delightedly in accord was not one for weak stomachs.

Packer was in the UK when the deal was announced but, unlike his visit two years before, preferred Scottish golf links to the World Cup cricketing haunts. He was back in Sydney by the time Taylor and Parish arrived in London to introduce the armistice: Taylor to WSC's players, Parish to ICC delegates.

Taylor had already been in touch with the Cricketers' Association to ensure that Dennis Amiss's deferred exile from Warwickshire was not hastily made permanent. Packer felt him to have been victimised and, according to Patrick Murphy, a tape of Taylor's telephone conversation with the Association played to Warwickshire officials was critical in renewal of Amiss's 1979 contract over the Easter weekend.

Taylor now paid most heed to disillusioned Springboks, who had left Australia in February after two contented years starring in a successful and well-paid World side. Mike Procter in particular felt he had received from Taylor after the Supertest Final an offer of a further three-year contract, and told Clive Rice: 'I've got another contract. Lynton and I have shaken hands on it.' He had even stored his kit in Australia, expecting to return.

A phone call in Bristol from Austin Robertson had given him a day's warning of the settlement, but he mourned: 'To this day I don't know why it disbanded so suddenly and why Kerry Packer packed it in.'

In Nottingham, Rice had wept in his wife's arms: 'It was as if someone had taken away my right arm . . . I never knew the truth of the old adage: "Tis better to have loved and lost than never to have loved at all". But I believe it now.'

But Taylor found his cricketers more receptive than Parish his administrators. When the ICC met at Lord's a week after the World Cup final, the ICC's Charles Palmer and Jack Bailey and TCCB chief George Mann saw little merit in the Taylor-Parish proposal. 'It was hard to avoid the sense of being hijacked twice in a couple of years,' wrote Bailey. 'First by Packer, now by the ACB.'

For West Indian Cricket Board of Control president, Jeff Stollmeyer, continued stand-off spelt doom. On 19 April he'd attended a WICBC meeting at Port-of-Spain's Holiday Inn, and perused a 1978 balance sheet showing an $EC584,324 loss. As a banker, he recognised a profitable West Indian tour of Australia in 1979–1980 as the WICBC's only route to solvency. 'Our overriding consideration was the financial salvation of West Indies cricket,' he recalled. 'Therefore we left no stone unturned to effect a compromise between the two foundation members so that a proposed joint tour could take place.'

The TCCB and ACB spent most of the rest of the English season working toward a *via media*. If the TCCB was to volunteer England for another Australian summer, the heavy World Series Cup program would have to be eased and PBL's 'abnormal conditions' waived. The ACB would have to offer Australia for six Tests in England in 1981, and accord England sole billing on its 1982–1983 visit to Australia.

The ACB and PBL argued the tariff down in turn, and eventually left a £30,000 tour profit guarantee on the table for the seventeen counties.

The counties fumed. Their costs had mushroomed in 1979 because of the basic cricketers' wage of £4500 they'd agreed. The World Cup had suggested that the ACB would prosper in 1979–1980. Half the Cup's £360,000 gross receipts had come from two Lord's games: Australia versus England and the West Indies versus England final. The sums didn't square: 1/17th of £30,000 equalled six weeks' wages for one average English cricketer.

There was an air of tit-for-tat in George Mann's phone call to Parish in Melbourne three weeks after the tour's confirmation on 4 October 1979, advising that the TCCB would not stake the Ashes in a three-match rubber a year after their retention over six Tests.

Packer gave only a mild murmur: he considered the decision 'small-minded'. It fell to Ray Steele to polemicise at the VCA. 'What are they trying to do?' he asked. 'Make our season look second-rate? All they in fact succeed in doing is to give the public the impression that they are chicken.'

It made an inauspicious backdrop to the Lord's farewell for Mike Brearley's Englishmen on 4 November. Brearley thought that the TCCB was wrong. His deputy Bob Willis believed it was right. But Derek Underwood, selected for the tour, finally felt at ease. It simply seemed a tad strange to be back so soon. 'Here we are again!' diarised Willis. 'It doesn't seem five minutes since we were here smiling the same smiles . . . and changing into the same school, sorry, team uniform. It is over 12 months since our last departure from HQ, but everything is so familiar.' It was the last familiar sensation Willis or his colleagues would have for some months.

20

'We were representing our country, but it wasn't important'

At London's Russell Hotel, Kim Hughes' tenderfoot Australians read all about it. The World Cup lay ahead, but now so did a grave new world set out in Melbourne while they had been in transit.

It had been a heady summer for Hughes, an aspirant Australian captain since his century on first-class debut in November 1975. Accepting another accolade a week before his team left – West Australian Cricketer of the Year – he told a dinner: 'I believe in myself, and I believe in the team.'

Who else did? Hughes' party had left Tullamarine for London on Sunday, 27 May 1979, with Dave Richards as manager promising a new spruceness abroad. Blazers would be de rigueur for the next month. But when a dapper Hughes and vice-captain Andrew Hilditch faced pressmen at the Russell on the Wednesday, all Australia's captain could say was that he wanted a 'piece of the action' in the World Cup.

Richards, too, was confused. At Lord's a week later a visiting Lillee – in England on a busman's holiday as a journalist – had the door shut in his face. 'A chill went through me,' Lillee wrote, 'as I thought of the problems to come in a compromise, if there was to be one.' Hughes rescued the situation by admitting Lillee warmly when he heard of the fast bowler's presence. But things could only improve.

'"There must be no recriminations" was the cry,' wrote English author David Lemmon at news of compromise, 'much in the way that Noel Coward used to sing: "Don't Let's Be Beastly To The Germans". But there had been a war ... When you have a war there are dead and wounded.'

The possible victimisation of WSC Australians as they reintegrated was anticipated with heavy emphasis in Parish's statement: The ACB will have exclusive responsibility for selection of Australian teams and has agreed that no player will be excluded by reason only of that player having participated prior to the commencement of the 1979–1980 cricket season in any match not authorised by the board.'

Packer took contractual care of his players. Their contracts were to be paid out fully, and Packer gratuitously bestowed an extra year's salary for no more than their good faith. Even Graeme Wood, the young ACB turk who'd signed for five years but not faced a single white ball, was paid out (albeit at an agreed discount rate).

The sole exception was ironically WSC's greatest discovery: the quasi-Australian Kepler Wessels. The peace jolted him. Hoping to qualify for Australian Test selection, he was to marry an Australian girl – former WSC publicist Sally Denning – in three weeks. He wrote anxiously to the Chappells and Marsh.

'Rod wrote back first,' Wessels recalled. 'And after criticising my handwriting said that he thought I should go to South Australia or Queensland as they had a history of using imported players. Ian wrote that he did not think I had ever written a letter in English before as the writing had been so disgusting, but he said he might be able to help me. Greg wrote that he thought he could organise something for me in Queensland.'

When Greg Chappell arrived in England to play a few invitation games in August, he couriered to Wessels an offer from Brisbane businessman Ron McConnell of three years' public relations work with time to play shield cricket.

PBL's attitude to 'rival promoters', however, was dim. Lynton Taylor called Wessels to remind him of his World Series Cricket contract. Wessels learned he had been 'promised' to New South Wales. He could sell insurance for The Brokers, a Consolidated Press arm that Tony Greig was setting up in Sydney. 'Discussions went on with Lynton, Greig and Kerry Packer himself all screaming at me and threatening to withhold payment on the second year of my contract,' Wessels wrote. 'I stood firm as I had given McConnell my word.' Wessels was eventually freed, but forfeited his second year's pay. The experience was formative: 'I felt it was unfair that I alone should miss out on the second year's payment. But that was the price I had to pay for not being a "true" Australian . . . It put me in a position with other people wanting to decide my future for me on the basis of what they wanted and not what was in my interests.'

Kim Hughes' Australians were 20–1 World Cup outsiders, with odds against their longer term international careers lengthening fast. The West Indies and Pakistan had enfolded WSC players with zeal and pundits salivated over a merged Australian team.

Their piece of the cup action, telecast on the 0-10 network, proved a fragment. Four execrable run-outs surrendered Australia's Lord's match against England. The team was then overrun by Pakistan's batting line-up at Edgbaston.

The latter match demonstrated how acutely the team's talent needed direction. 'I'd got it into my head that I could get a few of these guys out by bowling short,' Alan Hurst recalls. 'I kept at them and they kept hammering me. I was stupid, and I don't use it as an excuse, but it was really made worse by the inexperience of the side. I had the adrenalin flowing and I got no guidance at all.' John Arlott handed down a withering judgement: 'This defeat left Australia with little credit or dignity. There is now no escape for them.'

Gary Cosier was relieved that the team was spared meeting the West Indies: 'If we'd played them it would have been like the Battle of Little Big Horn. With the newness of our guys, we were probably lucky we had a game against Canada.' About 1200 people wondered at Edgbaston if they *were* lucky when Caribbean Canadian Glenroy Sealy pinched 26 from Rodney Hogg's two wayward overs but

Hurst came up with 5–21. The Australians watched the 23 June final – England's Little Big Horn – from home.

Even their captain now seemed on borrowed time. When eleven *Cricketer* experts picked preferred 1979–1980 sides it passed unremarked that not one included Hughes even as a batsman. Thoughts were so completely of the following summer that it was hardly noticed in July when Hughes and Hilditch were named to lead Australia's six-Test India tour. The ten-week trip departing on 22 August was ill-timed, in terms of both Indian meteorology and Australian cricket climate. Monsoons would soon hit India, and team members would return a fortnight into their domestic season, with two weeks to prove themselves before home internationals recommenced.

But the tour had been promised. 'If we wanted teams to come here,' says ACB treasurer Ray Steele, 'we had to visit them as well. We thought about cancellation, but we decided it had to go ahead. We had an obligation.'

'There are,' he adds, 'some things we probably should have done better.'

It was an Australian tour of Asia typical of the times. Local water was out, salads were hazardous and ice-cream untrustworthy. Tinned fruit sent by Australian Gold became at times the only reliable solid, and imported Swan Lager the only drinkable liquid. Aerogard dispensed by physiotherapist Frank Hennessy became a rationed valuable. From a *graffito* on a wall, Hughes and manager Bob Merriman took a tour slogan: 'To lose patience is to lose the battle.'

The team landed at Srinagar on a tarmac lined with tents billeting 2000 troops posted by Prime Minister Indira Gandhi as insulation against terrorists. 'Mr Singh', a Sikh carrying an ill-concealed machine pistol, joined the tour bus at the airport and did not leave the Australians' side. 'There is,' wrote first-time Test tourist Allan Border, 'no quicker education than a tour of India.'

The wickets were flat, the heat unremitting, the umpires sometimes intolerable and the balls like bearings: Yallop broke five bats. Plucked from winter at home, the Australians were overwhelmed by the crucible of Madras' Chidambaram Stadium, and rotated three and four sets of clothes a day.

Nagpur's Hotel Pravasi, a cross between Fawlty Towers and the Ettamoogah Pub, left an especial impression. 'The doors were like old dunny doors: boards and a cross-slat locked by a big brass padlock,' Hurst says. 'The bathrooms consisted of a concrete slab on the floor for a toilet, an open shower and a basin. There were no blankets and one ceiling fan in each room, and two inches of stagnant water on the bottom of the pool.'

Merriman mislaid his patience when lunch was served by white-gloved waiters fresh from the cesspit. 'The first course was soup, covered by a sludge of oil, and no one touched it,' Hurst recalls. 'Then they brought out chicken in gravy, except you couldn't see the chicken for all this gravy.' Bruce Yardley's discovery of half a cockroach prevented further exploration.

Hurst's was one of many careers that turned on an otherwise forgotten tour. He was at his theoretical peak, being wooed on the telephone by Glamorgan as he played, but the broken vertebrae he had nursed for five years finally buckled with the extra effort of stirring response from Indian pitches. After Australia slipped behind in the series at Kanpur, Hurst was repatriated a month early rather than risk Indian hospital traction. Orthopaedic surgeon Clark McNure, who'd badgered him since 1974 to forsake cricket, finally stopped him in his tracks: 'He started talking about wheelchairs.'

While the tour might have been typical, the times were not. At home, cricket composites changed hands like swap cards. Adrian McGregor visited Greg Chappell, prime candidate for Australia's captaincy, and asked him to pick a team. '"Sure", he said, and leaned back in his office armchair,' wrote McGregor. 'Laird, Wood, Darling and Hilditch for openers. Kent or Border first wicket down. Ian should bat at six to save the chronic collapse of Australian tails. He named seventeen players in all.'

In India, the feeling was one of rising helplessness. 'I couldn't get over the feeling that it was a pity we were there,' says Andrew Hilditch. 'That we were signed, sealed and delivered to India when everything was happening at home. We were representing our country, but it wasn't important. Everything we did was irrelevant. The result was that it was us who came back as outsiders rather than the other way round.'

The players had held no illusions and, as September ended, could hear the distant jostling for Sheffield Shield places. While their own Hughes and Kevin Wright were abroad as Australian captain and wicketkeeper, West Australian selectors appointed Rod Marsh as their captain cum keeper. Thirteen of the state shield squad had current official or unofficial international credentials: while Hughes, Wright, Wood, Yardley and twenty-three-year-old all-rounder Graeme Porter toured India, Marsh, Lillee, Laird, Langer and Malone were practising at the WACA with Serjeant, Clark and Mann. The handful of non-internationals included the supplanted captain Dr Ric Charlesworth, imported South African Ken McEwan and Australia's under-19 vice-captain Geoff Marsh.

Hilditch and Border had been joined in India by the twenty-one-year-old New South Wales tearaway, Geoff Lawson, when Hurst flew home. As McCosker, Pascoe, Walters, Davis, Gilmour, O'Keeffe, a relocated Ross Edwards and Trevor Chappell, and even Tony Greig prepared for the season in Sydney with Toohey, Dyson and Rixon, Hilditch's 'good luck Blues' telegram was pinned up in their dressing-room.

He was, after all, the state's captain. Hilditch recalls:

I could have enjoyed the tour far more and derived a lot more from it had I not felt locked away from what was happening in Australia. I had time off and I trained instead, in very poor conditions, when I could have benefited from getting away from cricket and seeing more of the country. But I was so desperate to get runs to keep my place. We were all thinking about doing something big in India and competing against each other to impress the selectors, and that inevitably had an effect on the way we played.

While Border, Hughes and Yallop made maiden Test centuries abroad and Dymock bowled with unwavering control, Australia played forty-four days of cricket on the trip without scenting victory. On the brink of a summer of unprecedented cricket publicity, Australia played Tests abroad covered by wire service writers if at all.

Information, though, came the other way: early Sheffield Shield scores were being studied for the last three Tests. 'The Australians played like young men under sentence of death,' recorded *Pelham Cricket Year*. 'Which is in fact, in cricketing terms, what they were.'

David Hookes chided Doug Walters as the pair stood at slip at Drummoyne Oval on the last Sunday in September 1979. While local stars in the annual Spastic Centre charity game were wearing green and gold, Walters had absent-mindedly slipped into old WSC togs. 'Well, there is meant to be a compromise,' Walters replied drolly.

This was the place to impress: Ian Chappell's XI versus Tony Greig's XI. Peter Toohey's 58 from 66 balls was exquisitely timed in all senses. 'I had the advantage of knowing the WSC guys before they signed,' he says. 'So it wasn't hard for me to go up to Doug Walters or Kerry O'Keeffe and have a beer with them, whereas with a few others it was probably a bit strained. That was an important game, though, and it was really good to get runs.'

Greig, a short-listed candidate for state captaincy, sang Toohey's praises: 'If Australia's selectors had seen his superb batting, they would have been embarrassed they'd not sent him to India. Peter is one of four or five players outside WSC with a chance of playing Tests this summer.'

As Toohey batted at Drummoyne that day, Andrew Hilditch had just finished captaining his country at Nagpur against Central Zone. A few Australian newspapers published unembellished scores. There'd hardly been space, what with St George beating Canterbury in the climax of the NSW Rugby League and Carlton pipping Collingwood in the VFL Grand Final, with Larry Holmes retaining the world heavyweight crown in between.

Hilditch, Border and Lawson attended their first state practice at the SCG six weeks later, and revelled in their state's depth. There was a week before the state's 18 November McDonald's Cup match at the Gabba, and Hilditch read that he was in the twelve although Rick McCosker had kept his early-season role as NSW captain. Never mind: he respected McCosker deeply and thought him a good leader. But a telephone call from state selector Dick Guy at home left him vaguely stunned.

After circling the captaincy issue, Guy continued. 'We've made you twelfth man for the one-day game in Brisbane,' he said. 'But don't tell anyone. We think you're still a chance to be picked for Australia this week.'

He was not, though the reversal of his fortunes – vice-captain of Australia to twelfth man for NSW without playing a game – did not sink in until after practice on the morning of the match in Brisbane. 'It wasn't until about twenty to ten that I realised just how far I'd fallen,' Hilditch recalls. 'It really knocked me over. I was a district cricketer again. Because these weren't exactly young, inexperienced players who'd been picked ahead of me. They were good cricketers and, once you got behind them, you just had no chance if the selectors gave them anything like a decent run.'

His friend John Dyson was not even in the twelve. Dyson's last innings the previous season had been his highest score, 197, and he'd top-scored in both state trial matches. 'When I got to 60 in the second one,' he recalls, 'they sent out the twelfth man to tell me to get out, that they'd seen enough. So I did. When Trevor Chappell and Ross Edwards were picked ahead of me, I just couldn't understand it. I felt that part of the deal in the settlement was that they'd play for NSW, and that I was the guy on the wrong end of the deal. I was pissed off to say the least.'

There was a lot of it going round. At the WACA the same day, the hosts were taking the field without Wood, Wright or Porter. 'I'd been to state practice when I got back,' says Wood. 'But I can still remember my Dad picking up the paper and reading me out the side, and I wasn't in it.'

But there was no particular death's head above the repatriated Australians. As the fates of dozens of Australian cricketers were decided in the next few weeks, it was with even less logic than usual. Pride, prejudice, caprice and raw guesswork were all that state selectors could work with. There was as much of a sense of loss for many of the lesser WSC Australians, now state players again and knowing better than to count on early call-up.

Malone was one already viewing WSC as a halcyon period:

I guess there were a lot of happy people. But I wasn't really one of them. If someone had said during those seasons that if I tore up my WSC contract then I'd be guaranteed a spot in the next Test team, I wouldn't have done it. I was a borderline Test player, and there was no guarantee I wouldn't have been injured or dropped. I think Greg and Dennis and David Hookes were really pleased to be back playing Tests but, if you were Mick Malone, or Ian Davis, or Kerry O'Keeffe, our Test careers were finished. We'd have been happy for WSC to go on another ten years.

Gary Gilmour and Kerry O'Keeffe, their faces and faculties no longer fitting, played Newcastle club cricket after lasting just two Sheffield Shield matches. WSC's fitness zealotry had worn on Gilmour through two seasons. 'We heard a lot of addresses about what was expected of professionals in terms of fitness and dedication,' he says. 'But it never made sense to me. The number of laps I could run shouldn't really make any difference. I'd always figured that if I didn't enjoy it, I wouldn't play cricket.' When the enjoyment left, so did he.

O'Keeffe, his right leg still lame, felt obsolete as a leg spinner. Trying a risky fourth on a strong outfield arm against Victoria, he was – literally and figuratively – run out. 'I knew there'd be a weight of opinion against picking me again, and that this was probably it,' he recalls. 'I took one lingering look at the SCG that day as I walked off, in case it was my last game. It was.'

Whatever their private feelings, ACB officials were publicly conciliatory. The first meeting of Sheffield Shield captains on the player's sub-committee on 20 August brought the Chappells together with Parish and Steele – for the first time since the split – in unblinking concord. Greg was seconded to the Test selection panel – an Australian first – while Ian escaped fairly mildly from two early skirmishes with umpires. Avuncular Jack Edwards was appointed Australia's full-time manager.

When that side was named for the first Benson & Hedges World Series Cup match against the West Indies at the SCG on 27 November, however, it could not help but creak. Kim Hughes was fraternally named Greg Chappell's vice-captain for 1979–1980, while Border and Rodney Hogg survived from the Bombay Test lost on 7 November. But statisticians seeking a linear progression will wonder at the mishap that apparently overtook Hilditch, Darling, Yardley, Whatmore, Sleep, Dymock, Yallop, Wright and Higgs in less than three weeks. Mass Bombay belly? Some horrid fate like that of 'Busby's Babes' twenty years earlier? In either case, the 1979 Australian team in India might be better recalled.

There were replays aplenty in the PBL highlights packages sold to the BBC for England's First Test in Perth on 14 December, and the sequence most rewound was that of umpires and in due course Greg Chappell bailing up Dennis Lillee for using a prototype aluminium bat called Combat. This he then threw defiantly onto the following day's front pages.

Even Lillee loyalists found it hard to accept the ten-minute exercise in pique; Derek Underwood commented that it was 'apparently a sign of weakness for an Australian Test cricketer to apologise or in any way regret such acts'.

The token reprimand that Lillee received at Parish's VCA House press conference left pundits dumbfounded. Never mind Lillee, what was Parish's board up to? David Frith, Thomson's biographer and as worshipful of Lillee as any critic alive, wrote: 'Any boy . . . must have thought it was all an acceptable part of the showbiz into which cricket is being transformed. And when that boy learned a fortnight later that the Australian fast bowler got off with a wagging of administration's forefinger, he must have felt that truly we do live in a "free world".'

The cricket of 1979–1980 became even harder to discern. In the fusion of Test tradition with PBL's mass-market priorities, a quick-change cricket cabaret ensued. International cricket's longest holiday was four days from 10 to 13 January. The Australians twice had Test matches separated by single days for travel.

Most simply felt there was too much cricket. 'Absolutely anything can be overexposed,' wrote Chris Martin-Jenkins, 'be it inanimate like the Mona Lisa or animate like the voice of Joan Sutherland. Even Viv Richards becomes ordinary when seen every day of the week.'

But that no stone was unsold intensified the congestion. Those not exposed to WSC's salesmanship were ambushed by PBL's hardsell, which new marketing manager Tony Skelton defined as 'hustling for the disposable dollar'. But even those who had been were taken aback. The 'three-way battle of the cricket gods' had no fewer than four 75-second versions of 'C'mon, Aussie' to ensure that every game was a 'big event'. Nullifying and negating all that had come before, almost

$2.5 million was spent by PBL and sponsors on cricket promotion in 1979–1980.

Everybody seemed to have a marketing itch. The ABC extolled Alan McGilvray, who called his hundredth Anglo-Australian Test match that summer, with a one-minute rhyme: 'The Game Is Not The Same Without McGilvray.' When the West Indies arrived in New Zealand in February 1980, they were serenaded by 'C'mon, New Zealand, We Can Do It'.

English players asked Lord's to intercede on learning that a composite poster of the three international teams was being given away with McDonald's hamburgers (the fast-food chain had replaced Gillette as sponsor of Australia's domestic one-day competition). 'Cornhill have put a great deal of money into English Test cricket but I don't think that gives them the right to use any player's name to sell their insurance,' wrote Geoff Boycott. 'And I don't hear Benson & Hedges . . . suggesting that every player was getting through a hundred of their special fags a day.'

The ACB's cohabitation with PBL, mutually admiring, obscured the reality that the ACB had been relegated to the role of administrator. It had ceased to be 'sole promoter'. The ACB took only one decision of consequence for the season: it raised Test admission prices from $3 to $5. With monopoly restored, daily Test attendances rose 47 per cent from 11,022 to 16,237 and the ACB banked $1.31 million from six Tests, against $807,043 from eight in 1978–1979. With about 20,000 people attending each World Series Cup match, ticket sales multiplied almost two and a half times in the space of a year. Almost $2.14 million replenished the depleted ACB treasury.

A few did, however, sense a discomfiture in the ACB's actions. It was Parish's valedictory season and, when Chris Martin-Jenkins interviewed him for the BBC on 6 February 1980, he appeared somewhat adrift. 'Parish commented on what a "long, hard season" it had been, yet seemed reluctant to accept that others shared his belief,' the broadcaster wrote. '"We must give the public what they want," he kept saying, like a man trying to convince himself.'

The weird itinerary was never publicly commented on, although Bob Willis diarised after a convivial dinner the same week with Dave Richards: 'He and I agreed that it is not really desirable to have two touring sides in the country for the whole season.'

When Willis, Mike Brearley and the Test and County Cricket Board's George Mann flew to Melbourne on 14 November 1979 to argue against using coloured clothing and field restriction circles – of which they had no experience – England's captain believed he was being subtly set up. 'Now there were those on the board who hoped privately that we would be stubborn,' he wrote, 'but not so stubborn that the series would be scrapped. They would then get their Anglo-Australian Tests (and revenues), Channel Nine would get its screens filled cheaply day after day, and we (the English) would get the blame. And that is exactly what happened.'

21

'These are professionals, and they'll behave as professionals'

'I'd never seen a man as big as this on a cricket field and his size, combined with his pace, frightened the hell out of me. The length of the pitch seemed to shrink to bloody near nothing as Big Bird ran into bowl. By the time the ball left his huge hand, he seemed to be breathing down your neck.' As twenty-four-year-old Allan Border faced Joel Garner at the Gabba on 1 December 1979, he glimpsed also the future shaped in Kerry Packer's forge. Cricket, so often a reminiscent game, had hit the 1980s a month early. Its new world order, in many respects, remains undisturbed.

For Clive Lloyd's West Indians, the summer of 1979–1980 was the first in a patterned procession of triumphs: the World Cup champions duffed the Australians in two of three Tests and seized the World Series Cup. With Roberts, Holding, Garner and Croft fit and available simultaneously, they spun not: despite playing their three Tests on lifeless surfaces in Brisbane, Melbourne and Adelaide, Lloyd tolerated only a dozen overs slower than medium pace. But neither did they toil: the Australians received 82 balls an hour, from which they scored an average 37. Within the year, the West Indians would be granting as few as 75 balls an hour on tour in England.

Touring Australia four years earlier, Lloyd's West Indians had managed 94 balls an hour, from which home batsmen had scored 45. Eighteen months had elapsed since Alvin Kallicharran's side at Sabina Park had lobbed 103 balls an hour at Bob Simpson's Australians. But, loitering with intent, the West Indies were now stomping a new, and contagious, cricket rhythm.

Viv Richards' command – absent much of 1978–1979 – returned in full measure in 1979–1980, reflected by a first-class average of 98 and one-day average of 97. Two-thirds of the former and almost half the latter accrued in boundaries, as Richards nursed groin and back injuries.

After his county upbringing, World Series Cricket had been a perfect finishing school for Gordon Greenidge. His recognition in 1979–1980 as a cornerstone of West Indian success 'made all the struggles of the past seem worthwhile, and confirmed the belief that I was now not merely a Test cricketer of some ability, but a world-class cricketer.' The free-style middle-order batting that followed Richards – mixing left-handers Kallicharran and Lloyd with right-handers Lawrence Rowe and Collis King – now had the bulwark of Roberts to follow. And Lloyd's span as captain grew a cubit: he would average more than 51 as Test captain, compared to 38 as Test player.

Packer pay had been banked with thanks. Privileged professional status would prolong careers. Michael Holding's 192 Test wickets after 1977 cost 24, the same as his first 57, but he was a changed cricketer. He married in 1980. His first child was born the following year. 'I did not take my money and spend it wildly,' he says. 'But I purchased things in a very short time that it would take most West Indians a lifetime to earn, and that I could not have afforded on $200 a Test match.'

Test cricket, all the same, still came as something of a tonic. To Joel Garner, the fragility of the WSC West Indies in 1978–1979 had been deeper than mere misfortune. 'There was a general feeling,' he wrote, 'something indefinable, that you couldn't even speak about for fear that you would . . . have applied a pin to the balloon of our pretended confidence. For me the feeling had something to do with ambition and national pride. I had become more realistic, more cynical . . . I missed playing for the West Indies.'

He had headed for England in 1979 to 'hunt for a lost feeling I once had for the game'. Cricket's division and its reconciliation brought him to a conclusion: 'I told myself that if I was to continue playing the game, then it would have to be a separate part of my life. I would have to control it . . . instead of it controlling me.' Joel Garner's cricket alter ego would blot out the sun in the 1980s: his post-WSC record of 234 wickets at 20 each places him at the very front rank of West Indian fast bowlers. To use the quiz show phrase, the West Indians had obtained money and box.

Ian Chappell left the game in 1979–1980 as Sheffield Shield cricketer of the year and, just as the shield itself was marginalised in Australia's new cricket structure, changes in which he'd been a prime mover had destined him to be the last of his line.

Under his brother, Australia entered the 1980s with a cricket of personality rather than of policy. Individual performances would shape its fortunes. Greg Chappell, at a peak of his powers, bookended that first summer of reconciliation with Test centuries. Lillee, bag of tricks stocked in WSC, took 11 English wickets with cutters at the MCG on a pitch that might in previous days have tamed him. Elaborately prepared by his two years Supertesting, Laird made a plucky Test debut at the Gabba with 92 and 75. Hughes made an unbeaten 130 there to book his place for the season. With 115 against England in Perth a week later, Border did the same.

The ball-in-glove affinity of Lillee and Marsh had been enriched by the wicketkeeper's suggestive semaphoring for particular deliveries. When David Gower interrupted the procedure one day at the SCG, he recognised the 'up the nostrils' gesture: 'When he realised I had spotted him, we both broke into broad smiles. I don't think the bowler obliged on that occasion but . . . the bouncer was never far away when you were facing those guys.' The collective ego, acumen and self-confidence could be so overpowering that, as England was taken by aggressive storm in the First Test at the WACA, Brearley felt his team 'lose touch with its combative powers'.

The seasonal structure, moreover, had turned Australia's cricket team into a capsule detached from the rest of the home season. The quintet of Greg Chappell, Lillee, Marsh, Ian Chappell and Gary Cosier had played eight Sheffield Shield matches each in 1975–1976.

Greg Chappell, Lillee, Marsh, Hughes and Border in 1979–1980 played eight between them.

As the ACB concentrated on the needs of that circle, there was frustration for those at the periphery. One-off World Series Cup trials that Walters, Yallop, Walker, Laughlin, Hookes, Whatmore and Darling were granted had reason but little rhyme. In their match on 11 December, Laughlin and Walters proved the most success-ful batsmen while Walker conceded only three runs an over, but none were recalled. Laughlin remembers a round of golf with Ian Botham, Ken Barrington and Australian selector Alan Davidson a few weeks later at which he almost broached the subject. 'I thought Davo might let something slip, but he didn't,' he says. 'All I heard was that Greg wanted to keep the Test side together in one-day games. I was disappointed because I feel I could really have devel-oped a role in one-day cricket.'

For WSC's participants, it was an unforeseen cost of revolu-tion. As Shayne Quick observes: 'Australian cricket players readily accepted the principles of capitalism into their arena . . . but it can only be speculated whether or not they fully realised the product maximisation involved . . . It is doubtful that they did.'

It was not a cricket world in which Ian Chappell fitted. Never again would a captain be told – as Ian Chappell had been before the 1972 tour by selector Neil Harvey – that he had been given 'a team of goers'. The Australian team in which he played in the Third Test against the West Indies at Adelaide was actually the oldest since 1952. His last bow the following week at the MCG in the Third Test against England could have been the scene for some romantic reflec-tion – a Chappell partnership seeing Australia to victory against the 'oldest enemy' – but Greg had a cab waiting outside to spirit him to the evening flight for Brisbane.

Greg Chappell felt a lot in common with John Cornell whom he piquantly met at Sydney airport a year later. When Cornell complained he was about to leave his family at home again for another screenwriting session abroad, Chappell lamented: 'If you were an Australian cricketer, you'd be seeing a damn sight less of them.'

Greg Chappell and Dennis Lillee's records pre- and post-WSC show an appealing symmetry: 4097 runs at 53 and 171 wickets at 23 before; 3013 runs at 55 and 184 wickets at 24 after. But every

Australian cricketer whom WSC had brushed was changed in some way.

From being the base of Australia's middle order before 1977, for instance, Rod Marsh became the top of its tail from 1979. 'Marshy got a few up the nostrils in WSC,' says Ian Chappell. 'I used to say: "You've a red ball up one, a white up the other. All you need's a blue ball and you'll have the set".'

Marsh posted his tenth first-class hundred against Essex in 1977. In another seven years' striving he made only two more. The result-ant search for an all-rounder to stiffen Australia's batting would have a marked effect on subsequent team balance.

Cricket's new whiff of danger was felt to suit some more than others. Laird, twenty-nine as 1979 ended, had all his twenty-one Tests ahead. Davis, twenty-six, would not add to his fifteen. Even WSC's successes paid a price. When Ray Bright took just seven first-class wickets at 64 in 1979–1980, Greg Chappell felt it a delayed reaction to two years' 'intimidatory batting'.

'A lot of spinners would probably have wilted in WSC, but Brighty stood up to it well,' notes Chappell. 'WSC, though, prob-ably changed his game a bit, got him bowling a bit more defensively and eventually cost him a bit of his bite. He'd had as tough a task as any young spinner could've had, bowling against the top twenty or thirty batsmen in the world day in, day out. And that eventually took its toll mentally.'

David Hookes' tour of Pakistan in mid-February 1980 simi-larly suggested the limits of his WSC 'master class'. His half-dozen innings on spin-friendly surfaces brought an embarrassing 10 runs, his one Test a mortifying pair. 'The only disappointment I have from WSC is that maybe my cricket education didn't proceed as it should have,' says Hookes. 'I faced a lot of quality fast bowlers, but I never really learned how to play spin. It was a setback for me not going to India in 1979. I saw guys like Border, Hughes and Rick Darling come back having learned an enormous amount about playing slow bowl-ers, experience I didn't get the benefit of.' Two and a half years would elapse before his next Test, and his remained a career unfulfilled.

If WSC had a spontaneous sequel, it was 1 February 1981, when Greg Chappell instructed brother Trevor to deliver his infamous MCG underarm to deny New Zealand an unlikely World Series Cup

Final tie. It was a tactic the captain had first considered three years earlier, after Wayne Daniel's twelfth-hour six at VFL Park.

And if WSC had a private echo, it could be regarded as Ian Chappell's divorce from Kay – his wife of fourteen years – at the same time. The second Mrs Ian Chappell would be the former Ms Barbara Loois, the ex-WSC tour co-ordinator.

Had he not been overwhelmed by the occasion of a World Cup fare-well for Andrew Hilditch in May 1979, meanwhile, Allan Border might never have got round to proposing to his wife Jane. While the faster lane of Test cricket took adjustment, Border would recognise WSC as a 'huge kickalong' for his game: 'I'd be silly to say that, although I wasn't involved in it personally, WSC wasn't the best thing that ever happened to my career.'

Border, though, was a singular man in Australian cricket. Young cricketers with whom he had propped Australia through the 1977–1979 Test summers became a lost patrol. Fifteen never played another Test.

In the five years it took Hilditch to rewin his Test place, the slaps of selectors stung severely. It was not until 1981, when he spent his honeymoon (after marrying Bob Simpson's daughter Kim) leading Forfarshire to the Scottish county league title, that he rediscovered his taste for cricket and resolved to press on with South Australia. Even then, cricket was never quite the same. Hilditch recalls:

> I realised that it was the guys who made a scene who got back in the side quickest. Much later, I was dropped from the South Australian side and it was so ridiculous that I thought I had to go and see the selectors, and say just how stupid it was. I got back in the team a couple of games later but I still felt: 'This is just not the way it should be. You're supposed to take these things like a man and quietly do your job.' If I was a selector I would admire the guy who just put things behind him and proved himself by performance. But it never worked out that way.

Graham Yallop would work his way back into Tests on Australia's 1980 Pakistan tour, but had the bitter experience at the subse-quent Lord's Centenary Test to be informed – by a journalist at the celebratory dinner – that in his absence he had been sacked as Victoria's captain. He stalked wordlessly from the room.

Most tangibly, however, Australia's Test captaincy would straddle a rift between the proud, prejudiced WSC circle of the Chappells, Lillee and Marsh, and Kim Hughes. WSC alumni never forgave Hughes his identification with the Australian Cricket Board during the seasons of split. Marsh's rebel streak was apparently never forgotten by the ACB.

In Greg Chappell's absences over the next four years, ill-concealed argument raged over the respective captaincy claims of Hughes and Marsh. The ACB's board meeting of March 1983 prior to that year's World Cup tied members at six-all with two apparently undecided, but Marsh was again overlooked. 'For them he was tarred with the same brush as Ian Chappell . . . of revolution and extremism,' Mike Brearley wrote. 'This was a major mistake; he might well have proved a more imaginative Test captain than Greg.'

Hughes' eventual inheritance of the captaincy was, without Greg Chappell, Marsh and Lillee, not so much a poisoned chalice as an empty one. It was telling comment on cricket peace's that, by 1985, Hughes and Yallop were leading an Australian team out of ACB bounds in South Africa's 'National Panasonic Test Series'. As he considered joining the 'rebel' team, Hughes reflected: 'I remember sitting down and thinking that throughout my whole cricket career I seemed to have been opposing people. Because of my stand against WSC, there were axes to grind and the situation just went from bad to worse . . . gradually it had eaten away at my confidence. In the end I had no one who I trusted.'

Those who would, with Border, shape Australian cricket in the 1980s, were a next generation in gestation during the WSC years. Sheffield Shield debutants in 1977–1978 included Geoff Lawson, Geoff Marsh and David Boon. Simon O'Donnell and Ian Healy were 'all-Australians' in the national under-16 competition at Rockhampton around the New Year in 1979. Australia's longest-serving Test umpire Tony Crafter adjudged the Hilditch 'handled the ball' during a maiden Test appointment at Perth three months later.

It was a global trend. Larry Gomes' emergence was as Viv Richards' stand-in against Australia in April 1978. He was then a key member of the team Kallicharran led to India in November, Malcolm Marshall's first tour. A seventeen-year-old Richie Richardson made his first England tour in 1979 with an Antiguan schools side.

India's Kapil Dev, having hinted at his abilities against a full-strength Pakistan, proved them against half-strength West Indian and Australian teams. Tony Greig's fall hastened Ian Botham's English rise, while Graham Gooch and David Gower flowered against Pakistan's innocents abroad in 1978 without the rivalries of Amiss or Woolmer. Knott's commitments finally cleared room for his thirty-seven-year-old understudy Bob Taylor. One Test in seven years became a career of fifty-seven. 'Of all the good and bad repercussions of the "Packer Revolution",' Chris Martin-Jenkins wrote, 'the happiest was that this perfect craftsman and ideal sportsman suddenly acquired a status which his exceptional ability warranted.'

Of the first crop of WSC's internationals, only Imran and Zaheer were destined to play more than a handful of Tests, as somewhat modified versions of their former selves. Zaheer – stance squared for composure against pace – would become one of his country's most sadistic scorers at home. His Test record after 1977 of 3062 Test runs at 53 dwarfs a relatively modest 1583 Test runs at 34 before WSC.

Greig ended WSC a shadow of the player who had begun. He was destined in 1979–1980 to find a corner in a crowded commentary box as he learned the insurance broking trade. While Greig's cricketing decline had been limited to his last two years, his intimacy with cricket's 'rival promoter' made retirement judgements harsher. 'The presence of the fallen idol with the feet of clay,' wrote his former champion Jim Swanton, 'had become an embarrassment to all.'

The English aftermath of WSC was the reverse of the Australian trend. Bob Willis's rise to England's captaincy in 1982 owed much to his stated allegiance. Underwood, Knott, Woolmer and Amiss had by this time severed their international cricket ties by joining the 'rebel' SAB England XI in South Africa in 1982.

The WSC repatriates watched instead as changes they had hastened permeated the game. When interviewed by Patrick Murphy for his *The Spinner's Turn* in 1983, all noted first-class cricket's brawnier feel as slow bowlers fell into disuse. Underwood believed that batsmen now tried to hit him harder: 'The high standard of fast bowling means they think: "We'd better get after the spinner now that the quicks are resting".' Amiss missed the challenge spinners posed: 'To play against a spinner is a pleasure, because in the last ten years the game's been about getting away from the ball to avoid being hit. When the spinners are on, it's a quieter game. No one's trying to knock off your head.' Knott remembered the way batsmen had of yore shouldered arms: 'Very few balls come to me behind the stumps now without the batsman trying to play a shot. They're all looking to run it down to third man, or go for the big drive.'

Amiss was denied another Test, despite a further forty first-class centuries, but his legacy as an innovator accompanied him at his finest hour. It passed almost unremarked that his first well-wisher on registering his one-hundredth hundred at Edgbaston in July 1986 was a wicketkeeper, Graeme Fowler, wearing a helmet.

Cricket's 1980s elite would follow WSC's footprints. They would wear helmets, whose development was spurred by WSC's original rash of head injuries. They would bat longer for their runs and face proportionally fewer deliveries. And on shorter, more congested tours as the limited-overs international became a genre in its own right, they would increasingly take one day at a time. Australian cricketers, in particular, would give up their nights as a result of WSC's signal week of success at VFL Park in January 1978.

WSC, of course, can claim no authorship for the one-day form. It merely worked its will upon it, through field restrictions, tougher prosecution of wides and repackaging as a technicolour blur. One-day international cricket went forth from WSC and multiplied.

Australia had been involved in sixteen one-day internationals in seven years before WSC, and hosted just three. Australia's first – the first anywhere – at the MCG had drawn 46,000 on a Tuesday in January 1971, but the experiment had not been repeated for another four years.

While the success of the 1975 World Cup was then minuted, further exploration of the format was not a priority. The ACB scheduled none between December 1975 and January 1979. And coloured clothing for the advent of colour television was beyond imagining. As ACB secretary Alan Barnes said when sounded out about sprinkling additional colour in the game for the sake of the cameras: 'Pardon me, but I've always thought people watched cricket for the play, not the decor.'

That state of affairs existed, it must be said, with thorough player blessing. Cricket containment went against Australian grain. When Australia met England in three Prudential games at the end of its 1972 tour, Ian Chappell thought seriously of golf instead. He went along with the gag only when deputy Keith Stackpole proved similarly uninterested.

Like county cricketers in their exploratory knock-out Gillette Cup in 1963, the Australians rarely mourned one-day defeat. Ian Chappell, moreover, resisted any programmed approach after second place in the 1975 World Cup buoyed his belief: 'I don't believe in altering your approach radically for these games. Perhaps teams could prepare themselves more intensely for the fielding aspect, but that's all . . . I've always felt that one-day cricket has its place and I think we all quite enjoy it.'

Two years later one-day cricket had a very big place and Chappell was straining to love it. WSC staged fourteen one-day matches in its first season and, when 60,000 attended the four night-time novelties, almost trebled that ration in New Zealand, Australia and the West Indies the following season. Those who neglected one-day cricket were clearly going to be poorer for it. The Australians missed out on $10,000 surrendering the International Cup final in 1977–1978, and $35,000 losing the best-of-five International Cup finals in 1978–1979.

Clive Lloyd's West Indians revelled in the format. 'There have probably been greater Test teams than this West Indian side, for they lack high quality spinners,' wrote Brearley in 1979. 'But I cannot imagine that, in the history of the game, there has been a side better equipped for one-day cricket. In fact their closest rivals were probably the winners of the 1975 World Cup!'

Australians, however, remained agnostic as the form grew more stereotyped and rehearsed. *Wisden* recorded of the 1979–1980 World Series Cup: 'Greg Chappell made it clear he disliked this defensive form of cricket. He attempted to win his matches without resorting to negative bowling or spreading his fielders round the boundary.' Lillee reflected the ambivalence of his countrymen when he wrote afterwards: 'I know it sounds un-Australian, and I almost find the idea offensive, but in limited-over cricket we must learn to think negatively.'

The different fitness demands of one-day cricket were recognised when Lillee's fitness guide Frank Pyke became an ACB consultant, and Cronulla physiotherapist Errol Alcott began accompanying teams from the 1984 West Indies tour. Probably until the 1987 World Cup, however, patriotic one-day defeat was an Australian trait.

Indeed as 'different' as WSC appeared, its status today as a kind of contra-cricket is almost too seductive. WSC's changes were stylistic rather than substantive. Colouring and illuminating cricketers were striking alterations to their entertainment package, but compared to rule changes for lbws and no-balls had relatively minor impact on the game's ritual.

WSC was less an initiator of change – reliance on fast bowling, one-day cricket, and even frequency of international competition were already increasing – than an expediter. WSC's participants were mature cricketers who, right to its conclusion, resisted too great a degree of difference from what they had known before. Bob Woolmer left Australia in February 1979, for example, worried that Packer seemed to want World players fitter the following season. 'We were set certain targets to achieve before the following year in weight reduction, mobility, stamina, wind and speed,' he wrote. 'So perhaps it was fortunate we never had to achieve them.'

In some respects, in fact, WSC's hard-sell disserved its personnel. The lexicon John Arlott opened with 'circus' was enlarged to denigrate those 'pirates' and 'pet monkeys' in their 'Packerball' and 'pyjama cricket'.

How thoroughly cricket was 'professionalised' is a moot point. There were assuredly radical short-term changes in cricket pay and conditions. In 1973, English Test cricketers received £150 a game. At the start of 1977, in spite of record wage inflation of up to 28 per cent, they were receiving £210.

The arrival of Cornhill Insurance as a sponsor and the need to head off further defections during 1977 saw the Test fee grow almost fivefold to £1000. By 1985 it was £1500. County wage bills, levered by the minimum wage negotiated by the Cricketers' Association, mushroomed threefold to £2 million over the same span.

While the focus also fell on pay in Australia, conditions there were as fundamental to WSC's rise. Australian players signed at a time when their match fees were on sharp incline and in spite of a tour fee for England (thanks to Benson and Hedges) four times as great as they had been paid two years earlier. Within three years, tobacco companies would be pouring $10 million into Australian sport.

The ACB, though, had dallied too long to remedy past grievance. Administrators had little understanding of players and, indeed, vice versa. The ACB's current chairman Alan Crompton recalls a conversation with Bruce Laird while managing Australia's 1982 New Zealand tour, when the player was surprised to learn that administrators were mostly unpaid. 'He'd gone through the whole of the WSC period thinking that administrators were fully professional. It emphasised to me how bad communications had been between the board and players in 1977.'

'The Boss' put them in good hotels. He welcomed their wives and let them pick their own teams. For all the talk of parity with other professional sports, the sums actually paid were derisory: as Rod Marsh earned $35,000 in 1977, his golfing brother Graham earned $US275,000.

Prior to the WSC Australians' tour of the West Indies in January 1979, they actually had their first pay dispute with WSC. They wanted less. When Lynton Taylor recognised that anticipated tour revenues would not satisfactorily cover salaries at the agreed contractual daily Australian rate, Chappell's team agreed to a pay cut reducing their aggregate salaries for the tour by $300,000.

It was Packer who dragged Taylor and Chappell into his office and told the Australian captain: 'Listen son, this organisation won't go broke over money like that. It will go broke if it starts dishonouring contracts over what it costs to buy a B-grade movie.' He told Taylor: 'Pay them their money.' The Chappells, Packer knew, were a far cheaper family than *The Sullivans*.

The gravest fear WSC raised in cricket board meetings was that of 'player power'. A genuine chill followed Justice Slade's High Court ratification of cricketers' free trade, and it recurred in the peace pact of June 1979. 'Much of the power of the international boards is with the cricketers,' wrote Trevor Bailey. 'Just how much will be seen in Australia when the England, West Indian and Australian teams appreciate the extent and start exploiting the new situation.'

Clive Lloyd's West Indians certainly wielded power. The WICBC's financial plight in April 1978 following the player's 'strike' had underscored its dependence on the success of their top cricketers.

The corrupting potential in that arrangement seemed in evidence when Lloyd's team beat a petulant path through New Zealand in March 1980, complaining of umpires, facilities, hotels, and even of having to carry their own luggage. Colin Croft's shoulder charge on umpire Fred Goodall, and Holding's chorus-line stump kicking made tin-bat tossing look tame. The tourists 'sat-in' their dressing-room at tea on the third day of the Second Test for twelve minutes, then four actually booked to fly home *during* the final day of the Third Test. By that stage, many New Zealanders would have been happy to see them go. Disciplinary action was apparently stifled, however, by the WICBC's need for a profitable England tour.

Indian cricketers dabbled in a professional association in 1978; Pakistan's Test players did the same in 1981. But 'player power' in international cricket really hinged on the existence of rival employers. WSC's impact has only been replicated since by the 'rebel tours' of South Africa. Post-WSC English and Australian players still depended on the generosity of a largely unchanged administration. While the former had the relative advantage of a gingering Cricketers' Association, the latter reverted to being un-unionised salaried employees who 'took it or left it'.

In Australia, moreover, the upward salary influence of WSC had become the downward commercial one of PBL. Although Packer conferred bonus salaries on his loyal subjects, he had always been an ironic patron for aggrieved workers. And, while a $10,000 loan from him in September 1977 had helped the Chappells set up an exploratory Professional Cricketers' Association of Australia, it led nowhere.

The brothers saw the PCAA protecting and preserving rights they appeared to have won when peace was agreed. Ian Redpath was made an 'acceptable' president when the PCAA registered on 17 January 1979 under the NSW Companies Act – coincidentally the day WSC staged its first match in pastels – and the Newcastle lawyer-cricketer Mick Hill later co-opted as an executive director. But the

Chappells were in the West Indies while truce terms were agreed and, in the climate of cricket reformation and the desperation merely to play, the PCAA struggled to gather members. Its territory was also annexed when the ACB broadened its two-year-old subcommittee to include elected members of Sheffield Shield teams as well as captains, and appointed Bob Merriman (an experienced industrial relations bargainer) as a further conduit for player-administrator communication. Merriman was well liked in his role, especially by Border, who knew him as manager on his first Australian tour in 1979 and later on his first Ashes tour as captain in 1985.

The limits of Packer's largesse were also discovered. When Hill and accountant Kim Butler visited Packer and Lynton Taylor at the SCG early in 1979–1980 to propose a tax-efficient scheme for the players' salary bonuses – in which a merchant bank would buy PBL's player contracts and distribute monies as capital rather than income – they received a robust response to the bank's request for Packer's personal guarantee.

'Change your merchant bank, son,' Packer advised.

As it happened, it was a Consolidated Press merchant bank, Pan Pacific Securities. 'You own the merchant bank,' Hill replied.

Packer was unmoved. 'Son, you've got more courage than sense,' he said. 'I haven't signed a guarantee since I was sixteen. I'm not starting now.'

As ACB and PBL interests converged, Packer even became a bizarre establishment ally acting against 'rival promoters'. That Packer and player interests had diverged completely was obvious in 1985–1987, when PBL put its money where the board's mouth was in resisting 'rebel tour' organiser Bruce Francis.

With official opposition and unofficial indifference, the PCAA stood a chance only if well funded. It wasn't. Although supported at its peak by three-quarters of Australia's first-class cricketers, its base proved too small. Industrial relations historian Braham Dabscheck concludes: 'Given the small size, wide geographic distribution of its membership and low income, the PCAA lacked the wherewithal . . . necessary to operate as a viable institution. It found itself a victim of the tyranny of distance.' After an unsuccessful attempt by Geoff Lawson to revive it, the PCAA was wound up in 1988. Although Packer was apparently happy to write off the loan, Ian Chappell found the $10,000 by selling a photo of his 1974–1975 Ashes team.

There is, of course, no need for anything as formal as a union or guild where the good intent of parties is absolute. And arguments about what players are paid invariably reduce cricket to sterilities from which the game is meant to be a relief. But by 1985, David Gower's unionised Englishmen were earning £1500 a Test and £500 a one-day match, against the $2200 and $700 being drawn by Allan Border's un-unionised but contractually bound Australians. And the dollar would depreciate 40 per cent between February 1985 and August 1986.

Popular perception is also that the better players were paid, the worse they behaved. The arguments are familiar, subjective, and often circular.

Players under WSC's flag were certainly more demonstrative. The VIP treatment it accorded, and the manner in which distant Test crowd worship gave way to active adulation from younger one-day crowds, was irrefutably reassuring and self-inflating. For Lillee, WSC was a transition from being told he was a hero in 1975 to knowing he was a hero in 1980. Greg Chappell told Adrian McGregor of his colleague: 'From a shy, gullible bloke when I first met him, he developed an unbelievably supreme ego. It's not a criticism. Most of us were the same.'

Actual WSC indiscretions, though, were rare. Players answered to a boss of a rather puritan sporting streak. 'There'll be no swear words,' he said at WSC's inception. 'These are professionals and they'll behave as professionals – or they're out.' Packer would, for instance, personally chide Greig for allowing Mike Procter's son to co-drive the drinks buggy at VFL Park.

While Ian Chappell committed probably the most serious offence of the WSC years with his haymaker at Vic Insanally at Bourda, Alan Knott remembered the period as one of the quietest stages of the cricketer's career. 'If you said well played when he got 50 or 100 he just wouldn't answer,' he wrote. 'The Aussies seemed to have this plan under the second stage of his captaincy. I used to say hello in the middle to Rod Marsh, for example, but in one match he didn't want to answer, obviously because he had been told not to.'

Television's increased keyholing and eavesdropping in cricket caused Richie Benaud one of his few misgivings in his summary of the lot of the post-Packer cricketer. 'Because of the glare of publicity from newspapers and television he cannot get away with anything,' Benaud wrote. 'An incident in which a player is involved today leads to him being called a larrikin. Years ago he was a personality. Bad language today means you're a loud-mouthed "yobbo". Years ago you were a character adding to the charm of the game.' Indeed, none of cricket's moral guardians has ever been heard celebrating how WSC's television breakthroughs enhanced the policing of on-field etiquette.

There is still little heard in favour of Kerry Packer's influence on cricket. Writing in 1979, Andrew Caro fantasised of a future in which he would attend a Lord's Taverners dinner on 11 June 1993 honouring Sir Kerry Packer for his contribution to cricket. It stayed a fantasy.

Packer, however, proved less a cricket revolutionary than a remarkable resurfacer. His influence there lingers in even his simplest insistences, like his loathing for 'batsmen's backsides'. To watch today BBC footage of Bob Massie's 16 wickets at Lord's in 1972 – filmed from *behind* the batsman – is to know the meaning of frustration. Brian Morelli, on the other hand, recalls the confusion of his young son at his first live cricket match at 'all the walking about' between overs: he had never noticed a change of ends on television.

WSC was also an education for cricket administrators, or at least should have been. Cricket's dependence on its broadcasters and sponsors has irrevocably altered the nature of cricket's revenue base. We remain wedded to crowd size as the prime pointer to cricket's financial health, but the sport's solvency today is more deeply rooted in the value of television rights and commercial support.

In 1977, the ACB was a strong financial institution, but its health was fragile. It had one profit centre (ticket receipts) derived from a single product (Test cricket), one growing but still small revenue stream (its Benson and Hedges sponsorship) and a host of loss-making operations (Sheffield Shield, club and junior cricket). It did not ultimately control its grounds, so its assets were predominantly intangible: a loyal clientele drawn mostly by the folklore of Test tradition, but increasingly by a particular generation of cricketers. Its 'monopoly' was unlegislated, depending wholly on high 'barriers to entry' for competitors. Once these were surmounted, its prosperity was in jeopardy.

The ACB and its brethren never grasped their rival's size and, to be fair, sport administrators have rarely appreciated sport's trifling costs in corporate terms. As Lamar Hunt's father warned him when World Championship Tennis began in 1967: 'If you're not careful Lamar, you'll go broke in a hundred years.'

Authorities failed also to appreciate WSC's different cost structure when integrated with Consolidated Press's broadcasting interests. But, as Justice Slade noted after hearing establishment testimony in the High Court that referred to 'legislation' and 'authorised cricket', there was a view that cricket existed somehow as an inviolable 'sovereign state'.

Packer received a similar reception in golf. The establishment Australian Golf Union was infuriated by his disrespect when he barred them from receptions at the Australian Open. Packer would walk away when the AGU demanded a bigger cut of gates. Cricket's telegenia, in contrast, made him persevere and he worked some undeniably brilliant business.

Where Hunt's WCT had only three slightly profitable years in its first twenty, for instance, Packer had his organisation in the black within three years. He had almost persuaded consumers that his 'Pepsi' tasted the same as ACB 'Coke'. With the pressure he exerted on the ACB, he actually won more than bargained for in 1976. Where Packer began only in pursuit of Test match telecast rights, he subsequently wrung changes in the 'monopoly market' that customised it for television.

In retrospect, Packer's personal attention to WSC is staggering. The cricket and golf balls (and lotto balls) he was juggling occasionally collided. WSC's initial signings were occurring as *The Young Doctors* and *The Sullivans* broke Australia's TV drama mould. John Crilly shared his Melbourne office with an ambitious group of journalists shaping *Sixty Minutes*. The floor beneath WSC's publicity centre housed Consolidated Press's 'think-tank', where engineering boffin Les Free worked on Packer's plans for Australia's domestic communications satellite.

Consolidated Press's *Australian Playboy* launch occurred at the Old Melbourne Inn during the Third Supertest in January 1979. Its promotional poster featured a bunny girl with bat. And as she spent $6 million overhauling *Australian Women's Weekly*, Ita Buttrose met her second husband at a WSC dinner.

Television's marriage with cricket has not been blissful. There have been obvious developments, where their interests have diverged and the former has prevailed. As Packer said in June 1977 when it was suggested to him that his interest in the game was 'half-philanthropic': 'That makes me sound more generous than I am.'

It was a period in which all sports were adjusting to television's intrusions. That year, for example, the American National Football League was agreeing to special protection of quarterbacks to improve the game's salesworthiness. 'Television time-outs' would arrive to accommodate commercials. Umpires, henceforth, answered to floor managers.

As Roger Angell remarked in October 1979 when baseball schedules were disastrously rewritten to allow a level of post-season play for each network: 'Keeping bad ideas out of baseball is like protecting democracies in Latin America; juntas and reschedulers are always hovering in the shadows, waiting for the next crisis or the next election, and when at last their shiny . . . new regime is given a trial term in office one somehow knows it is forever.'

Consolidated Press's decision that month, as it began work for the ACB, not to telecast Sheffield Shield matches was rigid, rationalistic commerce soiling what is still probably the best domestic competition in the world. It threatened to be the thin end of a very big wedge.

The group has profited mightily from its involvement with Australian cricket, paying a pin's fee as television rights prices worldwide have grown exponentially. PBL's promotion of the game has looked increasingly jaded and tatty, and there has been an ethnocentric arrogance to Australian cricket – not unlike that which prevailed at Lord's in 1977 – in demanding 'its' summers of international cricket in Australia. As Indra Vikram Singh wrote last year: 'This may have brought Australian cricket some extra bucks but it also turned a blind eye to the existence of India, Pakistan and Sri Lanka as Test-playing nations whose seasons conflict with Australia's.' The same potential conflict of seasons now applies with South Africa.

All the same, cricket has proceeded since in relative tranquillity, not to mention sleepiness. In their cost-consciousness in 1980, for instance, baseball's commissioners hired a bare-fisted General Electric executive to strangle player salaries. He precipitated a fifty-day strike in 1981.

With the help of such 'innovations' as an entirely nocturnal World Series to accommodate multiplying cable television systems, television revenues had certainly soared to reach $US1.4 billion by the end of the decade. But the cost was further lock-outs and strikes and an increasingly alienated 'old-fashioned' fan.

For all the complaints possible, there are many large mercies in our game's divergence from that path. There's been no Australian cricket 'strike'. No team has 'thrown' a game. Tests, uninventable today, do far more than merely survive. It may be cricket's good fortune to have natural advertising breaks: the quaint ritual of drinks has actually been consolidated, rather than corroded, by television's agenda. Kerry Packer is recalled as consoling the Australian team one evening after a narrow one-day defeat by telling them that they had topped the ratings.

'That was a great game of cricket,' Packer said. 'And great television.' The second still depends to a great extent on the first.

While it still seems fresh in the memory, WSC is history. As of 1993, Desmond Haynes, Kepler Wessels and Javed Miandad are the sole playing survivors. Sixteen years after the First Supertest, Mike Procter manages South Africa, David Holford the West Indies, while Majid Khan, Garth Le Roux, Dennis Amiss, Andy Roberts and Roy Fredericks are Test selectors. Every other ex-cricketer seems to commentate, while coaching appointments stretch from Bob Woolmer at Warwickshire to Haroon Rashid at United Bank and Rod Marsh at the Australian Institute of Sport. Among its principals, one has died (Brian Treasure), one has entered the House of Lord's (Robert Alexander, QC), one has become an ambassador (Rudi Webster).

As with Bagenal Harvey's Cavaliers in 1968, the TCCB pocketed ideas dry-run elsewhere. It introduced field restriction circles, dabbled in night cricket, has knitted its own variety of coloured clothing and even sold television rights to satellite broadcasters.

Martin Kent now finds himself telling young Queensland players of 'the old days' in the same way as he was once told of Hall, Griffith, Trueman and Statham. 'They never got to face Holding, Roberts, Garner, Croft, Daniel,' he says. 'And they want to know how we rate them. I reckon that team would have to be one of their best ever. I think Marshall at his peak would have got a game, but these guys were in their prime and trying like hell to keep their places.'

A book on WSC could just as easily be a text on television economics, or marketing, or sociology, even anthropology. Cricket was altered, for better and worse, in ways that would not have occurred under its previous institutional structures. Australia now has the first generation of Test cricketers weened on post-WSC product. Justin Langer's first recollection of cricket, for example, is watching uncle Rob play WSC at Gloucester Park, so it may only be in the next decade we achieve full measure of its consequence.

What stirred this book's writer was simply that for two seasons, the best players in the world played some remarkable, path-breaking cricket whose 56,126 runs and 2364 wickets, for reasons best known to the International Cricket Council, are not first-class. A skeleton of scores are to be found in the relevant *Wisdens* between pages 1001 and 1008 (1979) and pages 1095 and 1107 (1980) in less space than is devoted to county second XI averages. The business name World Series Cricket Pty Ltd, similarly, was struck off in November 1992, but it would be folly to consider its remains being so conveniently interred. Cricket faces a multitude of challenges as the next century approaches, and to treat WSC as though it never happened seems a wanton waste of its lessons.

SCORECARDS

Home team: WSC Australia
Away team: WSC West Indies
Competition: World Series Cricket Supertests 1977-78
Phase: 1st Supertest
Venue: VFL Park, Melbourne
Scheduled start date: 02 December 1977
Duration: 02, 03, 04 December 1977 (5-day match)
Balls per over: 8
Result: WSC West Indies won by three wickets
Won toss: WSC West Indies

Close of play: first day, WSC West Indies 47-2 (Greenidge 22); second day, WSC Australia 138-4 (Hookes 55, Walters 5).

WSC Australia

R. B. McCosker c Richards b Roberts	0	– c Fredericks b Daniel	47
I. C. Davis hit wkt b Holding	15	– b Roberts	0
*I. M. Chappell c Daniel b Holding	34	– lbw b Roberts	3
G. S. Chappell c Fredericks b Holding	0	– lbw b Daniel	28
D. W. Hookes b Holding	0	– c Lloyd b Roberts	63
K. D. Walters c Holford b Roberts	16	– lbw b Roberts	5
†R. W. Marsh c Holding b Daniel	23	– lbw b Holding	12
R. J. Bright c Greenidge b Roberts	69	– not out	16
D. K. Lillee c Fredericks b King	37	– c Allen b Holding	5
M. H. N. Walker c Richards b Daniel	30	– b Holding	1
L. S. Pascoe not out	26	– b Daniel	7
B 2, lb 3, nb 1	6	Lb 4, nb 1	5

1/0 (1) 2/33 (2) 3/39 (4) 4/39 (5)　(56.2 overs) 256
5/66 (3) 6/66 (6) 7/119 (7)
8/187 (9) 9/207 (8) 10/256 (10)

1/4 (2) 2/12 (3) 3/58 (4)　(36.6 overs) 192
4/126 (1) 5/139 (6) 6/158 (5) 7/158 (7)
8/168 (9) 9/171 (10) 10/192 (11)

Roberts 15–5–52–3; Holding 12–1–60–4; Daniel 11.2–0–51–2; King 8–0–46–1; Holford 10–2–41–0. *Second innings*—Roberts 13–1–52–4; Holding 12–1–72–3; Daniel 8.6–0–45–3; King 2–0–12–0; Holford 1–0–6–0.

WSC West Indies

R. C. Fredericks b Pascoe	24	– c Hookes b Walker	42
C. G. Greenidge lbw b Lillee	22	– c Lillee b Pascoe	16
M. A. Holding lbw b Pascoe	1		
I. V. A. Richards c Marsh b Hookes	79	– (3) c Hookes b Walker	56
J. C. Allen lbw b Walker	8	– (4) b Lillee	12
*C. H. Lloyd c I. M. Chappell b Walker	19	– (5) c Davis b Pascoe	44
C. L. King c Davis b Pascoe	5	– (6) c I. M. Chappell b Walker	4
†D. L. Murray c Hookes b Lillee	29	– (7) not out	36
D. A. J. Holford c Lillee b Bright	11	– (8) c Marsh b Lillee	0
A. M. E. Roberts run out	13	– (9) not out	13
W. W. Daniel not out	0		
W 2, nb 1	3	Lb 14	14

1/33 (1) 2/47 (3) 3/47 (2)　(49 overs) 214
4/68 (5) 5/150 (6) 6/156 (4) 7/165 (7)
8/185 (9) 9/214 (10) 10/214 (8)

1/30 (2)　(7 wkts, 50.7 overs) 237
2/113 (3) 3/116 (1)
4/130 (4) 5/147 (6) 6/186 (5) 7/196 (8)

Lillee 16–4–77–2; Pascoe 14–3–70–3; Walker 14–4–43–2; Hookes 2–0–6–1; Bright 3–0–15–1. *Second innings*—Lillee 20–1–100–2; Pascoe 13–2–56–2; Walker 13–3–43–3; Hookes 2–0–14–0; Bright 2.7–1–10–0.

Umpires: J. R. Collins and D. Sang Hue.

Home team: WSC Australia
Away team: WSC West Indies
Competition: World Series Cricket Supertests 1977-78
Phase: 2nd Supertest
Venue: Royal Agricultural Society Showground, Sydney
Scheduled start date: 16 December 1977
Duration: 16, 17, 18 December 1977 (5-day match)
Balls per over: 8
Result: WSC West Indies won by nine wickets
Won toss: WSC West Indies

Close of play: first day, WSC West Indies 33-0 (Fredericks 17, Greenidge 14); second day, WSC Australia 12-0 (McCosker 5, Laird 6).

WSC Australia

R. B. McCosker c Lloyd b Roberts	0	– c Fredericks b Garner	56
B. M. Laird lbw b Garner	28	– c Murray b Holding	18
*I. M. Chappell c Garner b Holding	29	– b Daniel	1
G. S. Chappell c Richards b Garner	9	– c Lloyd b Garner	31
M. F. Kent c Murray b Garner	2	– c Lloyd b Garner	0
D. W. Hookes retired hurt	81	– absent hurt	
†R. W. Marsh c King b Daniel	59	– (6) c Greenidge b Roberts	2
R. J. Bright c Murray b Roberts	4	– (7) lbw b Garner	0
D. K. Lillee b Roberts	1	– (8) c Richards b Holding	27
M. H. N. Walker not out	26	– (9) c Murray b Daniel	25
L. S. Pascoe run out	2	– (10) not out	13
B 1, lb 4, nb 5	10	Lb 4, nb 5	9

1/0 (1) 2/40 (3) 3/59 (4) (56 overs) 251
4/67 (5) 5/89 (2) 6/184 (8)
7/195 (9) 8/248 (7) 9/251 (11)

1/39 (2) 2/42 (3) (44.2 overs) 182
3/104 (4) 4/105 (5) 5/112 (1) 6/112 (7)
7/113 (6) 8/161 (8) 9/182 (9)

In the first innings Hookes retired hurt at 176-5.
Roberts 15–4–48–3; Holding 13–0–75–1; Daniel 10–0–50–1; Garner 13–2–55–3; King 5–0–13–0.
Second innings—Roberts 10–2–27–1; Holding 10–0–51–2; Daniel 8.2–0–36–2; Garner 13–2–58–4; King 3–2–1–0.

WSC West Indies

R. C. Fredericks lbw b Pascoe	25	– c Marsh b Pascoe	49
C. G. Greenidge lbw b Lillee	26	– not out	46
I. V. A. Richards c Marsh b Bright	88	– not out	5
L. G. Rowe c McCosker b Walker	7		
*C. H. Lloyd b Bright	58		
C. L. King c Marsh b Walker	28		
†D. L. Murray run out	46		
J. Garner c McCosker b Walker	25		
A. M. E. Roberts run out	16		
M. A. Holding c McCosker b I. M. Chappell	5		
W. W. Daniel not out	2		
Lb 6, nb 4	10	Lb 1	1

1/44 (1) 2/68 (2) 3/91 (4) (65.2 overs) 336
4/174 (3) 5/238 (6) 6/244 (5)
7/279 (8) 8/313 (9) 9/332 (10) 10/336 (7)

1/86 (1) (1 wkt, 16.7 overs) 101

Lillee 17–1–75–1; Pascoe 14–0–95–1; Walker 13–0–71–3; Bright 19–3–75–2; I. M. Chappell 2.2–0–10–1.
Second innings—Lillee 5–0–32–0; Pascoe 5.7–0–31–1; Walker 3–0–19–0; Bright 3–0–18–0.

Umpires: G. Duperouzel and P. R. Enright.

Home team: WSC Australia
Away team: WSC West Indies
Competition: World Series Cricket Supertests 1977-78
Phase: 3rd Supertest
Venue: Football Park, Adelaide
Scheduled start date: 31 December 1977
Duration: 31 December 1977, 01, 02, 03 January 1978 (5-day match)
Balls per over: 8
Result: WSC Australia won by 220 runs
Won toss: WSC Australia

Close of play: first day, WSC Australia 261-3 (I. M. Chappell 126, G. S. Chappell 55); second day, WSC West Indies 116-7 (Murray 5, Roberts 3); third day, WSC Australia 254-7 (Bright 2, Lillee 4).

WSC Australia

B. M. Laird c Lloyd b King	25	c sub (B. D. Julien) b King	106
R. B. McCosker c Murray b Holding	4	b Garner	0
*I. M. Chappell c sub (J. C. Allen) b Garner	141	c Murray b King	43
R. S. Langer c Murray b Garner	45	c sub (B. D. Julien) b King	8
G. S. Chappell c Greenidge b Roberts	90	b Garner	16
M. F. Kent c King b Roberts	43	b Garner	40
†R. W. Marsh c Richards b Garner	0	c Murray b King	19
R. J. Bright lbw b Padmore	15	lbw b Roberts	2
D. K. Lillee lbw b Padmore	1	not out	9
M. H. N. Walker not out	9	not out	8
W. Prior b Roberts	4		
Lb 8, nb 3	11	B 1, lb 14, nb 1	16

1/6 (2) 2/95 (1) 3/184 (4)   (105.2 overs)   388   1/4 (2)   (8 wkts dec, 75 overs)   267
4/304 (3) 5/315 (5) 6/316 (7)   2/80 (3) 3/100 (4) 4/122 (5)
7/348 (8) 8/352 (9) 9/382 (6) 10/388 (11)   5/216 (1) 6/238 (6) 7/248 (7) 8/254 (8)

Roberts 20.2–4–67–3; Holding 9–0–33–1; Garner 25–1–94–3; King 27–3–102–1; Padmore 21–3–71–2; Fredericks 3–0–10–0. *Second innings*—Roberts 13–3–41–1; Garner 17–1–48–3; King 19–1–78–4; Padmore 20–3–74–0; Lloyd 6–1–10–0.

WSC West Indies

R. C. Fredericks c Marsh b G. S. Chappell	38	c Laird b Prior	46
C. G. Greenidge c and b G. S. Chappell	40	lbw b Lillee	0
I. V. A. Richards c Marsh b Lillee	9	c Marsh b Walker	123
L. G. Rowe c Marsh b G. S. Chappell	12	c G. S. Chappell b Bright	12
*C. H. Lloyd lbw b Lillee	3	b Walker	9
C. L. King c and b G. S. Chappell	4	b Lillee	42
†D. L. Murray c McCosker b Prior	5	c and b Bright	7
J. Garner c Kent b G. S. Chappell	0	c G. S. Chappell b Bright	21
A. M. E. Roberts not out	24	b Bright	13
M. A. Holding c I. M. Chappell b Bright	8	c Prior b Lillee	5
A. L. Padmore c I. M. Chappell b Bright	0	not out	1
Lb 2	2	B 5, lb 6	11

1/79 (1) 2/82 (2) 3/92 (3)   (39.7   145   1/3 (2) 2/132 (1)   (62.3   290
                      overs)   3/167 (4) 4/188 (5)   overs)
4/100 (5) 5/105 (6) 6/112 (4)   5/197 (3) 6/210 (7) 7/245 (8)
7/112 (8) 8/116 (7) 9/145 (10) 10/145 (11)   8/271 (9) 9/282 (10) 10/290 (6)

Lillee 11–0–48–2; Walker 4–0–23–0; Prior 9–3–34–1; G. S. Chappell 12–2–20–5; Bright 3.7–0–18–2. *Second innings*—Lillee 14.3–0–61–3; Walker 15–0–61–2; Prior 8–0–58–1; G. S. Chappell 5–0–25–0; Bright 20–6–74–4.

Umpires: G. Duperouzel and D. Sang Hue.

Home team: WSC Australia
Away team: WSC World XI
Competition: World Series Cricket Supertests 1977-78
Phase: 4th Supertest
Venue: Royal Agricultural Society Showground, Sydney
Scheduled start date: 14 January 1978
Duration: 14, 15, 16, 17, 18, 19 January 1978 (5-day match extended to 6)
Balls per over: 8
Result: WSC World XI won by four wickets
Won toss: WSC Australia

Close of play: first day, WSC Australia 249-4 (G. S. Chappell 34, Kent 8); second day, WSC World XI 199-4 (I. V. A. Richards 79, Greig 33); third day, WSC Australia 13-2 (I. M. Chappell 0, Langer 4); fourth day, WSC World XI 78-1 (B. A. Richards 45, Greenidge 19); fifth day, no play.

WSC Australia

B. M. Laird b Garner	106	– lbw b Roberts	5
R. B. McCosker lbw b Procter	5	– b Procter	3
*I. M. Chappell run out	44	– c Fredericks b Roberts	19
R. S. Langer c Knott b Garner	39	– b Roberts	12
G. S. Chappell c I. V. A. Richards b Garner	35	– b Roberts	0
M. F. Kent c I. V. A. Richards b Underwood	10	– c Knott b Garner	31
†R. W. Marsh c Lloyd b Procter	8	– c Knott b Roberts	6
G. J. Gilmour c Knott b Roberts	10	– b Roberts	26
R. J. Bright c Knott b Procter	9	– c Knott b Garner	11
M. H. N. Walker b Procter	22	– c Knott b Garner	0
W. Prior not out	1	– not out	7
B 6, lb 3, nb 6	15	B 4, lb 4	8

1/8 (2) 2/113 (3) 3/203 (4)　　　　(82.7　　304　　　1/8 (1) 2/8 (2)　　　　　(28.4　　128
overs)　　　　　　　　　　　　　　　　　　　　　　　　overs)
4/204 (1) 5/252 (5) 6/252 (6) 7/270 (8)　　　　　　　3/25 (4) 4/25 (5) 5/44 (3) 6/54 (7)
8/270 (7) 9/303 (10) 10/304 (9)　　　　　　　　　　　7/86 (8) 8/113 (6) 9/113 (10) 10/128 (9)

Roberts 16–3–53–1; Procter 9.7–1–33–4; Garner 22–2–71–3; Greig 11–1–55–0; Underwood 24–4–77–1. *Second innings*—Roberts 12–2–69–6; Procter 9–1–25–1; Garner 7.4–1–26–3.

WSC World XI

R. C. Fredericks c Marsh b Gilmour	4	– b Gilmour	13
B. A. Richards b Gilmour	57	– c Marsh b Walker	48
C. G. Greenidge c Marsh b Walker	23	– b Gilmour	50
I. V. A. Richards c Gilmour b Walker	119	– c Marsh b Walker	18
C. H. Lloyd c I. M. Chappell b Walker	1	– (8) not out	0
*A. W. Greig c I. M. Chappell b Walker	38	– (5) c Langer b Gilmour	8
†A. P. E. Knott b Gilmour	2	– (6) b Gilmour	0
M. J. Procter c Marsh b Walker	6	– (7) not out	5
A. M. E. Roberts c Marsh b Walker	10		
J. Garner c Laird b Walker	24		
D. L. Underwood not out	3		
Nb 3	3	Lb 3	3

1/7 (1) 2/59 (3) 3/95 (2)　　　　(74.3　　290　　　1/15 (1)　　　　(6 wkts, 27.5　　145
overs)　　　　　　　　　　　　　　　　　　　　　　　　overs)
4/124 (5) 5/218 (6) 6/227 (7)　　　　　　　　　　　2/82 (2) 3/124 (4)
7/253 (4) 8/253 (8) 9/275 (9) 10/290 (10)　　　　　4/140 (5) 5/140 (6) 6/141 (3)

Prior 11–1–66–0; Gilmour 25–2–103–3; Walker 28.3–8–88–7; Bright 4–2–21–0; G. S. Chappell 6–1–9–0. *Second innings*—Prior 13–0–74–0; Gilmour 4–1–26–4; Walker 10.5–1–42–2.

Umpires: J. R. Collins and D. Sang Hue.

Home team: WSC Australia
Away team: WSC World XI
Competition: World Series Cricket Supertests 1977-78
Phase: 5th Supertest
Venue: Gloucester Park, Perth
Scheduled start date: 27 January 1978
Duration: 27, 28, 29, 30 January 1978 (5-day match)
Balls per over: 8
Result: WSC World XI won by an innings and 73 runs
Won toss: WSC World XI

Close of play: first day, WSC World XI 433-1 (I. V. A. Richards 72, Lloyd 30); second day, WSC Australia 73-4 (I. M. Chappell 25); third day, WSC Australia 373-9 (Bright 33, Walker 2).

WSC World XI

B. A. Richards c G. S. Chappell b Bright		207
C. G. Greenidge c Marsh b Bright		140
I. V. A. Richards c Walker b Lillee		177
C. H. Lloyd c G. S. Chappell b Lillee		37
Asif Iqbal c G. S. Chappell b Lillee		1
*A. W. Greig c Edwards b Lillee		14
Imran Khan c Walker b Bright		15
†A. P. E. Knott c Walker b Bright		20
A. M. E. Roberts c Davis b Gilmour		1
W. W. Daniel b Bright		1
D. L. Underwood not out		0
B 4, lb 4, nb 4		12
		—
		625

1/369 (1) 2/461 (4)   (114.3 overs)
3/481 (5) 4/551 (6)
5/571 (3) 6/587 (7) 7/613 (8)
8/622 (9) 9/624 (2) 10/625 (10)

In the first innings Greenidge, when 114, retired hurt at 234-0 and resumed at 587-6.

Lillee 27–1–149–4; Gilmour 33–3–141–1; Walker 14–1–115–0; Bright 31.3–3–149–5; I. M. Chappell 3–0–22–0; G. S. Chappell 6–0–37–0.

WSC Australia

B. M. Laird c Knott b Imran Khan	6	–	b Imran Khan		20
I. C. Davis c Knott b Roberts	2	–	b Daniel		7
*I. M. Chappell c sub (J. Garner) b Underwood	62	–	(8) not out		13
M. F. Kent c Knott b Imran Khan	0	–	(3) c Greig b Imran Khan		0
R. Edwards b Roberts	34	–	c Roberts b Underwood		39
G. S. Chappell c Knott b Imran Khan	174	–	(4) c B. A. Richards b Greig		26
†R. W. Marsh lbw b Roberts	27	–	(6) c Roberts b Underwood		23
G. J. Gilmour c Roberts b Underwood	9	–	(7) c I. V. A. Richards b Greig		13
R. J. Bright not out	41	–	b Greig		0
D. K. Lillee lbw b Greig	1	–	b Imran Khan		8
M. H. N. Walker c Asif Iqbal b Greig	10	–	b Imran Khan		4
B 8, lb 4, w 4, nb 11	27		B 3, nb 3		6

1/3 (2) 2/19 (1) 3/19 (4)   (92.4 overs)   393
4/73 (5) 5/156 (3) 6/201 (7)
7/251 (8) 8/367 (6) 9/368 (10) 10/393 (11)

1/28 (2) 2/28 (1)   (47 overs)   159
3/30 (3) 4/93 (5)
5/102 (4) 6/126 (6) 7/136 (7)
8/136 (9) 9/155 (10) 10/159 (11)

Roberts 17–2–65–3; Imran Khan 19–1–79–3; Daniel 10–1–59–0; Underwood 24–5–79–2; Greig 20.4–1–75–2; Asif Iqbal 2–0–9–0. *Second innings*—Roberts 8–2–18–0; Imran Khan 7–1–24–4; Daniel 7–1–30–1; Underwood 15–3–54–2; Greig 10–2–27–3.

Umpires: G. Duperouzel and P. R. Enright.

Home team: WSC Australia
Away team: WSC World XI
Competition: World Series Cricket Supertests 1977-78
Phase: 6th Supertest
Venue: VFL Park, Melbourne
Scheduled start date: 09 February 1978
Duration: 09, 10, 11, 12, 13 February 1978 (5-day match)
Balls per over: 8
Result: WSC Australia won by 41 runs
Won toss: WSC Australia

Close of play: first day, WSC Australia 175-1 (McCosker 68, Chappell 18); second day, WSC World XI 58-0 (Greenidge 38, B. A. Richards 17); third day, WSC World XI 370-8 (Knott 5, Roberts 1); fourth day, WSC World XI 37-2 (I. V. A. Richards 18, Roberts 0).

WSC Australia

I. C. Davis lbw b Garner	84	– b Garner 5
R. B. McCosker c I. V. A. Richards b Imran Khan	129	– b Imran Khan 5
*G. S. Chappell not out	246	– c Knott b Garner 6
R. Edwards c Zaheer Abbas b Imran Khan	0	– c Knott b Garner 8
D. W. Hookes c Asif Iqbal b Greig	57	– c Daniel b Garner 53
†R. W. Marsh c Knott b Greig	5	– c I. V. A. Richards b Roberts ... 5
R. D. Robinson c Knott b Imran Khan	2	– b Imran Khan 26
R. J. Bright (did not bat)		– b Imran Khan 25
M. H. N. Walker (did not bat)		– lbw b Garner 9
D. K. Lillee (did not bat)		– not out 8
L. S. Pascoe (did not bat)		– run out 7
Lb 12, nb 3	15	B 4, lb 4, w 1, nb 1 10

1/137 (1) 2/356 (2)   (6 wkts dec, 100.5 overs)   538
3/364 (4) 4/516 (5)
5/535 (6) 6/538 (7)

1/6 (1) 2/18 (3)   (35.7 overs)   167
3/18 (2) 4/34 (4)
5/79 (6) 6/98 (5) 7/141 (7)
8/152 (8) 9/152 (9) 10/167 (11)

Roberts 5–0–13–0; Imran Khan 21.3–1–134–3; Garner 27–0–134–1; Daniel 6.2–0–30–0; Greig 25–1–124–2; Asif Iqbal 14–1–77–0; I. V. A. Richards 2–0–11–0. *Second innings* — Imran Khan 12–1–57–3; Garner 14.7–1–52–5; Roberts 8–0–46–1; Greig 1–0–2–0.

WSC World XI

C. G. Greenidge c Marsh b Lillee	46	– c Edwards b Walker 19
B. A. Richards lbw b Walker	76	– c Marsh b Lillee 0
I. V. A. Richards lbw b Bright	170	– c Chappell b Lillee 18
Zaheer Abbas c Marsh b Walker	1	– (5) c Robinson b Walker ... 9
Asif Iqbal c Marsh b Pascoe	31	– (6) c Bright b Walker 35
*A. W. Greig c Robinson b Pascoe	0	– (7) c Edwards b Lillee 11
Imran Khan c Chappell b Bright	3	– (8) c Edwards b Lillee 19
†A. P. E. Knott lbw b Pascoe	15	– (9) not out 41
J. Garner c Marsh b Bright	13	– (10) c Bright b Lillee 1
A. M. E. Roberts not out	34	– (4) c Marsh b Walker 32
W. W. Daniel c Marsh b Lillee	14	– b Walker 36
B 8, lb 10, nb 13	31	Lb 6, w 2, nb 1 9

1/67 (1) 2/208 (2) 3/210 (4)   (86.1 overs)   434
4/285 (5) 5/287 (6) 6/299 (7)
7/348 (3) 8/368 (9) 9/410 (8) 10/434 (11)

1/1 (2) 2/37 (1)   (44 overs)   230
3/37 (3) 4/56 (5)
5/116 (4) 6/117 (6) 7/141 (7)
8/148 (8) 9/152 (10) 10/230 (11)

Lillee 27.1–2–141–2; Pascoe 24–2–113–3; Walker 13–1–51–2; Bright 22–4–98–3. *Second innings* — Lillee 15–2–82–5; Pascoe 12–0–64–0; Walker 14–2–62–5; Bright 3–0–13–0.

Umpires: J. R. Collins and D. Sang Hue.

Home team: WSC Australia
Away team: WSC World XI
Competition: World Series Cricket Supertests 1978-79
Venue: VFL Park, Melbourne
Scheduled start date: 08 December 1978 (day/night)
Duration: 08, 09, 10, 11 December 1978 (4-day match)
Balls per over: 6
Result: WSC World XI won by 102 runs
Won toss: WSC World XI
Man of the Match: G. S. le Roux.

Close of play: first day, WSC Australia 19-1 (Laird 6, Bright 5); second day, WSC World XI 74-1 (Majid Khan 33, Zaheer Abbas 34); third day, WSC Australia 27-1 (Wessels 18, I. M. Chappell 0).

WSC World XI

Majid Khan b Lillee	7	c I. M. Chappell b Lillee	77
D. L. Amiss c Marsh b Gilmour	0	c Marsh b Gilmour	6
Zaheer Abbas run out	14	run out	44
Javed Miandad b Bright	59	lbw b Gilmour	3
*Asif Iqbal c Gilmour b Lillee	8	c and b Bright	16
M. J. Procter c Marsh b Walker	4	lbw b Walker	66
C. E. B. Rice b Gilmour	41	c Wessels b Bright	5
Imran Khan c G. S. Chappell b Gilmour	24	not out	20
†A. P. E. Knott b Lillee	11	lbw b Gilmour	6
G. S. le Roux lbw b Lillee	0	b Bright	1
D. L. Underwood not out	1	run out	2
Lb 5, nb 1	6	Lb 7, nb 4	11

1/2 (2) 2/11 (1) 3/24 (3) (99.4 overs) 175
4/42 (5) 5/53 (6) 6/138 (4)
7/138 (7) 8/169 (9) 9/169 (8) 10/175 (10)

1/8 (2) 2/92 (3) (140 overs) 257
3/103 (4) 4/130 (5)
5/188 (1) 6/215 (7) 7/229 (6)
8/238 (9) 9/246 (10) 10/257 (11)

Lillee 32.4–13–51–4; Gilmour 21–8–28–3; Walker 23–5–55–1; Bright 20–9–28–1; Hookes 3–0–7–0. *Second innings*—Lillee 38–16–63–1; Gilmour 29–11–57–3; Walker 26–13–39–1; Bright 44–11–81–3; Hookes 3–1–6–0.

WSC Australia

B. M. Laird b le Roux	11	(2) b Underwood	9
K. C. Wessels c Knott b Procter	8	(1) c and b Underwood	46
R. J. Bright b le Roux	12	(8) lbw b le Roux	3
*I. M. Chappell b le Roux	48	(3) c Javed Miandad b Underwood	11
G. S. Chappell c Knott b Imran Khan	5	(4) c Rice b Imran Khan	81
D. W. Hookes c Knott b le Roux	15	(5) c Procter b Underwood	7
I. C. Davis b Underwood	9	(6) lbw b Rice	0
†R. W. Marsh c Imran Khan b Underwood	11	(7) b Imran Khan	17
G. J. Gilmour not out	12	b Imran Khan	0
M. H. N. Walker b Imran Khan	12	not out	2
D. K. Lillee c Majid Khan b le Roux	2	c Rice b Imran Khan	0
B 2, lb 3	5	Lb 3, nb 1	4

1/12 (2) 2/31 (1) 3/44 (3) (83.5 overs) 150
4/55 (5) 5/99 (4) 6/100 (6)
7/121 (8) 8/123 (7) 9/143 (10) 10/150 (11)

1/27 (2) 2/63 (3) (98.2 overs) 180
3/74 (1) 4/102 (5) 5/109 (6) 6/165 (7)
7/170 (8) 8/175 (9) 9/180 (4) 10/180 (11)

Procter 9–4–8–1; le Roux 25.5–7–39–5; Imran Khan 19–6–37–2; Underwood 22–8–36–2; Rice 4–0–8–0; Javed Miandad 4–0–17–0. *Second innings*—Procter 4–3–3–0; le Roux 24–6–53–1; Imran Khan 15.2–6–30–4; Underwood 37–18–59–4; Rice 18–6–31–1.

Umpires: J. R. Collins and G. Duperouzel.

Home team: WSC West Indies
Away team: WSC World XI
Competition: World Series Cricket Supertests 1978-79
Venue: Sydney Cricket Ground, Sydney
Scheduled start date: 21 December 1978 (day/night)
Duration: 21, 22, 23 December 1978 (4-day match)
Balls per over: 6
Result: WSC World XI won by an innings and 44 runs
Won toss: WSC World XI
Bowler of the Match: J. Garner.
Man of the Match: C. E. B. Rice.

Close of play: first day, WSC World XI 380-5 (Procter 56, Asif Iqbal 60); second day, WSC West Indies 11-0 (Greenidge 3, Haynes 6).

WSC World XI

B. A. Richards c Richards b Roberts	37	G. S. le Roux b Padmore		0
Majid Khan c King b Garner	17	D. L. Underwood c sub (B. D. Julien)		
Zaheer Abbas c Greenidge b Garner	91	b Padmore		7
Javed Miandad c Garner b Padmore	27	B 11, lb 4, w 1		16
C. E. B. Rice c Lloyd b Garner	83			
M. J. Procter c Lloyd b Roberts	56	1/56 (1) 2/56 (2)	(163.3	471
*Asif Iqbal c Rowe b Padmore	107	overs)		
Imran Khan b Garner	23	3/109 (4) 4/260 (3)		
†A. P. E. Knott not out	7	5/275 (5) 6/387 (6) 7/445 (8)		
		8/454 (7) 9/457 (10) 10/471 (11)		

Roberts 32–9–97–2; Holding 6–0–15–0; Garner 50–13–125–4; King 36–7–116–0; Padmore 39.3–8–102–4.

WSC West Indies

C. G. Greenidge b Rice	11	– c Knott b Imran Khan		7
R. C. Fredericks c Knott b Imran Khan	5	– (4) b le Roux		12
I. V. A. Richards c Majid Khan b Rice	13	– c Javed Miandad b Underwood		30
L. G. Rowe c Majid Khan b Procter	85	– (5) st Knott b Underwood		36
†D. L. Haynes c Javed Miandad b le Roux	14	– (2) run out		17
*C. H. Lloyd c Asif Iqbal b Underwood	36	– c Asif Iqbal b Rice		4
C. L. King run out	3	– lbw b Imran Khan		36
A. M. E. Roberts c Knott b Underwood	26	– c le Roux b Underwood		45
J. Garner b Procter	16	– c Rice b Procter		16
A. L. Padmore b Procter	0	– not out		0
M. A. Holding not out	0	– absent hurt		
B 6, lb 2	8	B 2, lb 3, w 1, nb 1		7

1/11 (2) 2/27 (1) 3/34 (3) (70.5 217
overs)
4/57 (5) 5/114 (6) 6/121 (7)
7/194 (4) 8/217 (8) 9/217 (9) 10/217 (10)

1/15 (1) 2/41 (2) (62.2 210
overs)
3/65 (4) 4/69 (3) 5/76 (6) 6/130 (7)
7/162 (5) 8/203 (8) 9/210 (9)

Imran Khan 10–1–27–1; le Roux 14–2–45–1; Rice 12–1–43–2; Underwood 22–7–41–2; Procter 8.5–0–36–3; Javed Miandad 4–0–17–0. *Second innings*—Imran Khan 12–3–38–2; le Roux 8–0–32–1; Rice 8–2–23–1; Underwood 24–8–68–3; Procter 10.2–1–42–1.

Umpires: G. Duperouzel and P. R. Enright.

Home team: WSC Australia
Away team: WSC West Indies
Competition: World Series Cricket Supertests 1978-79
Venue: VFL Park, Melbourne
Scheduled start date: 12 January 1979 (day/night)
Duration: 12, 13, 14, 15 January 1979 (4-day match)
Balls per over: 6
Result: Drawn
Won toss: WSC Australia
Man of the Match: L. G. Rowe.

Close of play: first day, WSC Australia 352-7 (Gilmour 26, Bright 14); second day, WSC West Indies 337-5 (Rowe 150, King 13); third day, WSC Australia 161-4 (Hookes 34, I. M. Chappell 30).

WSC Australia

B. M. Laird c Greenidge b Garner	2	– (2) st Murray b Austin	8
K. C. Wessels b Croft	126	– (1) c Lloyd b Austin	38
G. S. Chappell c Murray b Roberts	7	– lbw b Croft	33
I. C. Davis c Richards b Croft	31	– c Murray b Croft	8
D. W. Hookes lbw b Garner	116	– c Austin b Roberts	56
*I. M. Chappell run out	12	– c Croft b Roberts	65
†R. W. Marsh c Rowe b Garner	10	– c Greenidge b Austin	17
G. J. Gilmour c Murray b Roberts	26	– b Roberts	16
R. J. Bright c Murray b Croft	15	– c Lloyd b Austin	15
M. F. Malone c Murray b Roberts	0	– not out	7
D. K. Lillee not out	10	– not out	20
Lb 5, w 2, nb 4	11	B 6, lb 10, w 3, nb 2	21

1/15 (1) 2/35 (3) 3/112 (4) (121.5 366   1/26 (2) (9 wkts dec, 152 304
overs)   overs)
4/257 (2) 5/294 (5) 6/308 (7)   2/64 (1) 3/90 (4) 4/93 (3) 5/195 (5)
7/316 (6) 8/352 (8) 9/352 (10) 10/366 (9)   6/233 (7) 7/245 (6) 8/275 (9) 9/275 (8)

Roberts 26–4–83–3; Croft 33.5–11–91–3; Garner 32–5–79–3; Austin 19–4–60–0; King 11–2–42–0.
Second innings—Roberts 34–8–76–3; Croft 33–6–71–2; Garner 32–10–51–0; Austin 53–19–85–4.

WSC West Indies

C. G. Greenidge c Marsh b Lillee	10	– not out	58
R. A. Austin c Wessels b Bright	77	– b Malone	11
I. V. A. Richards lbw b Bright	7	– c G. S. Chappell b Malone	46
L. G. Rowe c G. S. Chappell b Bright	175	– not out	6
J. C. Allen b Lillee	0		
*C. H. Lloyd lbw b Malone	55		
C. L. King c Marsh b Lillee	27		
†D. L. Murray lbw b Gilmour	2		
A. M. E. Roberts not out	20		
C. E. H. Croft lbw b I. M. Chappell	11		
J. Garner b I. M. Chappell	6		
B 13, lb 14, nb 2	29	B 2, lb 2, w 1	5

1/22 (1) 2/50 (3)   419   1/39 (2) (2 wkts, 126
3/174 (2) (163.1 overs)   57 overs)
4/181 (5) 5/302 (6) 6/363 (7)   2/99 (3)
7/379 (8) 8/381 (4) 9/413 (10) 10/419 (11)

Lillee 42–16–91–3; Gilmour 25–2–84–1; Bright 49–13–113–3; Malone 27–5–68–1; Hookes 8–5–16–0;
I. M. Chappell 12.1–8–18–2. *Second innings*—Lillee 12–6–13–0; Gilmour 13–4–28–0; Bright 17–9–36–0;
Malone 13–6–41–2; G. S. Chappell 2–0–3–0.

Umpires: G. Duperouzel and D. Sang Hue.

Home team: WSC Australia
Away team: WSC West Indies
Competition: World Series Cricket Supertests 1978-79
Phase: Semi-Final
Venue: Sydney Cricket Ground, Sydney
Scheduled start date: 21 January 1979 (day/night)
Duration: 21, 22, 23, 24 January 1979 (4-day match)
Balls per over: 6
Result: WSC Australia won by ten wickets
Won toss: WSC West Indies
Man of the Match: R. J. Bright.

Close of play: first day, WSC Australia 50-3 (Redpath 7, Hookes 25); second day, no play; third day, WSC West Indies 78-7 (Murray 7, Padmore 6).

WSC West Indies

C. G. Greenidge c Pascoe b Bright	39	–	c G. S. Chappell b Lillee	8
R. A. Austin b Lillee	27	–	lbw b Lillee	0
I. V. A. Richards c I. M. Chappell b Bright	10	–	(5) c G. S. Chappell b Lillee	4
L. G. Rowe c and b Bright	4	–	c Redpath b Lillee	12
J. C. Allen c Gilmour b Bright	20	–	(3) b Lillee	10
*C. H. Lloyd not out	37	–	c Laird b Pascoe	29
†D. L. Murray c Marsh b Bright	0	–	c G. S. Chappell b Lillee	9
A. M. E. Roberts c Marsh b Pascoe	0	–	lbw b Pascoe	0
A. L. Padmore c Wessels b Bright	12	–	c Laird b Bright	11
W. W. Daniel b Pascoe	1	–	b Lillee	2
C. E. H. Croft c Marsh b Lillee	3	–	not out	0
Lb 4, nb 6	10		B 1, lb 2, nb 1	4

1/65 (2) 2/82 (1) 3/82 (3) (67 overs) 163
4/102 (4) 5/118 (5) 6/118 (7)
7/119 (8) 8/144 (9) 9/145 (10) 10/163 (11)

1/5 (2) 2/12 (1) (37.5 overs) 89
3/19 (4) 4/31 (5) 5/42 (4) 6/69 (6)
7/69 (8) 8/80 (7) 9/88 (10) 10/89 (9)

Lillee 15–4–33–2; Gilmour 10–3–26–0; Pascoe 19–4–42–2; Bright 23–6–52–6. *Second innings—* Lillee 14–3–23–7; Gilmour 11–3–30–0; Pascoe 5–0–20–2; Bright 7.5–2–12–1.

WSC Australia

B. M. Laird c Greenidge b Roberts	0	–	(2) not out	26
K. C. Wessels b Croft	5	–	(1) not out	40
G. S. Chappell lbw b Croft	8			
I. R. Redpath lbw b Padmore	9			
D. W. Hookes c Greenidge b Croft	69			
*I. M. Chappell b Croft	23			
†R. W. Marsh c Richards b Croft	23			
G. J. Gilmour c Austin b Roberts	3			
R. J. Bright b Daniel	18			
D. K. Lillee c Richards b Roberts	2			
L. S. Pascoe not out	5			
B 7, lb 6, nb 7	20		Nb 2	2

1/0 (1) 2/10 (2) 3/17 (3) (86.4 overs) 185
4/88 (4) 5/118 (5) 6/147 (6)
7/153 (7) 8/173 (8) 9/177 (10) 10/185 (9)

(no wkt, 24.5 overs) 68

Roberts 29–14–35–3; Croft 26–7–65–5; Daniel 14.4–4–21–1; Austin 2–0–9–0; Padmore 15–3–35–1. *Second innings—* Roberts 4–0–21–0; Croft 3–0–11–0; Daniel 4–1–14–0; Austin 5–1–7–0; Padmore 8.5–3–13–0.

Umpires: J. R. Collins and G. Duperouzel.

Home team: WSC Australia
Away team: WSC World XI
Competition: World Series Cricket Supertests 1978-79
Phase: Final
Venue: Sydney Cricket Ground, Sydney
Scheduled start date: 02 February 1979 (day/night)
Duration: 02, 03, 04 February 1979 (4-day match)
Balls per over: 6
Result: WSC World XI won by five wickets
Won toss: WSC Australia
Man of the Match: G. S. le Roux.

Close of play: first day, WSC World XI 100-8 (Knott 5, le Roux 9); second day, WSC Australia 198-6 (Hookes 93, Bright 4).

WSC Australia

K. C. Wessels c Richards b Procter	27	–	c Greig b Procter	1
B. M. Laird c Zaheer Abbas b le Roux	2	–	c Knott b Imran Khan	58
*I. M. Chappell c Imran Khan b le Roux	3	–	b Imran Khan	19
I. R. Redpath c Knott b Rice	4	–	c Knott b Rice	3
D. W. Hookes c Knott b Procter	33	–	b le Roux	96
M. F. Kent c Greig b le Roux	2	–	run out	4
†R. W. Marsh c Knott b le Roux	6	–	c Knott b Imran Khan	6
R. J. Bright not out	27	–	c Barlow b le Roux	10
G. J. Gilmour c Greig b Procter	27	–	c sub (R. A. Woolmer) b le Roux	0
D. K. Lillee c Procter b Rice	8	–	not out	9
L. S. Pascoe b le Roux	25	–	b le Roux	2
Lb 7, w 1	8		B 2, lb 9	11

1/7 (2) 2/11 (3) 3/25 (4)   (50.4   172
overs)
4/66 (1) 5/70 (6) 6/74 (5)
7/80 (7) 8/119 (9) 9/135 (10) 10/172 (11)

1/8 (1) 2/29 (3)   (87.3   219
overs)
3/32 (4) 4/166 (2)
5/172 (6) 6/179 (7) 7/203 (5)
8/203 (9) 9/211 (8) 10/219 (11)

Le Roux 18.4–3–57–5; Imran Khan 9–2–35–0; Rice 13–4–38–2; Procter 7–2–33–3; Underwood 3–2–1–0.
Second innings — le Roux 17.3–4–44–4; Imran Khan 22–5–60–3; Rice 12–2–26–1; Procter 18–2–45–1; Underwood 17–7–26–0; Greig 1–0–7–0.

WSC World XI

B. A. Richards c Wessels b Pascoe	28	–	not out	101
E. J. Barlow lbw b Lillee	0	–	c Gilmour b Lillee	0
Zaheer Abbas c Laird b Gilmour	18	–	c Wessels b Gilmour	37
C. E. B. Rice c Marsh b Gilmour	18	–	c Marsh b Pascoe	4
Asif Iqbal c Bright b Gilmour	8	–	lbw b Gilmour	3
M. J. Procter lbw b Lillee	1	–	b Bright	44
*A. W. Greig c Marsh b Lillee	0			
Imran Khan lbw b Lillee	6	–	(7) not out	17
†A. P. E. Knott b Gilmour	9			
G. S. le Roux not out	33			
D. L. Underwood b Lillee	32			
Lb 9, nb 6	15		Lb 3, w 4, nb 13	20

1/8 (2) 2/39 (3) 3/69 (1)   (64.5   168
overs)
4/71 (4) 5/80 (5) 6/80 (6)
7/85 (7) 8/86 (8) 9/104 (9) 10/168 (11)

1/3 (2)   (5 wkts, 57   226
overs)
2/57 (3) 3/70 (4)
4/84 (5) 5/175 (6)

Lillee 18.5–6–51–5; Gilmour 25–6–53–4; Pascoe 13–3–29–1; Bright 5–1–10–0; Hookes 3–1–10–0.
Second innings — Lillee 17–4–57–1; Gilmour 22–6–75–2; Pascoe 12–2–49–1; Bright 6–1–25–1; Chappell 0.0–0–0–0.

Umpires: J. R. Collins and D. Sang Hue.

Home team: WSC West Indies
Away team: WSC Australia
Competition: WSC Australia in West Indies 1978-79
Phase: 1st Supertest
Venue: Sabina Park, Kingston
Scheduled start date: 23 February 1979
Duration: 23, 24, 25, 26 February 1979 (5-day match)
Balls per over: 6
Result: WSC West Indies won by 369 runs
Won toss: WSC West Indies
Man of the Match: C. H. Lloyd.

Close of play: first day, WSC Australia 33-2 (G. S. Chappell 6, Bright 2); second day, WSC West Indies 228-5 (Lloyd 54, Roberts 0); third day, WSC Australia 91-4 (Bright 3, T. M. Chappell 3).

WSC West Indies

R. A. Austin c Gilmour b Lillee	18	– c G. S. Chappell b Lillee	2
D. L. Haynes run out	9	– c Laird b Lillee	8
R. C. Fredericks c Marsh b Gilmour	12	– c Marsh b Lillee	69
L. G. Rowe c Marsh b Gilmour	3	– retired hurt	0
I. V. A. Richards c Marsh b Lillee	31	– lbw b Thomson	48
*C. H. Lloyd c G. S. Chappell b Lillee	56	– c Marsh b Lillee	197
†D. L. Murray hit wkt b Lillee	11	– c Lillee b Thomson	28
A. M. E. Roberts c Gilmour b Thomson	6	– run out	89
M. A. Holding b Bright	10	– b Bright	0
C. E. H. Croft c Marsh b Bright	1	– not out	0
W. W. Daniel not out	17	– c Marsh b Bright	1
Lb 1, nb 13	14	B 3, lb 17, nb 19	39

1/25 (2) 2/38 (1) 3/45 (3) (56.2 overs) 188
4/50 (4) 5/88 (5) 6/103 (7)
7/119 (6) 8/138 (9) 9/148 (10) 10/188 (6)

1/3 (1) 2/44 (2) (109.4 overs) 481
3/111 (3) 4/166 (5) 5/227 (7) 6/453 (8)
7/460 (9) 8/480 (6) 9/481 (11)

In the second innings Rowe retired hurt at 44-2.

Lillee 18.2–3–68–4; Thomson 14–3–46–1; Gilmour 17–5–40–2; Bright 7–1–20–2. Second innings— Lillee 25–4–100–4; Thomson 22–2–68–2; Gilmour 20–2–93–0; Bright 28.4–1–108–2; Hookes 7–0–41–0; I. M. Chappell 4–0–15–0; G. S. Chappell 3–0–17–0.

WSC Australia

B. M. Laird lbw b Holding	14	– b Holding	5
T. M. Chappell lbw b Daniel	16	– (6) b Holding	3
*I. M. Chappell c sub (C. L. King) b Holding	5	– (2) c Roberts b Croft	41
G. S. Chappell c Murray b Roberts	6	– (3) c Haynes b Holding	20
R. J. Bright lbw b Roberts	10	– not out	47
D. W. Hookes b Daniel	23	– (4) c sub (C. L. King) b Daniel	15
M. F. Kent c and b Croft	9	– lbw b Croft	30
†R. W. Marsh c Fredericks b Daniel	3	– b Croft	3
G. J. Gilmour c Lloyd b Croft	14	– c Holding b Austin	11
D. K. Lillee c Austin b Croft	1	– c and b Roberts	12
J. R. Thomson not out	0	– c Holding b Austin	1
B 1, lb 2, nb 2	5	Lb 2, nb 4	6

1/18 (3) 2/29 (1) 3/33 (4) (37 overs) 106
4/42 (5) 5/76 (6) 6/87 (7)
7/87 (2) 8/92 (8) 9/106 (9) 10/106 (10)

1/22 (1) 2/46 (3) (51.4 overs) 194
3/79 (4) 4/83 (2)
5/92 (6) 6/158 (7) 7/162 (8)
8/175 (9) 9/193 (10) 10/194 (11)

In the first innings T. M. Chappell, when 4, retired hurt at 8-0 and resumed at 76-5.

Roberts 10–5–18–2; Holding 9–2–25–2; Croft 11–2–34–3; Daniel 7–2–24–3. Second innings—Roberts 8–2–14–1; Holding 10–1–37–3; Croft 13–2–70–3; Daniel 11–2–43–1; Austin 9.4–0–24–2.

Umpires: R. G. Gosein and D. Sang Hue.

Home team: WSC West Indies
Away team: WSC Australia
Competition: WSC Australia in West Indies 1978-79
Phase: 2nd Supertest
Venue: Kensington Oval, Bridgetown
Scheduled start date: 09 March 1979
Duration: 09, 10, 11, 12, 13 March 1979 (5-day match)
Balls per over: 6
Result: Drawn after play was abandoned on final day when the crowd threw bottles on the pitch
Won toss: WSC West Indies
Man of the Match: I. M. Chappell.

Close of play: first day, WSC Australia 240-6 (Marsh 12, Bright 13); second day, WSC Australia 294-7 (Bright 36, Lillee 3); third day, WSC Australia 48-2 (I. M. Chappell 27, G. S. Chappell 2); fourth day, WSC Australia 294.

WSC Australia

B. M. Laird c Greenidge b Croft	3	– (2) lbw b Holding	6
*I. M. Chappell c Lloyd b King	61	– (1) c Murray b Austin	86
M. F. Kent c Fredericks b Holding	78	– c Greenidge b Daniel	8
G. S. Chappell c Murray b King	45	– c Murray b Croft	90
D. W. Hookes c Austin b Holding	4	– run out	6
T. M. Chappell c Lloyd b King	10	– b Holding	22
†R. W. Marsh c King b Croft	31	– c Fredericks b Austin	24
R. J. Bright c Murray b Croft	37	– lbw b King	22
D. K. Lillee c Greenidge b Holding	6	– not out	8
J. R. Thomson not out	10	– b King	0
L. S. Pascoe b Holding	2	– b Austin	0
B 2, lb 12, w 1, nb 9	24	B 5, lb 12, w 1, nb 4	22

1/30 (1) 2/134 (2) 3/164 (3)   (106.1   311
overs)
4/170 (5) 5/206 (6) 6/213 (4)
7/283 (7) 8/297 (9) 9/301 (8) 10/311 (11)

1/11 (2) 2/30 (3)   (102.5   294
overs)
3/136 (1) 4/160 (5) 5/213 (6) 6/254 (4)
7/267 (7) 8/291 (8) 9/293 (10) 10/294 (11)

Holding 26.1–7–67–4; Croft 36–8–85–3; Daniel 14–3–29–0; Austin 10–0–50–0; King 20–4–56–3. *Second innings*—Holding 23–3–57–2; Croft 21–1–54–1; Daniel 15–0–50–1; Austin 24.5–13–59–3; King 18–3–50–2; Richards 1–0–2–0.

WSC West Indies

C. G. Greenidge c Laird b Lillee	4	– c Marsh b Pascoe	21
D. L. Haynes c Hookes b Thomson	4	– c Marsh b Lillee	9
R. C. Fredericks c Laird b Bright	89	– lbw b Pascoe	53
R. A. Austin c Marsh b Lillee	0	– c Marsh b Pascoe	4
I. V. A. Richards b Lillee	24	– not out	38
*C. H. Lloyd c Hookes b Thomson	14	– not out	0
C. L. King c I. M. Chappell b Bright	18		
†D. L. Murray b Pascoe	29		
M. A. Holding b Thomson	16		
W. W. Daniel b Pascoe	4		
C. E. H. Croft not out	9		
B 1, lb 9, nb 18	28	Nb 8	8

1/6 (1) 2/11 (2) 3/15 (4)   (58   239
overs)
4/88 (5) 5/107 (6) 6/175 (3)
7/206 (9) 8/221 (10) 9/222 (8) 10/239 (7)

1/19 (2)   (4 wkts, 29   133
overs)
2/41 (1) 3/47 (4)
4/133 (3)

In the first innings King, when 11, retired hurt at 160-5 and resumed at 222-9.

Lillee 13–2–56–3; Thomson 14–2–59–3; Pascoe 18–3–74–2; Bright 13–5–22–2. *Second innings*—Lillee 14–3–53–1; Thomson 9–3–36–0; Pascoe 4–2–20–3; Bright 2–0–16–0.

Umpires: R. G. Gosein and D. Sang Hue.

Home team: WSC West Indies
Away team: WSC Australia
Competition: WSC Australia in West Indies 1978-79
Phase: 3rd Supertest
Venue: Queen's Park Oval, Port of Spain
Scheduled start date: 16 March 1979
Duration: 16, 17, 18, 19, 20 March 1979 (5-day match)
Balls per over: 6
Result: WSC Australia won by 24 runs
Won toss: WSC Australia
Man of the Match: G. S. Chappell.

Close of play: first day, WSC Australia 204-7 (Laird 110, Lillee 11); second day, WSC West Indies 158-6 (Murray 8, Roberts 2); third day, WSC Australia 155-6 (G. S. Chappell 72, Bright 19); fourth day, WSC West Indies 119-1 (Fredericks 65, Rowe 6).

WSC Australia

B. M. Laird b Roberts	122	– (2) run out	0
*I. M. Chappell c and b Holding	1	– (1) c and b Holding	0
M. F. Kent c Richards b Roberts	7	– b Padmore	45
G. S. Chappell c Padmore b Holding	7	– c Roberts b Fredericks	150
D. W. Hookes c Murray b Holding	2	– c Lloyd b Padmore	6
T. M. Chappell c Rowe b Holding	3	– b Holding	2
†R. W. Marsh c Rowe b Padmore	34	– c Lloyd b Padmore	6
R. J. Bright b Holding	15	– lbw b Padmore	21
D. K. Lillee c Murray b Croft	30	– c Rowe b Padmore	12
J. R. Thomson b Roberts	7	– c and b Padmore	5
L. S. Pascoe not out	2	– not out	19
B 5, lb 8, nb 3	16	B 4, lb 9, nb 3	16

1/4 (2) 2/11 (3) 3/18 (4)   (100   246
overs)
4/26 (5) 5/32 (6) 6/93 (7)
7/137 (8) 8/232 (9) 9/234 (9) 10/246 (10)

1/0 (1) 2/0 (2)   (144.4   282
overs)
3/78 (3) 4/94 (5) 5/97 (6) 6/106 (7)
7/168 (8) 8/256 (9) 9/256 (4) 10/282 (10)

Holding 21–8–48–5; Roberts 21–8–39–3; Croft 23–7–71–1; King 10–6–12–0; Padmore 19–4–42–1; Fredericks 6–1–18–0. *Second innings*—Holding 28–6–49–2; Roberts 25–12–47–0; Croft 19–3–61–0; King 4–0–11–0; Padmore 54.4–21–81–6; Fredericks 7–4–9–1; Richards 7–1–8–0.

WSC West Indies

C. G. Greenidge c Lillee b Bright	21	– c I. M. Chappell b Lillee	37
R. C. Fredericks c Bright b Thomson	11	– b Lillee	72
L. G. Rowe b Thomson	8	– b Bright	11
I. V. A. Richards c Hookes b Thomson	44	– c Bright b I. M. Chappell	46
*C. H. Lloyd lbw b Thomson	39	– c Marsh b Pascoe	13
C. L. King b Lillee	19	– c Laird b Lillee	20
†D. L. Murray c Marsh b Pascoe	12	– run out	7
A. M. E. Roberts not out	50	– not out	21
M. A. Holding c Marsh b Thomson	10	– b I. M. Chappell	22
C. E. H. Croft b Pascoe	3	– c Laird b I. M. Chappell	0
A. L. Padmore b Pascoe	0	– b Pascoe	1
Lb 2, nb 11	13	B 2, lb 17, nb 5	24

1/24 (2) 2/32 (3) 3/80 (1)   (69.4   230
overs)
4/86 (4) 5/126 (6) 6/155 (5)
7/167 (7) 8/188 (9) 9/218 (10) 10/230 (11)

1/98 (1) 2/131 (3)   (89.5   274
overs)
3/133 (2) 4/187 (5) 5/199 (4) 6/222 (6)
7/226 (7) 8/267 (9) 9/267 (10)
10/274 (11)

Lillee 22–4–76–1; Thomson 20–5–78–5; Pascoe 10.4–3–35–3; Bright 17–4–28–1. *Second innings*—Lillee 31–5–77–3; Thomson 7–1–30–0; Pascoe 14.5–4–40–2; Bright 27–8–68–1; I. M. Chappell 10–2–35–3.

Umpires: R. G. Gosein and D. Sang Hue.

Home team: WSC West Indies
Away team: WSC Australia
Competition: WSC Australia in West Indies 1978-79
Phase: 4th Supertest
Venue: Bourda, Georgetown
Scheduled start date: 25 March 1979
Duration: 25, 26, 27, 28 March 1979 (4-day match, reduced from 5 when start rescheduled after rain)
Balls per over: 6
Result: Drawn
Won toss: WSC West Indies
Man of the Match: C. L. King.

Close of play: first day, no play; second day, WSC Australia 262-6 (Marsh 22, Bright 1); third day, WSC West Indies 288-5 (King 40, Murray 8).

WSC Australia

B. M. Laird c Murray b Croft	6	– lbw b Croft	13
T. M. Chappell c Murray b Holding	5	– b Croft	28
M. F. Kent c Murray b Garner	51	– b Roberts	28
G. S. Chappell c Murray b King	113		
*I. M. Chappell b Holding	9	– not out	11
D. W. Hookes b Croft	28	– (4) not out	23
†R. W. Marsh b Garner	49		
R. J. Bright not out	29		
D. K. Lillee c Richards b Garner	3		
J. R. Thomson c Richards b King	12		
L. S. Pascoe b Roberts	1		
B 5, lb 12, nb 18	35	B 3, lb 9, nb 2	14

1/17 (1) 2/25 (2) 3/111 (3)   (112.1   341
overs)
4/137 (5) 5/194 (6) 6/260 (4)
7/298 (7) 8/310 (9) 9/339 (10) 10/341 (11)

1/40 (1)   (3 wkts, 33   117
overs)
2/58 (2) 3/89 (3)

Holding 25–1–54–2; Roberts 21.1–2–53–1; Croft 22–2–74–2; Garner 26–5–60–3; Fredericks 4–1–18–0; King 14–0–47–2. *Second innings*—Holding 9–0–31–0; Roberts 7–3–12–1; Croft 8–1–32–2; Garner 5–0–14–0; Richards 3–0–10–0; Rowe 1–0–4–0.

WSC West Indies

R. C. Fredericks c Lillee b Thomson	12	M. A. Holding c Thomson b G. S. Chappell	20
C. G. Greenidge c Kent b Bright	52	J. Garner b Thomson	0
L. G. Rowe lbw b Thomson	64	C. E. H. Croft not out	6
I. V. A. Richards c G. S. Chappell b Thomson	54	B 3, lb 8, w 1, nb 24	36
*C. H. Lloyd c T. M. Chappell b Pascoe	31		
C. L. King c G. S. Chappell b Pascoe	110	1/37 (1) 2/116 (2) (113.1 476
†D. L. Murray c Lillee b Pascoe	82	overs)
A. M. E. Roberts c Marsh b Lillee	9	3/201 (3) 4/206 (4)

5/258 (5) 6/384 (6) 7/411 (8)
8/448 (9) 9/451 (10) 10/476 (7)

Lillee 24–4–98–1; Thomson 25–5–84–4; Pascoe 32.1–1–120–3; Bright 22–4–78–1; I. M. Chappell 4–0–33–0; G. S. Chappell 6–0–27–1.

Umpires: R. G. Gosein and D. Sang Hue.

Home team: WSC West Indies
Away team: WSC Australia
Competition: WSC Australia in West Indies 1978-79
Phase: 5th Supertest
Venue: Antigua Recreation Ground, St John's
Scheduled start date: 06 April 1979
Duration: 06, 07, 08, 09, 10 April 1979 (5-day match)
Balls per over: 6
Result: Drawn
Won toss: WSC West Indies
Man of the Match: G. S. Chappell.
Man of the Series: G. S. Chappell.

Close of play: first day, WSC West Indies 33-1 (Greenidge 20, Croft 0); second day, WSC West Indies 334-6 (Rowe 108, Murray 30); third day, no play; fourth day, WSC Australia 111-3 (G. S. Chappell 36, I. M. Chappell 13).

WSC Australia

R. B. McCosker c Holding b Roberts	35	– lbw b Croft	20
B. M. Laird c Haynes b Holding	2	– c Richards b Padmore	29
M. F. Kent b Roberts	40	– b Roberts	0
G. S. Chappell c Lloyd b Croft	104	– run out	85
*I. M. Chappell c Fredericks b Roberts	26	– b Holding	83
D. W. Hookes c Rowe b Roberts	2	– lbw b Holding	16
†R. W. Marsh b Croft	0	– not out	102
R. J. Bright lbw b Holding	0	– not out	56
D. K. Lillee lbw b Croft	6		
J. R. Thomson b Croft	4		
L. S. Pascoe not out	8		
B 4, lb 2, nb 1	7	B 5, lb 11, w 4, nb 4	24

1/15 (2) 2/65 (1) 3/93 (3)   (69.2   234   1/29 (1)   (6 wkts, 128   415
overs)   overs)
4/168 (5) 5/188 (6) 6/196 (7)   2/32 (3) 3/92 (2)
7/196 (8) 8/209 (9) 9/224 (4) 10/234 (10)   4/228 (4) 5/231 (5) 6/254 (6)

Roberts 20–3–73–4; Holding 17–2–60–2; Croft 18.2–2–56–4; Padmore 13–2–33–0; Richards 1–0–5–0. *Second innings*—Roberts 28–1–88–1; Holding 25–5–74–2; Croft 25–3–91–1; Padmore 40–12–101–1; Richards 6–0–15–0; Fredericks 4–1–22–0.

WSC West Indies

C. G. Greenidge c I. M. Chappell b Thomson	58		A. M. E. Roberts b Pascoe	17
D. L. Haynes lbw b Lillee	9		M. A. Holding c Marsh b Lillee	9
C. E. H. Croft c McCosker b Bright	47		A. L. Padmore not out	2
R. C. Fredericks b Lillee	45		B 9, lb 10, nb 4	23
L. G. Rowe c Marsh b Lillee	135			
I. V. A. Richards b Lillee	18		1/29 (2) 2/76 (1) (124.2	438
*C. H. Lloyd c Marsh b Lillee	1		overs)	
†D. L. Murray retired hurt	74		3/144 (4) 4/206 (3) 5/253 (6)	
			6/255 (7) 7/368 (5) 8/416 (9) 9/438 (10)	

Murray retired hurt at 428-8.

Lillee 33.2–2–125–6; Thomson 22–5–75–1; Pascoe 31–9–102–1; Bright 20–3–60–1; I. M. Chappell 12–3–41–0; G. S. Chappell 6–3–12–0.

Umpires: R. G. Gosein and D. Sang Hue.

BIBLIOGRAPHY

Interviews

Ray Bright, Andrew Caro, Greg Chappell, Ian Chappell, Wayne Clark, Gary Cosier, Tony Cozier, John Crilly, Ian Davis, John Dyson, Ross Edwards, Graham Ferrett, Gary Gilmour, Tony Greig, Tony Henson, Andrew Hilditch, Michael Hill, Michael Holding, David Hookes, Alan Hurst, John Inverarity, Martin Kent, Bruce Laird, Rob Langer, Trevor Laughlin, Mick Malone, Bill Macartney, Rick McCosker, Bruce McDonald, Dave McErlane, Graham McKenzie, Brian Morelli, Kerry O'Keeffe, Bob Parish, Barry Richards, Richie Robinson, Craig Serjeant, Ray Steele, Vern Stone, Peter Toohey, Mike Treloar, Alan Turner, Max Walker, Doug Walters, Phil Wilkins, Graeme Wood, Graham Yallop, Bruce Yardley.

Annuals

Bailey, Trevor (ed.), *World of Cricket,* MacDonald and Jane's, London, 1977–1980

Beecher, Eric (ed.), *Cricketer Annual,* Newspress, Melbourne, 1974–1977

Beecher, Eric (ed.), *Cricket Close-Up,* Newspress, Melbourne, 1978

Lemmon, David (ed.), *Pelham Cricket Year,* Pelham Books, London, 1979–1981

Piesse, Ken (ed.), *Cricket Digest,* Newspress, Melbourne, 1979

Piesse, Ken (ed.), *Cricket Year,* Peter Isaacson, Melbourne, 1980–1983

Wisden Cricketers' Almanack, 1970–1992

Books and Theses

Angell, Roger, *Late Innings,* Simon & Schuster, New York, 1982

Aris, Stephen, *Sportsbiz: Inside the Sports Business,* Hutchinson, London, 1990

Aylett, Allen and Hobbs, Greg, *My Game,* Sun Books, Melbourne, 1986

Bailey, Jack, *Conflicts In Cricket,* Kingswood, London, 1989

Beecher, Eric, *The Cricket Revolution,* Newspress, Melbourne, 1978

Belley, Peter (ed.), *Australian Television: The First Twenty-Five Years,* Thomas Nelson, Melbourne, 1981

Benaud, Richie, and others, *Ten Turbulent Years,* Swan Publishing, Sydney, 1987

Benaud, Richie, *Benaud on Reflection,* Collins Willow, London, 1984

Blofeld, Henry, *The Packer Affair,* William Collins, London, 1978

Bonney, Bill, *Packer and Televised Cricket,* Media Papers, NSW Institute of Technology, Sydney, 1980

Border, Allan, *Allan Border: The Autobiography,* Methuen, Sydney, 1985

Bose, Mihir, *A History of Indian Cricket,* Andre Deutsch, London, 1990

Boycott, Geoffrey, *Boycott: The Autobiography,* MacMillan, London, 1987

Boycott, Geoffrey, *Opening Up,* Arthur Barker, London, 1980

Boycott, Geoffrey, *Put to the Test,* Arthur Barker, London, 1979

Brearley, Mike and Doust, Dudley, *The Ashes Retained,* Hodder & Stoughton, London, 1979

Brearley, Mike and Doust, Dudley, *The Return of the Ashes,* Pelham Books, London, 1977

Brearley, Mike, *The Art of Captaincy,* Hodder and Stoughton, London, 1985

Butler, Keith, *Howzat!,* William Collins, Sydney, 1979

Buttrose, Ita, *Early Edition: My First Forty Years,* Macmillan, Melbourne, 1985

Caro, Andrew, *With a Straight Bat,* Sales Machine, Hong Kong, 1979

Cashman, Richard, *Ave a Go Yer Mug: Australian Cricket Crowds from Larrikin to Ocker,* Collins, Sydney, 1984

Chappell, Greg and Frith, David, *The Ashes '77,* Angus & Robertson, London, 1977

Chappell, Greg, *The 100th Summer,* Garry Sparke and Associates, Melbourne, 1977

Chappell, Greg, *Unders and Overs: The Controversies of Cricket,* Lansdowne, Sydney, 1981

Chappell, Ian and Robertson, Austin, *Chappelli Has the Last Laugh,* Lansdowne, Sydney, 1980

Chappell, Ian, *Chappelli,* Hutchinson, Sydney, 1976

Chappell, Ian, *The Cutting Edge,* Swan Publishing, Sydney, 1992

Dabscheck, Braham, 'The Professional Cricketers' Association of Australia', *Sporting Traditions,* Australian Society of Sports Historians, 1990

Denness, Mike, *I Declare,* Arthur Barker, London, 1977

Down, Michael, *Is it Cricket? Power, Money and Politics in Cricket since 1945,* Queen Anne, London, 1985

Egan, Jack, *Extra Cover,* ABC Books, Sydney, 1989

Fingleton, Jack, *Cricket Crisis,* Pavilion Books, London, 1985

Forsyth, Chris, *The Great Cricket Hijack,* Widescope, Melbourne, 1978

Frindall, Bill (ed.), *The Wisden Book of Test Cricket 1876-77 to 1977-78,* Macdonald and Jane's, London, 1979

Frindall, Bill (ed.), *The Wisden Book of Test Cricket Volume Two 1977 to 1989,* Macdonald Queen Anne Press, London, 1990

Frindall, Bill, *Frindall's Scorebook: Jubilee Edition,* Lonsdale Press, London, 1977

Frith, David, *The Ashes '79,* Angus & Robertson, London, 1979

Garner, Joel, *Big Bird Flying High,* Arthur Barker, London, 1988

Gower, David and Taylor, Bob, *Anyone for Cricket,* Pelham Books, London, 1979

Gower, David, *Gower: The Autobiography,* Harper Collins, London, 1992

Greenidge, Gordon, *Man in the Middle,* David & Charles, London, 1980

Greig, Tony, *My Story,* Stanley Paul, London, 1980

Hadlee, Richard and Brittenden, Dick, *Hadlee,* Reed, Wellington, 1981

Harding, Richard, *Outside Interference: Politics in Australian Broadcasting,* Sun, Melbourne, 1979

Imran Khan, *All-Round View,* Chatto & Windus, London, 1988

Imran Khan, and Murphy, Patrick, *Imran: The Autobiography of Imran Khan,* Pelham, London, 1983

Knott, Alan, *It's Knott Cricket,* Macmillan, London, 1985

Kowet, Don, *The Rich Who Own Sports,* Random House, New York, 1977

Laker, Jim, *One-Day Cricket,* Batsford, London, 1977

Lawson, Geoff, *Henry: The Geoff Lawson Story,* Ironbark Press, Sydney, 1993

Lee, Alan, *A Pitch in Both Camps,* Pelham Books, London, 1979

Lemmon, David, *Cricket Mercenaries,* Michael Joseph, London, 1987

Lillee, Dennis, *My Life in Cricket,* Methuen, Sydney, 1982

Lillee, Dennis, *Over and Out,* Methuen, Sydney, 1984

Lillee, Dennis, *The Art of Fast Bowling,* Collins, Sydney, 1977

Lloyd, Clive, *Living for Cricket,* Stanley Paul, London, 1980

Mallett, Ashley, *Spin Out,* Garry Sparke and Associates, Melbourne, 1977

Manley, Michael, *A History of West Indian Cricket,* Andre Deutsch, London, 1988

Marsh, Rod, *Gloves, Sweat and Tears: The Final Shout,* Penguin, Sydney, 1984

Marsh, Rod, *The Inside Edge,* Swan Publishing, Sydney, 1983

Marsh, Rod, *You'll Keep,* Hutchinson, Sydney, 1975

Martin-Jenkins, Christopher, *Cricket Contest: The Post-Packer Tests,* Macdonald and Jane's, London, 1980

Martin-Jenkins, Christopher, *In Defence of the Ashes,* Macdonald and Jane's, London, 1977

Martin-Jenkins, Christopher, *The Jubilee Tests,* MacDonald and Jane's, London, 1977

Mason, Tony (ed.), *Sport in Britain: A Social History,* Cambridge University Press, 1990

McDonald, Trevor, *Clive Lloyd: The Authorised Biography,* Granada, London, 1985

McDonald, Trevor, *Viv Richards: The Authorised Biography,* Pelham Books, London, 1984

McFarline, Peter, *A Game Divided,* Marlin Books, Melbourne, 1978

McFarline, Peter, *A Testing Time,* Hutchinson, Melbourne, 1979

McGilvray, Alan, *The Game is Not the Same,* ABC Books, Sydney, 1985

McGregor, Adrian, *Greg Chappell,* William Collins, Sydney, 1985

Meredith, Anthony, *Summers in Winter: Four England Tours of Australia,* Kingswood, London, 1990

Moran, Albert (ed.), *An Australian Broadcasting Reader,* Allen & Unwin, Sydney, 1992

Mosey, Don, *Laker,* Queen Anne Press, London, 1990

Murphy, Patrick, *Declarations,* Ringpress, London, 1989

Murphy, Patrick, *The Centurions,* J. M. Dent, London, 1986

Murphy, Patrick, *The Spinner's Turn,* J. M. Dent, London, 1982

Odendaal, Andre (ed.), *Cricket in Isolation,* self-published, Cape Town, 1976

Oram, James, *Hogan,* Penguin, Ringwood, 1987

Patmore, Angela, *Playing on Their Nerves,* Stanley Paul, London, 1980

Peel, Mark, *England Expects: The Life of Ken Barrington,* Kingswood, London, 1992

Pollard, Jack, *Australian Cricket: The Game and the Players,* Angus & Robertson, Sydney, 1988

Pollard, Jack, *From Bradman to Border: Australian Cricket 1948-1989,* Angus & Robertson, Sydney, 1989

Procter, Mike and Murphy, Patrick, *Mike Procter and Cricket,* Pelham Books, London,1981

Quick, Shayne, *World Series Cricket, Television and Australian Culture,* Ph D thesis, Graduate School of Ohio State University, 1990

Rader, Ben, *In Its Own Image: How Television Transformed Sports,* Free Press, New York, 1984

Redpath, Ian, *Always Reddy,* Garry Sparke and Associates, Melbourne, 1976

Richards, Barry, *The Barry Richards Story,* Angus & Robertson, London, 1978

Richards, Viv and Foot, David, *Viv Richards,* Star Books, London, 1982

Richards, Viv, *Hitting Across the Line,* Headline Press, London, 1991

Richardson, Victor, *The Vic Richardson Story,* Seal Books, Adelaide, 1969

Roberts, Randy and Olson, James, *Winning is the Only Thing: Sport in America Since 1945,* Johns Hopkins University Press, Baltimore, 1989

Robertson, Austin snr, *Ocker: The Fastest Man in the World,* Methuen, Sydney, 1986

Robertson, Austin, *Cricket Alight,* Swan Publishing, Sydney, 1979

Robertson, Austin, *Cricket Alive,* Swan Publishing, Sydney, 1978

Robinson, Ray, *On Top Down Under,* Cassell Australia, Sydney, 1981

Robinson, Ray, *The Wildest Tests,* Cassell Australia, Sydney, 1979

Scott, John, *Caught in Court,* Andre Deutsch, London, 1989

Simmons, Jack and Bearshaw, Brian, *Flat Jack: The Autobiography*, Queen Anne Press, London, 1986

Simpson, Bob, *Simmo*, Hutchinson, Sydney, 1979

Singh, Indra Vikram, *Test Cricket: End of the Road*, Rupa, Calcutta, 1992

Sissons, Ric, *The Players: A Social History of the Professional Cricketer*, Pluto Press, Sydney, 1988

Sloane, Peter, *Sport in the Market? The Economic Causes and Consequences of the Packer Revolution*, Hobart Papers, Institute of Economic Affairs, London, 1980

Sobers, Sir Garfield and Scovell, Brian, *Sobers*, MacMillan, London, 1988

Spence, Jim, *Up Close and Personal: The Inside Story of Network TV Sport*, Atheneum, New York, 1988

Stoddart, Brian, *Saturday Afternoon Fever: Sport in the Australian Culture*, Angus & Robertson, Sydney, 1986

Stollmeyer, Jeff, *Everything Under the Sun: My Life in West Indies Cricket*, Stanley Paul, London, 1983

Swanton, E. W., *As I Said at the Time*, William Collins, London, 1983

Thomson, Jeff and Frith, David, *Thommo*, Angus & Robertson, Sydney, 1980

Underwood, Derek, *Deadly Down Under*, Arthur Barker, London, 1980

Walker, Max, *Back to Bay 13*, Garry Sparke and Associates, Melbourne, 1980

Walker, Max, *Cricketer at the Crossroads*, Garry Sparke and Associates, Melbourne, 1978

Walker, Max, *Tangles*, Garry Sparke and Associates, Melbourne, 1976

Walker, Peter, *Cricket Conversations*, Queen Anne Press, London, 1976

Walters, Doug and Laws, Ken, *The Doug Walters Story*, Rigby, Sydney, 1981

Wellham, Dirk, *Solid Knocks and Second Thoughts*, Reed Books, Sydney, 1988

Wessels, Kepler, *Cricket Madness*, Aandbloom Publications, Port Elizabeth, 1987

Willis, Bob and Murphy, Patrick, *The Cricket Revolution: Cricket in the 1970s*, Sidgwick & Son, London, 1981

Woolmer, Bob, *Pirate and Rebel?*, Arthur Barker, London, 1984

Wooldridge, Ian (ed.) *The International Cavaliers' Cricket Book*, Purnell, London, 1969

Wynne-Thomas, Peter, *Cricket in Conflict*, Newnes Books, London, 1984

Wynne-Thomas, Peter, *Cricket Tours at Home and Abroad*, Guild Publishing, London, 1989

Yallop, Graham, *Lambs to the Slaughter*, Outback Press, Melbourne, 1979

Zaheer Abbas and Foot, David, *Zed*, Worldswork, London, 1983

Zimbalist, Andrew, *Baseball and Billions*, Harper Collins, New York, 1992

Magazines and Newspapers

Age, Australian, Australian Cricket, Australian Financial Review, Australian Women's Weekly, Broadcasting and Television, Bulletin, Cricketer (Australia), *The Cricketer* (UK), *Cricket Player* (NZ), *Daily Telegraph* (London), *David Lord's World of Cricket Monthly, Guardian, National Times, Pakistan Cricketer, Sportsweek* (India), *Sunday Times, Sydney Morning Herald, The Times, Wisden Cricket Monthly.*

INDEX